Perspectives on Discourse Analysis:
Theory and Practice

D1784890

Perspectives on Discourse Analysis:
Theory and Practice

By

Laura Alba-Juez

Perspectives on Discourse Analysis: Theory and Practice, by Laura Alba-Juez

This book first published 2009

Cambridge Scholars Publishing

12 Back Chapman Street, Newcastle upon Tyne, NE6 2XX, UK

British Library Cataloguing in Publication Data
A catalogue record for this book is available from the British Library

ISBN (10): 1-4438-0597-1, ISBN (13): 978-1-4438-0597-1

For Gustavo, Joaquín and Julian

TABLE OF CONTENTS

ACKNOWLEDGEMENTS

No present book on Discourse Analysis can boast of not having drawn on previous works on the subject. In this respect, I owe a special debt to all the authors whose work is cited or discussed in this book, and I hope not to have misrepresented any of them. In particular, my personal consultation with some of these researchers was of the greatest value and assistance. Thus my thanks go to:

1) Bruce Fraser, for generously sharing his work on discourse markers with me and for sending me his unpublished manuscripts.

2) Deborah Schiffrin, Deborah Tannen, Robin Lakoff, Heidi Hamilton, William Labov, Wallace Chafe and John Gumperz for clarifying many of my doubts about their approaches to discourse while I was a Visiting Researcher in the Linguistics Department at Georgetown University (U.S.A.).

3) Angela Downing, for being such a good teacher, and for generously giving and discussing with me some of her articles on coherence, thematic progression, topicality and discourse markers.

4) JoAnne Neff, for her perennial openness and her willingness in sending me her articles on political discourse, as well as for shedding light on my understanding of Critical Discourse Analysis during our conversations and discussions.

5) Teun van Dijk, for clarifying many of my doubts about Critical Discourse Analysis and the topic of ideology, by gently answering all my questions after one of his talks at my university, the UNED.

6) Irene Madfes, for sending me her articles on medical discourse.

My students of Discourse Analysis along the years have helped me with their comments and suggestions to try to provide clearer and more detailed explanations of certain topics, as well as to include a wider variety of sample analyses of the different phenomena discussed in the book. My sincere thanks go to them too.

I am especially grateful to my friend and colleague Gretchen Dobrott, for her thorough, detailed and invaluable work in proof-reading the manuscript. María Teresa Gibert also revised the manuscript and I profoundly appreciate her kindness and the time she took in doing it, as well as her wise and valuable comments and suggestions.

Also, this book owes much to the artwork (photography and drawings) of my art and computer wizard, Joaquín Armijo.

I would also like to thank *CNN International*, for granting me permission to reprint two fragments of the transcripts of one *Larry King Live* show. Likewise, I'm grateful to Lourdes Nafá, for giving me permission to reprint a fragment of her annotated corpus.

I also owe my friend and colleague Mónica Aragonés a debt of gratitude for reading and commenting on some of the chapters, as well as for her constant support and friendship.

Every effort has been made to contact the authors of the different fragments of discourse that are used for analysis in this book, and we would be glad to make any suitable arrangements with any copyright holders whom it has been impossible to contact.

Finally, but not less importantly, I would like to thank my husband, Gustavo, and my sons, Joaquín and Julian, for their understanding and unending help and support. The memory of my mother and the constant encouragement of my father, my sister and my two brothers have also been important forces accompanying me along the process of writing this book.

Needless to say, all deficiencies, mistakes and omissions are my own responsibility.

INTRODUCTION

1. Aims of this book

The main aim of this book is to provide the student/reader with the basic theoretical knowledge and empirical tools of some of the most relevant approaches to the analysis of discourse. It has been mainly conceived of as a general (university) course on Discourse Analysis, but it can also be useful for any person or group whose main concern is to acquire the basic necessary knowledge and skills for analyzing any type of discourse. The subject matter of the book could not only be of use for linguists or prospective linguists: given its interdisciplinary character, its findings can be (and in fact are) used and applied by practitioners and scholars from different fields, such as sociology, psychology, medical science, computer science, and so on.

The following are the general objectives that the student/reader is expected to reach after reading and studying the material in this book:

- Identification of the different theories and approaches to analysis discussed.
- Analysis of different types of text and discourse, taking into account the different perspectives, units of analysis, strategies and functions outlined in the book.
- Practical application of such analyses, with specification of their positive contribution to the fields of linguistics and humanistic studies in general.

A desirable and anticipated effect of the study of discourse is also the development of an open and tolerant mind which will eventually lead to a better understanding of the different and varied manifestations of language, culture and communication in human society.

2. Content of this book

The present book is a completely revised and updated version of *Discourse Analysis for University Students* (by Laura Alba-Juez, Madrid:

UNED), which was originally published in 2005. In this new version I have added material, two new approaches (*Narrative Analysis* and *Positive Discourse Analysis*), and new examples throughout, and I hope to have also added greater clarity. Both the referenced works and websites have been updated, and a new section with self-evaluation questions has been included at the end of each chapter.

It would be unwise to think that this work presents a complete picture of all possible aspects of, and approaches to Discourse Analysis. The discipline is a broad one, and consequently it would be impossible to review all related studies in a work of limited scope like the present book. Nor would it be possible to do justice even to the approaches I discuss[1]. Nevertheless, I have chosen several perspectives that are especially relevant (because of their remarkable influence), and I have tried to present and discuss them in a pedagogical way, considering the main aim of the book.

The book is divided into 12 chapters. **Chapters 1** (*Introducing Discourse Analysis*) **and 2** (*The Data*) are general chapters which describe and explain the basic tenets of Text Linguistics and Discourse Analysis. They also contain some introductory considerations about *corpus linguistics*, and the most common techniques for data collection and annotation, taking into account the necessary ethics for the job.

Chapters 3 to 11 cover the different approaches to be studied and compared, i.e., *Pragmatics* (Chapter 3), *Interactional Sociolinguistics* (Chapter 4), *Conversation Analysis* (Chapter 5), *The Ethnography of Communication* (Chapter 6), *Variation Analysis* and *Narrative Analysis* (Chapter 7), *Functional Sentence Perspective: Thematic and Information Structures* (Chapter 8), *Post-Structuralist Theory* and *Social Theory* (Chapter 9), *Critical Discourse Analysis* and *Positive Discourse Analysis* (Chapter 10), *Mediated Discourse Analysis* (Chapter 11).

Chapter 12 (*Further issues in Discourse Analysis*) covers some other issues, key concepts and aspects to be considered within discourse studies, such as the problem of choosing a unit of analysis, the identification and characterization of different genres or types of discourse, the analysis of text cohesion and coherence, and the use of discourse markers.

At the end of the chapters we find an extensive bibliography (References), containing all the works cited. The last section of the book provides the answers to the self-evaluation questions (*Key to Self-*

---

[1] I have to acknowledge that I am very much influenced by the American and some of the European schools of Discourse Analysis, and consequently my views on the subject, as well as my choice of approaches, reflect this fact.

evaluation Questions), as well as the key to the practice tasks in each of the chapters (*Practice Key*). The students/readers are advised to do the tasks first, and then check their answers in this section. The solutions given are by no means the only possible ones, considering the wide scope of Discourse Analysis and the multiple perspectives from which discourse can be approached. These answers are thus to be used as a guide, but by no means should they be viewed as complete and final solutions to the problems presented.

3. Chapter organization

Each chapter contains both a theoretical and an empirical part. All of the chapters are introduced by a *Chapter Outline* (whose content is closely connected to the main objectives of each chapter) followed by the theoretical development of the topic (main ideas and concepts) in question. A sample analysis of data is always provided in order to clarify the ideas and concepts explained. Lastly, all the chapters have the following sections:

- *SUMMING UP* (containing a summary of the main points studied in the chapter).
- *SELF-EVALUATION QUESTIONS* (containing multiple-choice questions which will assist the reader/student in studying the contents of each chapter. The answers to these questions are provided in the *Key to Self-evaluation Questions* section at the end of the book).
- *PRACTICE* (containing both open and semi-open activities whose main intention is to provide the student/reader with the opportunity to put all the theoretical knowledge into practice. The key to the semi-open tasks can be found at the end of the book in the *Practice Key* section).
- *FURTHER READING* (containing further references for those interested in studying the topics presented in the chapter in more detail).
- *USEFUL WEBSITES* (containing websites which might prove useful for doing further research on the subject matter of the chapter).

4. Final remark

I finally want to point out that this book does not claim originality in its content, in the sense that no new theory of Discourse Analysis is presented or outlined. The main aim in this respect has been to present a state-of-the-art description of some of the already existing approaches to the discipline, as well as its main issues or concerns. Notwithstanding, the general organization of ideas and approaches, the analysis of texts in the different chapters, as well as the pedagogical orientation and the practice exercises, intend to conform an original –albeit modest– contribution to the study of discourse.

1

Introducing Discourse Analysis

"Anyone who thinks we are close to final answers, or that we know how to find them, must surely be mistaken."

Wallace Chafe, *Discourse, Consciousness and Time.*

Chapter Outline:

- Defining *text* and *discourse*.

- Defining *Text Linguistics* and *Discourse Analysis*.

- Evolution of Text Linguistics and Discourse Analysis through time.

- Approaches to the phenomenon of discourse.

- The job and interests of discourse analysts.

1.1 Defining *text* and *discourse*. What is Text Linguistics? What is Discourse Analysis?

To define and describe the scope of study of Text Linguistics and Discourse Analysis and to establish the differences between them both is not an easy task. Suffice it to say that the terms *text* and *discourse* are used in a variety of ways by different linguists and researchers: there is a considerable number of theoretical approaches to both Text Linguistics and Discourse Analysis and many of them belong to very different research traditions, even when they share similar basic tenets.

In everyday popular use it might be said that the term *text* is restricted to written language, while *discourse* is restricted to spoken language. However, modern Linguistics has introduced a concept of *text* that includes every type of utterance; therefore a text may be a magazine article, a television interview, a conversation or a cooking recipe, just to give a few examples.

Crystal (1997) defines Text Linguistics as "the formal account of the linguistic principles governing the structure of texts". De Beaugrande and Dressler (1981) present a broader view; they define *text* as a *communicative event* that must satisfy the following seven criteria:

1) **Cohesion**, which has to do with the relationship between text and syntax. Phenomena such as *conjunction, ellipsis, anaphora,*

cataphora or *recurrence* are basic for cohesion.

2) **Coherence,** which has to do with the meaning of the text. Here we may refer to elements of knowledge or to cognitive structures that do not have a linguistic realization but are implied by the language used, and thus influence the reception of the message by the interlocutor.

3) **Intentionality,** which relates to the attitude and purpose of the speaker or writer.

4) **Acceptability,** which concerns the preparation of the hearer or reader to assess the relevance or usefulness of a given text.

5) **Informativity,** which refers to the quantity and quality of new or expected information.

6) **Situationality,** which points to the fact that the situation in which the text is produced plays a crucial role in the production and reception of the message.

7) **Intertextuality,** which refers to two main facts: a) a text is always related to some preceding or simultaneous discourse; b) texts are always linked and grouped in particular text varieties or genres (e.g.: narrative, argumentative, descriptive, etc.) by formal criteria.

In spite of the considerable overlap between Text Linguistics and Discourse Analysis (both of them are concerned with the notion of cohesion, for instance) the above criteria may help us make a distinction between them.

Tischer et al. (2000) explain that the first two criteria (cohesion and coherence) may be defined as *text-internal*, whereas the remaining criteria are *text-external*. Those approaches oriented towards 'pure' Text Linguistics give more importance to text-internal criteria, while the tradition in Discourse Analysis has always been to give more importance to the external factors, for they are believed to play an essential role in communication.

Some authors, such as Halliday, believe that *text* is everything that is meaningful in a particular situation: "By text, then, we understand a continuous process of semantic choice" (1978:137). In the "purely" text-linguistic approaches, such as the cognitive theories of text, *texts* are viewed as "more or less explicit epi-phenomena of cognitive processes" (Tischer et al., 2000: 29), and the *context* plays a subordinate role.

It could be said that the text-internal elements constitute the *text*, while the text-external ones constitute the *context*. Schiffrin points out that all approaches within Discourse Analysis view *text* and *context* as the two kinds of information that contribute to the communicative content of an utterance, and she defines these terms as follows:

> I will use the term "text" to differentiate linguistic material (e.g. what is said, assuming a verbal channel) from the environment in which "sayings" (or other linguistic productions) occur (context). In terms of utterances, then, "text" is the linguistic content: the stable semantic meanings of words, expressions, and sentences, but not the inferences available to hearers depending upon the contexts in which words, expressions, and sentences are used. […] Context is thus a world filled with people producing utterances: people who have social, cultural, and personal identities, knowledge, beliefs, goals and wants, and who interact with one another in various socially and culturally defined situations. (1994: 363)

Text in context

Thus, according to Schiffrin, Discourse Analysis involves the study of both **text and context.** One might conclude, then, that Text Linguistics only studies the text, while Discourse Analysis is more complete because it studies both text and context. However, as has been shown, there are definitions of text (like de Beaugrande's) that are very broad and include both elements, and that is why it would be very risky to talk about clear-cut differences between the two disciplines. De Beaugrande's (2002) definition of Text Linguistics (herinafter TL) as "the study of real language in use" does not differ from many of the definitions of Discourse Analysis (hereinafter DA) presented by Schiffrin within its functional approach, some of which are the following:

> The study of discourse is the study of any aspect of language use (Fasold, 1990: 65).

> The analysis of discourse is, necessarily, the analysis of language in use. As such, it cannot be restricted to the description of linguistic forms independent of the purposes or functions which these forms are designed to serve in human affairs (Brown & Yule, 1983: 1).

> Discourse... refers to language in use, as a process which is socially situated (Candlin, 1997: ix).

Thus, we see that the terms *text* and *discourse* are sometimes used to mean the same and therefore one might conclude that TL and DA are the same, too. It can be said, nevertheless, that the tendency in TL has been to present a more formal and experimental approach, while DA tends more towards a functional approach. Formalists are apt to see language as a mental phenomenon, while functionalists see it as a predominantly social one. As has been shown, authors like Schiffrin integrate both the formal and the functional approaches within DA, and consequently, DA is viewed as an all-embracing term which would include TL studies as one approach among others.

Slembrouck points out the ambiguity of the term *discourse analysis* and provides another broad definition:

> The term discourse analysis is very ambiguous. I will use it in this book to refer mainly to the linguistic analysis of *naturally occurring connected speech or written discourse*. Roughly speaking, it refers to attempts to study the organisation of language above the sentence or above the clause, and therefore to study *larger linguistic units*, such as conversational exchanges or written texts. It follows that discourse analysis is also concerned with *language use in social contexts*, and in particular with interaction or dialogue between speakers. (2005:1)

Another important characteristic of discourse studies is that they are essentially multidisciplinary, and therefore it can be said that they cross the Linguistics border into different and varied domains, as van Dijk notes in the following passage:

> ...discourse analysis for me is essentially multidisciplinary, and involves

linguistics, poetics, semiotics, psychology, sociology, anthropology, history, and communication research. What I find crucial though is that precisely because of its multi-faceted nature, this multidisciplinary research should be integrated. We should devise theories that are complex and account both for the textual, the cognitive, the social, the political and the historical dimension of discourse. (2002: 10)

Thus, when analyzing discourse, researchers are not only concerned with "purely" linguistic facts; they pay equal or more attention to language use in relation to social, political and cultural aspects. For this reason, discourse is not only within the interests of linguists; it is a field that is also studied by communication scientists, literary critics, philosophers, sociologists, anthropologists, social psychologists, political scientists, and many others. As Barbara Johnstone puts it:

... I see discourse analysis as a research method that can be (and is being) used by scholars with a variety of academic and non-academic affiliations, coming from a variety of disciplines, to answer a variety of questions. (2002: xi)

As noted above, not all researchers use and believe in the same definition of *text* and *discourse*. In this book, we are going to adopt the general definition of DA as **the study of language in use**, and we shall follow Schiffrin in including both *text* and *context* as parts of discourse, in which case we will consider the term *text* in its narrow sense, not in the broad sense that could place it on a par with the term *discourse*.

1.2. Origins and brief history of Text Linguistics and Discourse Analysis

Parallel to the Chomskyan Generative School (whose starting point is considered to be the publication of *Syntactic Structures* in 1957), other schools emerged in different parts of the world that supported different and even opposing ideas to those of Chomsky's.

All these new schools believed that a good linguistic description should go **beyond the sentence**, and pointed to the fact that there are certain meanings and aspects of language that cannot be understood or embraced if its study is limited to the syntactic analysis of sentences.

Thus, in the twentieth century, the following new disciplines emerged within the field of Linguistics:

- Functionalism (functional grammars)
- Cognitive Linguistics

- Sociolinguistics
- Pragmatics
- Text Linguistics
- Discourse Analysis

All these new disciplines are interrelated, and sometimes it is very difficult to distinguish one from the other, due to the fact that all of them have common denominators. Bernárdez (1999: 342) explains the basic tenets of these disciplines, which are summarized here as follows:

a) Language only exists in use and communication. It always fulfils certain functions in human interaction.
b) Language use is necessarily social.
c) Language is not autonomous. It shares some characteristics with other social and cognitive phenomena.
d) The description of language must account for the real facts of language. It should not postulate hidden entities only motivated by the needs of the formal system utilized.
e) Linguistic structures should be closely linked to the conditions of language use.
f) Language is natural and necessarily vague and inaccurate; therefore any prediction can only be probabilistic.

When performing DA, then, researchers may also engage themselves in Functional Grammar, Sociolinguistics, Pragmatics or Cognitivism, because all these fields are interrelated and have common tenets. As regards TL and DA, we may speak of a progressive "integration" of both disciplines, for, if we observe the evolution of language research through time, it will be noticed that many scholars have moved from TL into DA as part of the natural flow of their beliefs and ideas, as is the case with van Dijk, who, in his biographical article of 2002, explains how his research evolved from *Text Grammar* to *Critical Discourse Analysis*[1]. This author points out that the main aim of his studies in the 1970s was to give an explicit description of the grammatical structure of texts, and the most obvious way of doing so was by accounting for the relationship among sentences. A very important concept for Text Grammar at that time was the introduction of the notion of *macrostructure* (van Dijk, 1980).

---

[1] Another example can be found in de Beaugrande (1997: 68) when he comments on how his concepts of *text* and *discourse* evolved over a series of studies and expanded beyond the linguistic focus he first encountered.

undamental notion was that of *coherence* and the idea that texts ⸱ized at more global descriptive levels than that of the sentence. Later ⸱ ⸱, and under the influence of the cognitive theories, the notion of *strategic understanding* was developed, which attempted to account for what the users of a language really do when they understand a given text. Van Dijk also notes how several other new concepts were introduced in TL studies, such as *socio-cultural knowledge* and *mental models* (Johnson-Laird, 1983), as well as all the ideas and concepts coming from the field of *Pragmatics*. In his particular case, he took interest in the study of power and ideology, which places him within the DA stream-of-thought known as *Critical Discourse Analysis*[2].

Thus, after the early and uniform stage of "Text Grammar", TL went through a series of more open and diversified stages. The "textuality" stage emphasized the global aspects of texts and saw the text as a functional unit, larger than the sentence. This stage led into the "textualization" or "discourse processing" stage, where analysts "set about developing process models of the activities of discourse participants in interactive settings and in 'real time'" (de Beaugrande, 1997: 61-62).

The current aim now in DA is to describe language where it was originally found, i.e. in the context of human interaction. In this respect, it is important to point out that this interaction often involves other media besides language. Examples of these other semiotic systems may be *gesture, dance, song, photography* or *clothing*, and it is also the discourse analyst's job to explain the connection between these systems and language. In order to achieve these aims, different researchers have taken different approaches. We now turn to them.

1.3. Approaches to the phenomenon of discourse

Current research in DA, then, flows from different academic fields. This is one of the reasons why the terms *discourse* and *discourse analysis* are used to mean different things by different researchers. Schiffrin et al. note that all the definitions fall into three main categories:

1) Anything beyond the sentence
2) Language use
3) A broader range of social practice that includes non-linguistic and non-specific instances of language. (2001: 1)

---

[2] This approach is presented and discussed in Chapter 10.

Authors such as Leech (1983) and Schiffrin (1994) distinguish between two main approaches: 1) the formal approach, where *discourse* is defined as a unit of language **beyond the sentence**, and 2) the functional approach, which defines discourse as **language use.** Z. Harris (1951, 1952) was the first linguist to use the term *discourse analysis* and he was a formalist: he viewed discourse as the next level in a hierarchy of morphemes, clauses and sentences. This view has been criticized due to the results shown by researchers like Chafe (1980, 1987, 1992), who rightfully argued that the units used by people in their speech can not always be categorized as sentences. People generally produce units that have a semantic and an intonational closure, but not necessarily a syntactic one.

Functionalists give much importance to the purposes and functions of language, sometimes to the extreme of defending the notion that language and society are part of each other and cannot be thought of as independent (Fairclough, 1989; Focault, 1980). Functional analyses include *all* uses of language because they focus on the way in which people use language to achieve certain communicative goals. Discourse is not regarded as one more of the levels in a hierarchy; it is an all-embracing concept which includes not only the propositional content, but also the social, cultural and contextual contents.

As explained above, Schiffrin (1994) proposes a more balanced approach to discourse, in which both the formal and the functional paradigms are integrated. She views discourse as "utterances", i.e. "units of linguistic production (whether spoken or written) which are inherently contextualized" (1994: 41). From this perspective, the aims for DA are not only sequential or syntactic, but also semantic and pragmatic.

Within the category of *discourse* we may include not only the "purely" linguistic content, but also sign language, dramatization, or the so-called 'bodily hexis' (Bordieu, 1990), i.e. the speaker's disposition or the way s/he stands, talks, walks or laughs, which has to do with a given political mythology. It can thus be concluded that discourse is **multi-modal** because it uses more than one semiotic system and performs several functions at the same time.

Bodily hexis

Wetherell et al. (2001) present four possible approaches to DA, which are summarized as follows:

1.   The model that views language as a system and therefore it is important for the researchers to find *patterns*.

2.   The model that is based on the activity of language use, more than on language in itself. Language is viewed as a process and not as a product; thus

researchers focus on *interaction.*

3.   The model that searches for language *patterns* associated with a given *topic* or *activity* (e.g. legal discourse, psychotherapeutic discourse, etc.).

4.   The model that looks for *patterns within broader contexts,* such as "society" or "culture". Here, language is viewed as part of major processes and activities, and as such the interest goes beyond language (e.g. the study of racism or sexism through the analysis of discourse).

In spite of these categorizations, it would not be unreasonable to say that there are as many approaches to discourse as there are researchers devoted to the field, for each of them proposes new forms of analysis or new concepts that somehow transform or broaden previous modes of analysis. However, it would also be true to say that all streams of research within the field are related to one another, and sometimes it is difficult to distinguish among them. Precisely with the aim of systematizing the study of discourse and distinguishing among different ways of solving problems within the discipline, different traditions or schools have been identified. It would be impossible to embrace them all in only one work, and for that reason, in this book we are only going to concentrate on the main ideas and practices within some of the best-known schools, which are the following:

1. Pragmatics (Chapter 3)
2. Interactional Sociolinguistics (Chapter 4)
3. Conversation Analysis (Chapter 5)
4. The Ethnography of Communication (Chapter 6)
5. Variation Analysis and Narrative Analysis (Chapter 7)
6. Functional Sentence Perspective (Chapter 8)
7. Post-structuralist Theory and Social Theory (Chapter 9)
8. Critical Discourse Analysis and Positive Discourse Analysis (Chapter 10)
9. Mediated Discourse Analysis (Chapter 11)

A common characteristic of all these schools of thought is that they do not focus on language as an abstract system. Instead, they all tend to be interested in what happens when people **use** language, based on what they have said, heard or seen before, as well as in how they **do** things with language, such as express feelings, entertain others, exchange information, and so on. This is the main reason why the discipline has been called

"*Discourse* Analysis" rather than "language analysis".

1.4 What do discourse analysts do?

Broadly speaking, discourse analysts investigate the use of language in context, thus they are interested in what speakers/writers do, and not so much in the formal relationships among sentences or propositions. Discourse analysis, then, has a social dimension, and for many analysts it is a method for studying how language "gets recruited 'on site' to enact specific social activities and social identities" (Gee 1999: 1).

Even when a discipline is hard to delimit, as is the case with DA, we can learn a great deal about its field of concern by observing what practitioners do. If we look at what discourse analysts do, we will find they explore matters such as:

- Turn-taking in telephone conversations
- The language of humor
- Power relationships in doctor/patient interviews
- Dialogue in chat rooms
- The discourse of the archives, records or files of psychoanalysts
- The conversation at a dinner table
- The scripts of a given television program
- The discourse of politicians
- The study of racism through the use of discourse
- How power relations and sexism are manifested in the conversation between men and women
- The characteristics of persuasive discourse
- Openings and closings in different types of conversations
- The structure of narrative
- Representations of black/white people (or any race) in the written media (magazines, newspapers, etc.)
- The strategies used by speakers/writers in order to fulfil a given discourse function
- The use of irony or metaphor for certain communicative aims
- The use of linguistic politeness
- The discourse of E-mail messages
- Legal discourse used in trials
- How people create social categories like "boy" or "immigrant" or "lady" as they talk to, about, or among each other
- And a long *etcetera*…

These are just a few examples reflecting the concerns of discourse analysts, but they are sufficient to demonstrate that researchers in DA are certainly concerned with the study of **language in use**. As students/ readers progress through the different chapters of this book, they will encounter several other examples of possible DA areas of interest.

It is worth noting that, as Johnstone (2002) remarks, the discipline is called discourse *analysis* (and not, for instance, "discourseology") because it "typically focuses on the analytical process in a relatively explicit way" (2002: 3). This analysis may be realized by dividing long stretches of discourse into parts or units of different sorts, depending on the initial research question, and it can also involve looking at the phenomenon under study in a variety of ways, by performing, for instance, a given set of tests.

Thus, discourse analysts have helped (and are helping) to shed light on how speakers/writers organize their discourse in order to indicate their semantic intentions, as well as on how hearers/readers interpret what they hear, read or see. They have also contributed to answer important research questions which have lead, for instance, to the identification of the cognitive abilities involved in the use of symbols or semiotic systems, to the study of variation and change, or to the description of some aspects of the process of language acquisition.

In order to carry out their analyses, discourse analysts need to work with texts. Texts constitute the *corpus* of any given study, which may consist of the transcripts of a recorded conversation, a written document or a computerized corpus of a given language, to name a few possibilities. The use of corpora has become a very widespread practice among discourse researchers, and for that reason it is necessary for any discourse analyst to acquire some basic knowledge of how to handle the data and how to work with corpora. Chapter 2 is devoted to this enterprise.

SUMMING UP... (CHAPTER 1)

1. The terms *text* and *discourse* have been –and still are– used ambiguously, and they are defined in different ways by different researchers. In this book we are going to use the term *text* to refer to the 'purely' linguistic material, and we are going to consider *discourse* in a broader sense, defining it as **language in use**, composed of **text** and **context**.

2. *Text Linguistics* and *Discourse Analysis* share some basic tenets and, while some authors make a distinction between them, others use both terms to mean the same. However, it may be said that "purely" **Text Linguistic studies** are more concerned with the **text-internal factors** (i.e. cohesion and coherence), while **Discourse Analysis** focuses its attention more on the **text-external factors**, without disregarding the text-internal ones. The history of these disciplines shows that research has evolved, in many cases, from the narrower scope of *Text Grammar* (and later, *Text Linguistics*) into the broader discipline of *Discourse Analysis,* and therefore both disciplines have merged. For this reason and for clarifying and practical purposes, we shall consider DA as a macro-discipline that includes several sub-approaches, among which the 'purely' text-linguistic ones can also be found.

3. In this book we are going to touch on the main theoretical and practical tenets of the following traditions identified within discourse studies: *Pragmatics, Conversation Analysis, Interactional Sociolinguistics, Ethnography of Communication, Variation Analysis* and *Narrative Analysis, Functional Sentence Perspective, Post-structural and Social Theory, Critical Discourse Analysis/Positive Discourse Analysis and Mediated Discourse Analysis.*

4. In order to learn about a given discipline, it is useful to look at what practitioners do. Discourse analysts explore the language of face-to-face conversations, telephone conversations, e-mail messages, etc., and they may study power relations, the structure of turn-taking, politeness strategies, the linguistic manifestation of racism or sexism, and many, many other aspects of **language in use**. The sky is the limit.

5. Discourse analysts are interested in the actual patterns of use in naturally-occurring texts. These natural texts, once transcribed and annotated, are known as the ***corpus***, which constitutes the basis for analysis. Thus, discourse analysts necessarily take a corpus-based approach to their research.

SELF-EVALUATION QUESTIONS

Choose the answer that best suits the information given in Chapter 1.

1.   Modern Linguistics has introduced a concept of *text* that...
a) is very restrictive.
b) includes all types of utterances.
c) includes only written discourse.

2.   De Beaugrande and Dressler (1981)...
a)   view Text Linguistics from a broader perspective than that of Crystal's (1997).
b)   define text in terms of three main criteria.
c)   define text as a grammatical category.

3.   According to Tischer et al. (2000), the first two criteria that define *text* (De Beaugrande & Dressler, 1981)...
a)   are text-external.
b)   belong only to "pure" Text Linguistics.
c)   are text-internal.

4.   The tradition in Discourse Analysis has always been to...
a)   give more importance to the text-external criteria of *intentionality, acceptability, informativity, situationality and intertextuality.*
b)   give more importance to the text than to the context.
c)   consider context as playing a subsidiary role.

5.   According to Schiffrin (1994) and other authors, Discourse Analysis...
a)   involves only the study of context.
b)   is devoted to the study of text.
c)   includes the analysis of both text and context.

6.   De Beaugrande & Dressler's (1981) definition of Text Linguistics...
a)   differs widely from Schiffrin's (1994) definition of Discourse Analysis.

b) does not substantially differ from Schiffrin's (1994), Fasold's (1990), Brown & Yule's (1983) or Candlin's (1997) definition of Discourse Analysis.

c) is exactly the same as Schiffrin's (1994).

7. The tendency in Text Linguistics has been to…
a) present a more formal approach than that of Discourse Analysis.
b) present a more functional approach than that of Discourse Analysis.
c) be less formal than any other approach.

8. Functionalists see language…
a) mainly as a mental phenomenon.
b) as a predominantly social phenomenon.
c) as an acoustic phenomenon.

9. Many discourse analysts, like Schiffrin or Slembrouck …
a) integrate both the formal and functional approaches in their study of discourse.
b) do not mix the formal with the functional approach.
c) prefer the formal to the functional approach.

10. Discourse studies are…
a) restricted to the field of Linguistics.
b) devoted mainly to social phenomena.
c) essentially multidisciplinary.

11. Functionalism, Cognitive Linguistics, Sociolinguistic, Pragmatics, Text Linguistics and Discourse Analysis are…
a) all relatively new disciplines which are interrelated.
b) completely different from one another.
c) very easily distinguished from one another.

12. Many scholars' studies, like those of van Dijk or de Beaugrande…
a) have not changed substantially with time.
b) have evolved from Text Linguistics to Discourse Analysis.
c) do not show a natural flow of beliefs or ideas.

13. The current and main aim in Discourse Analysis is to…
a) study the formal aspects of texts.
b) discover the functions of language.

c)   describe language in the context of human interaction.

14. Zellig Harris (1951, 1952)…
a)   was a functionalist.
b)   was the first scholar that used the term *Discourse Analysis.*
c)   criticized Chafe's view of Discourse Analysis.

15. According to Schiffrin (1994), *utterances* are…
a)   written or spoken linguistic units that are inherently
      contextualized.
b)   units which are essentially and only sequential and syntactic.
c)   purely linguistic units.

16. Discourse is multi-modal because it…
a)   embodies one semiotic system.
b)   includes laughter in its study.
c)   uses more than one semiotic system.

17. Whetherell et al (2001) …
a)   write about four possible approaches to Discourse Analysis.
b)   write about only two models of analysis.
c)   do not distinguish between models.

18. Discourse analysts are…
a)   more interested in the grammatical aspects of language than in
      the details of its context.
b)   more concerned with the actions of speakers or writers than with
      the formal relationships between sentences.
c)   not particularly interested in body language.

19. In general, we may say that discourse analysts are…
a)   only interested in different types of conversations.
b)   not interested in the written language.
c)   mainly concerned with the study of language in use.

20. In order to carry out their analyses, discourse analysts…
a)   very frequently use linguistic corpora as their data.
b)   work only with written documents.
c)   always use recorded conversations as texts.

PRACTICE

A) *READING:* After reading the contents of this chapter, choose ONE of the following chapters[3] from books on Discourse Analysis and read it:

- Chapter 2 ("Definitions of discourse") and chapter 10 ("Text and context") in Deborah Schiffrin's *Approaches to Discourse*, 1994.
- Introduction ("What is Discourse Analysis?") to D. Schiffrin, D. Tannen & H. Hamilton's *The Handbook of Discourse Analysis*, 2001.
- Chapter 2 ("Toward a science of text and discourse") in R. de Beaugrande's *New Foundations for a Science of Text and Discourse: Cognition, Communication, and the Freedom of Access to Knowledge and Society,* 1997.
- Chapter 2 ("What is a text?") in S. Titscher et al.'s *Methods of Text and Discourse Analysis*, 2000.
- Introduction ("Perspectives on Discourse Analysis") to A. Jaworski and N. Coupland's *The Discourse Reader*, 1999.
- Chapter 3 ("Tools of inquiry and discourses") in J.P. Gee's *An Introduction to Discourse Analysis. Theory and Method*, 2005.
- Chapter 1 ("Interpreting Social Discourse") in *Working with Discourse. Meaning Beyond the Clause* by J.R. Martin and D. Rose, 2003.
- Chapter 1 ("Introduction") in Barbara Johnstone's
- *Discourse Analysis*, 2002.

B) *SUMMARY:* Make a written summary of the chapter you read, and then hand it in to your Tutor (if you are following a university course).

---

[3] The complete references to these chapters, as well as those of the books or articles included in the *Further Reading* section, can be found in the bibliography ("References") at the back of this book.

C) *DISCUSSION*: Discuss the content of your summary, giving special attention to the meaning of the terms *text* and *context* with five other students or people and/or with your Tutor (in person or in a computer conference).

FURTHER READING

- Brown, G. & Yule (1983), Chapter 1: Introduction.
- Fairclough, N. (1992).   Chapter 1: "Approaches to Discourse Analysis".
- Gee, J.P.[1999] 2005, Chapters 1 & 2.
- Van Dijk, T. (1977)
- Van Dijk (1985).   "Introduction: discourse as a new cross-discipline".   In *Handbook of Discourse Analysis, Volume 1: Disciplines of Discourse.*
- Van Dijk, T. (2004)
- Articles in journals that specialize in discourse analysis research, such as the following: *Text, Text & Talk, Discourse & Society, Discourse Processes, Discourse Studies.*

USEFUL WEBSITES

- Wikipedia entry for *Discourse Analysis*:
  http://en.wikipedia.org/wiki/Discourse_analysis
- Criticism.Com – Essays in Discourse Analysis:
  http://www.criticism.com/da/index.html
- Stef Slembrouck's page: "What is meant by discourse analysis":
  http://bank.rug.ac.be/da/da.htm
- Discourse Analysis online: http://extra.shu.ac.uk/daol/
- *Text and Talk* Journal website:

http://www.degruyter.de/journals/text/detail.cfm
- *Discourse & Society* Journal website:
  http://www.sagepub.co.uk/journalsProdDesc.nav?prodId=Journal
  200873
- *Discourse Processes* Journal website:
  http://www.tandf.co.uk/journals/titles/0163853X.asp
- *Discourse Studies* Journal website:
  http://www.sagepub.co.uk/journalsProdDesc.nav?prodId=Journal
  200865

2

THE DATA

"…no methodological preferences are reached in a vacuum: they are all the product of more general beliefs in what constitutes data and what counts as evidence and 'proof'."

Deborah Schiffrin, *Approaches to Discourse*

Chapter Outline:

- Techniques of data collection and annotation.
- The ethics of data collection.
- Defining the term *corpus*.
- Different types of corpora.
- The use of corpora for Discourse Analysis.
- Available tools for corpus querying.

2.1. Data collection

One of the first problems we encounter when facing discourse analytic research concerns the **data** to be used. Some questions arise, such as: *What type of discourse are we going to analyze? How are we going to collect the data we need? And, in the case of spoken discourse, how are we going to transcribe and annotate the data in such a way that we can show the features of both text and context as faithfully as possible?*

The answer to the first question depends completely on the objectives the researcher has in mind, which, in turn, depend on the *research question*. S/he may want, for example, to analyze spoken or written language, or both, or s/he may want to focus on a given genre or register: there are innumerable possibilities here. But once we know the type of discourse we want to analyze, we have to figure out how to collect the data; i.e. we need to decide upon the best possible way of getting a linguistic corpus which will provide the basis for our research. As Taylor remarks, "one of the processes by which material becomes data is **selection**" (2001: 24), and there may be several different criteria for selecting a *sample*. As noted above, these criteria depend on the goals of research. Schiffrin explains how the different approaches to Discourse Analysis (DA) take different perspectives and have different beliefs about methods for collecting and analyzing data:

> For example, some approaches focus intensively on a few fragments of talk (e.g. interactional sociolinguistics), others focus on distributions of discourse items across a wide range of texts (e.g. variationists). Some

require a great deal of social, cultural, and personal information about interlocutors and may use interlocutors as informants in analysis of their own talk (e.g. ethnography of communication); others assume an idealized speaker/hearer whose specific social, cultural, or personal characteristics do not enter into participant strategies for building text at all (e.g. pragmatics). Methodological differences such as these are due, partially, to different theoretical assumptions –assumptions that are based on the different origins noted above (1994: 13).

Thus, when it comes to data collection, our goals will guide us in the selection process and they are likely to lead us to choose different procedures, such as *recording* and *transcribing spoken discourse, keying texts in, scanning, using texts which are stored in machine-readable form, downloading material from the internet,* etc.

2.2. Transcribing the data

A very important aspect of data collection in research involving talk or spoken discourse is *transcription*. By means of the process of transcription the researcher turns the spoken discourse in question into a document called *transcript*. Transcribing is not an easy task and it is very time-consuming. If the researcher aims at some degree of objectivity (another difficult –if not impossible– task), s/he should try to use a system of transcription that shows, as faithfully as possible, all the variables that intervene in the studied phenomenon. There is no such thing as a totally neutral transcription, and, to the present, it has not been possible to create a system so perfect as to represent all variables and aspects. However, discourse analysts have always made attempts to contrive annotation systems that best suit the aims of their research, and that allow them to obtain reliable results to a reasonable extent. For instance, a conversation analyst who views talk as interaction would argue that the data will include not only the words, but also other aspects of the conversation, such as the sequential organization of the utterances of the different participants, as well as the interruptions and pauses. Another important requirement would be to work with a sample of 'naturally occurring'[1] talk,

---

[1] Taylor explains that, in the most idealized form, *naturally occurring talk* "would probably refer to informal conversation which would have occurred even if it was not being observed or recorded, and which was unaffected by the presence of the observer and/or recording equipment" (2001: 27).

rather than with data collected by means of research interviews[2]. Some **analysts include information about the text, such as genre, date and place** of publication, etc. Others include information about the pronunciation and intonation patterns, or about the speakers (sex, age, occupation, social class, etc.). They can also assign labelled brackets to each constituent of a sentence (parsing) or signal some features of spoken language such as laughter, interruptions or hesitations. In general, and as Johnstone (2005:20) notes, it is crucial to be able to uncover the many ways in which texts are shaped by contexts and the many ways in which texts shape contexts".

For the purpose of illustration, we will now examine the attempts made by a few authors to annotate their data.

2.2.1. Transcription conventions used by some discourse analysts

There is no single accepted way to transcribe or represent speech on the page. Each analyst chooses and annotates the features that best suit the purposes of his/her research, and consequently it can be said in all fairness that there are almost as many ways to transcribe speech as there are researchers who set about doing the task. Leech (2004) discusses this issue in the following passage:

> Any type of annotation presupposes a typology — a system of classification — for the phenomena being represented. But linguistics, like most academic disciplines, is sadly lacking in agreement about the categories to be used in such description. Different terminologies abound, and even the use of a single term, such as *verb phrase*, is notoriously a prey to competing theories. Even an apparently simple matter, such as defining word classes (POS), is open to considerable disagreement. Against this background, it might be suggested that corpus annotation cannot be usefully attempted: there is no absolute 'God's truth' view of language or 'gold standard' annotation against which the decision to call word x a noun and word y a verb can be measured.

However, it cannot be said that there is not a certain consensus. For example, when dealing with some syntactic categories, such as nouns, verbs and so on, people performing transcription will normally agree on

---

[2] *Research interviews* are supposed to be a more conventional method of data collection, by means of which the researcher initiates talk 'about' something and conducts an interview for the specific purpose of the research. The interviewer usually works with a prepared questionnaire or list of topics.

how to label them, whereas they will disagree on less clear cases. Hence the ideal procedure would be for the analyst to start from a consensual set of categories and only use his/her own for the cases in which there is no agreement whatsoever. In order to do this, it is first necessary to examine previous systems of annotation designed by other researchers.

Some important information about the speakers, necessary for analyzing their discourse.

There is no ideal transcription system which suits all purposes: highly detailed transcripts include more information but are often hard to read, whereas transcripts with less detail are easier to read but contain less information about the whole discourse situation. Transcripts including too many details may provide more information than people are able to process, and thus it is advisable not to include too much distracting extraneous detail in order to be able to concentrate only on the crucial elements or features of the speech event that will help us answer the research question.

According to Edwards (1993) three main principles should be observed when designing a transcription system, taking into account its readability for a human researcher or a computer:

1. Categories should be:

    - systematically discriminable
    - exhaustive
    - systematically contrastive

2. Transcripts should be readable (to the researcher)
3. For computational tractability, mark-up should be:

    - systematic
    - predictable.

In addition, the designer should make a decision as to whether the transcription is to be *orthographic*, *prosodic*, or *phonetic*, or more than one of these. Also, s/he will have to decide on how to represent non-verbal data, such as contextual information, paralinguistic features, pauses, and overlaps. This means that more than one level of transcription must be aligned, which will have obvious implications for mark-up of the data. As explained above, it is always useful to examine previous systems of annotation created by other researchers, and this is what we shall do in the next section of this chapter.

2.2.1.1. Notation used in the *London Lund Corpus* (Svartvik & Quirk, 1980)

The *London Lund Corpus* is a computerized corpus of spoken English which has been widely used by linguists and discourse analysts in different studies. It consists of 87 texts which are arranged in text groups (face-to-face conversation, telephone conversation, etc.) and, apart from the symbols used in their annotation, in some of the texts the authors provide the possible users of the corpus with some extra information about the speakers, concerning their age and occupation.

Let us now examine a fragment of one of the texts in this corpus with respect to its notation conventions:

Text S.11.1 Public, unprepared commentary, demonstration, oration. A trial (legal discourse)

```
11 1  1  10 1 1 a   11  ^Mr P=otter#                              /
11 1  1  20 1 1 a   11  ^did y/ou# - -                            /
11 1  1  30 1 1 a   11  ar^r\/ive#                                /
11 1  1  40 1 1 a   11  a^bout !two o`cl\ock#                      /
11 1  1  50 1 1 a   11  ^on [dhi] . !S\unday# .                    /
11 1  1  60 1 1 a   11  the ^date the 'will was . s\igned# .       /
11 1  1  70 1 1 b   11  ^y/es# - -                                /
11 1  1  80 1 1 a   11  and . did ^you . g\/o#                     /
11 1  1  90 1 1 a   11  and ^see your 'mother :straight aw/ay#     /
11 1  1 100 1 1 b   11  ^y\es I _did#                              /
11 1  1 110 1 1 a   11  ^what was she 'then d\oing# .              /
11 1  1 120 1 1 b   11  she was ^having her l\unch# - - -          /
11 1  1 130 1 1 a   11  ^what a'bout the :br\andy 'bottle#         /
11 1  1 140 1 1 a   11  ^where was th\at# - -                      /
11 1  1 150 1 1 b   11  ^I 'don`t kn\ow#                           /
11 1  1 160 1 1 b   12  ^I 'didn`t [s] . ![lu?] ^I 'didn`t !s\ee#  /
11 1  1 170 1 1 a   11  you ^didn`t s\/ee _it#                     /
11 1  2 180 1 1 b   11  ^w\ell# .                                  /
11 1  2 190 1 1 b   11  ^n\o {I ^d\idn`t#}#                         /
11 1  2 200 1 1 b   14  ^I ^I ^I ^all I kn/ow#                      /
11 1  2 210 1 1 b   11  was ^my !mother was :having her !l\unch# . /
11 1  2 220 2 1 b   21  when *I*                                   /
11 1  2 230 1 1 a   20  *((and))*                                  /
11 1  2 220 1 1(b   11  ar^r\ived# -                               /
11 1  2 240 1 1 a   11  ^how did she !s\eem {^th\en#}# -           /
11 1  2 250 1 1 a   11  ((at)) ^two o`cl\ock# -                     /
11 1  2 260 1 1 b   11  ^w/ell# .                                  /
11 1  2 270 1 1 b   11  she ^seemed 'all r/ight#                   /
11 1  2 280 1 1 b   11  I ^think she was a :little t\/ired# - - -  /
11 1  2 290 1 1 a   11  and ^how 'long did it :t\ake#              /
11 1  2 300 1 1 a   11  ^for her to com'plete her l\unch# - - -    /
11 1  2 310 1 1 b   11  oh ^I would !th=ink# - - -                 /
11 1  2 320 1 1 b   11  ^pr=obably# .                              /
11 1  2 330 1 1 b   11  ^f/ifteen 'minutes# -                      /
11 1  3 340 1 1 a   12  ^was it /any a ^meal of any s/ubstance# .  /
11 1  3 350 1 1 b   11  she ^had [@:m] . :ch\icken#                /
11 1  3 360 1 1 b   11  she ^didn`t 'eat very :m\uch of it# - - -  /
11 1  3 370 1 1 a   11  ^did !you s\/it with 'her#                 /
11 1  3 380 1 1 a   11  ^wh=ilst# .                                /
11 1  3 390 1 1 a   11  she com^pleted the m\/eal# -               /
11 1  3 400 1 1 b   11  I was ^in the r=oom#                       /
11 1  3 410 1 1 b   11  ^while she was :h\/aving _it#              /
11 1  3 420 1 1 b   11  ^y\es# .                                   /
11 1  3 430 1 2 a   12  and ^then [@] ( . coughs) - did she ^have it on a /
```

```
11 1  3 430 1 1 a   12  tr/ay# - .                                    /
11 1  3 440 1 1 b    11  ^y/es#                                        /
11 1  3 450 1 1 a    11  ^somebody took the !tr\ay out . {pre^s\umably#}# . /
11 1  3 460 1 1 b    11  [@:] ^my !w\ife 'took it 'out# -              /
11 1  4 470 1 1 a    11  and [?] . ^that`s . 'then a'bout 'two fift\een# - -/
11 1  4 480 1 1 b    11  [@] ^y/es#                                    /
11 1  4 490 1 1 b    11  [i?] ^y/es#                                   /
11 1  4 510 1 1 a    11  were ^y/ou 'then# .                          /
11 1  4 520 1 1 a    11  a^lone w/ith 'her# - -                       /
11 1  4 500 1 1 b    11  it ^w\ould be# .                             /
11 1  4 530 1 1 b    11  [@m] I was a^lone with m/other#              /
11 1  4 540 1 1 b    11  ^y/es#                                        /
11 1  4 550 1 1 b    21  ^after . my :wife left - - *[@m]*            /
11 1  4 560 1 1 a    11  ^*what* !took pl\ace#                         /
11 1  4 570 1 2 a    11  ^after your :wife 'left with the tr\ay . {be^tween /
11 1  4 570 1 1 a    11  'you and your m\other#}# .                   /
11 1  4 580 1 1 b    11  well my ^mother \asked 'me#                   /
11 1  4 590 1 1 b    11  ^when I "!g\ot th/ere# .                     /
11 1  4 600 1 1 b    11  ^if 'I had br\ought# -                        /
11 1  4 610 1 1 b    11  [@] this ^draft of her ":w\ill# .            /
11 1  4 620 1 1 b    11  and I ^said I h\ad# - -                       /
```

Transcription conventions:

A) PROSODY: *# End of Tone Group*   ^Yes   *Beginning of Tone Group*

Tones

Y\es	FALL	YⅤes	FALL-RISE	Y=es	LEVEL
Y/es	RISE	Y/\es	RISE-FALL		

Pitch

:Yes	Higher than the previous syllable		
!Yes	High	!!Yes	Very High

Stress

'Yes	Normal	"Yes	Strong

Pauses

Yes - -   Each dash is a unit pause of one stress unit or "foot"

Yes +   Brief pause

B) SPEAKERS

A	Speaker identity
(A)	Speaker continues where s/he left off
A, B	A and B
VAR	Various speakers
?	Speaker identity unknown
a	(low case letter) Non-surreptitious speaker

As can be seen, the specification of the notation used helps us learn many details, not only about the text, but also regarding the context of this fragment of legal discourse. There is both prosodic and pragmatic information, which allows us, for instance, to learn that both **a** and **b** are non-surreptitious speakers, which tells us that they knew they were being recorded. Also, by looking at the tones, pitch, stress, and other prosodic features used by the speakers, we may, among other things, infer information having to do with their attitude (e.g. if they are upset, or trying to be ironic, etc.).

2.2.1.2. Notation used by Deborah Schiffrin

The following data have been taken from D. Schiffrin and R. Lakoff's Data Packet for their "Discourse" class at Berkeley and Georgetown Universities (Spring 1998). As will be noticed, this notation has its peculiarities and is different from that used in the *London Lund Corpus* above. For example, this author uses square brackets ([]) to signal speech overlap, and a dot (.) to represent a falling intonation followed by a pause.

Debby: D   Zelda: Z

D: (1)   What does your uh daughter in law call you?
Z: (2)   Well, that's a sore spot.
D: hhhh
Z: (3)   My **older** daughter in law does call me Mom.=
D: Uh huh.
Z: (4)   My younger daughter in law right now is up to nothing.
    (5)   She [had said-
D: [Oh
Z: (6)   We had quite a discussion about it.
    (7)   We did bring it out in the open.
    (8)   She said that um…that she- just- right now, she's:- it'll take her

time.
(9)   Now they're marrie:d, it's gonna be uh... I think eh...five years,=
D: Um hmm.
Z: (10) that they'll be married.
    (11) and she said that eh it was very hard t's:-call someone else Mom beside her
            mother.
    (12) so I had said to her, "That's Okay!"
    (13) I said, "If you- if you can't say Mom, just call me by my [first name!
D:
            [Umhm
Z: (14) So, we had quite a discussion about it.
    (15) It was a little heated,   at one time.=
D: Yeh
Z: (16) She said, "All right", she'll call me Zelda.
     (17) But she still can't bring herself to say Zelda.
     (18) so she calls me nothing!
     (19) She do- but we're very cl- we're on very good terms,=

                                                                                Z
D:
    Yeh.

Transcription conventions

.   Falling intonation followed by noticeable pause (as at end of declarative sentence)
…   Noticeable pause or break in rhythm without falling intonation.
bold   Self interruption with glottal stop
CAPS   Very emphatic stress
[   ]   Speech overlap
=   Continuity of previous line of text (when lack of space prevents continuous speech from being
               presented on a single line of text)
Z   When speech from B follows speech from A without perceptible pause, then Z links the end of A with
               the beginning of B

When speech from B occurs during what can be heard as a brief silence from A, then B's speech is under A's silence:

A: I can't wait to go to the party!   It'll be fun.
B: Oh yeh!

2.2.1.3. Other annotation practices

The examples in 2.2.1.1. and 2.2.1.2. show only two possible ways of annotating corpora. Other authors have chosen different symbols or have taken into account some other, additional, variables. For instance, Jefferson (1979) marks the gaze of the speaker with a line above the utterance and the gaze of the addressee with a line below it. The line indicates that the interlocutor marked is gazing toward the other, while the lack of a line indicates the absence of gaze. Commas are used to indicate the dropping of gaze. Besides, some movements like head nodding are marked when they occur:

Ann: _____
      Karen has this new hou:se. en it's got all this

Beth: _____ ,,,   ((Nod))

Jefferson also marks applause by using strings of X's with lower- (for quiet applause) and uppercase (for loud applause) letters. In the following example, the amplitude of the applause increases at the end:

Audience: xxxxxxxxxXXXXXXXXXXXXXXXXXX

Deborah Tannen uses left arrows to highlight key lines, as in the following fragment taken and adapted from her well-known book *You Just Don't Understand. Women and Men in Conversation* (1990: 197):

STEVE: I think it's basically done damage to children. That what good it's done is outweighed by the damage

→ DEBORAH: Did you two grow up with
                                        television?

The examples of notation conventions presented in this section display only a few of the innumerable possibilities. As noted above, each researcher may choose his/her own conventions (which normally depend upon the needs and objectives of the analysis), provided they are explained and made clear to the reader.

2.3. Ethics of data collection

Another important aspect to be considered when doing discourse analysis is the **ethics** of the research, which necessarily affect the process of data collection.

Even though in an ideal world all participants in a project should have equal rights and power, it is a fact that, in general, the researcher has more power than the other participants in an experiment. This power may come, as Taylor notes, "from holding the status associated with being an academic and, supposedly, an expert" (2001: 20). In addition, the researcher has more information about the experiment than the subjects, a fact which also contributes to her power. Thus, for example, the discourse analyst will know that the publication of a given conversation might bring some negative consequences to the participants of the conversation if their identities are revealed, and therefore s/he should never publish the real names of the participants without their consent[3]. Researchers ought not to abuse their power. It is an ethical requirement that the researcher obtain the consent of the participants, not only to be involved in the study but also to use the data they provide. As a general rule, researchers have the obligation to a) protect all participants, b) not harm them in any way, and c) always observe their legal rights.

2.4.   Corpus Linguistics: The use of corpora for DA

Corpus is defined by Crystal as "a collection of LINGUISTIC DATA, either written texts or a TRANSCRIPTION of recorded speech, which can be used as a starting-point of linguistic description or as a means of verifying hypotheses about a LANGUAGE (**corpus linguistics**)" (1997: 95).

Corpus linguistics, thus, has to do with the practice and the principles of using corpora in language study. Biber et al. note that the essential characteristics of corpus-based analysis are:

- Empiricism (it analyzes the actual patterns of use in natural texts);
- Utilization of a large and principled collection of natural texts, known as a "corpus", as the basis for analysis;

---

[3] However, the principle of anonymity is not observed in DA when the intention of the analyst is to denounce and/or condemn the speech or writing of, for example, a given politician or institution. We find numerous instances of this type of analysis within the approach called *Critical Discourse Analysis* (Chapter 10).

- Extensive use of computers for analysis, using both automatic and interactive techniques;
- Use of both quantitative and qualitative analytical techniques. (1998: 4)

Corpora are excellent tools for discourse analysts, for they facilitate the investigation of language in use. Studies of language use require empirical analyses of large databases of authentic texts, a requirement that has been possible to meet, obviously, thanks to the aid of corpus linguistics. Using corpora allows researchers to analyze patterns of use, i.e. how some linguistic features are used in association with other linguistic and non-linguistic features. Linguistic and non-linguistic association patterns interact; they are not independent (Biber et al., 1998). For instance, if we consider the lexical associations for *thin*, *skinny* and *slim*, we can also consider their distribution across different registers. Thus, corpus-based studies aim at characterizing registers, dialects, etc. in terms of their linguistic association patterns.

Although some scholars (especially generative grammarians) have pointed to the limitations of corpus-based analysis (e.g. that it is limited to samples of *performance* only, or that no corpus can contain information about all areas of language), it cannot be denied that the use of corpora has proved to present considerable advantages when analyzing discourse: it has allowed researchers to deal with larger and more varied texts, bringing about a reliability of analysis never reached before; it has enabled them to make more objective and accurate descriptions of usage than would be possible through mere introspection. It also allows them, for instance, to come to reliable conclusions based on frequency of use of a given linguistic feature or pattern, to make comparative analyses about usage in different varieties, or to arrive at a total account of the linguistic features in any of the texts contained in the corpus. And, most important of all, a well-constructed general corpus can be an inexhaustible source of hypotheses about the way language works.

All the above advantages have been mainly made feasible thanks to the construction, in modern times, of computerized corpora, which permit the storage and analysis of a much greater number of natural language texts than would be possible if we had to store and analyze them by hand. However, the first large corpus of English-language data was entirely transcribed by hand and stored on index cards which were processed manually. This corpus was originally known as the *Survey of English Usage*, a project which started in the 1960s and which consisted of a million words comprising 200 texts of spoken and written material of

5,000 words each. The whole survey has now been computerized, and is currently known as the *London-Lund Corpus*[4].

2.4.1. Computer corpora and concordance programs

The first computerized corpus in the history of linguistics was the *Brown University Corpus of American English*. It was created in the 1960s by Henry Kucera and W. Nelson Francis, and it aimed to represent a wide range of genres of published written text in American English produced during a single year. The *Lancaster-Oslo/Bergen (LOB) Corpus of British English* was compiled in the 1970s to match the Brown corpus using British English texts.

Ever since the 1980s, increasingly large corpora have been compiled (especially of English) and are used in different fields, such as in the development of natural language processing software and in applications, including lexicography, machine translation, speech recognition, etc. Three examples of modern corpora are *The British National Corpus (BNC), The International Corpus of English (ICE)* and *The Bank of English*. Some online corpora can be found, such as the *Experimental BNC Website* (which offers a BNC online service allowing everyone with access to the internet to register for an account on the BNC server) or the *Shakespeare Online Corpus*. In addition, researchers can now benefit from concordance programs, i.e. programs which turn the electronic texts into databases which can be searched. Some examples of these programs are the *Word Cruncher* (which you get, for example, when you buy the ICAME corpora of modern and medieval English), *TACT* (a well-known, freeware program), *SARA* (specifically made for searches of the BNC) and *WordSmith Tools* (a program widely used by linguists, lexicographers and discourse analysts nowadays. It offers several possibilities, such as querying, searching for word combinations within a specified range of words, looking up substrings or parts of words, or accessing collocates and frequency lists).

2.4.1.   A possible classification of corpora

Once we have decided to use a computer corpus, we should decide what type of corpora will best suit our aims. We will not use the same corpus if we want, for example, to analyze spoken language as if we want to analyze written language (unless the corpus we choose is mixed and has

---

[4] See 2.2.1.1.

samples of both). Reich (1998) offers the following taxonomy, which classifies corpora according to *medium, national varieties, historical variation, geographical/dialectal variation, age, genre, open-endedness* and *availability*:

- *Medium*: **spoken** corpora (eg. London-Lund corpus) vs. **written** corpora (e.g. Lancaster Oslo/Bergen corpus (LOB)) vs. **mixed** corpora (British National Corpus (BNC) or Bank of English)
- *National varieties*: **British** corpora (e.g. Lancaster Oslo/Bergen corpus) vs. **American** corpora (e.g. Brown corpus) vs. an **international** corpus of English.
- *Historical variation*: **diachronic** corpora (Helsinki corpus, cf. the ICAME home page) vs. **synchronic** corpora (Brown, LOB, BNC) vs. corpora which cover only **one stage of language history** (corpus of Old or Middle English, Shakespeare corpora)
- *Geographical variation/dialectal variation*: corpus of **dialect samples** (e.g. Scots) vs. **mixed** corpora (The BNC spoken component includes samples of speakers from all over Britain)
- *Age*: corpora of **adult** English vs. corpora of **child** English (English components of CHILDES)
- *Genre*: corpora of **literary** texts vs. corpora of **technical** English vs. corpora of **non-fiction** (e.g. news texts) vs. **mixed corpora** covering **all genres**
- *Open-endedness*: **closed, unalterable** corpora (e.g. LOB, Brown) vs. **monitor** corpora (Bank of English)
- *Availability*: **commercial** vs. **non-commercial** research corpora, **online** corpora vs. corpora on **ftp servers** vs. corpora available on **floppy disks or CD-ROMs**

This taxonomy takes into account most of the types of corpora which are currently available, but it is not entirely comprehensive. Other variables might be considered depending on the research aims, which might bring about new types.

SUMMING UP... (CHAPTER 2)

1. The selection of the data for any given discourse analytic research depends completely on the objectives of the project, which, in turn, depend on the *research question.*

2. The different approaches to DA take different perspectives and have different beliefs about methods for collecting and analyzing data.

3. When discourse analysts use samples of the spoken language as their data, they generally turn the spoken discourse into a document called *transcript* by means of the process of *transcription.* There is no such thing as a totally neutral transcription, but researchers try to make their transcriptions as faithful as possible by using different systems of annotation depending on the goals of their research.

4. The *ethics* of data collection require that researchers protect all participants by not doing them any harm and by observing their legal rights.

5. *Corpus linguistics* has to do with the practice and the principles of using corpora in language study. A *corpus* is a collection of linguistic data used as the basis for linguistic description and analysis.

6. The use of computers has allowed for the storage and analysis of a much greater number of natural language texts than was ever possible. Computer corpora and concordance programs, which turn the electronic texts into searchable databases which are very widely used in linguistic research nowadays.

7. Corpora can be classified according to *medium, national varieties, historical variation, geographical/dialectal variation, age, genre, open-endedness, availability*, etc.

SELF-EVALUATION QUESTIONS

Choose the answer that best suits the information given in Chapter 2.

1. The type of discourse the analyst is going to study depends mainly on…
a) the research question.
b) what the researcher likes to do.
c) how the data are collected.

2. The different approaches to Discourse Analysis…
a) all share the same methods of collecting data.
b) take different views about collecting and analyzing data.
c) all work with naturally-occurring language.

3. Downloading material from the internet…
a) may be a procedure for data collection.
b) is a method of Discourse Analysis.
c) is the best method for data collection.

4. A *transcript* is…
a) a process of data collection.
b) a document that reflects the spoken discourse to be analyzed.
c) a complex type of discourse research.

5. Transcriptions …
a) are always completely neutral and objective.
b) try to show the different variables that intervene in the discourse studied.
c) always include contextual factors.

6. Each analyst…
a) uses various notation systems.
b) uses the notation system that best suits his/her objectives.
c) includes tone groups in the notation used.

7. Transcription conventions…
a) should always be explained and made clear to the reader.
b) should always be used in the same way by all researchers.
c) should be different for each study.

8. It is a well-known fact that, in an experiment…
a) the participants and the researcher have equal power.
b) there are no power issues.
c) the researcher has more power than the other participants.

9. It is an ethical requirement in discourse analysis that…
a) the researchers protect all the participants.
b) the researchers pay for the services of the participants.
c) the participants hide their names.

10. Corpus-based analysis …
a) normally uses both quantitative and qualitative techniques of analysis.
b) does not normally have an empirical nature.
c) is always theoretical in nature.

11. The use of corpora …
a) allows us to work with the spoken language only.
b) does not favor the analysis of small fragments of discourse.
c) allows the researcher to analyze patterns of use in language.

12. Corpus-based analysis…
a) has brought a reliability of analysis never reached before.
b) has many disadvantages.
c) can only be carried out by means of computers.

13. Concordance computer programs…
a) turn electronic texts into talk.
b) transform the texts into databases that can be searched.
c) are not used much by linguists nowadays.

14. The BNC is a corpus…
a)   that has been classified in terms of a national variety.
b)   of spoken British English.
c)   showing mainly historical variation.

15. The aims of research…
a)   have nothing to do with the corpus chosen for analysis.
b)   will vary if we use different corpora in the analysis.
c)   will determine the type of corpus used in the analysis.

PRACTICE

A) *COLLECTING SAMPLES OF SPOKEN DISCOURSE*:

a) *SEARCHING THE WWW*: THINK of a type of spoken discourse you would like to analyze in English (e.g. interviews, conversations, discussion panels, etc.) and SEARCH the World Wide Web to get samples of such a type. You can find it, for instance, on radio or TV programs, or the You Tube website.

b) ANNOTATING THE DATA: USE conventions for annotating the recorded data with the features you consider important for your future research (e.g. information about the text (genre, date of publication, place of publication), information about intonation patterns or pronunciation; information about the speakers (sex, age, occupation, social and geographical origin); parsing (i.e. assigning labelled brackets to each constituent of a sentence); discourse information of spoken material (laughing, interruptions, hesitations, etc). Reading "Appendix 2: Transcription Conventions" of D. Schiffrin's *Approaches to Discourse*[5] may help you in this enterprise.

c) *DISCUSSION*: SEND or HAND IN the sample data to your tutor (in case you are following a course) and DISCUSS the procedures and annotation used. Justify your decisions.

---

[5] See **References** at the back of this book.

FURTHER READING

- Johansson, S. & Stenström, Anna-Brita (eds.) (1991). *English Computer Corpora: Selected and Research Guide.*
- Mc Enery, T. & Wilson, A. (1996). *Corpus Linguistics.*
- Stubbs, Michael (1996*). Text and Corpus Analysis.*
- Wynne, M (editor). 2005. *Developing Linguistic Corpora: A Guide to Good Practice.* Oxford: Oxbow Books. Available online from http://ahds.ac.uk/linguistic- corpora/

USEFUL WEBSITES

Wikipedia entry for Corpus Linguistics:
http://en.wikipedia.org/wiki/Corpus_linguistics

Introduction to Corpus Linguistics:
http://www.essex.ac.uk/linguistics/clmt/w3c/corpus_ling/content/introduction.html

The British National Corpus site: http://www.natcorp.ox.ac.uk/
Freely-available, web-based corpora: http://corpus.byu.edu/

PRAGMATICS

A 'Beefeater' giving a guided tour at the Tower of London.

"*...within the history of linguistics, pragmatics is a remedial discipline born, or re-born, of the starkly limited scope of Chomskyan linguistics (while in philosophy, the interest in language use can in part be attributed to 'language reformism'). Pragmatics prior to 1957, it could be argued, was practised [...] without being preached.*"

Stephen Levinson, *Pragmatics*.

Chapter Outline:

- The scope of Pragmatics.
- *Speech Act Theory* and Grice's *Theory of Implicature.*
- *Reference, deixis* and *presupposition.*

3.1. Definition. What is the scope of Pragmatics?

Pragmatics is an indispensable source for discourse analysis. It is impossible to analyze any discourse without having a solid basic knowledge of pragmatic phenomena and the ways in which they work and interact.

To define *Pragmatics* and to delimit its scope is no easier task than to define *Discourse Analysis* or *Text Linguistics.* One thing we know for sure: when working within the field of Pragmatics we are dealing with MEANING. But, then, what is the difference between *Semantics* and *Pragmatics*? In a very simplified way, it could be said that if we think of Semantics as the area of study covering the truth-conditional meaning of utterances, then Pragmatics deals with all the other kinds of meaning. However, this would be a very broad definition, similar to the one given by Morris in 1938, considered to be the first modern definition of the term. As Levinson notes, Morris's definition of Pragmatics as "dealing with all the psychological, biological and sociological phenomena which occur in the functioning of signs" (1983: 108) is much wider than the scope of the work that is currently labelled as pragmatic. Levinson explains that the term *Pragmatics* was subject to a successive narrowing of scope and the definitions which were finally influential were those making reference to the **users** of the language.

Many authors have defined Pragmatics in different ways, and in these definitions, elements such as *context, meaning beyond literal meaning, speech acts, deixis, understatement* or *implicature* are presented as important components of this discipline.

Levinson argues that "the notion that pragmatics might be the study of aspects of meaning not covered in semantics certainly has some cogency" (1983: 15). Leech explains that both Semantics and Pragmatics are concerned with meaning, but the difference between them lies in two different uses of the verb *to mean* (1983: 6):

> [1] What does X mean?   [2] What did you mean by X?

Semantics would deal with [1], and Pragmatics with [2]. Therefore, semantic meaning is dyadic and has to do with words or expressions in a given language regardless of particular situations, speakers or hearers, while pragmatic meaning is triadic and is defined with respect to a speaker or user of the language.

Georgia Green's definition of Pragmatics is, like Morris's, a broad one:

> *Linguistic pragmatics* as defined here is at the intersection of a number of fields within and outside of cognitive science: not only linguistics, cognitive psychology, cultural anthropology, and philosophy (logic, semantics, action theory), but also sociology (interpersonal dynamics and social convention) and rhetoric contribute to its domain. (1989: 2)

As can be seen, Green's definition of Discourse Analysis is very similar to some of those that we examined in Chapter 1. In addition, one of Levinson's (1983) definitions of Pragmatics as "the study of utterance meaning" equates it to Schiffrin's definition of Discourse Analysis (see Chapter 1, 3). But, are Pragmatics and Discourse Analysis the same? Schiffrin notes that the scope of Pragmatics is wide and "faces definitional dilemmas similar to those faced by discourse analysis" (1994: 190).

In this book we see Pragmatics as one of the main sources and approaches to Discourse Analysis, thus we consider Discourse Analysis as a broader discipline that draws from the principles of Pragmatics but includes other perspectives within its scope. We regard Pragmatics, then, in a narrower sense. We shall certainly be concerned about the relationship of discourse to the users of the language (an essential aspect of the discipline) and we shall touch upon aspects of the speech situation which are typically regarded as pragmatic, such as *speech acts, deixis, reference, presupposition, implicature* and *politeness phenomena,* but we shall not place Pragmatics on a par with Discourse Analysis.

Although Pragmatics is a field of study that can be the subject matter of a complete linguistic course, in this book we are only going to cover the essentials and touch upon its basic tenets.

In the next section we shall discuss the so-called Gricean Pragmatics, which evolved from H. P. Grice's (1975) ideas about speaker meaning and the cooperative principle, and which has been most influential in the world of linguistics.

3.2. Grice's Cooperative Principle
and Theory of Implicature

As Horn & Ward note, "The landmark event in the development of a systematic framework for pragmatics was the delivery of Grice's (1967) William James lectures" (2004: xi). One of the basic concepts in Gricean Pragmatics is *speaker meaning*. Grice makes a distinction between natural meaning, which is devoid of human intentionality[1], and non-natural meaning (**meaning –nn**), which has to do with intentional communication. There is a second intention which is implicit in the definition of meaning - nn, i.e. the recognition, on the part of the addressee, of the speaker's communicative intention. Thus, for instance, if a child says *"I like that toy"* to her mother, the meaning –nn would be that she wants her mother to buy that toy for her (and therefore she expects her mother to recognize her "hidden" intention or wish of having that toy). This type of meaning is closely connected to another of the central concepts in Gricean Pragmatics: the notion of *conversational implicature*, which is considered to be one of the single most important ideas in Pragmatics. This notion has provided linguistic analysts with an explicit account of how it is possible to mean more than what is actually "said". Normally, what a speaker intends to communicate is far richer than what s/he says or directly expresses, and thus s/he exploits pragmatic principles that the hearer can invoke in order to bridge the gap between what was said (the literal content of the uttered sentence, determined by its grammatical structure) and what was meant (i.e. what was really communicated).

Conversational implicatures are a kind of inference that can be derived from an utterance in order to work out the "meant" from the "said", and they are related to what Grice called the *Cooperative Principle* and its *Maxims*. Given the fact that our talk exchanges do not normally consist of a succession of disconnected remarks (and would not be rational if they did), the remarks are characteristically cooperative efforts and each participant recognizes in them a mutually accepted direction (Grice, 1975: 45). Speakers are assumed to be cooperative and to follow the maxims, which are reproduced herein:

> A) THE COOPERATIVE PRINCIPLE:
> Make your contribution such as is required, at the stage at which it occurs, by the accepted purpose or direction of the talk exchange in which you are engaged.

---

[1] As in, for example, *Those dark clouds mean rain.*

1) THE MAXIM OF QUANTITY
- i) Make your contribution as informative as is required (for the current purposes of the exchange).
- ii) Do not make your contribution more informative than is required.

2) THE MAXIM OF QUALITY
Try to make your contribution one that is true, specifically:
- i) Do not say what you believe to be false.
- ii) Do not say that for which you lack adequate evidence.

3) THE MAXIM OF RELATION
Be relevant.

4) THE MAXIM OF MANNER
Be perspicuous, and specifically:
- i) Avoid obscurity of expression.
- ii) Avoid ambiguity.
- iii) Be brief (avoid unnecessary prolixity).
- iv) Be orderly.

(Grice, 1975:45-46)

Grice explains that people do not always follow these guidelines to the letter, and here is where conversational implicatures play their part. When a speaker violates or "flouts" one of the maxims, the hearer assumes that the speaker is nevertheless trying to be cooperative and looks for the meaning at some deeper level. In doing so s/he makes an inference, namely a *conversational implicature.*

One area in which conversational implicatures are fully at work is in the use of verbal irony. For example, if, after having a terrible argument with a friend, a woman responds:

You're a fine friend indeed!

the friend will readily understand that the woman is trying to get across a meaning which is different from the literal one, conveyed by her proposition. She is in fact violating the Quality Maxim, for her friend should reach the conclusion, by means of implicature, that the woman does not think she is a fine friend but, on the contrary, a bad/ disloyal/ selfish friend.

According to Grice, in order to work out the presence of a conversational implicature, the hearer will draw on:

- The conventional meaning of the words used, together with the identity of any references that may be involved.
- The Cooperative Principle and its Maxims.
- The context, linguistic or otherwise, of the utterance.
- Other items of background knowledge.
- The fact (or supposed fact) that all relevant items falling under the previous headings are available to both participants and both participants know or assume this to be the case   (1975: 50).

There are, however, cases in which the **conventional** meaning of the words used will determine what is implicated. Consider the following examples:

a)   *She is a woman and therefore she is not a good driver.*
b)   *The math problem was so easy that even Tom could solve it.*

By using the connector *therefore* in a) we support the notion that the fact of driving badly is a consequence of the fact of being a woman. Likewise, in b), the conventional meaning of the word *even* makes the hearer infer that Tom must not be very intelligent or at least is not very good at maths. This kind of inference, induced by *therefore* in a) and by *even* in b), is what Grice has called a *conventional implicature*. Conventional implicatures deal with detachable but non-cancellable aspects of meaning, and they are akin to pragmatic *presuppositions*[2].

One of the main characteristics of *conversational implicatures*, as opposed to *conventional implicatures*, is that they are *cancellable*, a feature that Grice explains in the following manner:

> To the form of words of the utterance of which putatively implicates that p, it is admissible to add "but not p", or "I do not mean to imply that p", and that it is contextually cancellable if one can find situations in which the utterance of the form of the words would simply not carry the implicature (1978: 115-16).

The fact that all conversational implicatures are non-conventional and therefore can be cancelled gives them a certain "slippery" condition. However, they constitute a crucial part of both speaker and hearer communicative competence: being able to work out implicatures, among

---

[2] See 3.6.

other things, makes a speaker proficient and capable of interacting successfully. It is a crucially important part of the pragmatic knowledge necessary to communicate efficiently in any language.

Many authors (e.g. Hirschberg 1991, Levinson 2000, Carston 1995) have debated the significance of two main kinds of conversational implicature, namely 1) *generalized* conversational implicature, and 2) *particularized* conversational implicature. Examples a) and b) illustrate the difference between the two types:

a) (A conversation between Robert and John, when talking about some beautiful, attractive women they met in their youth)

> Robert: Remember Paula?
> John: Ah!! Paula!! She was glorious, gorgeous! What a beautiful girl! She always hung out with Susan, remember?
> Robert: Yeah, **Susan was a nice person**.

Implicature a → **Susan was not attractive or beautiful (or glorious, or gorgeous)**

b) My brother is now in Rome or in Venice.

Implicature b → **I don't know for a fact that my brother is in Venice**.

The inferences induced in both a) and b) are non-conventional and therefore, cancellable. Thus, in both cases we are dealing with *conversational* implicatures. But what distinguishes *implicature a* from *implicature b* is the generality of the circumstances in which the inference was worked out. The inference drawn in a) is a case of ***particularized* conversational implicature** because it is only in the context of a conversation like the one between Robert and John (i.e. a conversation about beautiful women) that the hearer will normally be expected to infer the content of *implicature a*, i.e., that Susan was not beautiful. That is to say, the implicature is worked out in this particular context and would not apply to a general context (where nobody would question Susan's beauty and would just consider the fact that she was nice). On the contrary, the inference drawn in b), that the speaker does not know for sure whether her brother is in Venice or in Rome, is induced in the absence of a special context. Implicature b then, has a default nature and it represents the concept of ***generalized*** conversational implicature. It is important to note that in both examples the crucial elements to take into account for inducing the relevant implicatum are the **speaker** or **utterance**, NOT the proposition or sentence.

Having said the above, I want to remark that it is not within the objectives of this work to theorize about the difference between the two types of conversational implicature. For the sake of our analysis, it will suffice to be able to identify the conversational implicatures of a given discourse, whatever type they belong to, and thus from now onwards we shall simply refer to conversational implicatures as a general category, regardless of their type.

3.2.1. Examples and analysis

In the above section (3.2.) we saw an example of an implicature that was worked out after the violation of the Quality Maxim (*You're a fine friend indeed!*). The following examples show the violation of the other three maxims and the implicatures this violation triggers in each case.

1) Maxim of Relation: A: Could you pass me my jacket, please?
                                B: It's not cold.

In this example, speaker B flouts the maxim of relation by not giving the expected affirmative answer and simply passing A the jacket. Instead, B says something which, on the surface, does not seem to be relevant to the question asked; but on the assumption that B continues to observe the Cooperative Principle, it must be deduced that she intends to be relevant. Thus A has to infer that B implies that she does not need to wear her jacket because it is not cold.

2) Maxim of Quantity:

A: I'll call all my friends and ask them to come to my party next weekend.
B: Mark and Paula will be in town next weekend.
A: Great, I'll call Paula.

In this example, speaker A flouts the maxim of quantity because his response attends only to part of the topic initiated by A. Consequently, the deliberate omission can be said to imply that A is not going to invite Mark to his party, and even more, that he probably does not like Mark and that is why he does not want to invite him.

3) Maxim of Manner:

A: I don't think you've met Sally on the fourth floor.
B: No, what's she like?
A: Well, she's not of the kindest variety.

Here, speaker A is being ambiguous and a bit obscure (and therefore she is flouting the Manner Maxim) in order to avoid uttering a direct criticism, for she is not clearly saying that Sally is unkind. But this would precisely be the implicature triggered by the violation, i.e. that Sally is not a kind person at all.

Having touched upon Grice's central ideas, which are, in turn, central to Pragmatics, we now turn to other aspects of the speech situation which are considered to be essential within Pragmatic studies.

3.3. Speech Acts

Cheers! The speech act of making a toast

The basic belief that language is used to perform actions led John Austin and John Searle to develop a theory of *Speech Acts*. In the famous lectures[3] that were posthumously published as *How to Do Things with*

---

[3] The *William James Lectures*, delivered by Austin at Harvard in 1955.

Words, Austin (1962) set about demolishing the view that truth conditions should be considered as central to language understanding. He developed a general theory of illocutionary acts, which, in turn, became a central concern of general pragmatic theory. In saying something, Austin observes, we are also doing something, and, hence, three kinds of acts are simultaneously performed:

1. **Locutionary act**: the utterance of a sentence with a determinate sense and reference.
2. **Illocutionary act**: the making of a statement, offer, promise, etc. in uttering a sentence, by virtue of the conventional force associated with it.
3. **Perlocutionary act**: the bringing about of effects on the audience by means of uttering a sentence, such effects being special to the circumstances of utterance (Austin, 1962: 101-02).

In order to illustrate the difference between the three types of acts, consider the following utterance:
(A woman to her friend):
I have a new and very expensive diamond necklace. Would you like to borrow it?

Here, the **locutionary act** would simply be the uttering of a sentence meaning that the woman has a new and expensive necklace and that she asks her friend if she wants to borrow it. The **illocutionary act** would in a way be the effect of the locutionary act, i.e. the function fulfilled by the locution, which in this case is an offer. The intended **perlocutionary effect/act**, however, might be for the woman to impress her friend, or perhaps to show a friendly attitude. But perlocutions may be intended or unintended, so in this case an unintended possible perlocutionary effect could be for the interlocutor to feel offended because she interpreted that her friend was trying to belittle her by implying that she could never have or buy such an expensive necklace.

The term *speech act* has come to refer exclusively to the second kind of act, i.e. the illocutionary act, since this is the one that seems to present the richest developments and interpretations within pragmatic theory. In English (as in other languages), sometimes sentences contain linguistic expressions that serve to indicate the illocutionary force of the sentence. Consider the following examples:

1) I promise I will not do that again.
2) I order you to stop talking.

Only certain verbs (which Austin called *performatives*), like *order* or *promise*, have the property of allowing the speaker to do the action the verb names by using the verb in a certain way. Other verbs cannot be used in this way, and thus, for instance, saying "I nag you to pick up your clothes" is not nagging (Green, 1989: 67).

Searle's (1969) later systematization of Austin's work, in which he proposes a typology of speech acts based on *felicity conditions* (the social and cultural criteria that have to be met for the act to have the desired effect), became very influential. Austin and Searle's position can be formulated by saying that all utterances not only express propositions, but also perform actions. The *illocutionary act*, or, more simply, the *speech act*, is at a privileged level within these actions. Searle's typology of speech acts is rooted in the range of illocutionary verbs that occur in a given language. According to this author, then, there are five basic kinds of action that a speaker can perform by means of the following five types of utterance:

1) **Representatives**: Acts which commit the speaker to the truth of the expressed proposition (e.g.: concluding, asserting).

2) **Directives**: Attempts by the speaker to get the addressee to do something (e.g.: questioning, requesting, ordering, begging, forbidding, instructing, urging, warning).

3) **Commissives**: Acts which commit the speaker to some future course of action (e.g.: promising, threatening, offering, guaranteeing, pledging, swearing, vowing, undertaking, warranting, inviting, offering, swearing, volunteering).

4) **Expressives**: Acts which express a psychological state (e.g.: apologizing, welcoming, thanking, appreciating, congratulating, deploring, detesting, regretting).

5) **Declaratives**: Acts which bring about immediate changes in the institutional state of affairs and thus tend to rely on extra-linguistic institutions (e.g.: christening, declaring war, excommunicating, sentencing (a convict to Capital Punishment), pronouncing (a couple husband and wife), naming (e.g. a ship)).

Another contribution of Searle's (1975) is the development of a theory of indirect speech acts. He based his theory on the observation that by uttering, for instance, what appears to be a question (e.g.: *Don't you think that dress is beautiful?*) a speaker may be indirectly performing another type of illocutionary act, such as a request (e.g.: *Please, buy me that dress!*). In order to interpret indirect speech acts, hearers rely upon their knowledge of speech acts, as well as on the general principles of cooperative conversation, mutually shared factual information and a general ability to draw inferences (Schiffrin, 1994). All these facts led Searle to observe that we often do more than one thing at once in the same utterance, and this is part of the important issue of indirect speech acts. For instance, the sentence *I won't give you the candy unless you behave*, uttered by a father to his son, may be interpreted as both an assertion (Representative), which would be the "literal" act, and a threat (commissive), which would be the "primary" act. Even more, it could also be interpreted as a request or an order (directive) from the father to the child.

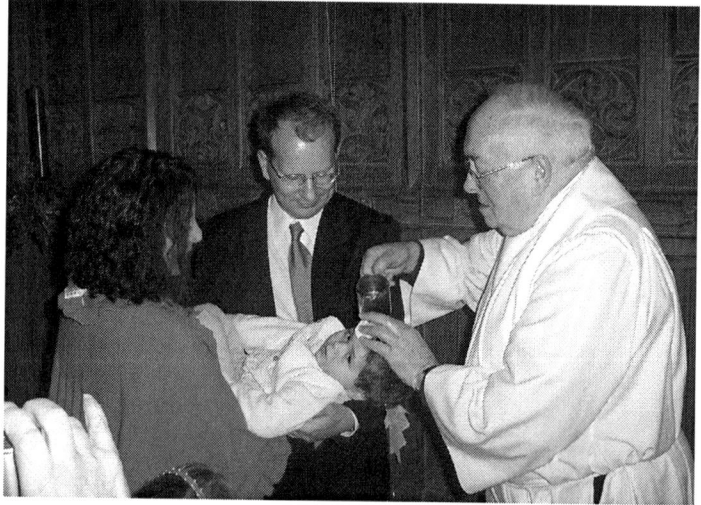

The declarative act of christening

In spite of the undeniable merits of speech act theory (which lie in advancing a view of language use as action), some authors have criticized the universalistic claims of Searle's version of the theory. For example, linguistic anthropologists such as Du Bois (1993) or Duranti (1993) have shown its limited applicability to non-Western modes of communication.

3.3.1. Examples and analysis

Examine the speech acts performed by the writer of the following letter to the "We hear you" column in the *Oprah* Magazine (December 2002 issue):

(1) Thank you for publishing the article on antibiotic-resistant bacteria ["The Microbe that Roared", September]. (2) My 77-year-old father just finished a six-week course of vancomycin to treat a bout of Staphylococcus aureus. This painful infection was initially misdiagnosed as arthritis. (3) The guidelines you provided for protecting ourselves and our loved ones were also particularly helpful. You have passed on information that may help save many lives.*

BTF, Boulder, Colorado

The above letter can be divided into three main discourse sequences containing three different types of speech acts:

a) Expressive (Thanking): *Thank you for publishing.....*

b) Representatives (Asserting: giving information about facts): *My 77-year-old father just finished... This painful infection was....*

c) Representatives/Expressives (Asserting and complimenting or acknowledging at the same time): *The guidelines you provided for protecting ourselves... You have passed on information that may help save many lives.*

(2) and (3) belong to the same broad category, but while the speech acts in the former fulfil the function of giving information, in (3) we can speak of a combination of two categories because by asserting (Representative act) that the guidelines provided were very helpful and may help save many lives, the writer is also complimenting the magazine and acknowledging its usefulness (Expressive act). We therefore see that the letter contains three clear speech act sequences: the first part aims at expressing gratitude for previously publishing the article in the magazine, the second part aims at informing about certain facts which somehow explain the writer's gratitude, and the third and last part is devoted to complimenting the editors for including such good articles in their magazine.

3.4. Reference

Many terms or expressions used in discourse have a referring function. This function seems to be exclusive of human language (as opposed to other animal communication systems), as Hockett and Altmann (1968: 63-4) note when dealing with the phenomenon of "aboutness", presented by these authors as one of the distinctive characteristics that define any human language. Thus, in using a human language we are able to talk **about** things that are external to ourselves which may be either in our immediate surroundings or at a distant location or time.

The prototypical words or expressions displaying reference are demonstratives and indexicals (e.g. *You, him, that woman, this house, here, there, his wife*), singular definite terms (e.g. *the man sitting at the corner, the author of* Paradise Lost, *my sons*) and proper names (e.g. *Rome, Peter Walsh, the Queen Mary (a ship), Picasso*). These terms refer to an entity within either the text or the context of utterance. Thus, "they unequivocally "pick out" some particular, definite individual or object" (Carlson, 2004: 76).

Referents are often introduced into discourse by using terms that are indefinite and explicit (e.g. *a man I met yesterday*) and continued with terms that are definite and inexplicit (e.g.: *he*). Definiteness has to do with the speaker's assumption that the hearer will be able to identify a single, specific entity to which the speaker intends to refer. Explicitness has to do with the presentation of information that actually enables H to correctly identify a referent (Schiffrin, 1994).

As Schiffrin notes, "scholars often view the process of referring to entities in the universe of discourse as pragmatic –simply because it is a process involving speakers, their intentions, actions, and knowledge" (1994: 197).

A group of engineers discussing technical facts based on mutual knowledge.

In effect, some types of reference depend on mutual knowledge. Referring to an entity with the expectation that the hearer will be able to make a similar identification depends upon mutual knowledge, beliefs and suppositions. Thus, the process by which referring expressions refer to an entity is not strictly semantic or truth-conditional; it is also pragmatic. For example, if I want to refer to my friend Gretchen, I may use definite or indefinite expressions like: *Gretchen, a workmate of mine, a woman I work with, Dr. Dobrott, someone I met six years ago, Professor Dobrott*, etc., and the use of one or other expression will depend on my intentions, as well as on my assumptions about the hearer's knowledge of my friend.

3.4.1. Types of reference

Following Martin & Rose (2007), we shall identify six types of reference, namely:

1) **Anaphoric**: reference that looks backward in the surrounding text. E.g.: *That's **my friend Sally**. **She** is an attorney* (where "She" refers back to "my friend Sally").

2) **Bridging**: reference that looks indirectly backwards; it is a kind of **inferred anaphoric reference**. E.g.: *The criminal **shot** a man in the street and **the gun** was found two days later* (where "the gun" refers indirectly backwards to the verb "shoot", since the most likely thing for someone to shoot with is a gun).

3) **Cataphoric**: reference that looks forward in the text. E.g.: *Immediately after **she** saw him, **Peggy** turned round and left the room* (where "she" refers forward to "Peggy").

4) **Esphoric**: reference that looks forward within the same nominal group. It identifies participants without us having to look elsewhere in the text; the elements point to themselves to be identified. This kind of reference occurs when one thing modifies another one and answers the question "Which one?" E.g. ***The house next door*** (where the referent "the house" points into itself and refers forward to the qualifier "next door")

5) **Homophoric**: reference that looks out to shared/cultural

knowledge, and may be realized through names or definite nominal groups whose reference is obvious.   E.g. *God, Leonardo Da Vinci, the President, the Pope, the Senate.*

6) **Exophoric**: reference that looks out to the situation, from language to outside the text. We refer to something outside that we can hear, see, touch, taste or feel. E.g. *Look!* ***The white car** crashed into a tree!* (where the white car is outside the text (because it was never mentioned before) but the interlocutors can see it).

3.4.2. Examples and analysis

Referring terms or expressions convey different types and different quantities of information which are somehow relevant to ongoing discourse. When reference is analyzed as a discourse process, not only referring terms and expressions but also *referring sequences* may become important, i.e. it is relevant to analyze how reference is initiated and continued in a given discourse such as a narrative or a letter, just to name but two possibilities.

Examine the use of referents in the following recipe:

MUSHROOM TART

6 ozs shortcrust pastry
8 ozs mushrooms
1 ½ ozs butter
¼ pt double cream
One eight pt single cream
2 eggs and 1 egg yolk
2 ozs grated Parmesan cheese
Coarse salt
Freshly ground black pepper
Cayenne

Line *an 8 inch flan ring* with *the pastry*. Fry *the chopped mushrooms* very lightly in *the butter*. Beat *the cream* with *the eggs* and *the extra egg yolk*. Stir in *the mushrooms and cheese*. Season with *salt*, *pepper* and a *tiny pinch of cayenne*. Pour into *the pastry case*. Sprinkle with *a little extra cheese*. Bake in *a moderate oven* (375° Gas N° 5) for about 40 mins, until

the filling is set and *the top* delicately browned.
(From: *Betchworth Village Recipes, U.K., 1978* [my italics])

Most of the referents in this recipe are introduced in bold type, as a list of ingredients. We may say that all of them are examples of *homophoric* reference, because they look out to real world food or ingredients that are well known by almost any person because they form part of their daily eating experience. The use of referents is then continued by using full noun phrases or zero pronouns which may constitute evoked, new, familiar or inferable referents. For instance, the referents *an 8 inch flan ring* and *a moderate oven* have not been evoked previously in the text and thus the noun phrase used is indefinite and explicit. However, they are both familiar referents for any person who has a bit of experience in cooking. Those referents which have been previously evoked are examples of *anaphoric* reference, but it can also turn *exophoric* at the moment the recipient is actually preparing the dish while following the instructions of the recipe, because he can see and touch the ingredients. The evoked referents here are definite and non-explicit to a certain degree (*the chopped mushrooms, the butter, the cream, the eggs, the extra egg yolk, the mushrooms and cheese, the pastry case, the filling*). There is one referent that was not previously evoked but is nevertheless definite, i.e. *the top*. This is due to the fact that it is an inferable item (and therefore, constitutes an example of *bridging* reference). The reader of the recipe has the necessary knowledge to understand that the writer is referring to the top of the mushroom tart. Inferable items can also be omitted, as illustrated in the sentences:

Season Ø with salt, pepper and a tiny pinch of cayenne.
Pour Ø into the pastry case.
Sprinkle Ø with a little extra cheese.

In all three cases, it is not necessary to add the pronoun "it", which would refer to the mixed ingredients at a given stage. We speak here of a "zero pronoun", which would be the direct object of the verbs *season, pour* and *sprinkle* but which is omitted because it can easily be inferred, considering it is a recent thematic product.

Thus, reference is initiated in this recipe by means of a list of evoked, homophoric referents which constitute the first sequence of this particular discourse. The reference is then continued in the body of the recipe (the second referring sequence), where the instructions contain referents that were mostly named in the previous (first) sequence, as well as a few inferable ones (whether present or omitted). These may be either inferable from the previous text (anaphoric reference, including bridging) or from the context (exophoric reference).

Many of the referents in the recipe can be labelled as *deictic*. **Deixis** is one of the central concerns in Pragmatics, since it introduces subjective, intentional, attentional and context-dependent properties into natural languages. We now turn to this phenomenon.

3.5. Deixis

The relationship between language and context is clearly observed through the phenomenon of *deixis*. Linguistic items such as demonstratives, pronouns, tense, place and time adverbs such as *now* and *here*, some verbs like *bring* and *take*, as well as other grammatical features which are tied directly to the context of utterance, are prototypically deictic. These items have also been called **indexical expressions** (Bar-Hillel, 1954), because they indicate or point to other entities within the text or context of utterance, or **shifters** (Jespersen, 1922), because their referential meaning shifts with every new speaker or occasion of use. As Levinson states:

> Essentially, deixis concerns the ways in which languages encode or grammaticalize features of the **context of utterance** or **speech event**, and thus also concerns ways in which the interpretation of utterances depends on the analysis of that context of utterance. Thus the pronoun *this* does not name or refer to any particular entity on all occasions of use; rather it is a variable or place-holder for some particular entity given by the context (e.g. by a gesture) (1983: 54).

In effect, utterances of sentences like the following cannot be fully understood or interpreted if there is no further indication of, for instance, when the sentence was uttered (1 and 2), where it was uttered (2), who did it (1, 2 and 3) and who the interlocutor was (1, 2 and 3):

1) **I**'ll call **you tomorrow.**
2) **(You)** Come **here, now**!
3) **I** don't like **you** at all.

Levinson (2004: 99) also points out that indexical reference introduces complexities into the relation between semantics and cognition, that is, between what sentences mean and what people mean when they utter them, and on the other hand, the corresponding thoughts they express. In effect, the use of indexicals in language is proof of the fact that the relation between meaning and thought is not transparent or direct: the context-dependent deictic system is semantically complex, because it is embedded in a context-independent descriptive system, where indexical reference is mediated by symbolic meaning. So deictics may contain both descriptive properties and contextual variables all in one, and even more, they are heavily dependent on pragmatic resolution "-*Come here* may mean come to this sofa or come to this city according to context" (Levinson, 2004: 104).

The group of indexical expressions is not clearly delimited, considering that most referring expressions depend on states of mutual knowledge holding between discourse participants for success, and therefore the vast majority of acts of reference depend on indexical conditions. Thus, there is more to deixis than what one might expect at first sight.

Having said the above, we shall now concentrate on the traditional division of deictic categories in three main types, namely: a) **person**, b) **place** and c) **time**.

Person deixis concerns the encoding of the role of participants in the speech event in which the utterance in question is delivered. This role is normally encoded in the first, second and third person pronouns.

Place deixis concerns the encoding of spatial locations relative to the location of the participants in the speech event. Demonstratives (like the English *this* or *that*) and deictic adverbs of place (like *here* or *there*) are the prototypical linguistic realizations of this type of deixis. *This* and *here* are examples of **proximal** (or close to the speaker) place deixis, while *that* and *there* constitute instances of **distal** (or non-proximal to speaker) place deixis.

Time deixis concerns the encoding of temporal points and spans relative to the time at which an utterance is spoken. This time is considered to be the **coding time** (Fillmore, 1971), which may be distinct from the **receiving time.** In English, time deixis is primarily encoded in tense[4] and in some adverbs of time like *now* and *then, yesterday, tomorrow* or *last year*.

Apart from these traditional categories, we also have to consider

---

[4] Thus, we may gloss the English present tense as specifying that the state or event is occurring at the coding time, or the past tense as specifying that it occurred before coding time, and so it is clear that there is a temporal element in most tenses. However, as Levinson (2004) observes, the system fails to capture much English usage (e.g. *The party is tomorrow*, where *is* does not refer to present time, or *Susan will be working now*, where *will* does not refer to future time).

discourse (or text) deixis and **social deixis:**

Discourse deixis refers to the use of expressions in an utterance which are used to refer to some portion of the discourse that contains the utterance. Both time and place deictic terms (such as: *the aforementioned, in the examples below, this* (used to refer to a forthcoming portion of the discourse) or *that* (used to refer to a preceding portion)) can be said to be discourse-deictic. Here, it is necessary to make the distinction between **discourse deixis** and **anaphora**[5]: Anaphora usually has to do with the use of a pronoun to refer to the same referent at some prior term, as in:

A woman opened the door. **She** was beautiful.

where *A woman* and *She* are said to be **co-referential** because they share the same referent. Discourse deixis usually involves a pronoun or expression which refers to a linguistic expression (or segment of discourse) itself, as in:

A: Believe me, I love you.
B: **That**'s the biggest lie I've ever heard!

where *That* refers to A's whole utterance.

Discourse connectors or pragmatic markers (in Fraser's (2004) terms), such as *however, besides, moreover, well, anyway*, when used in utterance-initial position, are also considered to be discourse-deictic, for they refer to or show a relationship with other segments of the ongoing discourse.

Social deixis concerns "those aspects of language structure that encode the social identities of participants (properly, incumbents of participant-roles) or the social relationship between them, or between one of them and persons and entities referred to" (Levinson, 1983: 89). The use of *honorifics* (such as the T/V pronouns –tu/vous in French or tú/usted in Spanish) is a prototypical example of social deixis, where a social relation concerning rank or respect is encoded in the grammar of the language.

It is interesting to note that deixis is generally organized egocentrically. In this way, the points constituting the **deictic center** (i.e. a "ground zero" or **origo** (Bühler, 1934)) are normally assumed to be as follows: The central person is the speaker, the central place is the speaker's location at utterance time, the central time is the time at which the speaker produces the utterance, the discourse center is the point which the speaker is

---

[5] See also 3.4.1.

currently at during the production of his utterance, and the social center is the speaker's social status and rank, to which the status or rank of addressees or referents is relative (Levinson, 1983: 63-64).

Levinson states that it is essential to distinguish different kinds of usage of deictic expression. Most deictic expressions also have **non-deictic usages**. In addition, we should distinguish between **gestural usage** and **symbolic usage**. These usages are illustrated in the following examples:

1) *You, you and you, but not you, have to do the exercise.* (Exophoric gestural, contrastive) –it can only be understood if the speaker is pointing at the different "yous").

2) What are **you** doing? (Exophoric symbolic –no gesture required, only knowledge of the basic parameters of the speech event).

3) **You** never know what to expect these days. (Non-deictic (general, non-specific use of the pronoun))

4) I want to put this desk **there.** (Exophoric gestural).

5) Hi **there**, what's up? (Exophoric symbolic).

6) **There** you go! (Non-deictic).

As Slembrouck (2005) notes, the phenomenon of deixis challenges the view of language as a self-contained, autonomous system given the fact that it ties up an utterance with contextually variable factors to such an extent that it can affect the meaning of other lexical items in the co-textual vicinity. Some scholars consider that indexicality played a crucial part in the evolution of language, prior to the symbolic system characteristic of modern human language, but what we now understand as deixis is better to be placed within the intersection of indexicality and the symbolic system, engendering a hybrid with complexities which go beyond the two contributing systems[6].

We now turn to the analysis of a few more examples of the different types and usages of deixis.

3.5.1. More examples and analysis

Consider the use of the pronouns *I* and *you* and the demonstratives *this* and

---

[6] See Levinson (2004) for a more detailed account of these complexities.

that in the following *Agnes* comic strip:

All the pronouns *I* and *you* in the strip are examples of the symbolic usage of personal deixis. Neither of the characters needs to point to the other to know who *I* or *you* is at a given discourse moment. As regards the use of *this* and *that* in the first exchange ("I think **this** would be a good quote to base my life on" and "Who said **that**?") it can be said that, even when both are cases of discourse deixis (both *this* and *that* refer to a fragment of the ongoing discourse[7]), we can also speak of symbolic place deixis. Agnes uses *this* because the quote seems proximal to her, since she has read it in the book and now she can recite it by heart. Her interlocutor feels the same quote is distal, for he has not read the book and the quote is both physically and psychologically non-proximal to him. In the second exchange, when Agnes says "I forgot to memorize **that** part", the distal place deictic (*that*) is used, due to the fact that, since she does not remember the author, this part or piece of information is not familiar and therefore non-proximal to her. The use of *that* by the man in the third exchange ("I like **that** one better) constitutes a similar example of symbolic, distal place deixis.

Another deictic element in this strip is the adverb *soon* ("It comes **soon** enough") which constitutes an example of time deixis, relative to the time of the speaker's utterance or to some psychological time that she has chosen as her deictic center. The use of *their* in Agnes' last intervention is an example of symbolic personal deixis (there are enough elements in both text and context for her interlocutor and the reader to know that *their* refers to the "creepy idiots" without her need to make any gesture).

---

[7] In the case of *this,* the reference is cataphoric; in the case of *that,* it is anaphoric.

3.6. Presupposition

Like implicatures[8], *presuppositions* are a kind of linguistic inference. But while implicatures cannot be said to be semantic (because they are based on contextual assumptions rather than being built into the linguistic structure of the sentences that trigger them), presuppositions are based more closely on the actual linguistic structure of sentences. However, they cannot be thought of as semantic in the narrow sense, considering that they are very sensitive to certain contextual factors (Levinson, 1983).

Presuppositions seem to be tied to particular words or aspects of surface structure in general, as shown in the following examples:

1) I was not able to see *the Side Show*. (**presupposition:** There exists a Side Show).
2) She didn't *realize* she had a big stain on her dress. (**presupposition**: She had a big stain on her dress).
3) Julia *stopped* smoking. (**Presupposition**: Julia used to smoke).

The definite description *the Side Show* in 1), the factive verb *realize* in 2) and the change of state verb *stop* in 3) are the linguistic expressions that trigger the presuppositions, and for that reason they are called **presupposition triggers.**

Green (1989: 71-74) presents a taxonomy of the phenomena that have so far been labelled as presuppositions, and she finds there are three main kinds:

- **Existence presuppositions**: This is the most representative case. It concerns the existence of definite descriptions. For example, the sentence *I met Susan's daughter at the market yesterday*, presupposes that Susan has a daughter and that there is a market in the area I was at yesterday. *Susan's daughter* and *the market* are the presupposition triggers.
- **Factive presuppositions**: There are several sorts of factive presuppositions. For example, the subject complements of *mean*, *be obvious* or *prove*, as well as the object complements of epistemic factives such as *know* or *realize* are considered to be presupposed true. So are the complements of emotive factive verbs such as *be glad*, *amaze* or *be surprised*. Thus, for instance, in the sentence: *She knows that Peter is in town*, the factive

---

[8] See 3.2.

presupposition is that Peter is in town. Another example can be found in the counterfactive verb *pretend*, whose use presupposes that the complement is not true (e.g. *Peter pretended that he was rich* → Peter was not rich).

- **Connotations:** The restrictions of use of some lexical items have been claimed to be or reflect presuppositions about the situation in which they are used. A typical example of a connotation is found in the verb *assassinate*, which carries the implicit presupposition that the killing was intended -it would make no sense to say: **He accidentally assassinated his wife.*

If we examine examples 1, 2 and 3 above, we shall see that they present, respectively, instances of an existence presupposition, a factive presupposition, and a connotation.

The phenomenon of presupposition is very complex indeed, and is still only partially understood. In this book, we are not going to analyze it in depth. Some authors (Stalnaker 1974, Karttunen & Peters, 1975, 1979, Horn 2004) put it on a par with the phenomenon of *conventional implicature*[9] (Grice, 1975). For our purposes, suffice it to say that it constitutes an important ground for the study of some aspects of the interaction between semantics and pragmatics, and that the study of the use or presuppositions may be of great help when doing discourse analysis. Some more examples are considered in the following section.

3.6.1. Examples and analysis

Examine some of the presuppositions in the following text:

Joanne, 47, **had worked her way through college (1)** as a bank teller, and by age 34 was a manager at **the Bankers Trust Company in Manhattan (2).** After her **first (3)** child was born, she **continued (4)** to commute three hours a day from **her (5)** Rahway, New Jersey, home. But when **she was told (6)** she had to travel repeatedly to Asia, she negotiated a severance package. [...] **Her career counselor (7)** inspired Joanne to think about how her skills could translate outside the banking industry –and Joanne **started (8)** to imagine becoming an outplacement expert herself. When she was **no longer (9)** a client, the outplacement firm, Lee Hecht Harrison, hired her as a part-time consultant.

From: "Recipe for Resilience", *The Oprah Magazine*, October 2002

---

[9] See 3.2.

The expressions in bold type are all *presupposition triggers*, and the triggered presuppositions are the following:

(1) Joanne once went to college (connotation).
(2) There exists a Bankers Trust Company in Manhattan (existence presupposition).
(3) Joanne has more than one child (connotation).
(4) Joanne had been commuting before (connotation).
(5) (It is a fact that) Joanne has a house in Rahway New Jersey, and that house exists, (mixture of factive and existence presupposition).
(6) Someone told Joanne she had to travel repeatedly to Asia (factive presupposition).
(7) (It is a fact that) Joanne had a career counsellor and this counsellor existed (mixture of factive and existence presupposition).
(8) Joanne hadn't imagined becoming an outplacement expert before (connotation).
(9) Joanne was once a client of the outplacement firm (connotation).

SUMMING UP... (CHAPTER 3)

1. Pragmatics is an indispensable source for discourse analysis. Many authors have defined pragmatics in different ways, but in most definitions it can be seen that elements such as *context, meaning beyond literal meaning, speech acts, deixis, understatement, implicature,* etc. are considered important components of this discipline.

2. **Gricean Pragmatics** is seen as one of the main contributions to the field of Pragmatics, for H. P. Grice's (1975) ideas about speaker meaning and the cooperative principle have been and still are extremely influential. A central concept in Gricean Pragmatics is the notion of *conversational implicature.* **Conversational implicatures** are a kind of inference that can be derived from an utterance, and they are related to what Grice called the **Cooperative Principle and its Maxims.**

3. *Speech acts,* or *illocutionary acts* (i.e. the making of a statement, offer, promise, etc. in uttering a sentence, by virtue of the conventional force associated with it) are central to pragmatic theory and discourse analysis.

4. Searle (1969) systematized Austin's work and developed a typology of speech acts. According to this author there are five basic kinds of speech acts: i) *Representatives,* ii) *Directives,* iii) *Commissives,* iv) *Expressives* and v) *Declaratives.* Searle (1975) also developed a theory of *indirect speech acts.*

5. Many terms or expressions used in discourse have a referring function. Some types of **reference** depend on mutual knowledge; thus, the process by which referring expressions refer to an entity is not strictly semantic or truth-conditional; it is also pragmatic.

6. The relationship between language and context is clearly observed through the phenomenon of *deixis.* Linguistic items such as demonstratives, pronouns, tense, place and time adverbs such as *now* and *here,* some verbs like *bring* and *take,* as well as other grammatical features which are tied directly to the context of utterance, are prototypically deictic. Traditionally, deixis has been divided into three main categories: a) **person,** b) **place** and 3) **time.** But two more types are considered: **Discourse** and **social** deixis. There are also three main kinds of deictic usage: **gestural, symbolic** and **non-deictic.**

7. *Presuppositions* are a kind of linguistic inference which is based more closely on the actual linguistic structure of sentences than on implicatures. Presuppositions seem to be tied to particular words or aspects of surface structure in general, and these particular words or expressions constitute the **presupposition triggers.**

SELF-EVALUATION QUESTIONS

Choose the answer that best suits the information given in Chapter 3.

1) Semantics and Pragmatics…
a) study the same phenomena.
b) are both concerned with meaning.
c) both focus on the users of a language.

2) Pragmatics deals with…
a) the truth-conditional meaning of utterances.
b) literal meaning.
c) all kinds of meaning different from the truth-conditional meaning.

3) One of the central concepts in Gricean Pragmatics is…
a) word meaning.
b) politeness.
c) speaker meaning.

4) Non-natural meaning (meaning –nn) has to do with…
a) the speaker's communicative intention and the hearer's interpretation of it.
b) literal meaning.
c) synonyms.

5) Implicatures are a kind of…
a) metaphor.
b) inference.
c) predicate.

6) Implicatures…
a) are triggered when a speaker flouts one or more of the maxims of the Cooperative Principle.
b) cannot be conventionalized.
c) are always conversational.

7) One of the main characteristics of *conversational implicatures* is…
a) their non-cancellability.
b) their cancellability.
c) their rigidity.

8) Specify which of the Gricean Maxims is flouted by Y in the following exchange:

   X: How old are you?
   Y: I'm younger than my oldest brother and older than my little niece.

a) Maxim of Quality.
b) Maxim of Relation.
c) Maxims of Quantity and Manner.

9) The term *Speech Act* has come to refer exclusively to …
a) the locutionary act.
b) the perlocutionary act.
c) the illocutionary act.

10) Which of the following is a *performative verb*?
a) Threaten.
b) Assure.
c) Bother.

11) Felicity conditions are conditions that have to be met for…
a) being happy after uttering a sentence.
b) the hearer(s) to understand what the speaker says.
c) the illocutionary act to have its desired effect.

12) Specify the type of action we perform when we thank a friend:
a) representative act.
b) expressive act.
c) declarative act.

13) Specify the type of action the Church performs when one of its members is excommunicated:
a) declarative act.
b) commissive act.
c) directive act.

14) The process of referring is essentially…
a) grammatical.
b) pragmatic.
c) phonological.

15) Deictic features, words or expressions…
a) are directly tied to the context of utterance.
b) do not shift with different speakers and contexts of use.
c) have nothing to do with the grammar of the language in question.

16) Specify the type of deixis encoded in the word in bold type:

Unluckily, I never learned to swim. **That**'s what prevents me from bathing in the sea.

a) time deixis.
b) discourse deixis.
c) place deixis.

17) Specify the type of deixis encoded in the expressions in bold type:

Her Royal Highness (1) is **now (2)** willing to receive **you (3)** in her office.

a) (1) social, (2) time and (3) person deixis.
b) (1) discourse, (2) time and (3) place deixis.
c) (1) social, (2) place and (3) person deixis.

18) Deixis is organized…

a)   so that the hearer is always the central person.
b)   so that the deictic center is always related to the speaker.
c)   so that the central aspects are alien to the speaker.

19) Specify the type of usage of the demonstratives in bold type:

I'd like to take **this** one and **that** one.

a)   Symbolic.
b)   Gestural.
c)   Non-deictic.

20) Identify the word or expression that triggers the presupposition
    that Janet used to smoke before 2001:

Janet quit smoking in 2001.

a)   in 2001.
b)   smoking.
c)   quit.

21) What type is the presupposition triggered by the word(s) in bold
    type?
    I was surprised to see that Linda came. → (Presupposition:
    Linda came)

a)   Existence.
b)   Factive.
c)   Connotation.

22) What type is the presupposition triggered by the word(s) in bold
    type?

She **started** playing golf when she was 12. → (Presupposition:
Before she was 12, she didn't play golf)

a)   Connotation.
b)   Factive.
c)   Existence.

PRACTICE

A) *READING*: READ Chapter 6 in D. Schiffrin's *Approaches to Discourse* and MAKE A SUMMARY of it. Send it or hand it in to your Tutor (in case you are a student following a course).

B) *ANALYSIS:*

    a) IDENTIFY AND ANALYZE the referents in the following recipe. Do you find any reference sequences? If so, EXPLAIN them.

SUPER FISH DISH

FILLETS OF LEMON SOLE
PRAWNS
HARD-BOILED EGGS
MUSHROOMS
TOMATOES
CHEESE SAUCE
GRATED CHEESE

Roll up the fillets of sole, enclosing a few prawns in each roll, and season. Lay them neatly in a fireproof dish. Slice the hard-boiled eggs and mushrooms and (or) tomatoes, and scatter them over the fish. Cover with cheese sauce and sprinkle liberally with grated cheese. Bake in oven 375 (Gas N° 5) for about 25-30 minutes and until golden brown. Serve hot.

---

    b) IDENTIFY AND ANALYZE the deictic terms or expressions in the following comic strips. SPECIFY the kind of deixis and the type of usage (symbolic, gestural or non-deictic) in each case.

1)

2)

c) IDENTIFY AND ANALYZE the speech acts in the following two fragments of a television interview (CNN's *Larry King Live*. Interview with Bill Maher, July 22nd, 2004). Can you find any pattern in the speech act sequences of the two fragments?

1)

1 KING: Toquerville, Utah, hello.
2 CALLER: Gentlemen, the honor is mine. Thank you for the call. Bill, what
3 do you think about the administration's Homeland Security Department's
4 little plan B to study to stop the election under threat of terrorist attack?
5 Does that remind you of our 2000 Florida deal?
6 MAHER: You mean you're talking about on election day?

7 KING: Yes, in case there's some big occurrence.
8 MAHER: Well, they've been pulling that card for how many...
9 KING: Wait a minute, you had some sort of disaster you don't want to
10 hold an election if you've got bombs dropping?
11 MAHER: That's true. And I agree with that. If there's really a problem on
12 election day. But, again, this is an administration that has always said,
13 OK, we're operating under this premise. You can't criticize the
14 administration during a time of war. Oh, and by the way, we're always at
15 war. The war is ongoing. So I mean, I don't trust them. Let me put it that
16 way. I don't trust them, or they haven't earned my trust.

2)

1 KING: Carbondale, Illinois.
2 CALLER: How do we get southern voters voting Democrat again? Thank
3 you, Bill. Thank you, Larry.
4 KING: Will the South ever vote Democratic?
5 MAHER: You know, that's a sore point with me, the south. The way that
6 they have the stranglehold over the electorate. Because, excuse me, and
7 I love playing to red states, because when I play the red states my
8 stand-up act I get all the people 40 don't usually have someone like me
9 come to their state. So there's a great bonding. And I feel for them,
10 because there's a lot of smart people in the south. But in general, it is
11 the dumbest part of the country. Excuse me. It is. And also, they're the
12 super patriots. The one part of the country that ever actually seceded.
13 The one part of the country that ever actually committed treason. And
14 they seem to lead in how we are supposed to think. Because they're
15 more religious, they're more patriotic and I think it's just a disservice to
16 our...
17 KING: You think in modern-day America you could still claim a whole
18 region is dumber than another region?
19 MAHER: They lead the region in dumbness, yes, they do. Because
20 there's just too many people who think that every problem can be solved
21 by either more guns or more Jesus. And like I said, I'm with the people
22 who are following the compass. Not the people who are reading the
23 entrails of the chicken. They're the people who are reading the entrails
24 of the chicken.

> d) IDENTIFY at least seven presupposition triggers in the
> two fragments of discourse in c) above and SPECIFY
> the presuppositions they entail as well as their type
> (*existence, factive* or *connotation*).

FURTHER READING

Leech (1983), chapters 1, 4, 8, and 9.

Green (1989), chapter 5.

Horn, L.R & G. Ward (2004), Introduction.

J.R. Martin & D. Rose (2007), Chapter 5.

USEFUL WEBSITES

Wikipedia entry for Pragmatics: http://en.wikipedia.org/wiki/Pragmatics

What is Pragmatics?
http://www.sil.org/linguistics/GlossaryOfLinguisticTerms/WhatIsPragmatics.htm

The Semantics-Pragmatics distinction :
http://userwww.sfsu.edu/~kbach/semprag.html

Journal of Pragmatics:
http://www.elsevier.com/wps/find/journaldescription.cws_home/505593/description

Books on Pragmatics:

http://books.google.es/books?id=wDg3jeB29ZkC&pg=PA82&lpg=PA82&dq=Linguistic+pragmatics&source=web&ots=kIuNzEKWEb&sig=vZvvieq2WS9PDqc7JhT8qQfNw0E&hl=en&sa=X&oi=book_result&resnum=10&ct=result

INTERACTIONAL SOCIOLINGUISTICS

"... language and context co-constitute one another: language contextualizes and is contextualized, such that language does not just function 'in' context, language also forms and provides context. One particular context is social interaction. Language, culture, and society are grounded in interaction: they stand in a reflexive relationship with the self, the other, and the self-other relationship, and it is out of these mutually constitutive relationships that discourse is created."

D. Schiffrin, *Approaches to Discourse.*

Chapter Outline:

- Main concepts and methods in Interactional Sociologuistics.

- Methodology and techniques used by Interactional Sociolinguists.

- Main concepts and principles of the Theory of *Politeness*.

- Approaches and perspectives on *Politeness*.

- Politeness strategies (as presented by Brown & Levinson, 1987).

4.1. Main concepts and methods

The interactional sociolinguistic approach to discourse analysis is multidisciplinary: it concerns the study of the relationships between language, culture and society and has its roots in Anthropology, Sociology and Linguistics. In spite of the diversity of disciplines upon which this approach is based, there is a consensus as to the basic beliefs about language, context and the interaction of self and other.

Interactional sociolinguists view discourse as a social interaction in which the emergent construction and negotiation of meaning is facilitated by the use of language, thus, they always resort to naturally occurring interactions as a source for data. They consider situated behavior to be the site where societal and interactive forces merge and they focus on how such interaction depends on culturally-informed but situated inferential processes, which play a role in the speakers' interpretative constructions of the kind of activity they are engaged in.

One of the main concerns of this approach is the study of the practices of *contextualization*, a concept based on a reflexive notion of context:

"context is not just given as such in interaction, but it is something which is made available in the course of interaction and its construal depends on inferential practices in accordance with conventions which speakers may or may not share" (Slembrouk, 2005: 14).

Two scholars have been the main contributors to the development of the interactional sociolinguistic approach: anthropologist John Gumperz and sociologist Erving Goffman. Their ideas and points of view have been extensively used and applied in the field of linguistics by different authors, such as Penelope Brown & Steven Levinson, Deborah Schiffrin or Deborah Tannen.

4.1.1. John Gumperz's contribution to Interactional Sociolinguistics

In his essays entitled *Discourse Strategies*, John Gumperz (1982) develops an interpretative sociolinguistic approach to the analysis of real time processes in face-to-face interactions. Gumperz emphasizes the fact that cognition and language are affected by social and cultural forces. What we thus need to understand and analyze the effects of society and culture on language is a "general theory of verbal communication which integrates what we know about grammar, culture and interactive conventions into a single overall framework of concepts and analytical procedures" (1982: 4).

A crucial concept in Interactional Sociolinguistics is that of *contextualization cue*, which Gumperz defines as:

…any verbal sign which when processed in co-occurrence with symbolic grammatical and lexical signs serves to construct the contextual ground for situated interpretations, and thereby affects how constituent messages are understood. (1999: 461)

Examples of contextualization cues are intonation or any prosodic choices, conversational code-switching, lexical or syntactic choices, style switching and facial and gestural signs. Gumperz notes that contextualization cues function indexically, i.e. they are deictic and thus share many of the characteristics of shifters; however, they are not necessarily lexically based: e.g. prosody or facial and body gestures sometimes signal relational values independently of the propositional content of utterances. Thus, human communication is seen as "channelled and constrained by a multilevel system of learned, automatically produced and closely coordinated verbal and non-verbal signals" (Gumperz, 1982: 141).

As Schiffrin (1994) notes, since contextualization cues are learned through long periods of close, face-to-face contact, many people in modern, culturally diverse societies are likely to interact without benefit of shared cues. And this is precisely one of the major strengths of Interactional Sociolinguistics: its insistence on the occurrence of asymmetries in the communicative background of speakers. Speakers and hearers do not always share the same inferential procedures, i.e. they do not contextualize cues in the same manner. This fact may cause misunderstandings which may have damaging social consequences for certain members of society, especially those belonging to minority groups.

In plain words, the main idea behind Gumperz's sociolinguistics of interpersonal communication is that speakers are members of social and cultural groups, and as such, the way they use language not only reflects their group identity but also provides indices of who they are, what they want to communicate, and how skillful they are in doing so. It is a great part of our communicative competence to be able to understand and produce these indexical processes as they occur in local contexts.

4.1.1.1. Examples and analysis of *contextualization cues*

The following example (taken from Gumperz), illustrates how the failure to interpret conversational code-switching (a typical contextualization cue) can lead to a misunderstanding:

> The graduate student has been sent to interview a black housewife in a low income, inner city neighborhood. The contact has been made over the phone by someone in the office. The student arrives, rings the bell, and is met by the husband, who opens the door, smiles, and steps towards him:
>
> Husband: So y're gonna check out ma ol lady, hah?
>
> Interviewer: Ah, no. I only came to get some information. They called from the office.
>
> (Husband, dropping his smile, disappears without a word and calls his wife.) (1982: 133)

Gumperz tells the readers that the student reported that the interview that followed was stiff and quite unsatisfactory. Being black himself, the student realized that he had "blown it" by failing to recognize the significance of the husband's speech style in this particular case. He should have responded with a typically black response like "Yea, I'ma git some info" so as to show familiarity with local values and etiquette. The student's use of Standard English was interpreted by the husband as a sign that he did not belong to his group, and therefore he was not to be trusted.

Another interesting example comes from my own experience. As a speaker of Argentinean Spanish living in Spain, I have often been involved in conversations in which one Argentinean person meets another without previously knowing where s/he is from, and thus the first speaker starts the interaction by using the second person singular pronoun *tú*, but the moment she notices that her interlocutor is also Argentinean (and she notices this because of her interlocutor's *accent* -another contextualization cue-), she starts using the equivalent (and typically Argentinean) pronoun *vos* to address her interlocutor, as a sign of camaraderie, or in order to show that she feels more at ease with someone who can speak "her own language". If the interlocutor "tunes in" to the use of *vos* and the special conjugation of the verbs accompanying it (e.g. *vos querés*, *vos tenés*, instead of *tú quieres*, *tú tienes*), then we can say that s/he has succeeded in recognizing the intention of the first speaker when using such a particular contextualization cue. If, on the contrary, the interlocutor does not "tune in" to this special use of the pronoun and prefers to adhere to the Peninsular, more standard *tú*, s/he will show s/he has failed to understand the meaning of the contextualization cue (*code switching* in this case). Such a reaction will thus be interpreted as cold and distant, or as a rejection of the first speaker's positive politeness strategies[1] and, consequently, of her intentions to include the interlocutor within her peer group. As in Gumperz's example above, the rest of the conversation may then turn stiff and quite uncomfortable or unsatisfactory for both interlocutors.

4.1.2. Erving Goffman's contribution to Interactional Sociolinguistics

Goffman has undoubtedly been one of the most influential authors in the study of spoken interaction. His sociology centers on physical co-presence rather than on social groups, and thus he focuses on aspects of *interaction order* such as:

  a) Particular settings (e.g. entering an elevator and how it affects talk).
  b) Forms of self-maintaining behavior such as the display of *focused interaction* and of *civil inattention*.
  c) Conduct in public situations involving embarrassment, face-saving behavior and/or public displays of competence (e.g. response cries such as *Oops*).

---

[1] See 4.2.

d) The role of temporal and spatial activity boundaries which result in inclusion and exclusion from talk in interaction.

Although Goffman takes talk as the basic medium of encounters, he also gives utmost importance to the state of co-presence, which draws attention to the body, its disposition and display. As Schiffrin (1994) notes, Goffman argues that the self is a social construction, and one way of viewing the self as a social, interactive construction is through the notion of *face*, i.e. "the positive social value a person effectively claims for himself by the line others assume he has taken during a particular contact" (Goffman, 1967: 5). One of the conditions of interaction is the maintenance of face. Interactants are expected to behave in a manner that is consistent with this image in order to *be in face* or to *maintain face*. Interpersonal rituals (both avoidance and presentational) contribute to the maintenance of face. The material resources available through social institutions also contribute to the maintenance of face, for they can not only be used to symbolize certain favored aspects of self, but can also facilitate the division of self into a public character and a private performer (Goffman, 1959). In Goffman's view, the study of interaction is not a study of motives but of rules: "to study face-saving is to study the traffic rules of social interaction" (Goffman, 1959: 13). As we shall see later in this chapter, Brown & Levinson's (1987) study of politeness takes Goffman's notion of face as one of its main tenets.

Another important concept in Goffman's analysis of interaction is that of *frame*. Goffman studies the way in which social actors organize their experience in terms of recognizable activities (e.g. a business meeting, a lecture, a game of chess) which are the frames through which people structure experience. Thus, the organization of framing activity is socially situated. Goffman's frame analysis shows how people can handle multiple, interdependent realities and therefore it reveals the complexity of mundane social activities. The concept of *footing* is tightly related to that of frame.

Footing stands for a speaker's shifting alignments in relation to the events at hand. This concept brings out the need to distinguish between different speaker roles. Goffman (1981a) identifies four roles or participation statuses: *animator* (the participant that produces talk), *author* (the one who creates talk), *figure* (the one who is portrayed by talk) and *principal* (the one who is responsible for talk). All these roles may be played by different people, but a single participant can also play two roles at the same time, or fill different position slots at different moments during the same interaction. The analysis of these roles is thus of utmost importance in situations where discourse production depends on coordinated teamwork with a particular division of labor which is to lead to a finalized product, as, for instance, "a television commercial, where a voice-over takes on the role of 'animator' for a message scripted by an advertising agency ('author') which expresses the position of the manufacturer ('principal')." (Slembrouck, 2006). For the sake of clarification, it may be said that the *animator* of this particular discourse is producing the talk for another, so s/he can neither be the *author* nor the *principal*. The *author*, i.e. the creator of the text to be broadcast on TV, is the advertising agency, which in the ad is delivering the essence of the original position taken by the *principal*, who in this case is the manufacturer of the product that is being advertised.

Goffman proposes similar distinctions for the category of hearer, revealing a range of participation statuses. He distinguishes between the *primary addressee* (a ratified hearer) and an *overhearer* (a non-ratified hearer, e.g., an accidental bystander). Again, the roles may vary depending on the situation, and thus *addressees* may be turned into *overhearers* or vice versa (e.g. when the talk becomes centered on only two of the interactants and discourages the involvement of others present in the frame).

The concept of *footing* has undoubtedly challenged the old conception of the communicative situation consisting of the presence of only a speaker and a hearer. In a similar way, the development of the category of *overhearer/bystander* forces us to consider the facts of interaction as relative to a 'gathering' rather than an 'encounter', i.e. to something wider, "namely 'the social situation', defining this as the full physical arena in which persons present are in sight and sound of one another." (Goffman 1981b: 136).

The concept of *footing* has been developed further in Pragmatics (e.g. Levinson 1983, 1988; Thomas 1986), as well as within Linguistic Anthropology (e.g. Hanks observes that this new concept "pushes beyond the simple dyad and opens up the possibility of a differentiated approach to multi-party talk" (1996: 219)).

4.1.2.1. Example and analysis

The following example and analysis have been taken from Schiffrin (1994: 107-08). The analysis is here summarized for the purpose of interpreting and understanding Goffman's concept of *footing* and how it provides situated inferences about the meaning of an interactional move:

(1)^2
Henry: (a)   Y'want a piece of candy?
Irene: (b)   No.
                        Z
Zelda: (c)   She's on a diet.
                                Z
Debby: (d)   Who's not on [a diet.
Irene: (e)   [I'm on-
                I'm on a diet.
          (f)   and my mother [buys-=
Zelda: (g)   [You're not!
Irene: (h)   = my [mother buys these mints. =
Debby: [Oh yes I amhhh!   /
                                          /_
Zelda: Oh yeh.

Schiffrin focuses on Zelda's remark and its alteration of the participation framework of talk. Zelda is "speaking for another", and one key feature of speaking for another is that it involves three participant roles.   In Goffman's terms, the spokesperson (who produces a message whose content is the responsibility of another) would be the *animator* for another person who is in the *principal* role. So when Zelda says "She's on a diet", she is an animator for Irene's *principal*. The remark "She's on a diet" alters the participation framework of ongoing talk and the way in which it is altered is tied to the social relationship among participants, the social acts being performed and the gender identities of participants (Schiffrin, 1994: 108). Normally, "speaking for" is a way of speaking that may be used with a person with whom one has a particular relationship (Zelda and Irene are friends). It is implicit in the interactional sociolinguistic approach that it is the social contextualization of an utterance that motivates and explains its use. Context, then, provides situated inferences about the meaning of an interactional move. Schiffrin also notes that one way that gender is realized and reflected in talk is through the differential construction of participation framework, so she suggests that Zelda's "She's on a diet" proposes an interactional alignment that is more typical of stances taken by women than those taken by men (gender identity).

   In short, Schiffrin situates the meaning of the single utterance "She's on a diet" in several different ways: as a participation framework within the microstructure of an interaction (one person "speaks for" another), as a socially motivated account within a sequence of acts (an offer issued

---

^{2} See transcription conventions in 2.2.1.

through a question is rejected), as a gender-based involvement strategy, and as a means of building sequential coherence by taking the role of the other.

4.1.3. Similarities in Gumperz's and Goffman's approaches

In spite of the obvious differences, there are enough similarities between both Gumperz's and Goffman's approaches to consider them both representatives of the Interactional Sociolinguistic approach to discourse analysis. Both scholars focus upon situated meaning. Two central issues that they share are the study of the interaction between self and other, and the study of context. Both authors see language as indexical to the social world: Gumperz conceives of language as an index to the cultural background knowledge which provides information as to how to make inferences and what is meant through an utterance. Goffman views language as an index to the social identities and relationships which are constructed during interaction.

Goffman's and Gumperz's work complement each other: Goffman tries to describe and understand the form and meaning of the social and interpersonal contexts from a sociological perspective. For Gumperz, language is a socially and culturally constructed symbol system that reflects, and at the same time creates, macro-level social meaning and micro-level interpersonal meanings.

To conclude, let us reflect upon the following segment from Goffman's essay on face-work:

> Throughout this paper, it has been implied that underneath their differences in culture, people everywhere are the same. If persons have a universal human nature, they themselves are not to be looked to for an explanation of it. One must look rather to the fact that societies everywhere, if they are to be societies, must mobilise their members as self-regulating participants in social encounters. One way of mobilising the individual for this purpose is through ritual: he is taught to be perceptive, to have feeling attached to self and a self expressed through face, to have pride, honour, and dignity, to have considerateness, to have tact and a certain amount of poise. These are some of the elements of behaviour which must be built into the person if practical use is to be made of him as an interactant, and it is these elements that are referred to in part when one speaks of universal human nature. (1967: 44-45)

The ideas expressed in this quotation were taken by Brown and Levinson (1987) as the general and fundamental tenets of their Theory of

Politeness. The next sections in this chapter are devoted to the different perspectives taken for the study of the phenomenon of politeness (but, in particular, to Brown & Levinson's perspective, for it is considered to be the most influential so far) as a line of analysis emerging from the interactional sociolinguistic approach.

4.2. Politeness

As many other concepts in Pragmatics and Discourse Analysis, the concept of politeness is not easy to define. There is a surprising amount of disagreement as to the criteria used to define it. Nevertheless, it has become an essential part of the knowledge required to analyze discourse.

Watts (2003) notes that, when people are asked what they imagine polite behavior to be, their usual way out of the dilemma is to resort to giving examples of behavior which they, personally, would consider "polite", such as "He always shows a lot of respect towards his superiors" or "She's always very helpful and obliging." Watts also remarks that "there are even people who classify polite behaviour negatively, characterising it with such terms as 'standoffish', 'haughty', 'insincere', etc." (2003:1). But politeness as a linguistic phenomenon has been researched by looking at it from wider perspectives than those attached to the everyday use of the term. Notwithstanding, there is not a uniform criterion to define and identify politeness phenomena.

Georgia Green explains that when we talk about politeness within pragmatic studies we refer to *strategies for maintaining or changing interpersonal relations* (1989: 141). The goals of the speakers when using these strategies may be ends in themselves (purely social conversation or "small talk") or they may be a link in a chain of goals whose ultimate end is to influence someone's behavior or attitude. Bruce Fraser (1990) analyzes the different points of view through which the phenomenon of politeness has been researched and studied in Linguistics, and he finds four main perspectives, to which we now turn.

4.2.1. Approaches to the phenomenon of politeness

In his famous article "Perspectives on politeness", Bruce Fraser (1990a) points to the fact that there is not a common understanding of the concept of politeness, and he reviews four of the best-known approaches to the phenomenon: 1) the social-norm view; 2) the conversational-maxim view; 3) the face-saving view; and 4) the conversational-contract view. Let us now briefly consider the four of them:

1) *The social-norm view* reflects the understanding of politeness embraced mainly by the English-speaking world in a general way. It assumes that each society has certain rules and norms that prescribe a particular behavior or way of thinking within a context. This sense of politeness is associated with what constitutes "good manners" as well as with a certain speech style, whereby a higher degree of formality implies greater politeness. Among the authors holding this view, Fraser cites Jespersen (1965) and Quirk (1985). This view does not have many adherents among current researchers.

2) *The conversational-maxim view* is principally based on Grice's work in his paper "Logic and Conversation" (1967, published 1975), in which he proposes his general Cooperative Principle (CP) and maxims. As we saw in Chapter 3, Grice assumes that the CP is always observed and that any real or apparent violation of the maxims signals conversational implicatures, i.e., non-explicit messages intended by the speaker to be inferred by the hearer. R. Lakoff (1973) and Leech (1983) are among the authors that subscribe to this approach.

3) *The face-saving view* is the best known of the approaches to

politeness. Its principles and tenets are found in Brown & Levinson's *Politeness: Some Universals in Language Use* (1987). This approach will be dealt with in more detail later in this chapter (4.2.1.2.), but for the purposes of this summary of perspectives, suffice it to say that Brown & Levinson assume the general correctness of Grice's view of conversational interaction, explicitly adopting a view that holds that there is a working assumption by conversationalists of the rational and efficient nature of talk. If there are deviations from this behavior, the recipient will find in considerations of politeness the reason for the speaker's apparent irrationality or inefficiency. As was noted in 4.1.3., these authors base much of their theory on Goffman's (1967) concept of *face* (the individual's self-esteem), which can be lost, maintained, enhanced or threatened. The fact that some acts can threaten face and thus require some kind of softening is the organizing principle of their theory.

4)   *The conversational-contract view*, an approach presented by Fraser (1975, 1990a) and Fraser & Nolen (1981), also adopts Grice's notion of a Cooperative Principle and recognizes the importance of Goffman's notion of face, but it differs in certain important ways from Brown & Levinson's view. Within this perspective, all the participants of an interaction enter into a conversation and continue within it with the understanding of a current Conversational Contract at every turn. "Being polite constitutes operating within the then-current terms and conditions of the Conversational Contract" (Fraser, 1990a: 233).

Views 2 (conversational-maxim) and 3 (face-saving) have had the most adherents among researchers. By and large, the most influential of all views has been Brown & Levinson's face-saving approach to politeness. We now turn to a more detailed account of these two views.

4.2.1.1. The conversational-maxim view

Before the year 1960 all semantic theories focused primarily on truth conditions. These theories were employed by logicians like Frege and Kripke, who recursively assigned to each sentence the conditions under which it would be true. The subsequent observations by linguists and philosophers of apparent differences in meaning between certain natural language words and their logical counterparts were the basis for the development of pragmatic reflection and studies, of which Grice's lectures at Harvard on the topic *Logic and Conversation* (1967) were considered to be crucial. Grice's construct of Conversational principles[3] has been adopted by some authors in an effort to account for politeness phenomena. Robin Lakoff (1973) and Geoffrey Leech (1983) are among these authors.

4.2.1.1.1. Leech's approach to politeness

According to Leech (1983), the Cooperative Principle and the Politeness Principle do not operate in isolation. They often create a tension in a speaker who must determine, for a given speech context, what message to convey and how to do it. The role of the Politeness Principle is "to maintain the social equilibrium and the friendly relations which enable us to assume that our interlocutors are being cooperative in the first place" (Leech, 1983: 82). Leech explains that politeness concerns a relationship between two participants, but speakers also show politeness to third parties who may or may not be present in the speech situation. In order to show politeness, the participants in a speech situation observe the following maxims (Leech, 1983: 132):

1) TACT MAXIM (in impositives and commissives):
   (a) Minimize cost to *other* [(b) Maximize benefit to *other*]
2) GENEROSITY MAXIM (in impositives and commissives):
   (a) Minimize benefit to *self* [(b) Maximize cost to *self*]
3) APPROBATION MAXIM (in expressives and assertives):
   (a) Minimize dispraise of *other* [(b) Maximize praise of *other*]
4) MODESTY MAXIM (in expressives and assertives):
   (a) Minimize praise of *self* [(b) Maximize dispraise of *self*]
5) AGREEMENT MAXIM (in assertives):
   (a) Minimize disagreement between *self* and *other* [(b) Maximize agreement between *self* and *other*]
6) SYMPATHY MAXIM (in assertives):
   (a) Minimize antipathy between *self* and *other* [(b) Maximize sympathy between *self* and *other*]

Fraser summarizes Leech's (1983) Principle of Politeness as follows:

> Other things being equal, minimize the expression of beliefs which are unfavorable to the hearer and at the same time (but less important) maximize the expression of beliefs which are favorable to the hearer. (1990: 225)

---

[3] For a detailed explanation of Grice's Theory of Implicature and Cooperative Principle, see 3.2.

Leech distinguishes between "Relative Politeness" and "Absolute Politeness". The former refers to politeness *vis-à-vis* a specific situation, and the latter to the degree of politeness inherently associated with specific speaker actions. Therefore, some illocutions (like *orders*, for instance) are inherently impolite and others (like *offers)* are inherently polite.

In Leech's view, *Negative Politeness* consists in minimizing the impoliteness of impolite illocutions, and *Positive Politeness* consists in maximizing the politeness of polite illocutions. The examples in the box below show how the speaker minimizes the impoliteness of a request by hedging it with the conditional clause *If it would not trouble you too much,* and how s/he maximizes the politeness of the assertive act delivering the good news by placing it within the subordinate clause of the main introductory clause *I am delighted to inform you*:

> *Negative Politeness*: **"If it would not trouble you too much,**
>
> could you lend me your car?"
>
> *Positive Politeness*: **"I am delighted to inform you** that you
>
> are the winner of the award."

Fraser (1990: 227) observes that Leech's conclusions seem too strong, when asserting, for example, that *to order* is inherently conflictive, reduces comity and requires negative politeness on the part of the speaker, because on occasions, this is not the case. For instance, in a situation where a teacher ordered a student to put her prize-winning solution on the board for the class, the order would not be conflictive at all and would not require the use of negative politeness strategies: the teacher could directly order the student to present the cause and results of her success without having to minimize any impoliteness, because the act of ordering would be regarded as polite (in this case, the obvious politeness of a teacher who wants to make the student 'feel good' about her achievement).

Another author who views Politeness from the conversational-maxim perspective is Robin Lakoff. Her approach is the subject of the next section.

4.2.1.1.2. Robin Lakoff's approach to Politeness

Lakoff defines Politeness as "a device used in order to reduce friction in personal interaction" (1979: 64) and proposes two Rules of Pragmatic Competence (1973: 296):

1) **Be clear** (this rule is in agreement with Grice's rules or maxims of conversation (1967))
2) **Be polite**

She explains that these two rules are at times reinforcing and at other times in conflict with each other. In general, when clarity is in conflict with politeness, politeness supersedes: avoiding offence in a conversation is considered more important than achieving clarity. In addition, she posits three Rules of Politeness (1973: 300):

1) **Don't Impose** (used when Formal/Impersonal Politeness is required)
2) **Give Options** (used when Informal Politeness is required)
3) **Make A Feel Good** – Be friendly (used when Intimate Politeness is required)

These three rules are applicable depending on the type of politeness required as understood by the speaker. For instance, if a participant assesses the situation as requiring **Formal Politeness (Don't Impose)**, he could ask the hearer about his personal life by introducing the question with another, non-imposing question:

Would you mind if I asked you a personal question?

If the speaker were in a situation requiring Informal Politeness, s/he might ask the personal question directly without asking for permission, but s/he would probably use *hedges* and/or an indirect question to mitigate the act as in:

I *guess* you have a boy-friend, don't you?

If the speaker wants to make the hearer 'feel good', to make her sense him/her as a friend, Intimate Politeness is needed, and therefore s/he might say:

Come on, sweetie; tell me about your boy-friend.

Lakoff herself summarizes her contribution to this topic in the following points:

1) ...we follow pragmatic rules in speaking, just as we follow semantic and syntactic rules, and all must be a part of our linguistic rules.
2) ... there are rules of politeness and rules of clarity (conversation), the latter a subcase of the former: rules of conversation are a subtype of R1 [Be clear].
3) ...the rules of politeness may differ dialectally in applicability, but their basic form remains the same universally.
4) ...these are not merely linguistic, but applicable to all cooperative human transactions. (1973: 305)

Lakoff undoubtedly sheds light on the phenomenon of politeness as a system which is relative to the level of formality holding in human relationships. However, some aspects in her approach are not made clear, and precisely one of the criticisms made of her politeness framework is the fact that "the reader is never told how the speaker or hearer is to assess what level of politeness is required" (Fraser, 1990a: 224).

4.2.1.2. The face-saving view: Brown & Levinson's Theory of Politeness

Undoubtedly, the most influential study on politeness phenomena so far is that of Brown & Levinson (1978 and 1987[4]) in their book *Politeness: Some Universals in Language Usage*, which is based on a particular interpretation of the work of E. Goffman (1967, 1971)[5] about the role of *face* in social interaction. With respect to this concept, Brown & Levinson (herinafter B & L) explain that:

Central to our model is a highly abstract notion of "face" which consists of two specific kinds of desires ('face-wants') attributed by interactants to one another: the desire to be unimpeded in one's actions (negative face), and the desire (in some respects) to be approved of (positive face). This is the bare bones of a notion of face which (we argue) is universal. (1987: 13)

B & L argue that there is a direct relationship between the *face* of the speaker and certain variables which they call *Sociolinguistic Variables*. These variables are:

---

[4] All the references in this book are made to the 1987 edition.
[5] See 4.1.2. and 4.1.3.

1)   The "social distance" (D) of S [speaker] and H [hearer] (a symmetric relation).
2)   The relative "power" (P) of S and H (an asymmetric relation).
3)   The absolute ranking (R) of impositions in the particular culture. (1987: 74)

According to B & L, all the speakers of a language have both a positive and a negative face. There are acts that intrinsically threaten the interlocutor's face, which these authors call *Face Threatening Acts* (hereinafter FTAs). In general, speakers try to minimize the face threat of these acts by using a series of strategies summarized and illustrated in the following figure (1987: 60):

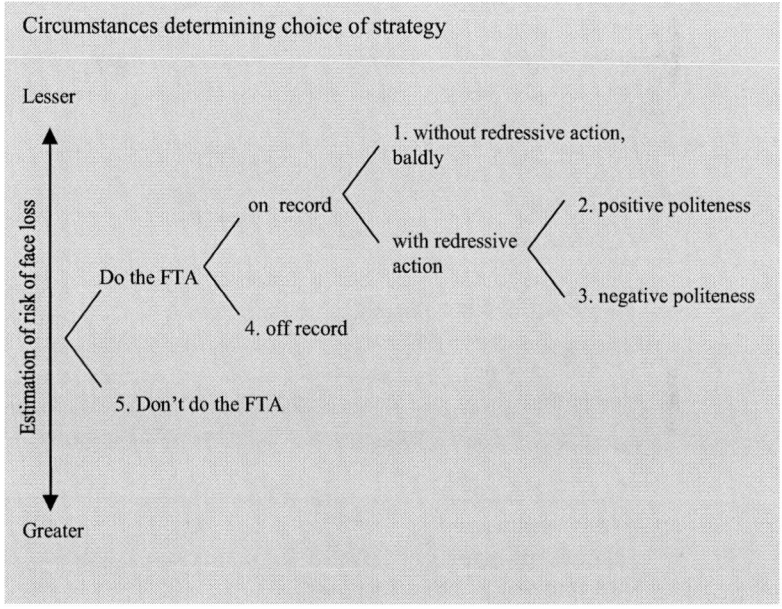

The more an act threatens S's or H's face, the more S will want to choose a higher-numbered strategy, given the fact that these strategies afford payoffs of increasingly minimized risk. This means that, if what the speaker has to say could in some way be offensive or impolite to the hearer, it is very likely that the speaker will use an *off record strategy*, characterized by the use of mitigating elements which convey certain meanings indirectly. If, on the contrary, S wants his/her utterance to be effective (because, for example, there is an urgency or the situation is task-oriented), it is most likely that S will use an on record strategy. When going on record, S may do it baldly or by using positive or negative politeness. Positive politeness strategies are oriented towards the positive face of H; they show S's desire for or approval of H's wants. Negative politeness strategies aim at H's negative face, i.e. his/her basic desire to maintain his/her terrain and self-determination.

4.2.1.2.1. Summary and examples:

To summarize and illustrate:

> ➤ If S uses an *on record strategy*, there is only one interpretation of his/her intention and there is no room for ambiguity. ***Bald on record*** *strategies* are considered to be in conformity with Grice's Maxims and they are used when maximum efficiency is required. Consider these examples:

> > • **Help!!** (Urgent, desperate situation. Compare to the non-urgent and non-desperate *Could you help me with the washing-up, please?*)
> > • **Don't move!!** (If S sees a Boa Constrictor approaching H)
> > • **Hands up!!** (When the police find a criminal)

> ➤ If the situation is not desperate, does not call for urgency or does not require maximum efficiency, S can still go *on record but with either positive or negative politeness*. Here are some **examples**:

> > • **What a beautiful hat you're wearing!** (On record with positive politeness)
> > • **Can you pass the salt?** (On record with negative politeness –conventionally indirect request–).

> ➤ If S wants to do an FTA, but for some reason wants to avoid the responsibility for doing it, s/he will most probably go off record and leave the interpretation to the addressee. By going off record S will always be flouting one or more of the Gricean Maxims, as can be seen in the following examples:

> > • **What a beautiful dress!** = *Please, buy me that dress.*

(Off record strategy: *Give hints*, which violates the Relevance Maxim).

- **John is a bit silly** = *John is **very** silly*. (Off record strategy: *Understate*, which violates the Quantity Maxim).
- **John is a real genius** = John is **stupid**. (Off record strategy: *Be ironic*, which violates the Quality Maxim).
- **I'm going you-know-where** = I'm going to the **bathroom**. (Off record strategy: *Be vague, use euphemisms*, which violates the Manner Maxim).

4.2.1.2.2.   Example of analysis

Alba-Juez (2002) analyzes the humorous FTAs in some episodes of two television comedy series, taking Brown & Levinson's (1987) model of politeness as the point of departure.

The use of politeness strategies and the interrelation of the sociological variables P (power), D (Distance) and R (Ranking of imposition of the particular culture) are shown in different fragments of the episodes. Consider the following example (Alba-Juez, 2002: 17-18):

Blanche: I've decided I can handle this relationship. I'm going out with Dirk Saturday night.

Dorothy: Was it ever in doubt?

Blanche: Momentarily. This is strictly off-the-record, but Dirk is nearly five years younger than I am.

Dorothy: In what, Blanche? Dog years??

The Golden Girls, 1991: 65.

This example is presented as another instance showing Dorothy's hostility towards Blanche by being sarcastic and implying that Blanche is a liar.   Dorothy flouts the Quantity Maxim by using an off record strategy (*Overstate*) when uttering her remark (*In what, Blanche? Dog years??*), which in turn triggers the implicature that Dirk is certainly much younger than Blanche asserts he is.   Instead of going on record, Dorothy chooses irony to tell her friend that she cannot fool her and that she should not fool herself, because it is obvious that Dorothy thinks that a relationship with so young a man is not likely to last long or end happily. Dorothy generally places herself as a realistic, down-to-earth woman, and she is the most educated of the four girls (she is a High School teacher and the other three girls look up to her as the most intelligent in the group), so she feels she is in a position of power to make fun of her room-mates and, in particular, of Blanche. Thus, the P value for Dorothy is high, while the D value is low, taking into account that the girls are friends and live in the same house, as a family. The R value for the realization of Dorothy's FTA in this example is rated high, considering the fact that in the American culture, as well as in many other western cultures, people still look at women who date or marry a younger man with a critical eye. It could be said, thus, that the male-dominant culture imposes its values upon Blanche's behavior and gives Dorothy the right to criticize and mock her friend.

Alba-Juez provides the formula for this particular example (2002: 17):

hP (S, H) + lD + hR , where:

hP (S,H) = High power of speaker with respect to hearer
lD = Low distance value between speakers
hR= High ranking of imposition of the culture as to doing or not doing the FTA.

By providing the formula for this and other examples, this author concludes that the context-dependency of the value of B & L's sociological variables is evident, for no single formula or combination of the variables seems to be *the* formula in cases of humorous FTAs, and, thus, other variables, such as *age, gender* or *level of education* should be considered when assessing the weightiness of an FTA.

The example above displays just one of the many instances in which scholars have used B & L's Theory of Politeness as a basis for Discourse Analysis. But in spite of its wide use, and even though it is the best-known of politeness theories, it has also been criticized. We now turn to this issue.

4.2.1.2.3.   Criticisms of Brown & Levinson's model of politeness

In spite of the fact that this theory has many supporters and has been the most influential Theory of Politeness up to now, B & L have been criticized, among other things, for claiming that their theory has a universal value, for being ethnocentric and for assuming an individualistic concept of face. The works of many scholars, such as Matsumoto (1988), Gu (1990), Nwoye (1992), Werkhoffer (1992), Mao (1994), O'Driscoll

(1996), Bravo (1999), Lee Wong (1999) and Watts (1992, 2003), point to these aspects.

The main underlying assumption in B & L's view of face is an individualistic view of the interactants as mainly sensitive towards a satisfaction of mutual face wants. Other scholars, on the contrary, have stressed the *situational* diversification of systems of politeness as well as their conventional nature. Pierre Bordieu[6] (1976, 1984, 1986), for instance, sees politeness in terms of conventions which reflect the determinate nature of power relations in a social space: the speaker who subscribes to these conventions is enacting political concession.

Lavandera (1988) criticizes other aspects of B & L's theory: she views politeness as a continuum and not as a dichotomy, in agreement with Fraser & Nolen's (1981) view, and she supplements the notion of *illocutionary force* (Searle, 1969) with that of *politeness force*, "emphasizing thereby the latter's obligatory nature" (1988: 1196). She also supports Fraser & Nolen's (1981) posits by emphasizing the conditions under which the expressions are used, i.e. the situation, and not the expressions themselves, for these conditions are crucial to determine the judgement of politeness (1988: 1196). Politeness, therefore, is a property of *utterances* and not of sentences. In her review of B & L's Theory of Politeness, she directs the reader's attention to what she describes as its weaknesses, which, in her opinion, are basically the following: 1) Brown and Levinson fail to see that politeness is a permanent component of all speech acts and thus they do not take into account any strategies aimed at *impoliteness*; 2) It is impossible to account for the fact that there can be an accumulation of similar strategies in the same speech act if we ascribe the degree of politeness to a strategy (as B & L do) and not to the entire speech act within which it occurs; 3) a distinction should be made between strategies like "Be pessimistic", which are purely pragmatic, and other strategies which contain a specific linguistic description such as "Employ a diminutive". Thus, in her view, even though B & L achieve some valuable and important aims, they do not succeed in providing a complete account of the phenomenon of politeness.

---

[6] See Chapter 9.

SUMMING UP... (CHAPTER 4)

1. The interactional sociolinguistic approach to Discourse Analysis is **multidisciplinary**: it concerns the study of the relationships between language, culture and society and has its roots in Anthropology, Sociology and Linguistics.

2. **Interactional Sociolinguistics** focuses upon situated meaning. Two central issues are the study of the *interaction between self and other* and *the study of context*.

3. One of the main concerns of this approach is the study of the practices of *contextualization*, a concept based on a reflexive notion of context.

4. John Gumperz and Erving Goffman have been the main contributors to the development of the interactional sociolinguistic approach: their ideas and points of view have been extensively used and applied in the field of linguistics by different authors, such as Brown & Levinson (1987), Schiffrin (1987) or Tannen (1989).

5. A crucial concept in Interactional Sociolinguistics is the concept of *contextualization cue*. Examples of contextualization cues are intonation, conversational code-switching, gestural signs, etc.

6. Goffman's sociology centers on physical co-presence rather than on social groups, and thus he focuses on aspects of *interaction order*. Key concepts in Goffman's interactional analysis are the concepts of *face, frame* and *footing*. Brown & Levinson's (1987) *Theory of Politeness* is based on a particular interpretation of the work of Goffman and the concept of *face*.

7. There is not a uniform criterion to define and identify politeness phenomena. From all perspectives on politeness, Brown & Levinson's *face-saving view* has undoubtedly been the most influential so far.

8. Brown & Levinson have been criticized, among other things, for claiming that their theory has a universal value, for being ethnocentric and for assuming an individualistic concept of face.

SELF EVALUATION QUESTIONS

Choose the answer that best suits the information given in Chapter 4.

1) The interactional sociolinguistic approach to discourse analysis…
   a) is based only on linguistics.
   b) draws information and concepts from several disciplines.
   c) is concerned mainly with the findings of anthropologists.

2) One of the main concerns of Interactional Sociolinguistics is…
   a) situated social interaction.
   b) written texts and their contexts.
   c) grammatical competence.

3) A crucial concept in Interactional Sociolinguistics is the concept of…
   a) linguistic performance.
   b) contextualization cue.
   c) minimal pairs.

4) One example of *contextualization cue* is…
   a) the place where a conversation occurs.
   b) the background noise of the room where a conversation occurs.
   c) code-switching within a given interaction.

5) Goffman argues that the self is…
   a) a social, interactive construction.
   b) a grammatical construction.
   c) the egocentric idea of one's being.

6) A crucial concept in Goffman's argumentation (1967) is the concept of…
   a) adjacency pairs
   b) proposition
   c) face

7) According to Goffman, one of the conditions of interaction is…
   a) the maintenance of face.
   b) the use of grammatically correct sentences.

c)   the use of politically-correct language

8)   An example of *frame* (another crucial concept in Goffman's
     analysis of interaction) could be...
a)   a relative clause.
b)   an academic lecture.
c)   body gestures.

9)   The concept of *footing* in Goffman's analysis...
a)   has to do with the different speaker roles.
b)   concerns the different codes used in an interaction.
c)   has to do with the turns taken by the different speakers .

10) According to Georgia Green, politeness has to do with...
a)   the use of appropriate language.
b)   being nice to everyone in an interaction.
c)   strategies for maintaining or changing interpersonal relations.

11) The most influential of the different politeness views has been...
a)   Fraser's conversational-contract view.
b)   Brown & Levinson's face-saving view.
c)   The social-norm view.

12) According to Leech, the Politeness Principle is mainly concerned
     with...
a)   maximizing the expression of unfavorable beliefs about the
     hearer and minimizing the expression of favorable ones.
b)   maximizing the expression of favorable beliefs about the hearer
     and minimizing the expression of unfavorable ones.
c)   always being generous and sympathetic, no matter what.

13) Robin Lakoff (1973) explains that, according to the rules of
     conversation...
a)   It is more important to be clear than to be polite.
b)   It is more important to be polite than to be clear.
c)   To be clear is never important.

14) Brown & Levinson's Theory of Politeness is based on an
     interpretation of the work of...
a)   J. Gumperz.
b)   E. Goffman.

c) G. Leech.

15) The three sociolinguistic variables, according to Brown &
    Levinson, are…
a) positive face, negative face and FTAs.
b) FTAs, negative politness and positive politeness.
c) Social distance, relative power (of speaker and hearer) and
    ranking of impositions in the particular culture.

16) Politeness strategies are normally used in order to…
a) minimize the face threat.
b) maximize the face threat.
c) lose face.

17) We normally use bald on record strategies when…
a) maximum efficiency is required.
b) there is no urgency of response.
c) we violate the maxims of the Cooperative Principle.

18) We normally use on record with positive or negative politeness
    strategies when…
a) maximum efficiency is required.
b) there is no urgency or when maximum efficiency is not required.
c) we violate the maxims of the Cooperative Principle.

19) We normally use off record strategies when…
a) we want to avoid certain responsibility for doing the FTA.
b) there is great urgency to do the FTA.
c) there is no need to flout the Gricean Maxims.

20) Brown & Levinson's Politeness Theory has been criticized for…
a) not being appropriate.
b) being pessimistic.
c) being ethnocentric.

PRACTICE

A) *ANALYSIS*: ANALYZE, from the interactional sociolinguistic perspective (combining both Gumperz's and Goffman's ideas and perspectives), the following segment from *Larry King Live*, which was examined in Unit 3 for the study of speech acts and presuppositions. Consider these aspects:

a)   The type and framework of interaction is an interview. Do you see any signs of behavior (e.g. hostility) which do not fit within this frame? Or, on the contrary, do you see any signs of sociability that fit within the frame? Are there any contextualization cues signaling shifts in participation structure? How and when are the participants being hostile/cooperating/ speaking for another?

b)   Can you identify the participant roles?

c)   How is face maintained?

1   KING: Toquerville, Utah, hello.
2   CALLER: Gentlemen, the honor is mine. Thank you for the call.
3   Bill, what do you think about the administration's Homeland
4   Security Department's little plan B to study to stop the election
5   under threat of terrorist attack? Does that remind you of our 2000
6   Florida deal?
7   MAHER: You mean you're talking about on Election Day?
8   KING: Yes, in case there's some big occurrence.
9   MAHER: Well, they've been pulling that card for how many...
10   KING: Wait a minute, you had some sort of disaster you don't
11   want to hold an election if you've got bombs dropping?
12   MAHER: That's true. And I agree with that. If there's really a
13   problem on Election Day. But, again, this is an administration that
14   has always said, OK, we're operating under this premise. You
15   can't criticize the administration during a time of war. Oh, and by
16   the way, we're always at war. The war is ongoing. So I mean, I
17   don't trust them. Let me put it that way. I don't trust them, or they
18   haven't earned my trust.

B) STUDY situations 1 to 5 and, in all of them, SPECIFY:

  a) The politeness strategies (positive, negative, off record, etc.)
      used by speaker B.
  b) The maxims (of Grice's Cooperative Principle) being flouted,
      when applicable.

  1) (Two sisters are having a conversation)

A: Tom has disappointed me. I discovered he has been lying to me ever
   since we met.
B: **Oh, what a fine friend he is!**

  2) (A and B are at the doctor's waiting room)

B: **It's cold in here, don't you think?**
A: Yes, indeed. I'll close the door.

  3) (A mother and her 10-year-old daughter are at a mall)

B: **I love that pair of jeans, Mom.**
A: O.K., I'll buy it for you.

  4) (A bear approaches B in the woods)

B: **Help!!!!!!**

  5) (A family is having dinner at home)

B: **Could you pass the olive oil, please?**
A: Sure!

C) *ANALYSIS*: ANALYZE the following scenes from the movie
Bicentennial Man and THINK about the interpretation Andrew gives to
the girl's comment "I think it sucks", as well as about the interpretation he
makes of Mr. Martin's comment "We're fine, Andrew" in Scene 2. Bear

in mind that Andrew is a robot and his mind is a computer.

SCENE 1: Mr. Martin shows Andrew (the robot) into the basement of the house.

Mr. Martin: Well, you'll be staying down here. Got everything you need?
Andrew: One only requires access to a power outlet.
       (pause)
Mr. Martin: Good Night, Andrew.
Andrew: It certainly is, sir.
Mr. Martin: No, no Andrew, the correct response to "Good night" is "Good night".
Andrew: Good night.
Mr. Martin: Yes.
Andrew: But the correct response to "Good night" is "Good night".
Mr. Martin: Good night, Andrew.
Andrew: Good night, sir.
Mr. Martin: You only need to say it once, Andrew.
Andrew: Or one should be saying it forever, sir, in an infinite verbal loop.
Mr. Martin: Exactly.
Andrew: Thank you, sir.
Mr. Martin: Good!
Andrew: Night! (Mr. Martin gazes at Andrew) Sorry, sir.

SCENE 2: The Martin family is having dinner. Andrew has served the dinner he prepared.

Mr. Martin: Mmmmm, Andrew, this is very good!
Andrew: Thank you, sir.
Mr. Martin: (addressing his daughter Grace ("Miss")) Don't you think…
Grace: I think it sucks!
Andrew: Sucks? How? Chickens do not have lips!
(Amanda, the "Little Miss", laughs)
Mrs. Martin: She's being rude (unclear comment to Grace)
  (pause)
Mr. Martin: We're fine, Andrew.
Andrew: Indeed you are, sir.
Mr. Martin: The kitchen!
Andrew: It's fine too, sir.
Mr. Martin: No, GO to the kitchen, now.

Now answer the questions in (1), and do (2):

(1) In what ways does Andrew lack "pragmatic knowledge"?
    i. Is he being cooperative?
    ii. Does he flout any of the Maxims of the Cooperative Principle?
    iii. Can he work out implicatures the same way humans do?
    iv. Is Andrew polite?
    v. Can he use all the rules of Politeness as described by B & L (1987)?
    vi. Can Andrew go off record? Why? Why not?

(2) WRITE a short essay with your answers to the questions in (1), making your point and justifying your analysis of Andrew's talk and linguistic behavior in general.

FURTHER READING

- Brown & Levinson, (1987), pp. 59-84, Chapters 4 & 5.
- Ferencik, (2007).
- Goffman, (1967, 1974).
- Gumperz, (1981).
- Holmes, 1995 (Also in Jarowski & Koupland, 2006; Chapter 23)
- Schiffrin, (1994), Chapter 4.
- Tannen, (1984), "Introduction to Linguists" and Chapter 1.
- Tannen, (2007).

USEFUL WEBSITES

Wikipedia entry for Interactional Sociolinguistics:
http://en.wikipedia.org/wiki/Interactional_sociolinguistics

Interactional Sociolinguistics useful links:
http://personal.cityu.edu.hk/~enrodney/Interact/links.htm

Wikipedia entry for Deborah Tannen:
http://en.wikipedia.org/wiki/Deborah_Tannen

Deborah Tannen's website at Georgetown University:
http://www9.georgetown.edu/faculty/tannend/

John Gumperz's biography:
http://www.mnsu.edu/emuseum/information/biography/fghij/gumperz_joh
n.html

Ervin Goffman's biography:
http://people.brandeis.edu/~teuber/goffmanbio.html

Bibliography on Politeness:
http://www.linguisticpoliteness.eclipse.co.uk/LingPolbib.htm

CONVERSATION ANALYSIS

"Conversation analysts use different approaches in developing analyses; there is no one right way. This presents a challenge in teaching others to do analyses since there are many paths to the final destination"

A. **Pomerantz and B. J. Fehr,** *Conversation Analysis.*

Chapter Outline:

- Scope and main tenets of Conversation Analysis (CA).

- Central concepts in CA (*turn-taking, adjacency pairs, preference organization, overall organization*, etc.) and their materialization in actual conversations.

- Sample analysis using the concepts and main techniques of CA.

5.1. Conversation Analysis: an approach to DA

Conversation Analysis (hereinafter CA) originated within Sociology as an approach to the study of the social organization of everyday conduct. It began with the work of Harold Garfinkel (1967, 1974) and his approach known as Ethnomethodology (which had in turn been influenced by the Phenomenology of Alfred Schütz[1]), and then it was applied to conversation by Harvey Sacks, Emanuel Schegloff and Gail Jefferson.

Ethnomethodological research suggests that knowledge is neither autonomous nor decontextualized; the actions of people produce and reproduce the knowledge through which individual conduct and social circumstance are intelligible. Thus, ethnomethodology avoids idealizations and argues that what speakers produce are categories that are continuously adjusted according to whether the anticipation of an actor is confirmed by another's actions or not. These categories are called *typifications*. Language (and action through language), as any other typification in social

---

[1] Alfred Schütz (1899-1959), was a philosopher and sociologist. His principal task was to develop the phenomenological philosophy of Edmund Husserl as a basis for a philosophy of the social sciences. Phenomenology seeks to understand how people construct meanings and "to study how human phenomena are experienced in consciousness, in cognitive and perceptual acts, as well as how they may be valued or appreciated aesthetically" (See Wilson, 2002).

conduct, is a situated product of rules and systems. The meaning of any given utterance is indexical to a specific context and purpose. As Schiffrin remarks, "the focus of CA on conversation, for example, arises out of the ethnomethodological distrust of idealizations as a basis for either social science or ordinary human action" (1994: 234).

CA has many things in common with other DA approaches, but it provides a particular way of analyzing and looking at talk. Schiffrin synthesizes this idea in the following passage:

> CA is like interactional sociolinguistics in its concern with the problem of social order, and how language both creates and is created by social context. It is also similar to the ethnography of communication in its concern with human knowledge [...] and its belief that no detail of conversation (or interaction) can be neglected *a priori* as unimportant. All three approaches also focus on detailed analysis of particular sequences of utterances that have actually occurred. But CA is also quite different from any of the approaches discussed thus far: CA provides its own assumptions, its own methodology (including its own terminology), and its own way of theorizing. (1994: 232)

CA is mainly differenciated from other approaches to DA in its particular approach to certain analytic issues. For instance, conversation analysts attempt to explicate the relevance of the parties to an interaction while they reject the use of investigator-stipulated theoretical and conceptual definitions of research questions. Sacks (1984) argues against too many idealizations in social science on the grounds that they produce general concepts that have only a vague relationship with a real set of events, and that is the reason why he chose to work on conversation: his intention was to deal with the details of actual events in order to remedy the idealizations of sociologists. Conversational analysts normally use tape-recorded conversation (which occurs without researcher prompting) as data, for they consider it to be objective data which can be available for many analysts and subjected to many analyses. Thus, CA avoids premature generalization and focuses on action as the locus of knowledge. All analyses must develop from the empirical conduct of speakers, considered to be the central resource for analysts.

In spite of the name of the field, conversational analysts do not engage solely in the analysis of ordinary conversation; rather, they are concerned with the study of *talk-in-interaction* (Schegloff, 2007), and this includes not only normal, casual everyday conversation but also institutionalized forms of talk (in the school, at the courts, at the doctor's office, etc.)

But even when CA is concerned with the contextual relevance that utterances always have for one another, some aspects of context are not assumed to have so much relevance. For instance, it can be noticed that CA transcripts of talk do not pay much attention to social relations or aspects of the social context such as setting, personal attributes or the occupation of a given participant. Thus, as Schiffrin notes, "although CA is an approach to discourse that emphasizes context, the relevance of context is grounded in text" (1994: 236).

5.2. Methods and central concepts of CA

One of the main assumptions of CA is that *interaction is structurally organized* (Heritage, 1984). Consequently, conversational analysts search for recurrent patterns, distributions, and forms of organization in large corpora of talk. Heritage lists two more assumptions: 1) contributions to interaction are contextually oriented, and 2) no order of detail in interaction can be dismissed a priori as disorderly, accidental or irrelevant.

The following are to be considered central criteria for CA:

- The data must be fully observable.
- Replicated analysis should look essentially the same.
- If data do not explain themselves, then more empirical data should be captured.

The core of CA is the exploration of sequential structures of social action. Sequential analysis can be made at different levels: *move, turn, exchange, transaction* and *interaction*. Sequential analysis is not interested in single utterances, but in how utterances are designed to tie with or fit prior utterances, or in how an utterance has significant implications for what kinds of utterances should come next (Wetherell et. al, 2001). One of the central structures of interaction (and a central concept in CA) is the *adjacency pair*, which is closely connected to that of *turn-taking*. We now turn to them.

5.2.1. Linear sequences: turn-taking and adjacency pairs

Sacks, Schegloff & Jefferson argue that "the organization of taking turns to talk is fundamental to conversation" (1974: 696). **Turn-taking** is used for talking in different *speech-exchange systems* such as interviews, meetings, debates or ceremonies. These authors, and conversational analysts in general, support the idea that there is a basic set of rules governing turn construction, which provide for the allocation of a next turn to one party, and coordinate transfer so as to minimize gap and overlap.

These rules are deduced from the following facts about turn-taking:

- Speaker change recurs, or at least occurs
- One party talks at a time.
- Occurrences of more than one speaker at a time are common, but brief.
- Transitions with no gap and no overlap are common. Together with transitions characterized by slight gap or slight overlap, they make up the vast majority of transitions.
- Turn order is not fixed, but varies.
- Turn size is not fixed, but varies.
- Length of conversation is not specified in advance.
- What parties say is not specified in advance.
- Relative distribution of turns is not specified in advance.
- Number of parties can vary.
- Talk can be continuous or discontinuous.
- Turn-allocation techniques are obviously used. A current speaker may select a next speaker (as he addresses a question to another party); or parties may self-select in starting to talk.
- Various turn-constructional units are employed (words, sentences, etc.).
- Repair mechanisms exist for dealing with turn-taking errors and violations (Sacks et al, 1974: 700-01).

Turn-taking is a form of social action and, therefore, it operates in accordance with a local management system. This system is conventionally known by members of a social group, and it is essentially a set of conventions for getting turns, keeping them or giving them away. A **Transition Relevance Place**, or **TRP** refers to any possible change of turn. The most obvious markers of a TRP are the end of a structural unit (a phrase or clause) and a pause (Yule, 1996). Speakers may hold the floor for extended periods of time. Within an extended turn, they normally expect their interlocutors to indicate that they are listening. This they do by means of head nods, smiles or other facial expressions, but they can also show attentiveness by using certain common vocal indications such as *uh-uh, yeah, mmm*, etc. These vocal indications are called **backchannels** and they are important because they provide feedback to the speaker regarding the positive reception of his/her message. Consequently, the absence of backchannels may be very frequently interpreted negatively, as lack of interest on the part of the interlocutor or as a way of withholding agreement.

Taking turns to speak in an elementary-school class

Thus, speakers having a conversation are viewed as taking turns at holding the floor, a fact that may be considered a common feature of all cultures and languages; however, the manner and frequency with which the floor is held and the turns are allocated may vary substantially from one social group to another.

Another central concept in CA is that of **adjacency pair**. An adjacency pair is a sequence of two utterances which are adjacent and produced by different speakers. These two utterances are ordered as a *first part* and a *second part* and they are generally typed, so that a first part normally expects and requires a given second part or range of second parts (Schegloff & Sacks, 1973). Prototypical examples of adjacency pairs would be the following:

1) *greeting-greeting:*   A: Hello.
                          B: Hello.

2)   *offer-acceptance*:   A: Would you care for more
tea?
B: Yes, please.

3)   *apology-minimization:* A: I'm sorry.
B: Oh, don't worry. That's O.K.

As Schiffrin notes, "adjacency pairs are organized patterns of stable, recurrent actions that provide for, and reflect, order within conversation" (1994: 236). As such, they provide a sequence for the specification of expectations about form and meaning across utterances. Levinson states the rule that governs the use of adjacency pairs as follows: "Having produced a first part of some pair, current speaker must stop speaking, and next speaker must produce at that point a second part to the same pair" (1983: 304). But this rule is not always followed to the letter in conversation. Frequently, **insertion sequences** occur (Schegloff, 1972) in which, for example, a question-answer pair is embedded within another, as seen in example 4:

4)
Child: Mom, can I play Nintendo now? (Question 1)
Mother: Have you cleaned up the playroom? (Question 2)
Child: No. (Answer 2)
Mother: Then, NO! (Answer 1)

Thus, we may speak of *nested adjacency pairs*, and in fact numerous levels of embedding are not infrequent, where, for instance, a question and its answer may be many utterances apart.

In addition, and again considering the *question-answer* pair, there are a great many responses other than answers which nevertheless count as acceptable seconds, such as "re-routes" (e.g.: *Better ask your father*), refusals to answer or challenges to the presuppositions or sincerity of the question (e.g.: *You've got to be kidding*). This fact, according to Levinson (1983: 307), seems "to undermine the structural significance of the concept of an adjacency pair". However, the importance of the concept is reassured by the equally important concept of **preference organization**, which will be analyzed and described in the next section.

5.2.1.1. Preference organization

The concept of **preference organization** underlies the idea that there is a hierarchy operating over the potential second parts of an adjacency pair. Thus, there is at least one **preferred** and one **dispreferred** category of response to first parts. This concept is a structural notion that corresponds closely to the linguistic concept of *markedness* (Levinson, 1983: 307), in such a way that preferred seconds are **unmarked** and dispreferred seconds are **marked**. For instance, the unmarked, preferred response to a request is a granting and not a rejection; the rejection being the dispreferred, marked second part, as shown in the following examples:

1) *Unmarked, preferred second:*

A: Hey Jack, can I borrow your car this afternoon?   (*First part: request*)
J: Sure!   (*Second part: granting*)

2) *Marked, dispreferred second:*

    A: Dad, could I borrow your car tonight for the prom? (*First part:*
                                                              request)
    B: Well…, I don't trust your driving skills yet. So maybe we'll leave
    it for some other time.   (*Second part: rejection*)

Levinson explains that dispreferred seconds normally exhibit one or more of the following features:

    a)   *Delays*: (i) by pause before delivery, (ii) by the use of a preface […] (iii) by displacement over a number of turns via use of *repair initiators* or insertion sequences.

    b)   *Prefaces*: (i) the use of markers or announcers of dispreferreds like *Uh* and *Well,* (ii) the production of token agreements before disagreements, (iii) the use of appreciations if relevant (for offers, invitations, suggestions, advice), (iv) the use of apologies if relevant (for requests, invitations, etc.), (v) the use of qualifiers (e.g. *I don't know for sure, but…*), (vi) hesitation in various forms, including self-editing.

c) *Accounts:* carefully formulated explanations for why the (dispreferred) act is being done.

d) *Declination component:* of a form suited to the nature of the first part of the pair, but characteristically indirect or mitigated. (1983: 334)

As the reader will observe, the example of a dispreferred second above has the four features described by Levinson, for the speaker uses the marker *Well* (*preface*) followed by a pause (*delay*), and at the same time he gives an explanation for his rejection (*account*: "I don't trust your driving skills yet") and provides a mitigated negative answer (*declination component*: "So maybe we'll leave it for some other time").

Example 4 in 5.2.1. above, however, only exhibits the declination component, which, as a matter of fact, is not indirect but quite the opposite. This is also a possibility, which occurs in some special contexts where the interactant that declines or rejects the request does not need to be indirect (because, as is the case in the example, there is a very close relationship (mother/son) between the interlocutors, or because the situation allows for the speakers to be direct and even impolite –as, for instance, in the discourse used among members of the armed forces[2]).

5.2.2. Other sequences: Repair, pre-sequences, insertion sequences and overall organization

Apart from the local organization operating in conversation by means of turn-taking and adjacency pairs, there are other orders of organization, such as certain recurrent kinds of sequence which can only be defined over three or four or more turns. We refer to **repair, pre-sequences** and **overall organization.**

5.2.2.1. Repair

A central conversational device which shows how preference organization operates within and across turns is the organization of **repair.** Repair is a device for the correction of misunderstandings, mishearings or non-hearings which has certain properties. **Self-initiated repair** is differentiated from **other-initiated repair**. Self-repair within a turn may

---

[2] See Culpeper 1996.

be signalled by phenomena such as glottal stops, lengthened vowels, etc. Repair initiated by a participant other than the speaker may be achieved by the use of echo-questions, repetitions of problematic items with stress on problem syllables, or by using expressions such as *What?, Pardon?, Excuse me?*, etc.

The repair system is set up in such a way that there is a tendency for self-initiated self-repair, the preference ranking being as follows:

> *Preference 1* is for self-initiated self-repair in opportunity 1 (own turn).
> *Preference 2* is for self-initiated self-repair in opportunity 2 (transition space).
> *Preference 3* is for other-initiation, by NTRI (Next Turn Repair Initiator) in opportunity 3 (next turn), or self-repair (in the turn after that).
> *Preference 4* is for other-initiated other-repair in opportunity 3 (next turn).
> (Levinson, 1983: 341)

Thus the first opportunity to make the repair would be immediately after the error, the second would be at the end of the turn, the third after recipient delay (transition space) at the end of the turn, the fourth at T2, the fifth at T3, and so on.

Here are some examples:

1) *Self-initiated self-repair in opportunity 1*:
A: She came to visit last month, **I mean last week**, you know.
B: Oh.

2) *Self-initiated self-repair in opportunity 2*:
A: I simply don't want to go to the cinema with him=
   = **Well, I mean, I don't like that movie, you know. I have nothing against him**.
B: I see.

3) *Other-initiation of self-repair in opportunity 3:*
A: What are your plans for tonight?
B: **Pardon?**
A: **What are your plans for tonight?**

4) *Self-repair in opportunity 4, following other-initiation by NTRI*
A: How about meeting at "Chez Pierre"?
B: **Where?**
A: **"Chez Pierre". It's a French restaurant.**

5) *Other-initiated other-repair in opportunity 3:*
A: Look at the bees!
  (pause)
B: **Wasps, I would say**.

5.2.2.2. Pre-sequences

Some sequences prefigure a turn which contains a reason for the sequence. For example, a summons prefigures a turn which contains the reason for the summons (Levinson, 1983), as in:

A: Jim!   (*Summons*)
J: Yes?   (*Answer*)
A: Could you come down here and help me with the washing up?
                    (*Reason for summons*)

Thus, summonses are generalized pre-sequences. Most pre-sequences can be said to prefigure the specific kind of action that they potentially precede. Other clear examples of pre-sequences are pre-closings, pre-invitations, pre-requests, pre-arrangements, pre-anouncements, etc., which are illustrated in the following examples:

1) *Pre-invitation:*
A: **Do you have any plans for tomorrow evening?**
B: **No, why?**
A: How about going to the theater?

2) *Pre-closing:*
A: ...and so this is what I wanted to tell you.
B: **O.K.   See you tomorrow, then**
A: **See you.   And remember to bring your camera!**
B: Don't worry, I will. Bye!

3) *Pre-request:*
A: **Will you be home tomorrow?**
B: **Yes, in the morning.**
A: So... would you mind if I come round and talk to you for a minute?

4) *Pre-announcement:*

A: **You won't guess the news.**
B: **No. What is it?**
B: I've been appointed Head of the Department.

5) *Pre-arrangement:*
A: **When are you free in the afternoon?**
B: **From 2:00 to 5:00 on Thursdays and Fridays.**
A: Let's meet on Friday at 2:00 pm, then.
B: O.K. Great.

5.2.2.3. Insertion sequences

At times, the distribution of the characteristic action is not exactly over the paradigmatic four-turn sequence, and we may find **insertion sequences** which may be concerned with, for instance, *repair,* or *establishing a temporary hold.* The following telephone conversation contains an example of an insertion sequence *establishing a temporary hold:*

T1	*Telephone rings* (T1: *Summons*)	
T2	A: Hello (T2: *Answer to summons*)	
T3	B: Hello I'd like to speak to Mr. Freeborn, please. (T3: *Request*)	
T4	A: **Could you hold on for a minute, please?**	
T5	B: **Yes.** (T4 & T5: *question/answer Insertion Sequence*)	
	(pause)	
T6	A: I'm afraid he's not in yet, Sir. Would you like to leave a message? (T6: *Answer to Request* in T3, and *Offer*)	
T7	B: No, thanks. I'll call later. (T7: *Rejection of Offer*)	

As can be seen, in this telephone conversation there is a two-turn insertion sequence which separates the request (T3) from its answer (T6), and which shows, at the same time, that the first and second parts of adjacency pairs do not necessarily have to be adjacent turns.

5.2.2.4. Overall organization

There is what conversational analysts call **overall organization,** due to the fact that it organizes the totality of the exchange within some specific kind of conversation. Thus, we may speak of classes of verbal interchanges (e.g. telephone calls, a talk over the garden fence, etc.) that have some special features, for example, in their opening or closing sections. The **openings** of telephone (and other related) conversations typically contain a summons-answer adjacency pair. This is normally followed by the **first topic slot**, which contains an announcement by the caller of the reason for the call. Then other topics are fitted to prior ones, until we finally get to the **closing section** of the overall organization of the call. Prototypical closings may include the making of arrangements, the giving of regards to family members, the use of markers such as *Okay, All right, So*, etc. organized in one or more pairs of passing turns and a final exchange of terminal elements (e.g. *Bye, Cheers, Take care*, etc.) Consequently, we may say that telephone conversations exhibit the following overall organization:

1.   **Opening section**
2.   **Main body**: Topic slot 1, Topic slot 2, Topic slot 3...
3.   **Closing section**

The first topic slot is normally the most important one, for it is the topic which caused the caller to make the call. Then there may be a succession of other topics which, according to Sacks (1971), in their preferred organization, should be related to one another. A high frequency of marked topic shifts, are signs of a 'lousy' conversation (Levinson, 1983: 313).

5.3. Example of analysis

We shall now go back to one of the fragments from *The Larry King Show* analyzed in Chapter 3, in which an outside caller has a short conversation with Bill Maher:

T1   (spectator call)
T2   KING: Toquerville, Utah, hello.
T3   CALLER: Gentlemen, the honor is mine. Thank you for the call.

Bill, what do you think about the administration's Homeland
Security Department's little plan B to study to stop the election
under threat of terrorist attack? Does that remind you of our 2000
Florida deal?

T4   MAHER: You mean you're talking about on Election Day?
T5   KING: Yes, in case there's some big occurrence.
T6   MAHER: Well, they've been pulling that card for how many...

T7   KING: Wait a minute, you had some sort of disaster you don't
       want to hold an election if you've got bombs dropping?
T8   MAHER: That's true. And I agree with that. If there's really a
       problem on Election Day. But, again, this is an administration that
       has always said, OK, we're operating under this premise. You
       can't criticize the administration during a time of war. Oh, and by
       the way, we're always at war. The war is ongoing. So I mean, I
       don't trust them. Let me put it that way. I don't trust them, or they
       haven't earned my trust.

This televised telephone conversation consists of eight turns. The first two
constitute the typical *summons-answer* **adjacency pair** of the opening of a
telephone conversation. We do not actually hear the telephone ringing, but
it is assumed that somebody behind the camera has notified Larry King
that there is a caller from Toquerville, Utah, and therefore he answers the
call by naming the place and by greeting. In terms of **overall
organization**, these two first turns constitute the *opening* of the telephone
conversation. Then the caller responds to the greeting and thanks them for
accepting his call, but quickly introduces the *first topic slot* (reason for the
call- T3), which is the first part of a *question-answer* adjacency pair that in
fact is not physically adjacent because there is a question/answer **insertion
sequence** in between (T4 and T5). This insertion sequence is concerned
with the *clarification of the question*. The answer to the question and the
second part of the pair started in T3 is found in T6, but before it is
completed, it is interrupted by another insertion turn (T7) which contains
another question related to the topic. Finally, in T8, Maher answers the
initial question as well as the previous question inserted in T7.

The telephone conversations in this television show are peculiar
because they do not normally have a **closing,** due to time constraints. The
callers only get the answer to their questions but they are not normally
granted the opportunity to go along with the talk until it reaches a normal
end. It is clear that it is always Larry King who is in **control of the floor.**
Even when Maher asks the caller a question (T4), Larry King feels entitled

to answer on behalf of the caller, without passing the floor on to him (T5).

In this short analysis we can see how CA sheds light on the structure of conversation, which in turn may help the analyst answer questions such as: *Who is in control of the floor, and therefore, who orients the conditional relevance of, for instance an answer after a question? What type of conversation structure and sequences do we find in conversations where one of the participants clearly exerts his/her power? How can the observations about conversation structure provide insight into particular instances of talk, such as, for example, pauses or silence?* In the fragment analyzed here, it is obvious that it is Larry King who controls the floor and who exerts his power over the other participants by interrupting and inserting sequences between adjacency pairs or by re-orienting the course of a question.

In spite of the fact that CA gives importance to context and participants, no further speculations can be made as to, for instance, the speakers' personality or what they really meant beyond their words. The analyst has to stick to what is there, to the actual conversation, and describe it in terms of its structure and overall organization, drawing conclusions based only on these elements and not on any other far-fetched assumptions.

SUMMING UP... (CHAPTER 5)

1. CA originated within Sociology with the work of Harold Garfinkel (1967, 1974) and his approach known as **Ethnomethodology,** and then it was applied to conversation by Harvey Sacks, Emanuel Schegloff and Gail Jefferson.

2. **Ethnomethodological research** suggests that knowledge is neither autonomous nor decontextualized; it avoids idealizations and argues that what speakers produce are categories that are continuously adjusted according to whether the anticipation of an actor is confirmed by another's actions or not. These categories are called **typifications**. Language is one of the typifications of social conduct.

3. One of the main assumptions of CA is that **interaction is structurally organized.**

4. The core of CA is the exploration of **sequential structures** of social action.

5. One of the central structures of interaction (and a central concept in CA) is the **adjacency pair**, which is closely connected to that of **turn-taking.**

6. **Turn-taking** is a form of social action which operates in accordance with a local management system. This system is essentially a set of conventions for getting turns, keeping them or giving them away.

7. **Preference organization** is a key concept in CA. It presupposes that there is a hierarchy operating over the potential second parts of an *adjacency pair.* Thus, there is at least one **preferred** and one **dispreferred** category of response to first parts.

8. There are other orders of organization, such as **repair, pre-sequences** or **overall organizations**, which can be defined only over three or more turns.

9. **Repair** is a device for the correction of misunderstandings, mishearings or non-hearings. **Pre-sequences** are turns which contain a reason for the next sequence. **Overall organization** refers to the organization of the totality of the exchange within some specific kind of conversation.

SELF EVALUATION QUESTIONS

Choose the answer that best suits the information given in Chapter 5.

1) Conversation Analysis originated within…
a) Linguistics.
b) Sociology.
c) Psychology.

2) Conversation Analysis began with…
a) the approach known as Ethnomethodology.
b) Psychoanalysis.
c) Sacks, Shegloff and Jefferson's approach.

3) Conversation analysts…
a) make use of many idealizations in their every-day work.
b) do not believe in the organized structure of interaction.
c) argue against too many idealizations in their analysis.

4) One of the main assumptions of CA is that…
a) social relations are of primary importance.
b) many details of conversation are *a priori* unimportant.
c) conversation is structurally organized.

5) It is essential for CA …
a) that the data be fully observable.
b) to analyze single utterances.
c) to specify what parties say in advance.

6) The concept of *adjacency pair*…
a) has very little to do with sequential analysis.
b) is in close connection with the concept of *turn-taking*.
c) always refers to utterances produced by only one speaker.

7) Turn-taking is a …
a) description of the making of errors.
b) local system.
c) a form of social action.

8) A *Transition Relevance Place* (TRP)…
a) is a structural unit.

b) has to do with possible changes of turn.
c) refers to a group of turns.

9) Interlocutors indicate that they are listening by means of…
a) backchannels.
b) adjacency pairs.
c) preference organization.

10) *Apology-minimization…*
a) is a backchannel.
b) refers to one of the prototypical adjacency pairs.
c) is one part of an adjacency pair.

11) In the following dialogue we find an example of…
a) a nested adjacency pair.
b) an incomplete adjacency pair.
c) repair.

John: Lucy, are you coming to Tom's party tomorrow evening?
Lucy: Who else will be there?
John: only his closest friends.
Lucy: Then yes, I'll go.

12) *Preferred seconds* in an adjacency pair…
a) are marked.
b) are instances of repair.
c) are unmarked.

13) *Dispreferred seconds* in an adjacency pair…
a) are marked.
b) are instances of repair.
c) are unmarked.

14) Within the repair system, there is a preference for…
a) self-initiated self-repair in opportunity 2.
b) self-initiated self-repair in opportunity 1.
c) other-initiation by NTRI in opportunity 3.

15) The sequence in bold type is an example of…
a)   pre-invitation.
b)   pre-announcement.
c)   pre-request.

A: **Do you like apple pie?**
B: **Yes, I love it. Why?**
A: I'll treat you to the best apple pie with ice-cream you've ever
      tried, at Clyde's this evening.

16) In the following exchange, there is an insertion sequence in…
a)   Turns 1 and 2.
b)   Turns 2 and 4.
c)   Turns 2 and 3.

T1   A: Do you love me?
T2   B: It depends on what you mean by the word "love".
T3   A: What could I mean? LOVE! Just that!
T4   B: Then I cannot give you an accurate answer.

17) The following could be considered as the typical overall
      organization of…
a)   Mass sermons .
b)   Business transactions.
c)   Telephone conversations.

1.   Opening section (with a summons-answer adjacency pair)
2.   Main body (with different topic slots)
3.   Closing section (farewell)

PRACTICE

A) *ANALYSIS*: The following is an adapted version of the transcription of a call made by a Police Officer at a private house in the U.S.A.. ANALYZE the sequence from the CA perspective, taking into account its *overall organization, turn-taking, adjacency pairs, insertion sequences*, etc.

T1   (Telephone rings)

T2 *Mr. Rowlings*: Hello?

T3 *Police Officer*: Hello, uhm… I'd like to talk to Mr. Rowlings, please.

T4 *Mr. R.*: Yes, this is he. Who's calling?

T5 *P.O.*: Good evening Mr. Rowlings. This is a police officer from the Maryland Troopers. We need some help for our people and families, and we are inviting you to collaborate with our Corps. Would you like to make your pledge?

T6 *Mr. R.*: Well… How much would that be?

T7 *P.O.*: Well, there's a minimum pledge of $36, but we would greatly appreciate it if you could contribute to our goals with a higher amount.

T8 *Mr.R.*: Oh, no, I think $36 is more than enough. I can't commit to giving you more.

T9 *P.O.*: O.K., thank you very much, Mr. Rowlings. We'll be expecting your check with your pledge of $36, no later than the end of this month.

T10 *Mr. R.*: O.K., You're welcome. Good bye.

T11 *P.O.*: Good bye now.

B) *ANALYSIS:* ANALYZE the following transcript of a fragment from the *Hannity & Colmes* show (*Fox News*, August 4th, 2004) with the CA perspective in mind.

T1

1   **HANNITY**: All right. Let's start with one. First of all, you
2   start with, in your book, page 193, you talk about "communism
3   is the control of business by government, fascism is the control
4   of government by business". My American Heritage dictionary
5   defines fascism as a system of government that exercises
6   dictatorship of the extreme right, typically through the merging
7   of the state and business leadership together with belligerent
8   nationalism. Sound familiar?
   (pause)
9   Are you accusing this president of being, and this administration
10 of being, fascist-like, Nazi-like?

T2

11 **ROBERT F. KENNEDY JR.**: The point is that if you read
12 that in context, is that Americans have to understand that
13 there's a huge difference between free market capitalism, which
14 is great for a democracy, which democratizes our country, that
15 brings efficiencies, and the corporate crony capitalism that has
16 been embraced by this administration, which is as antithetical

17 to democracy in America as it is in Nigeria. Today, you have
18 polluters running the agencies that are supposed to protect
19 Americans from pollution. The second in command at EPA is
20 a Monsanto lobbyist. The head of the air division at the EPA is
21 a utility lobbyist…

T3

22 **HANNITY**: I…

T4

23 **KENNEDY**: Let me finish.

T5

24 **HANNITY**: Go ahead. Go ahead.

T6

25 **KENNEDY**: …who for his lifetime has been defending the
26 worst polluters in America. The head of the public lands now,
27 Sean, is a mining industry lobbyist. The head of forest service
28 a timber industry lobbyist and on and on and on.

T7

29 **HANNITY**: I understand your point.

T8

30 **KENNEDY**: These people did not enter government for public
31 service. They entered to undermine and subvert the very laws
32 that they 're charged with enforcing.

T9

33 **HANNITY**: This is fundamental. Because I say the left today,
34 your leadership, including your uncle Ted Kennedy, has said
35 irresponsible things about our president and about our country.
36 And I find it here.

(pause)
37 Now I'm going to read a very long paragraph for the sake of
38 our audience because I don't want to take it out of context and I
39 want to make sure I get the full context in here. OK? This is
40 from your book.

T10

41 **KENNEDY**: Sure.

T11

42 **HANNITY**: You said, "these elected governments use the
43 provocation of terrorist attacks, continued wars"- You're talking
44 about Nazism and Fascism on page 193, OK?

T12

45 **KENNEDY:** No, no, no. Now you're…

T13

46 **HANNITY**: Wait a minute. Right here I have it in the book,
47 193 and 194, and you talk about Spain, Germany and Italy
48 reacting to the economic crises.

T14

49 **KENNEDY**: Sure.

The following questions and suggestions will guide you through the analysis:

a) LOOK FOR the turn-transition-places or turn-relevance-places (TRPs) relying on the linguistic cues that make them identifiable. They may be indicated by some of the following linguistic qualities or devices:

    i) *syntactic* (sentence, clause, or phrase completion)

    ii) *intonational* (final rise or fall), "trailing off", elongation and/or pause.

    iii) *semantic* (complete proposition –a verb and its argument(s)?)

    iv) *pragmatic* (complete speech act or larger "speaking" unit)

b) FIND, if possible, examples where all four of these linguistic cues converge, as well as examples where, even though these cues are partially or completely absent, a next speaker begins anyway.

c) IDENTIFY the *adjacency pairs* in the fragment and LOOK FOR any possible *insertion sequences*.

d) Do you find any instances of *repair*? If so, what type?

C) COLLECTING DATA: TAPE-RECORDING A CONVERSATION FOR ANALYSIS:

a) TAPE-RECORD a conversational exchange in a face-to-face interaction.

b) IDENTIFY the overall organization of the conversation (opening, closing, etc.) as well as the preferred organization of its adjacency pairs, indicating when the second parts are marked or unmarked.

c) DISCUSS and JUSTIFY your analysis with your teacher/tutor, your classmates, or anyone interested in the topic.

FURTHER READING

- Hutchby & Woofit (2008)
- Levinson (1983), Chapter 6
- Sacks, Schegloff & Jefferson (1974)
- Schlegloff (2007)
- Schiffrin (1984), Chapter 7
- Woofit, in Whetherell, Taylor & Yates (eds.) (2001), Chapter 2

USEFUL WEBSITES

Information on Ethnomethodology and CA: www.pscw.uva.nl/emca

Wikipedia entry for CA:
http://en.wikipedia.org/wiki/Conversation_analysis

Introductory tutorial to CA:
http://www-staff.lboro.ac.uk/~ssca1/sitemenu.htm

International Institute for Ethnomethodology and Conversation Analysis:
http://www.iiemca.org/

THE ETHNOGRAPHY OF COMMUNICATION

6

Socially situated cultural form: A display of Native-American
tradition in Arizona, U.S.A.

*"There are rules of use without which the
rules of grammar would be useless. Just as
rules of syntax can control aspects of
phonology, and just as semantic rules perhaps
control aspects of syntax, so rules of speech
acts enter as a controlling factor for linguistic
form as a whole."*

Dell Hymes, *On Communicative Competence.*

Chapter Outline:

- Main ideas and concepts of the ethnographic approach to DA.

- Hymes's concept of *Communicative Competence.*

- Sample analysis of a *speech event* using the SPEAKING grid.

6.1. An anthropological approach to DA

The ethnographic approach to DA is based on Anthropology and Linguistics. Even though these two disciplines have different goals and methods, they share a common interest in *communication*. The way human beings communicate is part of the cultural repertoire for making sense of – and interacting with– the world. Culture is perceived as a system of ideas that underlies and gives meaning to behavior in society (Schiffrin, 1994: 138).

The Ethnography of Communication (hereinafter EOC) can be thought of as the application of ethnographic methods to the communication patterns of a group (Cameron, 2001). Saville-Troike (2003) notes that EOC has two foci: a) the *particularistic* focus, and b) the *generalizing* focus. *Particularistic*, because it attempts to describe and understand communicative behavior in specific cultural settings; *generalizing*, because it is also within its scope to formulate concepts and theories which are to be taken as the basis for a global metatheory of human communication.

Duranti (1997) explains that EOC is mainly a method which offers a set of valuable techniques that allow researchers to connect linguistic forms with cultural practices. The starting points for all analyses are *involved participation* and *distanced observation*. **Dell Hymes** is the key figure in the development of ethnographic studies. The main tenets of his approach are found in a series of papers written in the 1960s and 1970s, many of which are collected in his 1974 *Foundations in Sociolinguistics: An Ethnographic Approach*. However, the origins of this perspective to

DA can be traced back to Sapir (1933) and the Prague School of Linguistics, which emphasized the penetration of language structure by function.

Hymes characterizes EOC as an interactive-adaptive method of enquiry:

> It [Ethnography] is a mode of enquiry that carries with it a substantial content. Whatever one's focus of inquiry, as a matter of course, one takes into account the local form of general properties of social life – patterns of role and status, rights and duties, differential command of resources, transmitted values, environmental constraints. It locates the local situation in space, time and kind, and discovers its particular forms and center of gravity, as it were, for the maintenance of social order and the satisfaction of expressive impulse. (1980: 100)

Environmental constraints: time, location, resources, etc.

Ethnography, thus, encourages a participant-oriented rather than a narrowly text-oriented approach to meaning. This fact contrasts with many European traditions in DA in that the latter show a tendency to isolate texts as 'objects' for analysis. On the contrary, the ethnographic approach values the treatment of context -which is in itself an epistemological problem- emphasizing the idea that it is impossible to separate speech data from the history under which they were obtained.

6.2. The concept of Communicative Competence

Hymes (1970) argues that, since the speakers of a language form part of a given community or culture, in order to function in that language, they possess an ability that goes further than grammatical competence. He notes that up to that time linguists (such as Chomsky 1957, 1965) had ignored the study of the communicative patterns and systems of language use. Hymes insists that scholars focus on *communicative competence*, which not only involves the knowledge of abstract linguistic rules, but also the ability to use language in concrete situations of everyday life, such as the ability to *check in at a hotel, argue, pray*, or even *use silence* appropriately. His definition of the term takes into account four elements:

- whether and to what degree something is grammatical,
- whether and to what degree something is socially appropriate,
- whether and to what degree something is feasible (psycholinguistic limitations),
- whether and to what degree something is done (actual language use).

Thus, his main concern was not the structure of isolated sentences, but the **rules of speaking** within a community.

Hymes' concept of *communicative competence* has had a far-reaching influence in the world of Linguistics, Applied Linguistics and most discourse analytic traditions (especially in Interactional Sociolinguistics[1]), to such an extent that no present-day scholar would deny its relevance, as it constitutes one of the single most important concepts in discourse research and linguistics in general.

6.3. Main concepts and notions in ethnographic research

Hymes presents a descriptive orientation for the accumulation of data on the nature of ways of speaking within speech communities. He lists the fundamental notions and concepts within an adequate descriptive theory for sociolinguistic enquiry, which are essentially the following:

- ***Speech community***: a primary concept defined as "a community

---

[1] See Chapter 4.

sharing rules for the conduct and interpretation of speech, and rules for the interpretation of at least one linguistic variety" (Hymes, 1972: 54). A *speech community* alludes, then, to a group of people who share the same rules for using and interpreting at least one communication practice. A communication practice might involve specific events, acts, or situations. Notice however, that the term *speech* here refers to various means of communication, verbal and nonverbal, written and oral, and that the term *community* typically involves a great diversity of communication practices.

A family reunion

- ***Speech situation***: An activity which is bounded or integral in some recognizable way. It may have verbal or non-verbal components and it may enter as context into statements of rules of speaking, albeit not in itself governed by such rules. It refers to the social occasion in which speech may occur, e.g. *a family reunion*.
- ***Speech event***: This concept is restricted to activities which are directly governed by rules or norms for the use of speech, e.g. *a conversation during the family reunion*.
- ***Speech act***: This is the smallest unit and the most fundamental level for the management of discourse. E.g. *Telling a joke within*

the conversation at the family reunion.

- **Ways of speaking**: This is the most general term, based on the premise that a community's communicative conduct entails determinate patterns of speech activity. The communicative competence of people presupposes knowledge regarding such patterns. These patterned *ways of speaking* – e.g., about the weather, about politics, or the ways of speaking in education or medical encounters – identify the community a given group of people belong to. Thus, ethnographers of communication explore various ways of communicating, i.e. the situated variety according to the events, acts, and situations of communicative life.

- **Fluent speaker**: A relative term, underlying the notion that different communities can hold distinct ideals of speaking for different statuses, roles and situations. It draws attention to differences in ability. Therefore, the expectations for a speaker to be considered fluent in one community may be different from the expectations in another community.

- **Rules of speaking**: These rules focus on the observation that shifts in any of the components of speaking (See 6.4. below) may mark the presence of a rule and should be taken into consideration. For instance, a shift from Standard English to slang, or from normal tone to whisper, may mark important strategies or norms of use of a given sociolinguistic system.

- **Functions of speech**: These are determined by the relationships among components such as choices of code, topic or message form. EOC falls within the functionalist paradigm of research, which is concerned with the stylistic and social functions of language. Not all functions apply equally to all languages and all speech communities. Diversity is assumed and the differences between communities are explored.

6.4. The SPEAKING grid

Once ethnographers of communication identify a specific event, act, situation, or community for study, their next step is to analyze the selected practice as a multi–faceted phenomenon. This entails the systematic analysis of the practice as it occurs in its normal social contexts, and as it is discussed by participants. Hymes (1972) proposed a classificatory grid as a descriptive framework for EOC, which is known as the SPEAKING grid, a mnemonic device where each letter is the starting letter for one of the different components of communication. As Hymes explains, each component invites us to ask certain questions about the communication practice of concern:

SITUATION → **What are the *setting* (i.e. the physical location where the practice takes place) and *scene* (i.e. the participants' sense of what is going on when this practice is active) of the communication practice?** The focus here is on the physical and temporal circumstances defining the speech event. The consideration of both the setting and scenic qualities of the practice helps ground the analysis in the specific contexts of social life.

PARTICIPANTS → **Who are the *participants* in this practice?** Communication is seen as an event in which people participate, and thus the key concept is *participant* (in the event). This moves away from typical encoding and decoding models, or others which focus only on senders and receivers of messages.

ENDS → **What are the *ends* of this practice?** This component asks about two ends: the goals and purposes participants may have in doing the practice, and the outcomes actually achieved. Communication practice may target some goals, yet attain different outcomes (e.g. when a man asks a girl out with the intention of spending an unforgettable evening with her, but she rejects the invitation).

ACT SEQUENCE → **What *act sequence* is involved in and for this practice?** This component involves an analysis of the sequential organization of speech acts of the practice, its message content and form.

KEY → **How is the practice being *keyed*? What is the emotional pitch, feeling, or spirit of the communication practice?** This component refers to the tone or manner of speaking. Some events are keyed as reverent and serious (e.g. religious ceremonies or funerals). Other events may be keyed, for instance, as ironic, humorous or light–hearted.

INSTRUMENTALITIES → **What is the *instrument* or channel being used in this communication practice?** The channel could be oral, written or just gestures or bodily movements. **Is a technological channel preferred, or prohibited?** (Some practices may be normally conducted via a synchronous, face-to-face channel (e.g. a doctor/patient encounter), and some others, for instance, via an asynchronous written channel (e.g. e-mails). The language or variety (e.g. American English) being used should be taken into account within this component as well.

NORMS OF INTERACTION AND INTERPRETATION → **What *norms* are active when communication is practiced in this way and in this community?** This component refers to both the norms attached to speaking and interaction (e.g. organization of turn-taking), and the norms within the cultural belief system, which may be of two kinds: 1) the norm as a matter of habit (e.g. Few people go to church) and 2) the appropriate thing to do (e.g. One should go to church). Thus, standards of normalcy are distinguished from the morally infused dimension of communicative practices.

GENRE → **Is there a *genre* of communication of which this practice is an instance?** This involves identifying the textual category involved in the practice, as well as its level of formality. For instance, the genre in a given practice could be that of *informal oral narrative*. The properties of the genre become relevant to its analysis, for the practice might be understood as part and parcel of, for example, a folk genre, and be analyzed accordingly.

This grid is a tool researchers have at their disposal for discovering the culturally relative taxonomies of the three communicative units described in 6.3. above (*speech situation, speech event* and *speech act*). The larger units in the set embed the smaller, e.g., a speech act, such as *insulting*, may be included in the speech event of *a debate*, which is in turn embedded in the speech situation of *a television program*.

6.5. Method of analysis

As noted in 6.1., doing ethnographical research involves mainly field work (observing, participating in group activities, asking questions, checking the validity of the researcher's perceptions by learning about native-speaker intuitions, etc.). Researchers have to rid themselves of their cultural prejudices and be open to new modes of thought and behavior. However, Ethnography is not restricted to the study of "other" cultures. The researcher's own community may be studied as well, but s/he has to be conscious of the fact that such a study may present problems regarding objectivity. A positive outcome of the study of one's own community and of its assessment with respect to other communicative practices is the inevitable revelation that what is assumed to be 'normal' or 'natural' in one's own community may be regarded as totally foreign or abnormal in another. This idea leads to a deeper understanding of *cultural relativism*, which constitutes an essential feature of all ethnographic studies.

6.6. Further remarks on EOC

The ethnographic approach to DA has shed light on the fact that the uses of language and speech in different societies have patterns of their own which are worthy of description and which are comparable and related to other patterns in social organization and other cultural domains. As anticipated in 6.1., the particularistic focus of this approach is directed at the description and understanding of communicative behavior in specific cultural settings, whereas the generalizing focus is directed toward the formulation of concepts and theories upon which to build a global metatheory of human communication (Saville-Troike, 2003). Thus, cross-cultural studies are very common within this approach, and the result of these studies may lead researchers to interesting and valuable conclusions about the universals of language.

Socially situated cultural form: gathering at Piccadilly Circus

All that has been said in this chapter can lead us to the central research question of EOC, which could be worded as follows: *What knowledge does a speaker need to have in order to communicate appropriately in a particular speech community and what skills does s/he need to acquire in order to make use of this knowledge?* This question takes for granted that language form cannot be separated from how and why it is used. Understanding the patterns of use is essential for the recognition and understanding of linguistic form. In this respect, it seems timely to quote Saville-Troike:

While recognizing the necessity to analyze the code itself and the cognitive processes of its speakers and hearers, the ethnography of communication takes language first and foremost as a socially situated cultural form, which is indeed constitutive of much of culture itself. To accept a lesser scope for linguistic description is to risk reducing it to triviality, and to deny any possibility of understanding how language lives in the minds and on the tongues of its users. (2003: 3).

Recent studies on EOC have looked into matters such as intercultural communication around the globe (e.g. Carbaugh 2005), the problem of intertextuality (e.g. Bauman 2004), mass media texts in various societies (e.g. Katriel 2004), interpersonal communication in many cultural settings (e.g. Fitch 1998), communication in various contexts such as work or education (e.g. Covarrubias 2005), processes of power, and so on.

Finally, some remarks about the significance of this approach, which goes beyond a simple taxonomy of communicative facts and behaviors. EOC has been significant for different fields of research. For Anthropology, it has helped understand the relationship between language, social organization, values, beliefs and other aspects of the socialization process. For psycholinguistics, ethnographic research has contributed to studies of language acquisition, in understanding that we must not only recognize the innate capacity of children for language, but also must account for the particular ways of speaking of particular societies and how these are developed in the process of social interaction. As was suggested above, EOC can even contribute to the study of both form and use universals, as well as to the formulation of an adequate theory of language and linguistic competence.

6.7. Sample analysis of data

The following conversation is an example of a service encounter conversation between a bookshop assistant and a customer. The **speech situation** can be classified thus, as a *service encounter*. The **speech event** could be defined as a *shopping/bargaining for books* exchange or conversation.

1 M: Good morning. Can I help you?
2 W: Oh, good morning. Yes, I hope so… I'm looking for a copy of
3 Somerset Maugham's *The Razor's Edge.*
4 M: Well, I think I may be able to help. Bear with me for a minute or
5 two, will you…yes… let me see… blast! Confounded machine… Now
6 what's it doing?
7 W: Computers! You know what they say… to err is human… but to
8 really foul things up you need a computer.
9 M: Oh very good… yes… I must remember that one… now oh… here

10 she comes... yes...oh... no that's sold...well it looks like I've got...

11 oh yes... what luck... a signed first edition. Signed first edition!

12 W: Oh, well... er...how much would that be...?

13 M: Urm... let me... let me... that's £110.

14 W: Oh... I see... well really I didn't want anything quite... so... first

15   edition did you say?

16 M: Yes, and signed by the author.

17 W: Oh, by Somerset Maugham himself?

18 M: That's right.

19 W: Well of course that's splendid but £110 did you say?

20 M: That's right... I could I could er... make that a £105 I suppose...

21 W: Well that's very good of you but really... you see I just wanted the

22 book to read not as a collector's item if you see what I mean...

23 M: Well, I imagine it is still in print perhaps your local, er, bookstore

24 might oblige with a, ahem, paperback edition. Perhaps with, er,

25 footnotes and a learned introduction by a Cambridge don.

26 W: Yes, still, I mean it would be nice... it's a present you see for my

27 nephew...

28 M: Well really madam what could make a more wonderful gift for the

29 young man! A first edition signed by the great man himself. Food for

30 the mind AND a splendid investment.

31 W: An investment you say?

32 M: Oh undoubtedly madam. Undoubtedly. Such a volume can only

33 increase in value.

34 W: Ooh well if you put it like that. But all the same I mean £105 -it's

35 a lot of money, I mean, it's more money than I had planned to pay you

36 see.

37 M: Madam, had I known that the work was intended as a birthday gift

38 for a young man... ... I could certainly make it a round £100.

39 W: 70.

40 M: I beg your pardon?

41 W: 70. I'll give you £70.

42 M: £70? No really madam... I'm afraid I simply couldn't part with it

43 for less than... for less than shall we say £90?

44 W: 80.

45 M: 85 cash.

46 W: Done. £85. Here we are... 60...80... and a fiver makes £85.

47 M: Thank you madam and many happy returns to the young gentleman.

(Aragonés, Medrano & Alba-Juez (2002 [2007]), *Lengua Inglesa I*; dialogue
Chapter 18, by Jim Lawley)

In order to identify this event as a certain kind of discourse occurrence and to discover the communicative features and qualities that underlie our knowledge about service encounters, we are going to use Hymes' SPEAKING grid. It is important to take into account the fact that bargaining is a key part of many service encounters, and therefore it will be useful to pay attention to the structure of the speech events in which this communicative practice is used.

	Shopping/bargaining for a book
SETTING	Bookshop in an English town, sometime during shopping hours in the early 2000s
PARTICIPANTS	**M**: Bookshop assistant/owner **W**: customer (a middle-aged woman)
ENDS	Buying/selling. W wants to buy a not very expensive book as a present/ M wants to sell at best possible price. Outcome: the book is sold at best possible price.
ACT SEQUENCE	**M**: greeting/offer **W**: greeting/response to offer/ request **M**: positive response to request/ complaint (about computer) **W**: Comment (about computer) **M**: provides information (about book) **W**: request for information (about price) **M**: provides information **W**: requests clarification **M**: provides clarification **W**: requests clarification **M**: provides clarification **W**: requests clarification **M**: provides clarification/offers lower price **W**: rejects offer

	M: accepts rejection/suggestion **W**: provides further information (about present) **M:** provides further information (about book) **W**: requests clarification **M:** provides clarification **W**: bargains (still rejecting last offer) **M**: offers (a lower price) **W**: bargains/ requests (an even lower price) **M**: bargains/ offers (lower price than last offer but higher than previous request) **W**: bargains/ requests (lower than last offer but higher than previous request) **M**: bargains/ offers (higher than previous request but lower than last offer) **W**: accepts final offer/ makes payment **M**: greeting.
KEY	Serious but not solemn/ ironic (on the part of the assistant) when bargaining
INSTRUMENTALITIES	Oral, face-to-face, colloquial British English
NORMS	Interaction based on needs for buying and selling. Norms for bargaining: Bookseller should sell at highest possible price, and customer should buy at cheapest possible price.
GENRE	Service encounter/ buying-selling transaction discourse. Narrow range (the talk is mainly directed at the main and specific goal of buying and selling).

As can be noted in the table, the range of ACTS, the KEY, and the GENRE are all relatively narrow, because both participants direct their conversation toward the specific goal (END) of buying and selling, which is mutually known by M and W. This is one example of the way in which the different components of communication are related.

Regarding the sequence of acts, it can be noticed that, apart from the normal *greetings* at the opening and closing of the exchange, we find sequences of acts requesting and giving information mainly at the initial stages of the encounter. These sequences lead on to the core sequence of *requests* and *offers*, which form part of the real negotiation and bargaining for the assistant to sell the book and for the customer to buy it. The acts at this stage of the exchange may be interpreted and used in different ways, according to the participants. In this analysis, the customer's proposal to pay less has been interpreted as a *request* (she requests a lowering of the price) and the assistant's lowering of the price has been interpreted as an *offer* (he offers the book at a lower price). However, the customer's proposals could also be interpreted as *offers*, depending on the viewpoint taken (she offers to pay less than requested), which the assistant may accept or reject. An interesting thing that the analysis of act sequences in this service encounter sheds light on, thus, is the essence of bargaining: somehow the participants are striving for power, and hence make their *requests* sound like *offers* in a more or less lengthy negotiation until they come to an agreement. In this particular case, we find a sequence of six acts of request/offer within the broader act of bargaining before making the final deal. This lengthy sequence can be said to be related to the NORMS of this type of encounter. A bargain would not be a bargain if there were no such sequence of acts during the service encounter. The KEY is also connected with the sequence of ACTS, the GENRE and the SETTING: the participants expect this type of exchange to be serious to a certain extent,, but a bit of irony and/or deviation from the truth is expected in the bargaining (the customer knows the first price given is higher than the actual price and the assistant knows that the first price requested by the customer is lower than what she will eventually agree to pay). The INSTRUMENTALITIES always have a relationship with the other elements: the goals (ENDS) and SETTING, as well as the other elements of communication, determine whether it is a verbal or a written exchange, and the type of English (in this case) to be used.

Thus, the analysis of all the components of the SPEAKING grid will help the researcher understand the essence and nature of the communicative practice/s being analyzed, which could in turn be compared to similar practices in a different culture. In such a case, the comparison of these practices across cultures would contribute to the acceptance or rejection of hypothetical global generalizations about certain human discursive behaviors, and the conclusions reached by means of the comparison would eventually lead the researcher to consider whether these practices have a universal character or not.

SUMMING UP... (CHAPTER 6)

1. The ethnographic approach to DA is based on Anthropology and Linguistics.
2. The starting points for all ethnographic analyses are *involved participation* and *distanced observation*.
3. **Dell Hymes** is the key figure in the development of ethnographic studies.
4. Hymes insists that scholars focus on *communicative competence*, which not only involves the knowledge of abstract linguistic rules, but also the ability to use language in concrete situations of everyday life.
5. Fundamental concepts within EOC are the concepts of *Speech Community, Speech Situation, Speech Event* and *Speech Act*.
6. Hymes (1972) proposed a classificatory grid as a descriptive framework for the Ethnography of Communication, which is known as the **SPEAKING** grid, where each letter is the first letter of one of the different components of communication (Situation, Participants, Ends, Act sequence, Key, Instrumentalities, Norms of interaction and interpretation, and Genre).
7. An essential feature of all ethnographic studies is the profound conviction and belief in *cultural relativism*.
8. The central research question of EOC could be worded as follows: *What knowledge does a speaker need to have in order to communicate appropriately in a particular speech community and what skills does he need to acquire in order to make use of this knowledge?*
9. The findings of the EOC have been significant for different fields of research, such as Anthropology, Psycholinguistics, Applied Linguistics or Theoretical Linguistics.

SELF EVALUATION QUESTIONS

Choose the answer that best suits the information given in Chapter 6.

1) The ethnographic approach to Discourse Analysis is based on...
a) Psychology and Linguistics.
b) Linguistics and Sociology.
c) Linguistics and Anthropology.

2) Ethnography...
a) is a method that helps see the connection between linguistic forms and cultural practices.
b) is a cultural technique to understand language.
c) has nothing to do with Sociolinguistics.

3) The focus of Ethnography is mainly oriented towards...
a) texts.
b) participants.
c) places.

4) *Involved participation* and *distanced observation*...
a) are basic in all ethnographic analyses.
b) are not considered appropriate in ethnographic analysis.
c) can not be carried out from the ethnographic perspective.

5) What type of knowledge does *Communicative Competence* entail?
a) grammatical and syntactic rules.
b) linguistic rules and rules of appropriateness (to situations of everyday life).
c) phonological and semantic rules.

6) Hymes' main concern was...
a) the structure of isolated sentences.
b) the structure of conversation.
c) the rules of speaking within a community.

7) The telling of a joke within a conversation at a family reunion constitutes…
a) a speech event.
b) a speech act.
c) a speech situation.

8) The speakers of *Estuary English* constitute…
a) a speech event.
b) a speech community.
c) a speech act.

9) Which of these concepts is an essential feature of ethnographic studies?
a) mediated action.
b) cultural relativism.
c) grammatical competence.

10) The Ethnography of Communication takes language as…
a) a set of grammatical and syntactic rules.
b) a psycholinguistic phenomenon.
c) a socially situated cultural form.

11) The SPEAKING grid…
a) constitutes a descriptive framework for ethnographic analysis.
b) is useful for syntactic analysis.
c) is a grid for classifying speech acts.

12) In the speaking grid, **G** stands for…
a) Grammar.
b) Gender.
c) Genre.

13) In the speaking grid, **A** stands for…
a) Analysis.
b) Act sequence.
c) Approach.

14) In the speaking grid, **P** stands for…
a)   Participants.
b)   Power.
c)   Pattern.

15)   The findings of the Ethnography of communication…
a)   have only been used in Linguistics.
b)   have been significant for different fields of research.
c)   are not considered to be relevant nowadays.

PRACTICE

A) *ANALYSIS:* ANALYZE the following television interview from the EOC perspective.

1 **W**: Hello, good evening and welcome to tonight's edition of *Lifestyle*. On
2 tonight's program we have Edwin Lewis, the poet and novelist… Mr
3 Lewis…
4 **E**: Edwin… please call me Edwin.
5 **W**: Edwin.. here we are on the Island of Mull. A beautiful, lonely island off
6 the North West coast of Scotland. We're looking out across the bay… the
7 mountains behind us… the sea gulls cawing and wheeling in the sky… the
8 waves rolling in and breaking on the beach below. Why? Why have you
9 come to such a remote spot to live?
10 **E**: Well… I feel… I feel that… that when you set out on adulthood…
11 when you leave home and finish full-time education whether it's school or
12 university… that's when you first accept responsibility for the whole of the
13 rest of your life… and that's when you have to ask yourself some pretty
14 basic questions.
15 **W**: What sort of questions?
16 **E**: Well 'what', 'who' and 'where' questions for example… questions like:
17 what do I want to do; who do I want to be with; and where do I want to be?
18 **W**: You mean what work do you want to do, who do you want to share
19 your life with, and where do you want to live?
20 **E**: That's right. I'd say those were sort of the three basic questions… And
21 of course you've got to put them in some sort of order…give them some
22 sort of, you know, priority…
23 **W** Yes?
24 **E**: Yes… I mean, decide which is the most important… if I'd been madly

25 in love perhaps I'd... perhaps I'd have given priority to the 'who'
26 question... and that would have overridden everything else...
27 **W**: But that wasn't the case.
28 **E**: No, that wasn't the case... and quite suddenly one day... I was on the
29 tube... waiting for a train at Piccadilly Circus... I just knew... it came to
30 me in a flash... with utter certainty I knew that for me the most important
31 thing was *where*... that I had to be in the right place...
32 **W**: Here?
33 **E**: That's right. Here. I feel right here... this is the place for me... It's
34 here that I can think my thoughts all the way to the end –bigger thoughts
35 than I ever had in London. I look out at the Atlantic... the waves... have
36 you ever read Unamuno's book "Cómo se hace una novela"?
37 **W**: No, I'm afraid...
38 **E**: Well, there's a book... read that... read about the waves... "paciencia y
39 barajar"...
40 **W**: And... you've stayed here ever since?
41 **E**: Basically, yes... I do travel... I travel a lot but this is home... my place.
42 **W**: and when you travel?
43 **E**: Yes, I like to go to Spain. Do you know the gardens of the Alcazar in
44 Seville? That's another place... another special place for me... whenever
45 I'm there I always feel I'm in the right place...

(Aragonés, Medrano & Alba-Juez (2002 [2007]), *Lengua Inglesa I*; dialogue Chapter 8, by Jim Lawley)

a) SPECIFY and ANALYZE the different communicative components of the interview (SPEAKING grid).
b) FIND the relations between the different components (*ends, participants, acts*). In what ways are the components influenced by one another?
c) EXAMINE the *act sequence* of the interview. Do you find any pattern that could characterize this type of interview?

B) *ANALYSIS*: ANALYZE the different components of communication in the following fragment of a computer-mediated exchange (taken from a chat-room on the Internet) from the EOC perspective, by using Hyme's **SPEAKING** grid.

1 Kimberly-Todd presents the speaker with question #241 from SalemTheCat:
2 What motivated you to start a career in acting?
3 MelissaJH says, "i was 4 and wanted to be on romper room"

4 MelissaJH says, "my mom got me into commercials"
5 MelissaJH says, "and it took off from there"
6 Kimberly-Todd presents the speaker with question #263 from lindauer: How old
7 are u?
8 MelissaJH says, "i turned 23 in april"
9 Kimberly-Todd presents the speaker with question #252 from MDi:
10 What kind of music do you listen to?
11 MelissaJH says, "i like all kinds, some of my favorites are nine inch nails, tribe
12 called quest, smashing pumpkins"
13 Kimberly-Todd presents the speaker with question #242 from SalemTheCat:
14 How many different shows have you starred in?
15 MelissaJH says, "well i have a big body of work, but i have starred in 2 regular
16 tv series, clarissa and sabrina"
17 Kimberly-Todd presents the speaker with question #279 from A. Lopez: Have
18 you seen any of the new movies out now?
19 MelissaJH says, "i returned from australia on Wednesday after shooting sabrina
20 down under for ABC, and have not had a chance to catch up with movies
21 yet"
22 MelissaJfl says, "but i want to see star wars and election"
23 Kimberly-Todd presents the speaker with question #294 from Mster Magoo:
24 What's your fav. NIN album?
25 MelissaJH says, "pretty hate machine of course"
26 Kimberly-Todd presents the speaker with question #297 -from Mmy: How do
27 you feel about bike safety?
28 MelissaJH says, "i feel bike helmets and safety are important simply because
29 head injuries related to bike accidents are an easy thing to avoid".

FURTHER READING

- Bauman (2004).
- Carbaugh (2005).
- Covarrubias (2005).
- Hymes 1962, 1964 a & b, 1970.
- Katriel (2004).
- Saville-Troike (2003).
- Schiffrin (1994), Chapter 4.

USEFUL WEBSITES

Wikipedia entry for EOC:
http://en.wikipedia.org/wiki/Ethnography_of_communication

Wikipedia entry for Dell Hymes:
http://en.wikipedia.org/wiki/Dell_Hymes

Dell Hymes website: http://www.virginia.edu/anthropology/dhymes.html

Bibliography on Anthropology:
http://print.google.com/print?id=io94HFih5FQC&pg=23&lpg=23&prev=h
ttp://print.google.com/print%3Fq%3Dthe%2Bethnography%2Bof%2Bco
mmunication%26ie%3DUTF-
8%26lr%3D%26sa%3DN%26start%3D50&sig=Ma182tNdZmewuDpeJO
q97JOVxM0

VARIATION ANALYSIS
AND
NARRATIVE ANALYSIS

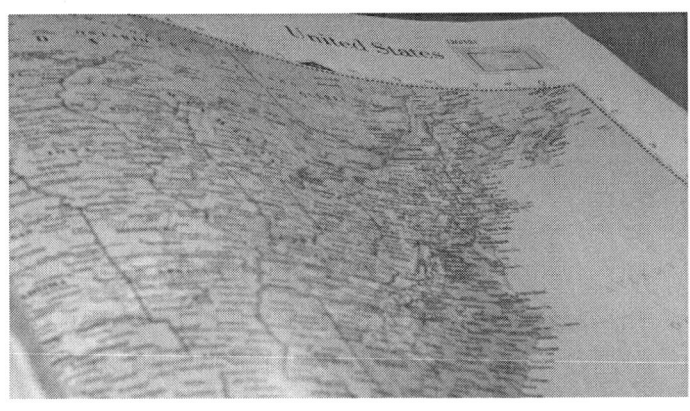

"In 1987, I had another opportunity to test the usefulness of linguistics on a matter that was vital to a single person. A number of bomb threats were made in repeated telephone calls to the Pan American counter at the Los Angeles airport. Paul Prinzivalli, a cargo handler who was thought by Pan American to be a "disgruntled employee," was accused of the crime, and he was jailed. The evidence was that his voice sounded like the tape recordings of the bomb threat caller. The defense sent me the tapes because Prinzivalli was a New Yorker, and they thought I might be able to distinguish two different kinds of New York City accents. The moment I heard the recordings I was sure that he was innocent; the man who made the bomb threats plainly did not come from New York at all, but from the Boston area of Eastern New England. [...] It was almost as if my entire career had been shaped to make the most effective testimony on this one case. The next day, the judge asked the prosecuting attorney if he really wanted to continue. He refused to hear further statements from the defense. He found the defendant not guilty on the basis of the linguistic evidence, which he found 'objective' and 'powerful'."

William Labov, *How I got into linguistics, and what I got out of it.*

Chapter Outline:

- The phenomenon of linguistic change.

- Techniques of data collection and analysis within both the Variation Analysis and Narrative Analysis approaches to discourse.

- Main concepts and techniques of Narrative Analysis.

- The construction of individual and/or global identity through narrative.

7.1. Variation Analysis: The study of linguistic change

Although the origins of the variationist approach are solely within the field of Linguistics, this approach differs from traditional Linguistics in many ways. The basic assumption of variationists is that there are patterns of language which vary according to the social environment and therefore such patterns can only be identified by studying a given speech community. Variation Analysis, thus, is concerned with the variation and changes observed in language along different speech communities.

Originally, prototypical variation analyses were limited to the study of semantically equivalent variants, i.e., to the different words used to refer to the same thing according to geographical location or social level. However, such analyses have been extended to texts. The variationist approach has developed "in the search for text structure, the analysis of text-level variants and of how text constrains other forms" (Schiffrin, 1994: 282).

The most prominent figure within this approach is William Labov, who developed the initial methodology and theory. Data collection and field work play an important role in Variation Analysis. Labov (1996) argues in favor of the inadequacy of intuition as a source of information about language structure as well as of the importance of the vernacular language (Labov 1972a) of a speech community as the variety showing the most systematic grammar of a dialect. Thus, Labov holds a materialistic conception of language, which views language as "a property of the speech community, an instrument of social communication that evolves gradually and continuously throughout human history, in response to a variety of human needs and activities" (2004: 1). The materialist approach starts by observing the variability which is characteristic of speech production and then applies formalisms based on probability theory to this variation. Multivariate analyses are then applied to the data in order to find out how each element of the environment contributes to the application of a rule. An adequate description of language should contain a dynamic and evolutionary perspective, and that is the reason why much of the research within this perspective has to do with the study of linguistic change.

Labov demonstrated how language changes spread through society. He showed that linguistic changes are normally carried out by certain social groups, and that dialect variation is by no means free or haphazard. On the contrary, it is governed by "orderly heterogeneity" or structured variation (Weinreich, Labov and Herzog, 1968).

One of Labov's most important endeavors is the Telsur/Atlas project, which deals with the linguistic changes in progress in North-American English. It defines the major dialects of North-American English on the basis of some phonological characteristics, and contains regional maps where the phonological features of these dialects can be examined in detail. The interpretation of the data is based on the acoustic analysis of hundreds of linguistic interviews with speakers of the different North-American regions.

Variation Analysis combines both qualitative and quantitative techniques. Quantitative analyses are basic within this approach, and they require the definition of the variants (or different realizations of a type), a classification of the conditions under which those variants may be found, and frequencies of occurrence of the different variants in relation to some factors of the environment.

In addition, certain assumptions have to be made as to the relationship between text and context which necessarily limit the interpretation of such analyses. Therefore, even when quantitative studies of variants are of crucial importance, they also present some limitations, such as, for example, the lack of attention given to particular cases that might be of interest, because variationists generally focus on general trends or patterns. In general, researchers avoid making statements about typical patterns unless they are based on frequency of occurrence and evaluated by statistical tests.

An important notion in Variation Analysis is that of **constraint**. Thus, it is assumed that the overall information structure of a text imposes certain constraints on its parts, and so we see, for example, that the overall temporal structure of a narrative places constraints on its composing elements and even on the syntactic forms used to form those elements. Another instance can be found in recipes: recipes normally have to contain a list of ingredients, and therefore they always present constraints on the referring terms of the list, which necessarily have to be terms related to food. At the same time, their overall structure is normally constrained to the use of both descriptive structure (lists) and narrative structure (the steps followed for making the dish, which are generally presented in temporal order).

According to Patrick, a typical sequence of analysis for variationists would be the following:

1) Establish which forms alternate with one another –i.e., which are "the same".
2) Delimit the environments in which this alternation-with-sameness occurs, and classify the factors within those environments exhaustively.
3) Propose hypotheses for contextual factors which might constrain the variation.
4) Compile a data set that allows for investigation and (dis-)confirmation of the alternations and co-occurrences predicted by hypotheses in (3).
5) Compare the frequencies/probabilities with which the different variants co-occur with the different (environmental) factors.
6) Typically, place primary emphasis on internal linguistic factors, and only secondary importance on external social explanations.
7) Typically, consider analysis primarily exploratory rather than confirmatory (due to lack of precisely predictive sociolinguistic theories) (2004:3).

As Labov explains, variationists focus upon different units of analysis:

It is common for a language to have many alternate ways of saying "the same" thing. Some words like *car* and *automobile* seem to have the same referents; others have two pronunciations, like *working* and *workin'*. There are syntactic options such as *Who is he talking to?* vs. *To whom is he talking?* Or *It's easy for him to talk* vs. *For him to talk is easy.* (1972b: 188)

Thus, variation or linguistic change can not only be studied at the level of semantically equivalent words, but also at other levels, such as the phonological, the syntactic or even the textual level, as Labov himself has demonstrated through his analysis of narrative.

Labov regards the study of narrative as "a privileged area of discourse, because this discourse type is the closest to the vernacular"[1], and that is the reason why he has devoted a great part of his research to the study of narrative syntax.

7.1.1. The vernacular

The linguistic analysis made by variationists is not based on linguists' intuitions of grammatically correct sentences, but mainly upon what people actually say. Therefore, it is of utmost importance for researchers to collect samples of authentic speech data. However, when people know that their language is being recorded or observed, they may alter their register and use different forms, structures or strategies than when not being observed. This fact made variationists seek the mode of speech called the **vernacular**. The vernacular is the variety acquired in pre-adolescent years that is used by speakers of a given language when they pay minimum attention to speech (Labov, 1984: 29). In order to collect samples of the vernacular, variationists resort to *sociolinguistic interviews*, which allow them to discover the regular rules of language and the social distribution of variants. As Schiffrin explains, respondents to these interviews are encouraged to tell narratives of personal experience:

> Sociolinguistic interviews are a mixed genre of talk […]. One way in which they differ from other interviews is that they encourage topic shifting and group interactions among people present. Another difference is that respondents are encouraged to tell narratives of personal experience. This is not only because narratives reveal community norms and styles of personal interaction, but also because speakers regularly shift toward the vernacular when telling a story (Labov 1984: 32). (Schiffrin, 1994: 289-90)

The work with narratives of personal experience within Variation Analysis is considered to be the basis for the analysis of narrative from a linguistic point of view. We now turn to this approach.

7.2. Narrative Analysis

The first steps in narrative analysis from a linguistic perspective were taken by William Labov and Joshua Waletzky as a by-product of the

---

[1] Excerpted from a talk given at Georgetown University, 1998.

sociolinguistic field methods that had been developed in the survey of the Lower East Side of New York (Labov 1966) and in the work that engaged them at the time -- the study of African-American Vernacular English in South Harlem (Labov, Cohen, Robins and Lewis 1968).

Labov's concern with "verbal deprivation" was the trigger for his interest in narrative. He argued against the generalized idea that black children were verbally deprived and consequently genetically inferior. He fought to eradicate the prejudices against Black English Vernacular (the dialect of English used by black people in America) in favor of "a more adequate notion of the relations between standard and non-standard dialects" (Labov, 1972a: 201-02). By studying the verbal behavior of black people in narratives of personal experience, Labov was able to demonstrate that, far from being verbally deprived, some black people used Black English Vernacular in a very talented and effective way. As explained in 7.1.1., Labov considered the vernacular to be the form of language "first acquired, perfectly learned, and used only among speakers of the same vernacular" (1997b). Thus, this is a type of language that speakers normally use when there are no other participants of a different variety, which led Labov to reflect upon the so-called **Observer's Paradox**, i.e. the effort made by researchers to observe how speakers talk when they are not being observed. The elicitation of narratives of personal experience within the face-to-face interview was found to present at least a partial solution to this paradox[2], and proved to be a very effective technique to gain considerable insight into the entrails of narrative and the vernacular language used in them.

Labov & Waletsky (1967) and Labov (1972a) provided a framework for the analysis of oral narrative which illustrates their approach to discourse units in a systematic way. These authors define a narrative as a particular unit in discourse which contains smaller units having particular syntactic and semantic properties. As Schiffrin notes, "narratives are a discourse unit with a fairly regular structure that is largely independent of how they are embedded in surrounding talk" (1994: 284). The different sections of a narrative present different kinds of information which fulfil different functions within the story. Labov defines narrative as "one method of recapitulating past experience by matching a verbal sequence of clauses to the sequence of events which (it is inferred) actually occurred" (1972b: 359-60). The skeleton of a narrative, then, consists of a series of

---

[2] This is due to the fact that, when asked to narrate personal experiences, speakers tend to use the vernacular, and consequently to handle more natural and "careless" forms of speech.

temporally ordered clauses which Labov calls *narrative clauses*.

Broadly speaking, narratives contain a beginning, a middle, and an end, but if we study them in detail, we shall find all or some of the following elements:

1. **Abstract** (one or two clauses summarizing the whole story).
2. **Orientation** (a clause or clauses giving information about the time, place, persons, their activity or the situation).
3. **Complicating action** (sequential clauses describing the different events).
4. **Evaluation** (the means used by the narrator to indicate the point of the narrative: why it was told, and what the narrator is aiming at, i.e. to give information on the consequences of the event for human needs and desires. Evaluative clauses are normally in an *irrealis* mood, because they make reference to events that did not occur, might have occurred, or would occur, by comparing the real events with events in an alternative reality that was not in fact realized. The evaluation section is typical of narratives of personal experience).
5. **Result or resolution** (the set of complicating actions that follow or coincide with the most reportable event).
6. **Coda** (a free clause at the end which signals that the narrative is finished; a final clause that returns the narrative to the time of speaking, precluding the potential question: "And what happened then?"). (Labov, 1972b, 1997b).

Not all narratives contain all six elements, their basic characteristic being their *temporal sequence*, which is an important defining property proceeding from its referential function. In Labov's view, not all recapitulation of experience is a narrative. In order for a recapitulation of experience to be a narrative it must recapitulate experience in the same order as the original events (Labov, 1997c: 13). All complicating action clauses (as well as the resolution clauses) are necessarily *sequential clauses*, while those of abstracts, orientations and codas are not. By **sequential clause** Labov means "a clause that can be an element of a temporal juncture", and "two clauses are separated by a **temporal juncture** if a reversal of their order results in a change in the listener's interpretation of the order of the events described" (1997b: 399).

According to Labov, the simplest possible narrative consists of the single line of the complication without a clear resolution (1997c: 37). Minimal narratives often have both complication and resolution (e.g. *Jane fell down and broke her arm*). In more complex narratives, the structure *O (Orientation) - C (Complicating action) - E (Evaluation) – R (Resolution) – C (Coda)* appears to be the most common, the most frequent variant being the case in which the evaluation ends the resolution (as in jokes, ghost stories or stories with surprise endings).

Examine the different components of narrative in the following example, taken from Labov (1997c: 10):

1 (Did you ever have a feeling, or a premonition, that
2 something was gonna happen, and it did?)
3 Yes, I did. (Tell me about it)
4 I was goin' with a girl, one time; we were
5 layin' on a bed –we weren't doing anything, we
6 were talkin' –and, I don't know, I looked into her
7 face, and I saw, like, horns coming out of her
8 head. You know. You know – like– I said,
9 "You look like the devil!"
10 She said, "What do you mean, I look like
11 the devil?"
12 Don't kid around." I said. "I'm not kiddin'.
13 I saw horns comin' out of your head."
14 And the girl got very angry and walked
15 out. But, we got together, and we went together
16 for about four months.
17 And, like, this girl tried to put me in a
18 couple of tricks. Like she tried to get some boys
19 to hurt me. You know. And she was a devil.
20 So, now, anything I see I believe it's going
21 to happen.

This narrative presents all the elements described above except for the abstract, which is in some way given by the interviewer's question (*Did you ever have a feeling...?*). The other five elements appear in the following order:

Lines 4-6: **Orientation**
Lines 6-16: **Complicating action** (notice the sequential clauses)
Lines 17-19: **Result or resolution**

Line 19 ("She was a devil"): **Evaluation**
Lines 20-21: **Coda**

An important contribution of this approach is the insight gained into the capacity of a narrative to transfer the experience of the narrator to the audience, which has also provided some explanation about the defining property of personal narrative that events are experienced as they first became known to the narrator (Labov, 1997b: 415).

The analysis of narrative shows, among other things, how variationists extend beliefs about language structure to the analysis of texts. Social context influences the construction of speech actions and rules and thus it becomes an important part of the study of discourse units: the display of linguistic competence is affected by the setting where a story is told. Narrative is a social phenomenon and, as such, it varies with social context; consequently, the data extracted from narratives will vary depending on the social context within which they are collected.

Thus, Labov and Waletzky demonstrated that the effort to understand narrative is amenable to a formal framework, a framework that "proved to be useful in approaching a wide variety of narrative situations and types, including oral memoirs, traditional folk tales, *avant garde* novels, therapeutic interviews and most importantly, the banal narratives of every-day life" (Labov, 1997b: 396).

As the reader will surely have noticed by now, narratives are privileged forms of discourse which play a central role in almost every conversation and, consequently, they also play an important role in people's construction of identity[3]. This is the reason why so many scholars have approached the subject not only from the linguistic point of view, but from other perspectives (e.g. that of psychology, sociology or literary criticism) as well.

An essential concept within narrative analysis (especially within the analysis of narratives of personal experience) is that of **reportability**. This concept has to do with the fact that telling a narrative requires a person to hold the floor longer, and the narrative to carry enough interest for the audience to justify its telling. Otherwise, as Labov remarks, "an implicit or explicit 'So what?' is in order, with the implication that the speaker has violated social norms by making this unjustified claim"[4]

---

[3] We shall deal with this particular aspect of narrative in 7.2.3.

[4] Namely, the claim that the story was worth telling, and consequently that the speaker had the right to occupy more social space than the other participants in the conversation.

(1997b: 405). Thus, a **reportable event** is defined as "one that justifies the automatic reassignment of speaker role to the narrator", and a **most reportable event** as "the event that is less common than any other in the narrative and has the greatest effect upon the needs and desires of the participants in the narrative (is evaluated most strongly)" (1997b: 406). Therefore the most reportable event of a narrative can be said to be the semantic and structural crucial point around which the narrative is organized.

Another important concept is the notion of **credibility**, which refers to "the extent to which listeners believe that the events described actually occurred in the form described by the narrator" (Labov, 1997b: 407). If credibility is not achieved when telling a narrative of personal experience, the narrative will be considered to have failed and its narrator's claim to reassignment of speakership will most probably not be attended to.

Considerations of credibility lead to the issue of **causality**, which is another of the characteristics of narratives. Every narrative requires a personal theory of causality, where the sequence of events is explained by (a series of) explicit or implicit causal relations. In other words, there is a proposed chain of events that links the orientation to the most reportable event through a web of causal relations.

The narrator's **point of view** is normally reflected in the **assignment of praise or blame** to the actors or actions involved in the narrative. This viewpoint constitutes the ideological framework within which events are presented or seen by the narrator, and it is rarely a conscious process.

Related to these issues is the concept of **objectivity**. In Labov's terms, an **objective event** is "one that became known to the narrator through sense experience", and a **subjective event** is "one that the narrator became aware of through memory, emotional reaction, or internal sensation" (1997b: 412). Labov observes (in contrast to therapeutically oriented writers) that the narratives of personal experience that have the greatest impact upon audiences are those that use the most objective means of expression, mainly due to the fact that, normally, objectivity increases credibility. However, as we shall see in 7.2.1., a great deal of subjectivity can be found in successful narratives, especially in their evaluative structure. So it might be concluded that it is probably in the sequence of events (complicating action and resolution) where the audience expects the narrator to be more objective, whereas greater degrees of subjectivity are expected and tolerated within the evaluative clauses of the narrative. In plain words, the story is more likely to succeed if the events can be proved to be true, irrespective of whether the point of view of the narrator (with which the audience may agree or not) seems to be objective or subjective.

7.2.1. Information structures

One of the main concerns of variationists is to search for the information structures that prevail in discourse, considering that syntactic and semantic differences among linguistic items are sensitive to text structure. Such differences may be analyzed within one text type or across text types. Therefore, differences among text types can be discovered by examining how certain linguistic forms fit a given distributional pattern.

As anticipated in 7.2., **temporal structure** is a central criterion for the definition of narrative. The linear presentation of event clauses in a narrative is crucial for the assignment of reference time. However, in a different type of text, the temporal structure may be of no importance or may fulfil a completely different function. Schiffrin (1994), for instance, compares the temporal structures of narratives and lists, and concludes that, whereas the temporal structure of a narrative is central to its identity as a discourse unit and to its semantic interpretation, it has little relevance in the structure of lists.

Descriptive structures can also form part of narratives, but they are not central to them, since description in narratives is typically assigned to a background orientation function (Labov 1972b). Narrative descriptive orientation may preface the narrative action itself, or it may be embedded within the complicating action. A speaker might, for example, interrupt the narration of sequential events in order to describe the physical and/or spiritual features of a given character in the story.

Schiffrin notes that, since stories are often said to be constructions of an experience rather than representations of a reality, narrators may impose their own subjectivity on what happens at a variety of levels (1994: 306). A lot of subjectivity is involved in the process of making a point when telling a story, and the point of a story is indicated by means of some sort of *evaluation*. **Evaluative structures** are then important in the construction of narratives. Whereas evaluation is normally necessary and required in stories, it may be optional and less important in other types of text, like, for example, recipes or the manual instructions to use an appliance.

The different information structures of texts display the arrangements of units in recurrent patterns. These units are related to one another so as to make texts *coherent*. This leads us to reflect upon one of the key tasks of variationists: the comparison and contrast of the use of the different information structures across text types, as well as within a given text type. This type of analysis leads to a more systematic study of the characteristics of different texts and their functions, which in turn leads to a basic assumption in both variation and narrative analysis: that equivalence (or difference) in syntactic form does not always imply functional equivalence (or difference). Likewise, equivalence (or difference) in function does not always presuppose equivalence (or difference) in form. To put it in a simpler way, there is not a biunivocal relationship between form and function in linguistics: a given form may fulfil different functions, and a given function may be realized by different forms.

7.2.2. Sample analysis of data

Examine the following narrative, in which a High School student tells what happened to his English teacher one of the times he (the teacher) was at gunpoint.

> A: Did you ever meet a real brave person?

> B: Oh, yeah. That's my English teacher. You know, he's the one that's uh… been four times at gunpoint. One time there was this guy who uh, wanted him to get out of his property, so uh…he got out his rifle and threatened to shoot him. My teacher just got pissed, went up to him and put his hand on the barrel. The guy was drunk and didn't even know what he was doing so he fired the rifle. But then when he actually saw a bullet come out, he was surprised 'cause he thought the gun wasn't loaded. The bullet went through my teacher's hand and left a terrible wound. If you look now, uh… you can see he has quite a scar there.

> (Personal communication with a student at the *American School of Madrid*, January 2005)

Albeit not very long, this story contains many of the elements and devices of narratives. It has an **abstract** (*You know, he's the one that's uh… been four times at gunpoint.*) which summarizes the point the student wants to make (that his teacher is brave because he was at gunpoint four times and faced the events). The abstract is followed by a short **orientation** as to one of the times he was at gunpoint (*One time there was this guy who…*) followed in turn by a succession of events related to this time, which constitute **the complicating action.** The **result or resolution** is expressed by means of the clause *The bullet went through my teacher's hand and left a terrible wound,* and the final clause functions as a **coda**, showing how the effect of the actions described in the narrative has been extended to the present moment (*If you look now, uh…you can see he has quite a scar there*).

If we compare this narrative to that of Labov's reproduced in 7.2., we shall see that they do not have exactly the same elements. As explained in

7.2., the one element all narratives do seem to have in common is their **sequential structure**, manifested in the **complicating action** and the **resolution**, because that is the characteristic that, according to Labov and many authors following him, defines a narrative[5]. The other elements may vary, as is the case with some of them in these two particular narratives. Labov's story in 7.2. does not have an **abstract** proper, but it does have some clauses fulfilling the function of **orientation**. While Labov's narrative has an evaluative clause (*She was a devil*), the narrative in this section does not strictly contain any explicit evaluative clause: the student seems to limit himself to the telling of the events. However, the response to the interviewer's question (*Oh, yeah. That's my English teacher*) could be considered as an evaluative introductory clause, and, also, it is clear that every subsequent clause contributes to the main point of the story, i.e. that the English teacher is brave, which in itself constitutes an implicit **evaluation**.

This type of discourse analysis, if taken further and done in more detail, can lead the researcher to draw conclusions as to the different types of narratives there are, as well as to the different devices used in each type. If the analysis were to be intended within Variation Analysis (following all the steps, as we saw in 7.1.), we would need a more extensive corpus (containing numerous narrations) and we should go through the process of quantifying the occurrences of the variants and dealing with statistical tests, a procedure we shall not follow in this book because it goes beyond the scope of the objectives set for this chapter.

7.2.3. Further discussion on Narrative Analysis

Some authors have pointed out (e.g. Cortazzi and Jin, 2003) that Labov's model does not take into account the relationship between teller and listener, that it does not pay sufficient attention to context, or that it does not fully consider features of narrative performance or culture. Thus, they argue in favour of the analysis of narrative in the light of wider socio-cultural dimensions.

In effect, as was noted in 7.2., narrative and the broader field of storytelling have become the focus of attention of many scholars, not only within linguistics but also in many other academic and literary disciplines. The storyteller is seen as someone who can make something out of nothing, who is capable of a fascinating elaboration of detail that is entertaining and amusing, who is, in short, a gifted user of the language.

---

[5] However, see comment on Mishler's (2006) work in 7.2.3.1.

Thus, narrative analysis is acknowledged to be an "empowering" social science, for it gives the narrators the opportunity to present their own viewpoints and evaluative standards. During interviews, the respondents make an effort to organize their temporal experience into meaningful wholes, using the pattern of narrative form as a means to make sense of the events of their lives, and that is the reason why the analysis of narrative is taken by many scholars as a useful tool for the study of the construction of identity, a topic to which we now turn.

7.2.3.1. Narrative and identity

Discourse practices such as narrative have a central role in social practices, as Foucault (1984) has pointed out. Both social and discourse practices constitute a frame within which individuals and groups present themselves to others, and in so doing they find themselves in the process of building their identity. Thus, narrative discourse has proved to be a very fertile ground for the study of the construction of both individual and/or social/cultural identity.

One basic way of looking at the phenomenon of identity is through the prism of *social constructionism* (e.g. Zimmerman and Wieder 1970, Hall 1996, Kroskrity 2000), whose main assumption is that identity is neither a given nor a product. This perspective conceives of identity as a process that presupposes *discursive work* and takes place in concrete interactional situations, and as a process that comes out as the result of negociation and entextualization (Bauman and Briggs 1990).

Narrative analysis provides a systematic way of understanding how people make events in their lives meaningful and how they engage in the ongoing construction of their identities. Through this type of analysis, we can see how interlocutors build their identity by assuming stances not only towards ideologies, but also with respect to each other or to absent third parties. Numerous scholars have committed themselves to this enterprise. One of them is Susan Bell (2006), who analyzes how a woman positions herself in relation to the dominant ideology of intensive mothering, as well as how she produces herself as a mother. Another one is Mike Baynham, who, in his study of Moroccan narratives of migration and settlement, shows "how different kinds of narrative, personal and generic, imply different kinds of speaking position and corresponding identity choice" (2006: 395).

Some authors have drawn on Goffman's work (1981) on participation frameworks and the deconstruction of the notion of speaker into more subtle distinctions[6] for their analysis of narrative. These studies show, for example, how speakers may make use of a variety of linguistic means (e.g. reference, quotation, use of pronouns) to assume an authoritative identity with respect to interlocutors, by claiming expertise in certain fields of knowledge or experience (e.g. Schiffrin 2006, Ribeiro 2006). Other studies (e.g. De Fina 2006, Kiesling 2006) show how speakers are able to implicitly convey their position on social problems such as gender, race or ethnicity by resorting to narratives of personal experience in which they play a protagonistic role.

Bakhtin (1981) showed how the narrator's voice could be separated from that of the speaking character, thus obtaining a blend of different voices (which are sometimes very difficult to distinguish) within the same narrative. Bakhtin's views on voice and dialogism[7] have been used by other authors (e.g. Wortham and Gadsden 2006, Moita Lopes 2006) to argue in favor of the idea that narrators can borrow the voices of others in order to construct their own identity. In fact, the study of narrative allows us to understand and see how both individual and global identities are constantly intertwined in discourse. Global identities may emerge from local, individual identities or they can be constructed simultaneously in the ongoing discourse or interaction.

An interesting contribution to the study of narrative is that of Mishler (2006), because it defies the dominating and prevailing view of narrative as a chronologically-ordered set of clauses. This author takes a critical look at the privileging of linear time in the structure of narrative and the formation of identity by arguing that many narratives do not represent temporal and causal chains leading toward the present. On the contrary, our constructions of identity may flow recurrently between the present and the past.

In short and to conclude, this section has tried to show and to call the reader's attention to how recent scholarship in linguistics has proved that it is largely within discourse, and in particular, within narrative, that we find the answers to many questions about the construction of local and global identities.

---

[6] See 4.1.2.
[7] See 9.5.

SUMMING UP... (CHAPTER 7)

1. The origins of the **variationist approach** are solely within the field of Linguistics.
2. Variation Analysis is concerned with the **variation** and changes observed in language along different speech communities.
3. The most prominent figure within this approach is **William Labov**.
4. Labov holds a **materialistic conception of language**. The materialist approach starts by observing the **variability** which is characteristic of speech production and then applies formalisms based on **probability theory** to this variation.
5. Variationists focus upon **different units of analysis**: phonological, syntactic, semantic and textual.
6. Differences among **text types** can be discovered by examining how certain linguistic forms fit a given **distributional pattern**.
7. The different information structures of texts display the arrangements of units in recurrent patterns. These units are related to one another so as to make texts *coherent*.
8. An important notion in Variation Analysis is that of **constraint**. A given text type (for instance, a medical prescription, a recipe, or a narrative of personal experience), poses constraints upon the syntactic units used in the text.
9. Labov considers that the study of narrative is a priviledged area of discourse, because it is the closest to the **vernacular**. The vernacular is *the variety acquired in pre-adolescent years and which is used by speakers of a given language when they pay minimum attention to speech* (Labov, 1984: 29).
10. The skeleton of a narrative consists of a series of *temporally ordered* clauses which Labov calls **narrative clauses**.
11. The elements (Labov, 1972b, 1997b) that are normally found in the **structure of a narrative** are: *Abstract, Orientation, Complicating action, Evaluation, Result or resolution* and *Coda*.
12. Narratives are privileged forms of discourse which play a central role in almost every conversation and, consequently, they also play an important role in people's **construction of identity**.

SELF EVALUATION QUESTIONS

Choose the answer that best suits the information given in Chapter 7.

1) The origins of Variation Analysis are found…
a) in Anthropology and Psychology.
b) solely in Linguistics.
c) both in Linguistics and Anthropology.

2) Variation Analysis is concerned with the language changes observed…
a) between different speech acts.
b) within the same community.
c) along different speech communities.

3) The most prominent figure within Variation Analysis is…
a) Dell Hymes.
b) William Labov.
c) Deborah Schiffrin.

4) The vernacular language is…
a) the standard variety.
b) the most grammatically correct variety.
c) the variety which is first acquired and perfectly learned.

5) Variation Analysis…
a) combines both qualitative and quantitative techniques.
b) is only concerned with qualitative analysis.
c) is only interested in the quantitative results.

6) Variationists study linguistic change…
a) only at the semantic level.
b) at both the semantic and syntactic levels.
c) at all linguistic levels.

7) According to Labov, narrative is a privileged area of discourse because…
a) it is closer to the vernacular than any other type of discourse.
b) it is the most grammatically correct type of discourse.
c) it does not contain any mistakes.

8) Through the sociolinguistic interviews…
a) the researchers analize the interviewees' social lives.
b) the respondents speak about their private lives.
c) conclusions about the social distribution of variants can be drawn.

9) Labov argued in favor of the idea that…
a) black children were verbally deprived.
b) white children were genetically superior.
c) black children were not verbally deprived.

10) The *observer's paradox* has to do with …
a) the effort made by researchers to observe how speakers talk when they are not being observed.
b) how to make observants speak while the observer is not speaking.
c) the contradiction between speaking and observing at the same time.

11) A narrative is a discourse unit…
a) surrounded by other, dependent units.
b) that contains smaller units and has a fairly regular structure.
c) with an irregular structure.

12) According to Labov, the basic characteristic of all narratives is…
a) their temporal structure.
b) their descriptive structure.
c) their evaluative structure.

13) Which are the elements of the following short narrative?

> Melissa was in bed when she felt everything was moving and realized it was an earthquake, so she jumped out of bed, rushed down the stairs, and managed to get to the street before the building collapsed.

    a)   abstract – orientation – resolution – coda
    b)   complicating action – resolution
    c)   orientation – complicating action – resolution

14) *Reportability* in a narrative has to do with…
a) how long the narrative is.
b) the interest it elicits from the audience, so as to justify its telling.
c) how interesting the speaker thinks the narrative is.

15) In narratives of personal experience…

a) credibility and causality are closely related.

b) no causal relations can be found within the sequence of events.

c) it is not important whether the hearer believes the story or not.

16) According to Labov, the more objectively the events in a narrative are presented …

a) the more credibility they will receive from the audience.

b) the less credibility they will receive from the audience.

c) the more subjective the point of view of the narrator will be.

17) The analysis of narratives and their functions leads to the basic assumption in both variation and narrative analysis that…

a) syntactic equivalence implies functional equivalence

b) syntactic equivalence does not imply functional equivalence.

c) equivalence in function presupposes equivalence in form.

18) Narrative discourse has proved to be a fertile ground for the study of…

a) all kinds of social practices.

b) personal opinion.

c) individual and social/cultural identity.

PRACTICE

A) *ANALYSIS:*   Many jokes adjust to the structure of narratives. ANALYZE the following jokes (a and b) and compare their structure following Labov's main lines for narrative analysis. Do the elements vary from one joke to the other?

a)

Don't Leave' Em Hanging

Ralph and Edna were both patients in a mental hospital.
One day while they were walking past the hospital swimming pool, Ralph suddenly jumped into the deep end. He sank to the bottom of the pool and stayed there. Edna promptly jumped in to save him. She swam to the bottom and pulled Ralph out.
When the Head Nurse became aware of Edna's heroic act she immediately ordered her to be discharged from the hospital, as she now considered her to be mentally stable.
When she went to tell Edna the news she said, "Edna, I have good news and bad news. The good news is you're being discharged; since you were able to rationally respond to a crisis by jumping in and saving the life of another patient, I have concluded that your act displays sound-mindedness. The bad news is, Ralph, the patient you saved, hung himself right after you saved him with his bathrobe belt in the bathroom. I am so sorry, but he's dead."
Edna replied "He didn't hang himself. I put him there to dry. How soon can I go home?"

b)

Take Off My Clothes

My wife came home the other night and told me to take off her blouse. Then she told me to take off her skirt. Then she told me never to wear her clothes again.

B) *ANALYSIS*: The jokes presented in A are clear examples of narratives. However, not all jokes adjust to the structure of narratives. EXAMINE the structure of the following joke and COMPARE it to those of the jokes in A. How do they differ?

White House Visitors

A: What do you call someone in the White House who is honest, ethical, intellectual, law-abiding, and truthful?
B: A tourist.

C) ANALYZE the elements of the following narrative, indicating the *information structure* that prevails in it (temporal, descriptive or evaluative). Which is the most reportable event? Justify your answer.

"When I was younger, I dated a guy named Ethan who was really critical of me. He constantly made little snide comments about my weight, how stupid I was and how clumsy I was. For whatever odd reason, I was into him, despite the fact that all of my friends and family hated him. One weekend when he was away, I met Will at a party and we completely hit it off. He was the complete opposite of Ethan –kind, sweet and generous, yet completely cool and fun, too. We hung out all weekend and it was like a light bulb went off in my head: This is how mature, relationshipworthy guys act. I hooked up with Will the night before he left, and broke up with Ethan soon after. Will and I dated for three years and now we're married".

FURTHER READING

- Bell (1999)
- De Fina, Schiffrin & Bamberg (2006)
- Labov (1972b).
- Labov (1972a), (1981), (1984), (1997b & c), (2004).
- Labov & Waletzky (1967).
- Schiffrin (1981) & (1996).

USEFUL WEBSITES

Variation Analysis: http://www.orlapubs.com/AL/L32.html
http://www.orlapubs.com/AL/L59.html
http://privatewww.essex.ac.uk/~patrickp/TDbiblio.html

Narrative Analysis (Labov, Univ. of Pennsylvania):
http://www.ling.upenn.edu/~wlabov/sfs.html
http://www.blackwellpublishing.com/specialarticles/jcn_8_674.pdf
http://www.clarku.edu/~mbamberg/LabovWaletzky.htm

William Labov's home page:
http://www.ling.upenn.edu/~wlabov/home.html

8 FUNCTIONAL SENTENCE PERSPECTIVE: THEMATIC AND INFORMATION STRUCTURES

The city of Prague, the native town of Functionalism.

"A scientist in the true sense needs to be in love with a rich store of data. As one who sought to understand language and the mind, I would aim to find out all I could about as many languages as I could, not just by reading grammars and hearing what others said about languages, but especially by coming in contact with diverse languages themselves. I would also continue to observe more and more about my own language. I would want to pay particular attention to what people really do when they use language, my own or another, in order to sensitize myself to the distinction between natural and artificial data. I would carefully observe not just linguistic form, but also function."

William Chafe, *Discourse, Consciousness and Time.*

Chapter Outline:

- Main tenets of Functionalism.

- *Functional Sentence Perspective* as a theory of linguistic discourse analysis.

- The concept of *communicative dynamism.*

- Analysis of thematic and information structures.

8.1. Functionalism

Functionalism was one of the great linguistic paradigms of the 20th century, still in force, which grew as an alternative to the abstract, formalized view of language presented by Transformational Grammar, an approach to language that, according to functionalists, could not explain certain linguistic facts. Functionalism relies, contrary to Formalism, on a pragmatic view of language as social interaction, and therefore the approach focuses on the rules which govern verbal interaction. These rules are seen as a form of co-operative activity, and their study helps the researcher describe the linguistic structures of language in relation to the context in which they occur. Meaning, rather than form, is taken into account, and both the extra-linguistic context and the purpose of communication play a crucial role in this approach.

The origins of functionalism can be traced back to the Linguistic School of Prague, in the work of scholars such as Vilèm Mathesius, Frantisek Danes or Jan Firbas. These scholars emphasized the functional aspects of the organization of information. Danes (1974) developed the concept of *Communicative Dynamism* and Firbas (1964, 1986) was the father of the theory of *Functional Sentence Perspective*, which studies the distribution of information, organized in more or less dynamic elements called *theme* and *rheme*.

8.1.1. Functional Sentence Perspective

Functional Sentence Perspective is a theory of linguistic analysis which refers to an analysis of utterances or texts in terms of the information they contain. The role of each part of a given utterance is evaluated for its semantic contribution to the whole. The notion of *communicative dynamism* is a key concept in this theory, for it attempts to rate the different levels of contribution within a structure, in particular those related to the concepts of *theme* and *rheme*. Firbas defines *communicative dynamism* as "the relative extent to which a linguistic element contributes towards the further development of the communication" (1992: 8). He also explains that:

> It is an inherent quality of communication and manifests itself in constant development towards the attainment of a communicative goal; in other words, towards the fulfillment of a communicative purpose. Participating in this development, a linguistic element assumes some position in it and in accordance with this position displays a degree of communicative dynamism. (1992: 7)

Thus, communicative dynamism assumes that when speakers say something, they have a communicative purpose and that the elements of their language contribute to that purpose. It is important to note, however, that even when functional sentence perspective relies on introspections regarding the goals of communicative acts, any broader social or cognitive commitments are avoided.

Functional Sentence Perspective provides a functional explanation for word order: all other things being equal, the order of words in a sentence corresponds to an increase in communicative dynamism. There are four factors which determine communicative dynamism: 1) **linear modification**; 2) **the contextual factor**; 3) **the semantic factor** and 4) **prosodic prominence** (in spoken language) (Chafe, 1994: 162).

Linear modification[1] is a term used by Firbas to depict the relation between word order and communicative dynamism, as illustrated in the following example:

> A: Any news about your mom?
> B: Yes, she has travelled to Brussels.

---

[1] The term *linear modification* was first used by Dwight Bolinger (1952: 1125) to explain a somewhat different phenomenon from that explained by Firbas under the same term.

B's response might have different purposes, but the most obvious seems to be "to state the destination of B's mom's trip". In B's reply, then, the word *she* contributes the lowest degree of communicative dynamism; *has travelled* contributes an intermediate degree, and *to Brussels* the highest degree, since it serves the purpose of the response (destination).

The contextual factor has to do with the concepts of "retrievability and irretrievability from the immediately relevant context" (Firbas 1992: 21), which have created the opposition *context-dependent* versus *context-independent*.

The semantic factor deals with the so-called *dynamic functions*. The notions of *theme* and *rheme* are crucial here. The **theme** is considered to be the part of a sentence which adds least to the advancing process of communication, having the lowest degree of communicative dynamism. By contrast, the **rheme** carries the highest degree of communicative dynamism. We shall deal with these two concepts in more detail in section 8.1.1.1.

Prosodic prominence is a factor which can be studied only in spoken language, and it integrates functional sentence perspective with intonation studies. It deals, for example, with the function that certain tones or other prosodic features (such as pitch prominence) fulfill in discourse.

8.1.1.1. Thematic Structure: Theme vs. Rheme

The thematic structure of a clause contains two main elements: **theme** and **rheme.** Following Halliday (1967: 212), we shall say that the *theme* of a clause is what speakers/writers use as the 'point of departure'. The rest of the message constitutes the other element of the thematic structure, namely, the *rheme.*

Different elements can be chosen as the point of departure or initial constituent of a clause, as illustrated in the following examples:

	THEME	**RHEME**
a)	Peter	doesn't like that car
b)	That car	Peter doesn't like
c)	What Peter doesn't like	is that car
d)	It's that car	Peter doesn't like

The four clauses in the examples above have the same propositional content; however, the choice of theme made by the speaker or writer in each case changes its meaning to a certain extent, because it shows the angle from which the speaker projects his/her message. From the point of view of discourse analysis, the possibility of making these choices is proof of the fact that a speaker producing one or other choices will be making different assumptions about the stage of knowledge of his/her hearer. It is clearly the case that all four clauses could not be the answer to the same question, and therefore each of them assumes different presuppositions on the part of the interlocutor. For example, **d** seems to presuppose the shared belief of both interlocutors that Peter does not like something, and **c** restricts what Peter does not like among other things the hearer might consider 'not likeable'.

The theme always contains an ideational element. This element is some entity which functions as subject, object, complement or circumstantial adjunct. Halliday (1985: 54) refers to this entity as the *topical theme* (due to the fact that it generally corresponds to the element identified as topic in topic-comment analysis). The ideational function represents our experience of the world, namely, processes, actions, events, processes of consciousness and relations, and that is why this type of theme has also been called *experiential theme.*

Apart from the clausal/experiential themes, we may find what Downing and Locke (2006: 234) call *non-experiential themes*, which can be divided into two main kinds: a) *interpersonal* themes and b) *textual* themes. Within **interpersonal themes** we find **continuative themes**, manifested as pragmatic markers of attention, response, request, surprise, hesitation, etc. (such as *Oh, Well, Please, Hey!*), **Adjuncts of stance** (such as *apparently, surely, certainly*) and **vocatives** and **appellatives** (such as *Dad! Mr. Wilson! Ladies and gentlemen*). **Textual themes** include **connective adjuncts/discourse markers** (such as *anyway, however, first, finally*, etc.) which connect a clause to the previous part of the text by indicating relations of consequence, addition or concession, among others.

Table 1 presents these main kinds of theme more schematically, with illustrative examples:

Table 1: Experiential and non-experiential themes

TYPES OF THEMES	
A) EXPERIENTIAL	**Examples**
1. Subject	**Tom** is coming for dinner.
2. Object	**"No!"** I said.
3. Circumstantial adjuncts	**This morning at the cafeteria** we had a lot of fun. (Time and place adjuncts)
4. Complement	**A terrible fiasco** it was. (subject comp.) **General Director** he was appointed. (object comp.)
5. Verb	**Coming up** is the latest news. (thematized verb)
B) NON-EXPERIENTIAL	**Examples**
1. *INTERPERSONAL*	
a) Continuative pragmatic markers	**Well**, see you tomorrow.
b) Adjuncts of stance	**Frankly**, I don't understand your point.
c) Vocatives and appellatives	**Peter**, call your Mom, please.
2. *TEXTUAL* (connective adjuncts/ discourse markers)	She is sick. **Consequently**, she won't go to work today.

8.1.1.1.1. Multiple Themes

As Table 1 shows, the three macro-functions of language (experiential, interpersonal and textual) can be represented within the Theme. Two or the three types of theme may be concurrent in the same utterance, and in such cases we may talk of **multiple themes**. When the three of them appear together, the typical sequence of these elements is textual/ interpersonal/experiential, although the interpersonal theme may be *marked* (see 8.1.1.1.4) in certain circumstances, and thus it may appear before the textual theme. But the experiential theme always has to be the final one. Here are some examples of **multiple themes**:

Well	*then*	*you little brat*	*what*	*do you want?*
continuative	connective adjunct	vocative	object	
Interpersonal theme	Textual theme	Interpersonal theme	Experiential theme	
THEME				**RHEME**

Unfortunately	*though*	*she*	*rejected my offer*
adjunct of stance (evaluative)	connective adjunct	subject	
Interpersonal theme	Textual theme	Experiential theme	
THEME			**RHEME**

8.1.1.1.2. Detached Themes

Some themes are **detached** from the main clause in one way or another. Downing & Locke (2006) note that a subtype of these does not function as a constituent of the clauses that follow them. They are normally detached lexical noun phrases which stand outside the clause, and are called **Absolute Themes.** Absolute themes are common in the spoken registers of many European languages, such as English or Spanish. Consider this example:

The financial crisis, we are all aware that some measures have to be taken.
Absolute Theme

Here the noun phrase *the financial crisis* is completely detached and thus has no grammatical relations with the second part of the message. This is to say that *the financial crisis* is neither the subject nor the object, nor any other constituent of the clause that follows (*we are all aware that some measures have to be taken*). However, there is still a connection between both parts: the absolute theme provides a pragmatic framework which allows the hearer to infer the relationship between them. This is one of the many instances in linguistic communication where grammatical competence is not enough, and the interlocutors have to resort to the wider pragmatic/discursive/communicative competence in order to sort out meanings.

Dislocations are another subtype of detached themes. They are different from Absolute Themes "in that the 'dislocated' element is a constituent of the clause, frequently subject [...], and is repeated by a co-referential pronoun [...] in its normal position within the clause" (Downing & Locke, 2006: 232). In this type of theme, then, the connection is encoded grammatically. When the dislocated element is placed at the beginning of the clause, it is known as *left-dislocation*; when it is placed at the end of the clause, it is called *right-dislocation*. Consider these examples:

a) Left-dislocations:

That scream,   where did **it** come from?
Left-dislocated Theme

That house,   **that** is the one I've always dreamed of!
Left-dislocated theme

Here, the normal, non-dislocated forms would be, respectively: *Where did that scream come from?* and *That is the house I've always dreamed of!*

b) Right-dislocations:

Is **it** yours, **that jacket?**
       Right-dislocated theme

It's fantastic, **this book**.
       Right-dislocated theme

The normal non-dislocated forms for these examples would be, respectively, *Is that jacket yours?* and *This book is fantastic.* Not being initial, this kind of theme is more problematic to analyze, but as Downing & Locke suggest, the cognitive motivation for such a structure could be that of making explicit a referent (*that jacket* and *this book* in our examples) which was accessible to the speaker in the context, but perhaps not so obvious to the hearer, or not in the speaker's mind at the moment he uttered the first part of the clause (2006: 233).

Two or more detached themes may co-occur, in which case the relationship between them must be pragmatically relevant, as in the following example:

Your friend, the car outside her house, they've stolen **it**.
Absolute theme + left-dislocated theme

The co-occurrence of detached themes is more likely to be found in spoken English than in written English. Downing & Locke explain that the function of double or multiple detachments "is to 'anchor' the final referent to other related referents which are presumed to be accessible to the hearer" (2006: 234).

8.1.1.1.3. Thematic clauses

When two or more clauses are joined together in a complex clause, the clause that is placed first is said to be thematic with respect to the whole complex clause. This applies for cases of coordination as well as for cases of subordination. Examine these examples:

1) **Coordination**

Tommy hit his sister	and she burst into tears.
THEME	**RHEME**

2) **Subordination**

When I saw her	I realized she had been crying.
THEME	**RHEME**

Clauses related by coordination are said to be *paratactically*[2] related. Clauses related by subordination are said to be *hypotactically*[3] related. Paratactically related clauses are typically placed in the chronological order in which the events described occur. In example 1, the event described in the rheme clause (Tommy's sister bursting into tears) is understood to have occurred after the event described in the theme clause (Tommy hitting his sister). In hypotactically related clauses, however, the speaker/writer does not necessarily have to maintain chronological order,

---

[2] A paratactic relationship is that holding between clauses of equal status. It is, thus, a relationship of equivalence.
[3] A hypotactic relationship is that holding between clauses of unequal status. It is, thus, a relationship of non-equivalence.

thus in example 2 both the main and the subordinate clauses could be used as the starting point of the message (or theme). Therefore, *I realized she had been crying when I saw her* is equally possible, the only difference being the intention, on the part of the speaker/writer, to place what he considers to be new and important information at the end, and as part of the rheme in each case.

The thematic organization of the different clauses in a text is of great importance to the discourse analyst, because it reveals the method of textual development: "...by analyzing the thematic structure of a text clause by clause, we can gain an insight into its texture and understand how the writer made clear to us the nature of his underlying concerns" (Halliday, 1985: 67).

8.1.1.1.4. Theme, subject and topic

It is important to note that *theme* is a different category from syntactic *Subject* and from *Topic*, even though "these three tend to coincide in one wording" (Downing & Locke, 1992: 222). Whereas *theme* is the starting point of the message, *subject* is a syntactic element of clause structure (the other elements being *Predicator, Complements, Objects* and *Adjunct*) and *Topic* refers to what the text is about (it may refer to the whole or only to a given part of the text). The following examples illustrate the fact that the three elements may coincide (a) or, contrariwise, may not (b):

a) **The new president** has been strongly criticized for his foreign policy.
   Subject
   Theme
   Topic

b) **In Spain, the people** criticized **the new president** for his foreign policy.
   Theme   Subject   **Topic**

As can be seen in **b**, the theme does not coincide with the syntactic subject. Instead, the theme is, syntactically, an *adjunct* (circumstance) which is realized by a prepositional phrase (*In Spain*). The topic does not concur with the subject either: when turning **a** into its active counterpart in **b**, the agent (*the people*) that was not named in **a** appears as the subject of the clause and the topic is now the direct object (*the new president*). However, clauses may have more than one type of topic. Those topics which are introduced into the discourse for the first time are called *new topics*. New topics may become *old* or *known topics* as the discourse proceeds, or they may be abandoned completely. In **b**, for example, *the people* could be taken as an old topic and *the new president* as the new topic. We may also speak of *global* and *local* topics (Downing & Locke, 2006: 225). The former refer to those that organize a whole piece of language; the latter, to the topics of utterances and sentences, and these are the only ones that have a direct grammatical realization. In between global and local topics it can be said that paragraphs or sections in writing, as well as episodes in talk, each have their own topic. All levels of topic help to build up the coherence of discourse as a whole.

8.1.1.1.5. Marked and Unmarked Themes

Depending on the purposes of communication, certain types of information may be foregrounded or *thematized*. When the theme does not coincide with the expected first constituent of each mood structure,[4] we speak of a **marked theme**. If, on the contrary, the theme co-exists with such a constituent, it is an **unmarked theme**. For example, the expected first constituent of a *declarative clause* is the *subject*, so if in such a clause the subject appears as the first constituent, the theme will coincide with the subject (as is the case in example **a** in 8.1.1.1.4.), and we shall say that the theme is *unmarked*. Contrariwise, in example **b** the adjunct *In Spain* has been *thematized* or foregrounded, and thus we say that the theme is *marked*. Here are two more examples:

1)

Sally	will never pass that exam.
UNMARKED THEME	**RHEME**

Never	will Sally pass that exam.
MARKED THEME	**RHEME**

---

[4] The different mood structures with their corresponding (normal or expected) first constituents are: a) **Declarative → subject** (e.g. *Tommy fell off his bike*); b) **Polar interrogative → Finite + subject** (e.g. *Do you believe in ghosts?*); c) **Wh-interrogative → Wh- element** (e.g. *Who told you such a thing?*); and d) **Imperative → Predicator or *let* + Subject** (e.g. *Do it now!/ Let's do it now!*). For a more detailed description of this topic see Downing and Locke (2006:224-25).

2)

He	popped the question.
UNMARKED THEME	**RHEME**

The question	he popped.
MARKED THEME	**RHEME**

In example 1, the adjunct *never* is fronted and thus thematized; in example 2, it is the direct object (*the question*) that is thematized, both fronted elements thereby turning into **marked themes**. If we go back to Table 1 (in 8.1.1.1.) we shall see that in all the examples, except for the first one (*Tom is coming for dinner*), the themes are marked.

8.1.1.1.6. Thematization/Staging

As has been suggested so far, sentence word order is of capital importance for the organization of the information. The same applies for the order in which sentences are put into texts, because this order will influence the hearer's or reader's interpretation of the whole discourse in question. The speaker/writer always has to choose a beginning point: what s/he puts first will influence the interpretation of the text which follows it. This process, which has to do with the *linear organization* of sentences and texts, has been called **thematization.** A more inclusive and more general term than *thematization* is **staging**[5], a term that, according to Grimes, refers to the fact that "Every clause, sentence, paragraph, episode, and discourse is organised around a particular element that is taken as its point of departure" (1975: 323).

It is interesting to note how the linear organization can be manipulated to bring certain items or events into greater prominence than others by means of the process of *thematization* or *staging*. The title of a newspaper article, or the title of a book can be considered a powerful thematization device used by the author. Thematization creates certain expectations in the readers or hearers in that the thematized elements provide a starting point which constrains their interpretation of the discourse that follows. Brown & Yule illustrate this by presenting the results of an exercise they

---

[5] Although some authors, like Brown & Yule (1983), make no distinction between these terms (*thematization* and *staging*).

conducted using the following text:

A Prisoner Plans His Escape

> Rocky slowly got up from the mat, planning his escape. He hesitated a moment and thought. Things were not going well. What bothered him most was being held, especially since the charge against him had been weak. He considered his present situation. The lock that held him was strong, but he thought he could break it (1983: 139).

Brown & Yule used this text to conduct an exercise in which they asked their subjects several questions, and they found that "there was a general interpretation that Rocky was alone, that he had been arrested by the police and that he disliked being in prison" (1983: 139). Another group of subjects were given the same text to read but with a different title, namely, *A Wrestler in a Tight Corner*. This group gave very different answers to the questions: they said Rocky was a wrestler who was being held in some kind of wrestling 'hold' and was planning to get out of it. They also thought that Rocky was not alone and that that he had had nothing to do with the police. This experiment shows how, by providing different themes or starting points in the thematized elements of the two different titles, the authors constrained the ways in which the texts were interpreted by the subjects.

8.1.1.2. Information Structure: Given vs. New

In his search for correspondences between linguistic elements and their functions, Halliday found that the *tone group*, apart from being a phonological constituent, "functions as the realization of something else, namely, a quantum or unit of information in the discourse" (1985: 274). Halliday explains that spoken discourse takes the form of a sequence of *information units*, and he uses the term *information* to mean "a process of interaction between what is already known or predictable and what is new or unpredictable" (1985: 274-75). The information unit, thus, is a structure made up of two functions: the **New** and the **Given**. From a structural point of view, it can be said that all information units have an obligatory *new element* and an optional *given element*. The latter is concerned with information which is presented by the speaker as 'recoverable' (either from the linguistic co-text, from what has been said before, or from the situational or cultural context). The former (the new element) concerns whatever information the speaker presents as not recoverable by the hearer.

We say that the Given is optional from the structural point of view because, by its own nature, this element is referential or 'phoric' (i.e. it refers to something already present in the verbal or non-verbal context), and reference is often achieved through *ellipsis*. Ellipsis is a grammatical form in which certain features are not realized in the structure.

The Given typically precedes the New, and the New is always marked by tonic prominence. The element which has this prominence is said to be carrying *information focus*. Consider this example, in which the syllable in capitals represents the intonation nucleus of the tone unit:

A: Where have you guys been?
　　　B: Well, I've been to the **GRO**cery store, and Tim to the **LI**brary.
　　　　　GIVEN　　　　　　　**NEW**　　　　　　　**GIVEN**　　　**NEW**

In A's utterance, *you guys* is a deictic expression that refers to B (*I*) and to Tim, so by the time of B's reply, *I* and *Tim* are a Given, and the New elements are found towards the end of each coordinate clause.

As noted above, on many occasions the Given is ellipted, and therefore the clause structure consists only of the New element, as in the following example:

　　　A: What are you writing?
　　　B: (I am writing)　　　An essay for my English class.
　　　　(Ellipted Given)　　　NEW

Here the first part of B's response has been ellipted, since it would involve a repetition of part of A's clause, and therefore would be redundant and unnecessary. Thus, the whole of B's response can be said to be New.

8.1.1.2.1. Marked and Unmarked Focus

Regarding the information focus in normal, unemphatic discourse, the unmarked distribution starts with the Given and progresses towards the New. Downing & Locke (2006: 241) explain that this is often called the principle of **end-focus**. The focus normally marks where the New element ends (because it typically falls on the last lexical item in the clause) but it is not always clear where it begins, or where the boundary between Given and New would be. The distinction of such a boundary is highly dependent on other elements of the text or context, which are not always available to the analyst. If, for example, we take an utterance out of context, we will be able to tell that it culminates with the New, but will not be able to tell whether there is a Given element first. Suppose you overhear the following statement:

All the people were running for their LIVES.
← NEW →

Here we know that *their lives* is New, because the prominence falls on that element, but we would not be able to tell whether the New extends also to *were running* and *all the people*. The whole statement would be New if it were the answer to the following question: *What happened immediately after the 9/11 attacks in New York?* However, if the questions changed as shown in Table 1, the New (in bold type) would also vary:

Table 1

What were all the people doing immediately after the 9/11 attacks in New York?	(All the people) **were running for their lives.**
What were all the people running for immediately after the 9/11 attacks in New York?	(All the people were running for) **their lives.**
Who were running for their lives immediately...	**All the people** (were running for their lives...).
Where were all the people running for their lives?	(All the people were running for their lives...) **in New York.**
When were all the people running for their lives in New York?	(All the people were running for their lives...) **immediately after the 9/11 attacks.**

The principle of end-focus allows us to say that the **unmarked** option for the focus is to fall on the last lexical item of the clause. The focus will be **marked**, therefore, when it does not fall on the last lexical item. The third example in Table 1 (*All the people*) illustrates an instance of marked focus, placed at the beginning of the clause. A focus is marked when the speaker wants to contrast or correct something which has been said or implied in the previous discourse or in the situational context. It can also be marked for emotive purposes. Consider example 1, which has an **unmarked focus**, in contrast with examples 2, 3 and 4, which contain **marked foci** for contrastive purposes:

1.   Sarah took her car to the ga**RAGE**. (unmarked focus)
2.   Sarah took her **CAR** to the garage. (not her motorbike)

3. Sarah **TOOK** her car to the garage. (not "brought it from there")
4. **SA**rah took her car to the garage. (not Susan)

Table 2 displays examples of foci marked for emotive purposes.

Table 2

UNMARKED FOCUS	MARKED FOCUS
It sounds **ODD.**	It **DOES** sound odd.
She is **SHY.**	She **IS** shy.
You will see me in the **FU**ture.	You **WILL** see me in the future.

8.1.1.2.1.1. But how do we identify the focus?

It was explained in 8.1.1.2. that speakers divide their messages into segments of information, namely, *information units*. These are features of the spoken language, for they are not realized by any given grammatical unit but by a phonological unit called **tone unit**. Tone units always contain one syllable which is more prominent. This syllable contains the **intonation nucleus** of the unit and constitutes the **focus** of information. Prominence can be given by means of pitch movement, increased duration and tonic stress. **Pitch movement** corresponds to the different **tones** of intonation, which may be falling, rising or level.

The information focus represents the *peak* or *highest point* of the unit, and its correct placement is of utmost importance in English, due to the fact that it constitutes the main strategy used by speakers for communicating contrast and emphasis in the spoken language.

It must be emphasized that there is not a one-to-one correspondence between the tone unit and any grammatical unit. Downing & Locke (2006) pinpoint the fact that speakers may lengthen or shorten their tone units according to their communicative needs, and that variations in the length of tone units also depend on other factors, such as speed of utterance, the syntactic structures and/or the lexical items chosen, familiarity with the content of the message and the consequent relative need to plan ahead, acoustic conditions, self-confidence, etc.

Considering all these factors, it is not surprising that the identification of the information focus is not always as easy and clear-cut a task as one would wish it to be. Several authors have pointed this out, and have therefore proposed new alternatives to the analysis of the phenomenon of information structure (see 8.3.).

8.1.1.2.1.2. Cleft Constructions: it-cleft and wh-cleft

Speakers often re-organize the content of a single clause into two related parts or units in order to place the focus on a new element that always follows a form of the verb *be*. This is called **clefting**, and it can be done by using two different constructions: the *it-cleft* and the *wh-cleft*. Thus, a simple clause like "I want a hamburger" may be re-organized as:

a) It's a HAMBURGER (that) I want.   (It-cleft)
    New   **Given**

b) What I want is a HAMBURGER.   (Wh-cleft)
   Given   **New**

The focus of both clefts in a) and b) is *hamburger*, which is thus marked with tonic stress. In a) the focus is near the front of the first unit; in b) it is at the end of the second unit. The verb *want* contains Given or presupposed information and for this reason it has a lesser stress.

The main discourse function of cleft constructions is to mark contrastive focus, but they may also be used to highlight expressions of time or place (e.g. *It was in December that I met her*), to signal the beginning of an episode in discourse (e.g. *It is with pleasure that I introduce you to Dr. Stephens tonight*), to signal a shift to a new episode (e.g. *It was only after some years that I realized I had to change*); or to suggest exclusiveness (e.g. *What I want is care and attention* = (Care and attention is the only thing I want = I don't want money or anything else))

8.2. Information Structure and Thematic Structure: Given + New, and Theme + Rheme

Information and thematic structures are closely related from the semantic point of view. Under normal conditions, the speaker/writer will choose the Theme from within what is Given and will locate the New within the Rheme. However, neither Given and Theme nor New and Rheme are the same. As Halliday puts it, "The Theme is what I, the speaker, choose to take as my point of departure. The Given is what you, the listener, already know about or have accessible to you. Theme + Rheme is speaker-oriented, while Given + New is listener-oriented" (1985: 278). Thus, the speaker can use thematic and information structure to produce a wide variety of **rhetorical effects**; s/he can play with the two systems by using different strategies which will bring about different results in the interpretation of the message on the part of the hearer. Example 1 shows a prototypical case, where the Given information is found within the Theme and the New within the Rheme. Example 2, on the contrary, shows an example in which B plays with the two systems in order to produce a contrastive effect, and in some way contradict or correct his/her interlocutor's statement.

1)   A: What does Mary think of John?
    B: She   HATES him.
       Theme   **Rheme**
       Given   **New**

2)   A: Bill likes tennis
    B: GOLF   is what he really likes.
       Theme **Rheme**
       New   **Given**

In these examples it is clear that the New has not been mentioned before and therefore did not appear in the previous structure of discourse. However, it is important to note that it is not the structure of discourse which determines whether information is treated as New or Given. On the contrary, the factor determining this choice is the speaker's moment-to-moment assessment of the relationship between what he wants to say and his/her hearer's informational requirements. For instance, and as Brown & Yule state, "it is not the case that if a speaker has just mentioned a referent he must necessarily repeat it low in pitch, treating it as a given" (1983: 168). Consider example 3:

3) (A mother is upset when she sees her youngest son bothering her older son and eventually fighting with him.)

Mother: Please, don't fight with your BROther any more. Your BROther,
       Theme   **Rheme**   **Theme**
       Given   **New**   **New**

sweetheart, is one of the most important people in your life.
       Rheme
       Given

Your BROther, will always love and protect you, even after dad and I die.
Theme   **Rheme**
New   **Given**

This example shows how, if the speaker so judges it, she can treat information that has already been mentioned in the discourse as New by giving it phonological prominence. In this case, the mother wants to stress the fact that it is Tommy's older brother (and nobody else) who will always care for and love him, especially when she and their father eventually die. Thus she gives the highest prominence to the word *brother* in all the clauses of her discourse in order to signal, in each case, a new aspect of the importance of brotherhood as it affects Tommy. Even when the information in the Rheme portion of her clauses might be considered partially new, it is more important for the mother to single out Tommy's brother as a key person in his life, and therefore treat him as the New information in each case.

8.3. Some Considerations Related to Halliday's Information Structure Analysis

Brown & Yule (1983) note that Halliday makes the simplifying assumption that the sole function of pitch prominence is to mark the focus of new information within the tone group. Indeed, if we examine pitch prominence carefully, we shall see that it may have several other discourse/pragmatic functions, such as marking the beginning of a speaker's turn or the beginning of a new topic. Brown & Yule very graphically explain that phonological prominence has "a general *watch this!* function" (1983: 164), that is, it is used by speakers to mark any kind of information that requires being paid attention to, but by no means does it only and exclusively mark the information focus.

In addition, some scholars have found that it is very difficult to find such perfect tone groups as the ones Halliday describes (constituted around a tonic syllable). It is, on the contrary, common to find tightly rhythmically bound structures with several peaks of prominence. Experiments such as those made by Brown, Currie & Kenworthy (1980) have shown that the phonetic cues which were traditionally thought to mark the tonic syllable rarely cumulate on one word in spontaneous speech. Contrariwise, they tend to be distributed separately or paired over words which introduce new information. Therefore, many scholars who do research on conversational speech do not believe that the information unit should contain only one focus and that it should then be realized with only one tonic.

Furthermore, some authors such as Ward & Birner (2001) have noted that the term *focus* means different things to different people, and that a two-way division of information into Given and New is inadequate. Prince (1992), for instance, classifies information by means of a pair of cross-cutting dichotomies: on the one hand information may be *discourse-old* or *discourse-new*, and, on the other hand, it can be either *hearer-old* or *hearer-new*. Such a distinction sheds light on the fact that what is new to the discourse need not be new to the hearer. Consider this example:

Yesterday the sun was shining, so I invited a neighbor to go to the pool.

Here, *the sun* represents information that is discourse-new but hearer-old, while *a neighbor* refers to information that is both discourse-new and hearer-new.

In very general terms, however, Halliday's approach is accepted by most information structure analysts: it can be said that the information that is felt or judged to be New is going to be prominent, while the Given information will be produced without prominence. However, it seems reasonable to suggest that information structure is not only realized by the phonological system, but also by the syntactic system (e.g. by word order and thematic organization) and the textual system (e.g. the organization of the different paragraphs in a given text).

All in all, the analysis of discourse is not an easy task, and the approach studied in this chapter, as well as all other approaches, is but one more attempt to describe and understand the different ways human beings organize their linguistic messages. No approach is perfect or all-embracing, but each and all of them contribute with different and useful tools for linguistic analysis. It is up to analysts to choose a given approach or certain elements from different approaches in order to best suit the needs of their research.

8.4. Sample analysis of data

8.4.1. Thematic structure

From the information given in 8.1.1.1., we can infer that the analysis of the thematic structure of a text helps us draw conclusions as to the way the writer or speaker has organized the information s/he wants to convey. Likewise, thematic analysis can help us identify the topic area as well as the discourse type of the text in question. It can be used to establish the relative coherence of a text and to show how paragraphs can be arranged across sentence boundaries by means of patterns of theme and rheme development. Consider the thematic structure of the following letter in a financial advice column of a very well-known American magazine:

> *After 12 years of marriage*, I have just begun divorce proceedings. *We* have three children ranging from 1 to 10, and *I*'ve been a stay-at-home mom for the entire marriage. *My physician husband* has a substantial income, and *our expenses* are high because of our large mortgage. *I* know that we will have to sell our beautiful house. *My attorney* says that, taking into account child support and alimony, I should be able to stay home until the baby is in kindergarten or first grade. *My question* is this: *How*, after never having taken care of myself, do I plan for my future? *I* don't want to end up as my mom did after my father died –living on a $500 Social Security check.
> (*The O Magazine*, January 2005, p. 30)

Several interesting conclusions can be made from the thematic analysis of this letter. Firstly, if it were presented in isolation (without a title, introduction or context), by merely looking at the themes (which are in italics), the reader/analyst could easily identify this text as coming from an advice column, and thus its genre or type of discourse could be pinpointed. In the very first clause of this letter we see an instance of *thematization*, where a circumstancial adjunct of time (*After 12 years of marriage*) is fronted, probably in order to give the proper frame to the situation the writer is going to present: having been married for 12 years, this woman is now divorcing and needs advice as to what to do with her house and finances, because throughout those twelve years she was financially protected by her husband and thus did not develop skills to protect herself in that respect.

The first themes (*After 12 years of marriage, We, My physician husband, our expenses, My attorney*) clearly show that the writer is talking about herself, narrating some aspect of her personal experience. The last themes (*My question, How, I*) point to the fact that she is asking a question which is centered on her particular problem (described at the beginning of the letter), and consequently needs some advice. Secondly, if we look at the themes of this text, we will observe that most of them are related to the writer or to some aspect of her life, which gives this letter the characteristics of a narrative of personal experience. In this type of narratives there is often a tendency to thematize the teller or narrator. Thirdly and consequently, we may say that most of the themes in this letter have an interactional nature. McCarthy & Carter explain that "a theme is interactional if it contains words or phrases which specifically refer to the sender or receiver(s)" (1994: 71). The fact that most of the themes are interactional also tells us something about the features of this text: we can infer that the writer's intention is to interact with someone who will read the letter and somehow try to help her. The way in which the interactant is going to help can be inferred from the last themes, which show that the writer is asking for some type of advice. The two types of theme found in this letter lead us to reach the conclusion that we are facing a case of 'mixed register' (Fairclough, 1989), i.e., it contains the characteristics of a narrative of personal experience but at the same time it communicates with the recipient of the letter on a different plane, asking for advice, which also makes it a multifunctional and multivalent discourse.

8.4.2. Information Structure

The following fragment has been taken from Nafá (2005) and is an accurate phonological transcription of a part of a lecture given at the European Parliament. We shall examine how the speaker treats the New and Given information by assigning prominence to certain words and not to others. The bold type indicates the focus in each information unit.

> DO4 // [p] ´how ´**important** // [p] is the ´New Delhi ´Conference? // [p] Now, // [o] the ´Commissioner is ´writing ´down: // **[hk]** [p] "´**very** // [r] ´**important**". // [p] But of ´course, // [p+] the ´answer // [p] to the ´question // [r] I ´then asked: // [p] if it is ´**very** important, // [r] ´why is she ´here? // (2005: 395).

As can be observed, the speaker wants to give rhetorical importance to the adjectival phrase *very important*, and therefore, in all cases, the focus is placed either on the word *important* or on the word *very*. In the first clause (*How important is the New Delhi Conference?*) we may clearly speak of a *marked focus* because it is placed at the beginning and not at the end: the word *important* is stressed and treated as New, while *the New Delhi Conference* is treated as Given information. In the successive clauses, *very important* and then *very* are treated as New, even when both words were mentioned before, due to the fact that the speaker uses her rhetorical skills in order to give a final ironic effect. She uses a final rhetorical question in relation to the Commissioner's comment on the New Delhi's Conference being 'very important', thus signalling the Commissioner's inconsistency in being present at the parliamentary discussion instead of at the 'very important' Delhi Conference. The analysis of this example sheds light on the fact that speakers may play with information structure (i.e. the organization of the Given and the New in discourse) in order to produce certain effects, such as irony or indirect criticism.

SUMMING UP... (CHAPTER 8)

1. Functionalism relies, contrary to Formalism, on a **pragmatic view of language as social interaction**, and therefore the approach focuses on the rules which govern verbal interaction. Both the **extra-linguistic context** and the **purpose of communication** play a crucial role in this approach.

2. The origins of Functionalism can be traced back to the Linguistic School of Prague.

3. Danes (1974) developed the concept of *Communicative Dynamism* (the relative extent to which a linguistic element contributes towards the further development of the communication) and Firbas (1964, 1986) developed the theory of *Functional Sentence Perspective*, which studies the distribution of information, organized in more or less dynamic elements called **Theme** and **Rheme**.

4. The *Theme* of a clause is what speakers/writers use as the 'point of departure'. The rest of the message constitutes the *Rheme*.

5. Considering the three macro-functions of language, there are two main types of themes: **experiential** and **non-experiential**. Experiential themes contain an ideational element and they represent our experience of the world (experiential macro-function). Non-experiential themes contain textual and/or interpersonal elements (textual and interpersonal macro-functions).

6. When non-experiential themes co-occur with the obligatory topical/experiential theme, we speak of **multiple themes**.

7. Depending on the purposes of communication, certain types of information may be foregrounded or **thematized**. When the theme does not coincide with the expected first constituent of each mood structure, we speak of a **marked theme**. If, on the contrary, the theme coincides with such a constituent, it is an **unmarked theme**.

8. Spoken discourse takes the form of a sequence of **information units**. The information unit is a structure made up of two functions: the **New** and the **Given**.

9. The New is always marked by **tonic prominence**. The element which has this prominence is said to be carrying **information focus**. The **focus** is **unmarked** when it falls on the last lexical item of the clause. The focus is **marked**, therefore, when it does not fall on the last lexical item.

10. **Information structure** is closely related to **thematic structure** from the semantic point of view. A speaker can play with the organization of the thematic and the information structures in order to produce a wide variety of rhetorical effects, bringing about different results in the interpretation of the message on the part of the hearer.

11. Some scholars have found that it is very difficult to find such perfect tone groups as the ones Halliday describes (constituted around a tonic syllable). Furthermore, some authors, such as Ward & Birner (2001) have noted that the term *focus* means different things to different people, and that a two-way division of information into Given and New is inadequate. However, and in very general terms, Halliday's approach is accepted by most information structure analysts: it can be said that the information that is felt or judged to be new is going to be prominent, while the given information will be produced without prominence.

SELF EVALUATION QUESTIONS

Choose the answer that best suits the information given in Chapter 8.

1) Functionalism relies on…
a) a formal view of language.
b) a pragmatic view of language.
c) an anthropological view of language.

2) Communicative dynamism has to do with the extent to which a linguistic element contributes towards …
a) the development of communication.
b) the grammaticality of the clause.
c) the accuracy and truth of a proposition.

3) A tenet within Functional Sentence Perspective is that…
a) themes and rhemes are always marked options.
b) the rheme carries the lowest degree of communicative dynamism.
c) the relative order of constituents in a clause serves different functions in discourse.

4) What is the type of theme in this clause?

   Honestly, *I don't understand what you say.*

        a)   Experiential.
        b)   Non-experiential.
        c)   Detached.

5) Choose the appropriate combination of themes corresponding to the following clause containing multiple themes:

   O.K., then I *will do what you want.*
   1 + 2 + 3

    a)   Non-experiential (Textual) + experiential (object) + Non-experiential (interpersonal).
    b)   Non-experiential (interpersonal) + Non-experiential (Textual) + experiential (subject).
    c)   Experiential (subject complement) + Non-experiential (interpersonal) + Experiential (object).

6) What sub-type of detached theme is *your sister* in the following clause?

Does she like music, **your sister**?

a) Left dislocation.
b) Absolute theme.
c) Right dislocation.

7) The *theme*, *subject* and *topic* of a clause...
a) always coincide in the same wording.
b) do not necessarily have to coincide.
c) never coincide.

8) The themes in i, ii, and iii are, respectively...
a) marked, marked, unmarked.
b) unmarked, marked, unmarked.
c) unmarked, unmarked, marked.

i) What I want is to know your secret.
ii) Under no circumstances will I tell you my secret.
iii) Can you tell me your secret?

9) The information unit is made up of...
a) four elements: theme, rheme, given and new.
b) two elements: theme and given.
c) two elements: given and new.

10) The *Given* is optional from the structural point of view because...
a) the speaker knows what s/he is talking about.
b) it is marked by tonic prominence.
c) it is referential or phoric.

11) The focus of a clause...
a) is always at the end.
b) always coincides with the rheme.
c) does not necessarily coincide with any of its grammatical units.

12) The foci (marked in capitals) in i, ii and iii are, respectively:
a) marked, marked, unmarked.
b) unmarked, unmarked, marked.
c) marked, unmarked, marked.

     i)   I DO like your new car. It's beautiful.
     ii)   I like your NEW car, not the old one.
     iii)   She came here to ask for a FAvor.

13) In the clause:

She wants to BORROW your car, not just see it.

a) both Theme and New coincide in the word *borrow*.
b) the Theme does not coincide with the New element.
c) the Rheme coincides with the Given element.

14) Pitch prominence...
a) fulfills the sole function of marking the focus of new information within the tone group.
b) fulfills several discourse/pragmatic functions.
c) fulfills the sole function of marking a speaker's turn.

15) Information structure...
a) is only realized by the phonological system.
b) is realized by the syntactic and semantic systems.
c) is realized by the phonological, syntactic and textual systems.

PRACTICE

A) *ANALYSIS:* IDENTIFY the themes in each of the following examples and say whether they are marked or unmarked. If marked, specify which clause constituent has been thematized in each case:

a) Out she came in a rush.
b) Susan called to say good-bye.
c) Are you for or against McCain?
d) Never say never again.
e) Right you are!

B) *ANALYSIS*: IDENTIFY the type of theme: Experiential/non-experiential/detached?

a)   Hey dude, give me my pen-drive.
b)   I love him. However, I don't want to talk to him.
c)   She will never forgive you.
d)   That kid, is he your child?
e)   The Rolling Stones. There will be a concert tomorrow night.

C) *ANALYSIS*: The following is a fragment of a Joint Debate on Pharmaceutical Products at the European Parliament, which is part of the anotated corpus found in Nafá's (2005) study. ANALYZE the thematic structure of the fragment, as well as its organization structure (Given-New) and explain how both structures (Theme-Rheme & Given-New) are used to cause certain rhetorical effects. Pay attention to tonic prominence (see notation conventions below) in the text.

1	/// [HK] [p+] President, ′I have ′admiration // [p] for the
2	′accomplishment // [p+] of ′scientific research // [p] in developing
3	′medicines // [p] which have ′proved // [r] of ′great ′benefit. // [hk]
4	[p+] Yet ′also, // [r] I have a ′healthy ′scepticism // [r] ′both of our
5	′pharmaceutical industry // [o] and ′our... // [p] of our
6	′exaggerated ′confidence // [p] in ′some of its ′products, // [o]
7	′many of which ′cause // [hk] [r] a ′great deal more ′harm // [r] than
8	the ′illegal // [hk] [r] ′recreational drugs // [lk] [p] which ′attract //
9	[p] the ′bulk of ′public ′attention. // [p+] And for ′that reason, //
10	[hk] [p] it would be ′wrong // [p] to place ′more ′unnecessary
11	burdens // [r] and ′regulations // ′[o] upon // ′[p] food ′supplements
12	// [p] and the ′health-′food shops // [lk] [r] that ′sell them. // ′[o]
13	Many ′believe // [p] these ′products // [r] to be ′beneficial, // [r] and
14	at ′least // [p] they ′don′t cause ′harm. // [p] I ′regard ′homeopathic
	′medicines // [p] in the ′same ′way. [LT] ///
15	
16	/// [HK] ′[r+] Today // [p] we have ′more ′patients // [o] who ′are //
17	′[r] better ′informed // [r] than ′ever ′before // [lk] [p] –and ′that′s a
18	′good thing. // [p] I ′want people // [r+] to have ′access to // [r]
19	′objective ′information // [p] about ′medicines // [p] and ′YAB18
20	about ′treatment. // [p] But ′that′s quite ′different // [p] from
21	′opening the ′door // [p] to the ′direct ′advertising // [lk] [p] of
22	′medicines. // [p] The ′result, // [r+] I ′fear, // [r] will ′not be better
23	public ′information, // [r] but ′greater public ′confusion, // [o]
	′stimulated // [r] by the ′marketing techniques // [p] of a ′used-′car
	salesman. [LT] ///

Notation conventions:

[**HK**] Initial High pitch pitch

[**MK**] Initial Medium pitch

[**LK**] Initial Low pitch

[**HT**] Final High pitch

[**MT**] Final Medium pitch

[**LT**] Final Low pitch

[**hk**] Internal High pitch

[**lk**]   Internal Low

[**p**] Falling tone

[**r**]   Falling-rising tone

[**p+**]   Rising-falling tone

[**r+**] Rising tone

[**o**] Level tone.

D) *DATA COLLECTION AND ANALYSIS*: LOOK FOR an article in any newspaper in English (or search the web for newspaper sites), CHOOSE a fragment of the article (no less than three paragraphs) and ANALYZE the thematic structure of the text.

E) *DATA COLLECTION AND ANALYSIS*: RECORD (directly from a lecture, a television or radio program, etc.) a fragment of oral discourse. ANNOTATE the fragment in order to mark information units and tonic prominence and ANALYZE its information structure (Given and New information). How does it intertwine with its thematic structure?

FURTHER READING

- Chafe, 1994 (Chapter 14).
- Downing, 1991, 1996, 1992, 2006.
- Downing & Locke (2006).
- Firbas, 1992.
- Halliday, 1985.
- Ward & Birner, 2001.

USEFUL WEBSITES

Functionalism: http://papyr.com/hypertextbooks/engl_126/style1.htm

Theme/Rheme // Given/New:
http://courses.nus.edu.sg/course/ellibst/lsl15.html
http://www.wordiq.com/definition/Theme_and_rheme
http://ling.kgw.tu-berlin.de/discourse&grammar/Text/d131.htm

On-line exercises on Theme and Rheme:
http://www.tki.org.nz/r/esol/esolonline/secondary_esol/classroom/ncea/fat
_tax/task12_e.php

POST-STRUCTURALIST THEORY
AND
SOCIAL THEORY

"Linguistic exchange – a relation of communication between a sender and a receiver, based on enciphering and deciphering, and therefore on the implementation of a code or a generative competence – is also an economic exchange which is established within a particular symbolic relation of power between a producer, endowed with a certain linguistic capital, and a consumer (or a market), and which is capable of procuring a certain material or symbolic profit. In other words, utterances are not only (save in exceptional circumstances) signs to be understood and deciphered; they are also signs of wealth, intended to be evaluated and appreciated, and signs of authority, intended to be believed and obeyed."

Pierre Bourdieu, *Language and Symbolic Power.*

Chapter Outline:

- Main ideas and concepts of Post-structuralist Theory and Social Theory.

- Most important contributions made by these theories to DA.

- Post-structuralist Theory and Social Theory as a basis for Critical Discourse Analysis (Chapter 10) and Mediated Discourse Analysis (Chapter 11).

9.1. Post-structuralism

A number of structural theories regarding human existence which were in vogue around the mid-20th century intended to explain and describe different aspects of human knowledge. These theories, belonging to the so-called **structuralist movement**, were based in France and synthesized the ideas of Marx, Freud and de Saussure. Marxists argued that the truth of human existence could be understood by an analysis of economic structures. Within the field of psychology, psychoanalysts (following Freud) tried to describe the structure of the psyche in terms of the unconscious. As far as the study of language was concerned, the structural linguistics of Ferdinand de Saussure suggested that meaning was not to be found in the analysis of individual words but rather within the structure of a whole language.

Post-structuralism, as the term suggests, was subsequent to Structuralism, and even though it shared some ideas with it, the former originated as a reaction against the "absolutism" and totalizing concepts of Structuralism. Thus the practices of Post-structuralism are grounded on the following basic assumptions:

- the concept of "self" as a singular and coherent entity is a fictional construct, because each individual comprises conflicting tensions and knowledge claims (e.g. gender, race, class, profession). Consequently, in order to study a text or discourse, a reader/hearer must understand how this discourse is related to the writer's/speaker's own personal concept of self. Thus the perception of the self plays a critical role in one's interpretation of meaning.
- The idea of a text having a single purpose or a single meaning is rejected. It is believed that every individual reader/hearer creates a new and individual purpose, meaning, and existence for a given text. Therefore the author's intended meaning is secondary to the meaning that the reader perceives. This displacement is often referred to as the "destabilizing" or "decentering" of the author.
- Thus, it is crucial to analyze the way in which the meanings of a text shift in relation to the variables related to the reader's identity. A variety of perspectives have to be utilized in the analysis of texts so as to create a multifaceted interpretation of them, even if these interpretations turn out to be in conflict with one another. None of the possible interpretations is considered to be the right one. All of them contribute to a better understanding of the text in question.

The French philosopher and historian Michel Foucault, originally labelled a structuralist, came to be regarded as the most important representative of the post-structuralist movement. He had views in common with the structuralists, for he believed that language and society were shaped by rule-governed systems. However, he did not share all their tenets: he did not believe that there were definite underlying structures that could explain the human condition, nor did he think it possible to survey and study discourse from an objective point of view.

Post-structuralism conceives of the social space (organizations, institutions, identities and relationships, etc.) and the world of material objects as discursive in nature. Thus, although post-structuralist thinkers believe that *there is nothing outside the text*, this does not entail a denial of the material world. Laclau & Mouffe clarify this aspect in the following excerpt:

The fact that every object is constituted as an object of discourse has nothing to do with whether there is a world external to thought, or with the realism/idealism opposition. An earthquake or the falling of a brick is an event that certainly exists, in the sense that it occurs here and now, independently of my will. But whether their specificity as objects is constructed in terms of 'natural phenomena' or 'expressions of the wrath of God' depends upon the structuring of a discursive field. What is denied is not that such objects exist externally to thought, but the rather different assertion that they could constitute themselves as objects outside any discursive conditions of emergence. (1985: 108)

As has been suggested, a basic tenet of the post-structuralist theory of discourse is that the process of meaning-making in relation to people and objects is never ultimately fixed; on the contrary, it is viewed as an unstable flux. This view challenges the 'closure' of the structuralist linguistic model, which reduces all elements to the internal moments of the system.

Thus we see that post-structuralism is against any kind of totalizing concept. There is an underlying relativism in all post-structuralist ideas, which suggests that no signifying system is completely stable and/or unproblematic. Post-structuralists see reality as much more fragmented, diverse and culture-specific than structuralists; consequently, they give greater attention to specific histories and to the local contextualizations of concrete instances. Besides, there is a greater emphasis on the body, which is seen as the actual insertion of the human-being into the texture of time and history. Greater attention is also given to the specifics of cultural working, the arenas of discourse and cultural practice, and to the role of language and textuality in our construction of reality and identity.

In sum, there is a deep sense that we live in a **linguistic universe,** which implies the rejection of the phenomenalist assumption that language is a transparent medium. 'Reality' in a linguistic universe is only **mediated reality,** which is governed by things such as the structure of ideology, the world of discourse, the various cultural codes, etc. We live in a world of language, discourse and ideology. None of these elements is transparent, and all of them structure our sense of being and meaning. All meaning is textual and intertextual. Meaning circulates in economies of discourse, for every text exists only in relation to other texts.

It seems appropriate herein to quote Slembrouck's words on the achievements of post-structuralism:

One of the achievements of post-structuralism is the radical way in which it has placed discourse analysis at the heart of the social-scientific endeavour. Its consequences for disciplines as diverse as anthropology, history, law, social psychology, sociology, etc. have been enormous. For instance, a post-structuralist logic advocates the view that "historic facts" or "legal facts" are discursive constructions. As a consequence, scientific historic writing falls within the scope of, say, narrative analysis, while judicial decisions can be viewed as outcomes of discursive practices which are socio-historically contingent (in this respect, post–structuralism shares a number of characteristics with conversation analysis and ethnomethodology–despite obvious differences in the underlying assumptions). Needless to add, a "truth/rationality"-crisis has been one of the effects. (2004: 18)

The works of Michel Foucault (1973, 1980, 1984), Jacques Derrida (1967, 1981) and Jacques Lacan (1977) have been conventionally associated with post-structuralist theory. Roland Barthes' work *Elements of Semiology* (1967) is of great importance as well, because he advanced the concept of the *metalanguage* as a systematized way of talking about concepts like meaning and grammar beyond the constraints of a traditional (first-order) language. Barthes argues that *deconstruction*[1] itself is in danger of becoming a metalanguage, thus exposing all languages and discourse to scrutiny. Also, the work of M. Bakhtin (1986) became very influential throughout the post-structuralist movement (from the late 1960s onwards), although he cannot be considered a post-structuralist in the strict sense of the term, because his writings date from the first half of the 20th century (but were not published until the 1970s). Bakhtin's critique of Saussurean linguistics, based on his dialogic view of language use, is to be highlighted (see 9.5).

9.1.1. Major Weakness of Post-structuralist Discourse Theory

In spite of its achievements, it is undeniable that post-structuralist discourse theory has its weaknesses, the main one being its failure to

---

[1] Jacques Derrida (1930-2004) developed *deconstruction* as a technique for uncovering the multiple interpretations of texts. He suggests that every text contains ambiguity and therefore the possibility of a final and complete interpretation is impossible.

present an explicit method for the analysis of actual instances of text or social interaction-in-context. However, some authors, like Howarth (2000) or Carabine (2001) have attempted to apply some aspects of this theory to the analysis of real discourse in action. Howarth (2000) proposes a method based on an elaboration of Michel Foucault's *genealogical method*,[2] which focuses on the deconstruction of power/knowledge complexes (Derrida). Carabine (2001) presents a practical method of analysis (also based on Foucault's genealogical theory) consisting of eleven steps to be followed succesively. Carabine's guidelines to analysis are outlined in 9.3.1.

9.2. Social Theory

Social Theory is used as a generic term to describe an attempt to theorize the modern social world in any of its spheres (cultural, legal, political, etc.). It is a discipline considered to be outside the mainstream of Sociology (where the theory is "correctly" tested), for it does not follow the scientific method. Indeed, it is essential to the enterprise of "social theory" to challenge the hegemony of a scientific method. Sharing its core commitment to truth, the social theorist points to the radical difference in phenomena between the subject matter of Physics and that of Sociology. Thus the social theorist is suspicious of "objectivity".

Social Theory is different from Sociology in that the sociologist looks for neat, predetermined problems to which s/he can apply equally neat methodologies, while the social theorist places emphasis on the less objective and brute fact of human suffering. However, some social theorists, such as **Pierre Bourdieu** (see 9.4.), have shown that Social Theory can be very empirical, as long as there are true stories to be told and as long as we believe that listening can be a profoundly empirical act.

Social Theory has been affected by recent developments in feminism, critical race theory, multiculturalism and other movements associated with groups that are somehow perceived as oppressed.

As has been suggested, some social theorists and/or post-structuralist thinkers, such as Foucault or Bourdieu, have made important contributions to the study of language and discourse. We

---

[2] See 9.3.

now turn to them.

9.3. Michel Foucault

The popularization of the concept of *discourse* and of *discourse analysis* as a method can partly be attributed to Foucault's great influence upon the social sciences and humanities.

A philosopher, social theorist, historian and literary critic, Foucault is also included within the post-structural school of thought. His main interest is in the origins of the modern sciences (e.g. medicine, sexology or psychiatry), their affiliated institutions (the clinic, the asylum, etc.) and how the production of truth is governed by discursive power regimes (Slembrouck, 2006).

Foucault's important contribution to the theory of discourse is mainly found in such areas as the relationship of *discourse and power, the discursive construction of social subjects and knowledge,* and *the functioning of discourse in social change.*

Foucault's work is divided into three main stages, each showing a shift of emphasis with respect to the previous one: 1) Archeological work; 2) Genealogical studies; and 3) Ethics.

His early **archaelogical work** (1972) includes a **constitutive view of discourse**, a view that conceives discourse as actively constituting or constructing society on various dimensional planes. Thus, discourse constitutes social subjects and forms of self, social relationships and conceptual frameworks, as well as the objects of knowledge. Special emphasis is placed on the interdependency of the discourse practices of a society or institution. There is always influence of historically prior texts upon new texts, and any given type of discourse practice is created out of the combination of other types and is defined in terms of its relationship to others. Foucault's insistence on the fact that the subject has to conform to the conditions of the statement before s/he can become the speaker of it (a reversal of the subject-statement relationship) is particularly relevant to discourse analysis. This view, then, insists on the prevailance of discourse structures over human agency, and has the following implications (adapted from Slembrouck, 2006: 20):

- Meaning is governed by the formative rules of discourse; therefore it does not originate in the speaking subject. Speaking is, thus, "de-centered".
- Social identity is "dispersed". The "whole", "unique",

social subject is replaced by a "fragmented" subject that is constituted in the unstable role identities enabled by discursive formations.

- The acquisition of social identities is a process of immersion into discursive practice and submission to discursive practice. For instance, the process of becoming a teacher is a process in which a novice gradually adopts and subjects him/herself to the multiple modes of speaking and writing which are available in the teaching profession.[3]

All these implications are of major significance, for discourse is seen in an active relationship to reality. Language signifies reality in the sense that it constructs meanings for it; it does not merely refer to objects which are taken to be given in reality.

In the second stage of Foucault's work, the stage of his **genealogical studies**, discourse is put on a secondary plane. He now shifts his focus to truth/power regimes and how they affect the bodily disposition. Indeed, an interesting and primary concern of genealogical analysis is how the techniques of power work upon bodies, habits or movements. Foucault argues that the modern technology of discipline is geared toward producing "docile bodies", i.e., bodies which are adapted to the demands of modern forms of economic production:

> The body is the inscribed surface of events (traced by language and dissolved by ideas), the locus of a dissociated self (adopting the illusion of a substantial unity), and a volume in perpetual disintegration. Genealogy, as an analysis of descent, is thus situated within the articulation of the body and history. Its task is to expose a body totally imprinted by history and the processes of history's destruction of the body. (1984: 83)

Thus, Foucault analyzes two major 'technologies' of power: *discipline* and *confession*. Discipline is manifest in diverse forms, such as the architecture of schools, prisons or factories (designed to allocate a given space to each inmate), the division of the educational or working day into strictly demarcated parts, and so on. **Discipline** (whose main technique is *examination*) is a technology

---

[3] However, as Slembrouck (2006) and McNay (1994) point out, it is probably not correct to ascribe such a view on the socializing capacities of language use to Foucault himself.

for handling masses of people, which, according to Foucault, 'objectifies' the subject, thereby transforming the indivicual into a describable, analyzable object and producing the manipulation of records to arrive at generalizations about populations, averages, norms, etc. **Confession** is a ritual of discourse, and is, on the contrary, a technique that subjectifies people. The need to talk about oneself (e.g. one's sexuality) seems to be a liberating resistance to the objectifying bio-power. However, Foucault believes that this is an illusion, for confession draws the person more into the domain of power.

In his third stage, Foucault shifts his focus to the **ethics of the postmodern subject**, and he develops an ethical orientation for the postmodern era which is based on the idea that an analysis of the techniques of domination can be counterbalanced by an analysis of the techniques of the self (Slembrouck, 2004).

Foucault's ideas may seem very abstract at first sight, but they brought significant contributions to DA as a discipline. Let us summarize them in the following points:

- Foucault did not focus on language, but on **discourse as a system of representation**, i.e. the rules and practices that produce meaningful statements and regulated discourse in different historical periods.
- Discourse is a way of representing the knowledge about a particular topic at a particular historical moment.
- All practices have a discursive aspect. Discourse constitutes the social (objects and subjects), thereby its constitutive nature.
- Since we can only have a knowledge of things if they have a meaning, it is discourse, not the things in themselves, which produces knowledge.
- All discursive practices are defined in terms of their relations to others, and depend upon others in complex ways.
- The practices and techniques of modern 'biopower' (such as *examination* and *confession*) are discursive to a significant degree.
- Discourse has a political nature: the exertion of power occurs both in and over discourse.
- Social change is discursive in nature: changing discursive structures are a sign of social change.

9.3.1. Applying Foucauldian Theory to the Analysis of Actual Discourse: Guidelines and Example

In spite of all his theoretical findings, Foucault's analysis of discourse does not include discursive and linguistic analyses of real texts, a major weakness of his work that has been attempted to be resolved by other scholars, such as Carabine (2001). This author proposes the following steps to apply genealogy to the analysis of real texts, in order to explore and trace the power/knowledge networks which are evident in social policy:

Guide to doing Foucauldian genealogical discourse analysis:

1) *Select your topic* – Identify possible sources of data. If you were undertaking a social policy analysis, then sources might include policy documents, discussion papers, parliamentary papers, speeches, cartoons, photographs, parliamentary debates, newspapers, other media sources, political tracts, and pamphlets from local and national government, quangos, and political parties. You might also wish to include an analysis of counter-discourses and resistances; here you might use material from campaigning and lobbying groups, activists and welfare rights organizations, etc.
2) *Know your data* – read and re-read. Familiarity aids analysis and interpretation.
3) *Identify themes* – categories and objects of discourse.
4) Look for evidence of an *inter-relationship* between discourses.
5) Identify the discursive strategies and techniques that are employed.
6) Look for *absences* and *silences*.
7) Look for *resistances* and *counter-discourses*.
8) Identify the *effects* of the discourse.
9) *Context 1* – outline the background to the issue.
10) *Context 2* – contextualize the material in the power/ knowledge networks of the period.
11) Be aware of the *limitations* of the research, your data and sources. (2001: 281)

Carabine uses this guide to illustrate the steps she took when doing her research on the representations of sexuality in social policy material, for which she chose the *Commissioners' Reports of the Poor Laws*[4] as data. Some excerpts of this document are reproduced here, which show how the Commissioners refer to unmarried mothers:

[1]
... the female in the very many cases becomes the corruptor.
[2]
...continued illicit intercourse has, in almost all cases, originated with the females.
[3]
...the women, ...feel no disgrace, either in their own eyes, or in the eyes of others, at becoming mothers of bastards, have still less reluctance in allowing the claims of a husband to anticipate the marriage ceremony, in fact they are almost always with child when they come to the church.
[4]
I met with a striking instance, which proves that the female in these cases is generally the party most to blame; and that any remedy, to be effectual, must act chiefly with reference to her. (2001: 289-90)

It is obvious from these excerpts that the Commissioners' report showed a negative bias towards women. Here is a brief summary of Carabine's genealogical analysis (2001: 281-85) of the document:

Select your topic: Carabine explains that there is no single starting point for doing genealogical discourse analysis, and that she chose to begin her project about sexuality and social policy by visiting the local university and city libraries. There she read different parliamentary papers, reports and legal statutes until she finally selected the *Commissioners' Reports of the Poor Laws*. She focused on this document for a number of reasons, primarily because the 1834 Poor Law is considered to have had a considerable impact on the form of welfare provision provided in the U.K. over a hundred year span.

---

[4] The complete reference of the document is: *Reports of His Majesty's Commissioners on the Administration and Practical Operation of the Poor Laws and Assistant Comissioners' Reports 1834 with Appendices, Parts I, II & III Reports from the Assistant Commissioners (1834 (44) vol. xxvii-xxxviii).* The version used by Carabine was the 1971 British Parliamentary Papers Series (vols. 8-18), published by the Irish University Press.

Know your data: The next step for Carabine was to spend several months reading and examining a range of secondary and original sources on the *Poor Laws* and eighteenth and nineteenth century sexuality, gender relations, working class and family life, marriage, and other related topics. This step was necessary in order to get a 'sense' of what the documentation was about, as well as to establish where sexuality entered the discussion and to identify the objects of discourse.

Identify themes, categories and 'objects' of discourse: Here the author tells us that she found out that, in her data, sexuality was 'spoken of' in a number of ways, such as *fears about population growth, marriage, the need for celibacy, bastardy, unmarried mothers and female immorality*, among others. She subsequently decided to focus on the sections known as the *Bastardy Clauses* and proceded to analyze the ways in which bastardy was spoken of. Thus she identified different themes (e.g. morality, sexuality or class) categories (e.g. men, women or illegitimate children), representations in, and objects of, the discourse. An interesting finding developed from the fact that the Commissioners initially indicated that their concern was with the support of illegitimate children, the relief afforded to mothers, and the attempts to obtain payment from fathers. The Commissioners' concerns about these three topics were expressed through a discourse of bastardy, which focused mainly on unmarried mothers and their lack of sexual morality (neglecting the illegitimate child and absolving the father of any moral, sexual or financial liability or responsibility for his actions), thereby contradicting their initial claim of concern about the children and the relief of the mothers.

Absences and silences: As an example, Carabine notes that in the *Poor Laws* Commissioners were primarily concerned with increased levels of illegitimacy, while there were three important omissions: 1) the bastard child was rarely mentioned; 2) illegitimacy amongst the middle or upper classes was not discussed; 3) while female sexuality was discussed, male sexuality was neither explored nor judged. These are evident examples of significant absences or silences.

Inter-relationship between discourses: Categories and themes were interrelated in the *Poor Laws*. There was a process of cross-referencing. One key influence was Thomas Malthus' ideas about population.

Context: Carabine explains that in order to become familiar with the context for the document she was studying, she established the background to the policy or issue in question and analized the key influences, a process that was partly developed in the sections *Know your data* and *Identifying themes and categories*. For this reason, she points out as a final remark, that it is difficult to identify the different stages as though following a recipe, because in practice some processes occur simultaneously or at a different stage than expected, so we have to consider discourse analysis as a dynamic process of interpretation and reinterpretation.

We shall now turn our attention to Pierre Bourdieu, another social theorist whose findings, like Foucault's, have had a remarkable impact upon discourse studies.

9.4. Pierre Bourdieu

Pierre Bourdieu is considered to be an intellectual who challenged French social thinking. A philosopher, social theorist and teacher, he is the author of more than 25 influential books. From a language studies perspective, he is primarily associated with the following key concepts:

A) The metaphor of **symbolic capital**, which establishes an analogy between **financial capital** and **symbolic resources** (such as the access to discourse situations and the ability to mobilize sets of linguistic conventions), for he argues that they are both unequally divided over groups within a given population. Symbolic capital, like financial capital, is subject to laws of supply and demand. Certain groups in society possess more symbolic capital than others, and the more capital one possesses, the easier it becomes to invest it profitably.

B) The notion of **habitus**, which refers to individual differences in practical linguistic competence. Speakers are considered to be strategic players who have the ability to put language resources to practical use, as well as to anticipate the reception of their words. The formation of a habitus is permanently modified and sanctioned by the relative success or failure in the market of linguistic exchanges. The concept of *habitus* presupposes a **theory of linguistic practice** rather than a theory of the linguistic system, for Bourdieu is against any abstraction that is detached from social action. *Habitus* is a social construct that motivates and arranges social practices and whose evidence is shown through language use and forms within organizations, cultures and communities.

C) The notion of **bodily hexis**, which associates linguistic practices with deep-rooted bodily dispositions. Bourdieu explains that language is a body technique and that linguistic competence is "a dimension of bodily hexis in which one's whole relation to the social world, and one's whole socially informed relation to the world, are expressed" (1999: 510). Thus, for example, members of the upper-social classes will have a different bodily disposition[5] associated to their use of language than members of the lower classes.

Different bodily dispositions associated to the use of language
and the discourse situation

An interesting point made by Bourdieu is the following:

A speaker's linguistic strategies (tension or relaxation, vigilance or condescension, etc.) are oriented (except in rare cases) not so much by chances of being understood or misunderstood (communicative

---

[5] This bodily disposition has to do with the way of articulating the different sounds of the language, as well as to the way they move or the bodily postures they adopt.

efficiency or the chances of communicating), but rather by the chances of being listened to, believed, obeyed, even at the cost of misunderstanding (political efficiency or the chances of domination and profit). (1976: 654)

From Bourdieu's words we conclude that, in his view, communicative efficiency is subsidiary to political efficiency and the desire to dominate and gain profit, and thus *comprehension is not the primary goal of communication*. As can be inferred, this view is opposed to that of other linguists and/or philosophers, such as Grice[6], whose *Cooperative Principle* is based on the assumption that speakers' efforts are always geared towards achieving understanding.

Another important conclusion to be made from Bourdieu's theory is the idea that authority and credibility in a particular situation do not necessarily imply an impeccable use of a standard language. In other words, a good command of the standard language does not guarantee success in the market of symbolic exchanges. There are other 'ingredients' which, when mixed with an inclination towards standard use, characterize a successful habitus in influential social domains. The value of any given utterance depends highly on the ability and the capacity of speakers to impose their criteria, and this capacity can not be said to be determined only in linguistic terms: "the whole social structure is present in each interaction (and thereby in the discourse uttered)" (Bourdieu, 1999: 503).

We also infer from Bourdieu's proposals that linguistic capital is a field-specific form of capital which can be transformed into other forms. For example, a certain linguistic disposition will result in the acquisition of certain educational qualifications which will eventually give the subject access to a given prestigious job and to a valuable social position. Thus it can be said that the processes of control over the value of symbolic resources (which in turn regulate access to other social, cultural and economic assets) are very important from a sociolinguistic perspective.

To summarize and conclude, we may say that Bourdieu's sociological critique of linguistics entails a three-way displacement of concepts (1976: 646):

    1.   He replaces the concept of *grammaticalness* by

---

[6] See Chapter 3.

the notion of **acceptability** (or, it can also be said that *"the"* language (Saussure's *langue*) is replaced by the notion of **legitimate language**).

2. He speaks of **relations of symbolic power,** rather than of *relations of communication,* thereby replacing the question of the *meaning of speech* by the question of **value and power of speech.**

3. Instead of *linguistic competence,* he uses the term **symbolic capital,** which is inseparable from the **speaker's position in the social structure**.

Bourdieu's social critique and concepts have been widely used by discourse analysts, especially within the approach known as Critical Discourse Analysis, to which a whole chapter is devoted in this book. Hence, the reader is referred to Chapter 10 in order to study how these ideas have been put into practice in actual analysis.

9.5. Mikhail Bakhtin

Bakhtin was a theorist writing in the Soviet Union during the Stalinist era. Although his books on language, literature and psychoanalysis date from the 1920s and 1930s, Bakhtinian posits only became influencial and achieved recognition after the 1960s, when his works were published in the western world.

Although Bakhtin cannot exactly be considered a Marxist (he had problems with the regime and was exiled), he shares with Marxist theorists an interest in the historical and social world, in how human beings act and think, and in language as the means in which ideologies are articulated (Klages, 2001).

Bakhtin's view of language clearly opposes Saussurean structuralist linguistics. He argues that language should be studied not as an abstract system, but as a concrete lived reality, for language is "essentially social and rooted in the struggle and ambiguities of everyday life" (Maybin, 2001: 64).

Some of the basic ideas in Bakhtin's work are:

- Language is **dialogic,** which entails the consideration of the **utterance** as the basic unit of language, as well as the fact that there is always one other respondent voice implicit in any utterance. In his conception, utterances can never be isolated from the sequence in which they occur and they always hold a dialogic relationship with previous utterances which have been voiced or which are presupposed. A dialogic view of language opposes the Saussurean idea that language is an autonomous system describable in terms of relationships between internal signs, and it gives priority to texts which are 'impure' (i.e. texts which contain traces of various voices that have been involved in their production, be they clearly reported voices or voices that are taken on as if they were the author's own).

- Discursive practice is essentially **heteroglossic**, which requires that language is normally patterned into **speech genres**[7] (which are associated with particular kinds of contextual features and social purposes) and that two or more genres normally co-exist in a given discourse practice. "**Heteroglossia** might be defined as the collection of all the forms of social speech, or rhetorical modes, that people use in the course of their daily lives" (Klages, 2001: 3). Texts often contain the various voices that have been involved in their production (reported voices or voices that are taken on as if they were the author's own). But not all texts have the same level of heteroglossia; some are more heteroglossic than others (Maybin 2001). For example, a film text normally includes the voice of the screenplay writer, the director and all the people involved in its realization and production, while a kitchen recipe may only contain the voice of its creator (although, again, it depends on the historic and contextual conditions of the particular discourse practice in question).
- There is an internal struggle in language which is conceptualized in terms of a conflict between **centripetal** and **centrifugal forces**. *Centripetal forces* are associated with political centralization and a unified cultural canon. They produce authoritative and inflexive discourses such as those of scientific truth, religious dogma, fathers, teachers, etc. *Centrifugal forces*, on the other hand, allude

---

[7] Bakhtin defines speech genres in the following way: "Each separate utterance is individual, of course, but each sphere in which language is used develops its own *relatively stable types* of these utterances. These we may call *speech genres*" (1986: 60).

to the stratification and diversification of language into varieties associated with different genres, professions, age groups and so on. These forces are more associated with everyday informal conversations and people's inner dialogue or reflections upon their own experience than centripetal forces.

- The essentially dialogic and heteroglossic nature of language ensures that our views and understanding of the world, as well as our relations with others and our sense of our own identity, are always evaluative and **ideological** (Bakhtin, 1981).

- **Genres** are viewed as the drive belts between the history of language and the history of society (Fairclough, 1992b), and thus **any shift or transformation in genre conventions contributes to, and therefore indicates, social change**. Therefore, social changes are first perceived at genre level, and languages change through the transformations of genre conventions.

The theoretical ideas expressed by Bakhtin in his writings have exerted a considerable influence upon literary analysis, as well as upon some European forms of discourse analysis and the Northern American approaches covered under the term "linguistic anthropology"[8]. Many authors have applied the concept of heteroglossia in their linguistic analysis of texts (e.g. Fairclough, 1992b; Keith Sawyer, 1995; Baynham & Slembrouck, 1999; Iedema et al, 2004), an analysis which has proved useful to explain why people appeal to other voices and what functions are fulfilled by the different voices in a text. We now turn to one of these studies, in order to illustrate how Bakhtin's theoretical findings can be used as tools for analyzing actual discourse.

9.5.1. A Sample of Heteroglossic Analysis

In order to illustrate how Bakhtinian analysis can be carried out, we shall borrow the following situation and analysis from Baynham & Slembrouck (1999). A social worker is interviewed by a senior

---

[8] Linguistic anthropology is a cover term for mainly Northern-American approaches which contextualize language use in socio-cultural terms (See Chapter 6).

colleague about a particular instance when a baby was diagnosed as being underweight for its age. The interview is part of a policy review in the domain of child care:

> [...] it turned out that there was a further four weeks before the child was taken to hospital for an appointment on being taken there erm (1) *the hospital felt that this was a clear picture of failure to thrive* (2) *the child was as I recall off the top of my head I think it was two and a half kilos underweight was very dehydrated* and in fact had the situation been left for longer the child would have died the child was admitted and what then happened was that the mother [...]   (1999: 439-40).

Baynham & Slembrouck explain that there are two strings (1 & 2) of speech representation in this fragment of discourse, which are rhetorically implicated in a structured display of evidence. String (1) gives the conclusion: *a clear picture of failure to thrive*, while string (2) presents the detailed observations which lead to this particular conclusion: *The child was (...) was two and a half kilos underweight (...)*. Thus, the reported speech counts as a rhetorical device which must help persuade the listener that the institutional intervention was appropriate, but at the same time it shifts the responsibility away from the social worker (speaker).

The diagnosis *a clear picture of a failure to thrive* is attributed to a voice of medicine, referred to collectively as *the hospital*, and by introducing the medical voice, an interprofessional working relationship (with a division of responsibilities in the domain of child care and corresponding institutional action) is evoked. Thus we have the voice of medical diagnosis versus that of the assessment of the social circumstances, which, within the context of the policy interview, help justify the statement referring to the child as being potentially at risk.

Also, it is interesting to note how the specific way in which the reported medical voice is projected contributes to its credibility, which is made clear in the second string of speech representation, where social work voice and medical voice become one (the worker attributes clear medical facts to his own memory: *As I recall off the top of my head...*).

Finally, Baynham & Slembrouck argue that, while grammatical/stylistic studies of reported speech tend to be mostly concerned with the classification of the speech representation strings as belonging to a particular category type (direct/indirect speech, etc.), such taxonomies may say very little about why people appeal to other voices or about the functions which such reporting fulfills in a particular context of use. In contrast, they observe that by doing heteroglossic analysis, we may learn that whenever one represents what someone else has said or written down, a network of social relationships comes into play. In this particular case, the relationship was between social work and medical work, as well as between the social worker/reporter and the interviewer/reportee.

9.6 Final Remarks on Post-structural and Social Theories

Post-structural and social theories have not been accepted by some linguists and discourse analysts (e.g. Schegloff[9]) as a model to follow on the grounds that these theories are politically-oriented and biased. However, it cannot be denied that they have had a considerable influence upon other and subsequent schools or approaches to discourse, such as *Critical Discourse Analysis, Positive Discourse Analysis* and *Mediated Discourse Analysis*. For this reason, in this book, **Post-structuralism** and **Social Theory** have been included prior to these other three approaches. In this way, the reader will more easily understand the reach of Post-structuralism and how its ideas have been used and developed by other researchers for the analysis and further understanding of the complex phenomenon of discourse. We will consider these last three approaches in the next two chapters (10 & 11).

---

[9] See key for practice exercise B in this chapter (at the back of the book), as well as 10.5. in Chapter 10.

SUMMING UP... (CHAPTER 9)

1. The structuralist movement, which was based in France, synthesized the ideas of Marx, Freud and Saussure. **Post-structuralism** shares some ideas with Structuralism, but it stands against its 'absolutism' and its totalizing concepts.

2. Post-structuralist thinkers view the social space and the world of material objects as discursive in nature, based on their belief that *there is nothing outside the text*. All meaning is textual and intertextual. Meaning circulates in economies of discourse, for every text exists only in relation to others.

3. Post-structuralists see reality as much more fragmented, diverse and culture-specific than structuralists; consequently, they give greater attention to specific histories and to the local contextualizations of concrete instances. Some post-structuralist thinkers and/or social theorists, such as **Foucault, Bourdieu** and **Bakhtin,** have made important contributions to the study of language and discourse.

4. Foucault's contribution to the theory of discourse is mainly found in such areas as the relationship of **discourse and power, the discursive construction of social subjects and knowledge**, and **the functioning of discourse in social change**.

5. Bourdieu is mostly associated with such key concepts as **symbolic capital** (an analogy between financial capital and symbolic resources), **habitus** (which refers to individual differences in practical linguistic competence and presupposes a theory of linguistic practice, rather than a theory of the linguistic system), and **bodily hexis** (which associates linguistic practices with deep-rooted bodily dispositions).

6. Bakhtin's view of language clearly opposes Saussurean structuralist linguistics, arguing that language should be studied not as an abstract system, but as a concrete lived reality. Bakhtin argues that language is **dialogic** and that discursive practice is essentially **heteroglossic**, which entails that language is normally patterned into **speech genres**.

SELF EVALUATION QUESTIONS

Choose the answer that best suits the information given in Chapter 9.

1) Post-structuralism originated as…
a) a reaction against Foucault's ideas.
b) a result of Marxism.
c) a reaction against the absolutism of Structuralism.

2) One of the main assumptions of Post-structuralism is that…
a) every text has a single purpose and meaning.
b) the meanings of a text vary according to the reader's identity.
c) there is only one possible interpretation of texts in general.

3) Michel Foucault thought that…
a) discourse could be studied from an objective point of view.
b) discourse could not be studied from an objective point of view.
c) the material world did not exist.

4) All post-structuralist thought…
a) has an underlying relativism.
b) views meaning-making as stable.
c) sees reality as a unified whole.

5) Post-structuralist thinkers…
a) view language as a transparent medium.
b) are phenomenalists.
c) believe that reality is mediated by ideology and cultural codes.

6) One of the effects of post-structuralism was…
a) a truth/rationality crisis.
b) a rejection of reality.
c) a negation of our sense of meaning.

7) One of Foucault's contributions to discourse theory is in the area
   of…
a) formal grammar.
b) discourse and power.
c) social dialects.

8) Foucault's archaeological work includes a view of discourse…
a) as a separate level in linguistic studies.
b) as independent from other practices.
c) as constituting social subjects and social relationships.

9) In Foucault's view…
a) speaking is considered central.
b) the subject is considered unique.
c) speaking is de-centered.

10) In his genealogical studies, Foucault focuses on…
a) truth/ power regimes.
b) spoken discourse.
c) written texts.

11) Pierre Bourdieu's metaphor of symbolic capital…
a) shows the similarities between the access to discourse situations and the access to financial capital.
b) makes an analogy between financial capital and cultural knowledge.
c) symbolizes different language metaphors.

12) The concept of habitus presupposes a theory of …
a) linguistic system.
b) linguistic practice.
c) psycholinguistics.

13) The notion of bodily hexis…
a) associates linguistic practices with bodily dispositions.
b) applies only to the upper-social classes.
c) applies only to the lower classes.

14) In Bordieu's view…
a) comprehension is the primary goal of communication.
b) communicative efficiency is not so relevant as political efficiency.
c) the desire to be understood is greater than any other aim in discourse.

15) According to Bordieu, a good command of the standard
language…
a) guarantees success in the market of symbolic exchanges.
b) is a necessary condition to communicate effectively.
c) does not guarantee success in the market of symbolic exchanges.

16) Bourdieu displaces grammaticalness in favour of…
a) power.
b) ideology.
c) acceptability.

17) One of the basic ideas in Bakhtin's work is that…
a) language is dialogic.
b) speakers have different tones of voice.
c) there is only one genre in each discourse.

18) According to Bakhtin…
a) all texts have a unified cultural canon.
b) language is patterned into speech genres.
c) the speaker's voice pitch is central to communication.

19) According to Bakhtin social changes…
a) are first perceived at genre level.
b) are not perceived at the genre level.
c) indicate a corruption of language.

20) The concept of heteroglossia…
a) has not been understood by authors other than Bakhtin.
b) has not been used in America.
c) has been used and applied by many authors in their analysis.

21) Some authors have not accepted Post-structural and Social
Theories as valid for discourse analysis on the grounds that they
are…
a) too complex.
b) biased.
c) too rigorous.

PRACTICE

A) *SUMMARY*:   CHOOSE any of the articles or books in the *FURTHER READING* section below and make an outline with its main points.

B)   *REFLECTION AND COMPARISON*: COMPARE the methods and concepts used by post-structuralists and social theorists to those of conversation analysts (Unit 5). In what ways do they differ?   Do you find any similarities between them? EXAMINE each approach in terms of the following elements:
  a)   The context: which aspects are considered relevant or not?
  b)   The relationship of discourse with the real world, the objective truth and the results of its generalization.
  c)   The position of analysts with respect to the topic: are they politically engaged?

C) *CHATROOM AND DISCUSSION*: DISCUSS the results of the comparison made in B with two or three classmates/friends over the Internet in a synchronic mode.

D) *ANALYSIS*: In the following narrative, a joke that circulated on the web among friends who wanted to entertain one another, we can identify more than one 'voice'.   From a Bakhtinian perspective, IDENTIFY these voices and briefly COMMENT on the reason why these voices are included in the narrative, as well as on the function they fulfill in the total context of the occurrence of the narrative:

> A Spanish teacher was explaining to her class that in Spanish, unlike English, nouns are designated as either masculine or feminine. "House" for instance, is feminine: "la casa." "Pencil," however, is masculine: "el lápiz."
> A student asked, "What gender is 'computer'?"
> Instead of giving the answer, the teacher split the class into two groups, male and female, and asked them to decide for themselves whether "computer" should be a masculine or a feminine noun.
> Each group was asked to give four reasons for its recommendation.
> The men's group decided that "computer" should definitely be of the feminine gender ("la computer"), because:
>
> 1. No one but their creator understands their internal logic;
> 2. The native language they use to communicate with other

computers is incomprehensible to everyone else;
3. Even the smallest mistakes are stored in long-term memory for possible later retrieval; and
4. As soon as you make a commitment to one, you find yourself spending half your paycheck on accessories for it.

(No chuckling... this gets better!)

The women's group, however, concluded that computer should be masculine ("el computer"), because:

1. In order to do anything with them, you have to turn them on;
2. They have a lot of data but still can't think for themselves;
3. They are supposed to help you solve problems, but half the time they ARE the problem; and
4. As soon as you commit to one, you realize that if you had waited a little longer, you could have gotten a newer and better model.

The women won!

FURTHER READING

- Bakhtin, 1986
- Baynham & Slembrouck, 1999; 2006
- Bourdieu, 1976; 1999
- Carabine, 2001
- Fairclough, 1992; 1999
- Foucault, 1980
- Laclau & Mouffe, 1985
- Maybin 2001
- O'Farrell, 2005

USEFUL WEBSITES

Generalities about Post-structuralism:
www.philosopher.org.uk/poststr.htm
www.brocku.ca/english/courses/4F70/poststruct.html
http://en.wikipedia.org/wiki/Poststructuralism

http://www.mtholyoke.edu/courses/sgabriel/post_structuralism.htm

Social Theory:
http://en.wikipedia.org/wiki/Social_theory
http://solomon.soth.alexanderstreet.com/
http://www.socialtheory.info/
http://www.ashworth-
program.unimelb.edu.au/about/social_theory.html

Michel Foucault :
www.csun.edu/~hfspc002/foucault.home.html
www.qut.edu.au/edu/cpol/**foucault**
www.synaptic.bc.ca/ejournal/**foucault**.htm

Pierre Bourdieu:
http://es.wikipedia.org/wiki/Bourdieu
http://en.wikipedia.org/wiki/Pierre_Bourdieu
http://www.guardian.co.uk/news/2002/jan/28/guardianobituaries.bo
oks

Mikhail Bakhtin
http://bank.rug.ac.be/da/Bakhtin.htm
http://www.colorado.edu/English/courses/ENGL2012Klages/bakhti
n.html
http://dialogic.blogspot.com/2006/06/mikhail-m-bakhtin-life-by-its-
very.html
http://www.infoamerica.org/teoria/bajtin1.htm

CRITICAL DISCOURSE ANALYSIS
AND
POSITIVE DISCOURSE ANALYSIS

"If powerful speakers or groups enact or otherwise 'exhibit' their power in discourse, we need to know exactly how this is done. And if they thus are able to persuade or otherwise influence their audiences, we also want to know which discursive structures and strategies are involved in that process. Hence, the discursive reproduction of dominance, which we have taken as the main object of critical analysis, has two major dimensions, namely that of production and reception.[...] Discursive (re)production of power results from social cognitions of the powerful, whereas the situated discourse structures result in social cognitions. That is, in both cases we eventually have to deal with relations between discourse and cognition, and in both cases discourse structures form the crucial mediating role. They are truly the means of the 'symbolic' reproduction of dominance."

Teun van Dijk, *Principles of Critical Discourse Analysis*

...we do need to move beyond a preoccupation with demonology, beyond a singular focus on semiosis in the service of abusive power – and reconsider power communally as well, as it circulates through communities, as they re-align around values, and renovate discourses that enact a better world. Good question, of course, what better is! And how to achieve it? We can start to ask.

James R. Martin, *Positive Discourse Analysis: Solidarity and Change*

Chapter Outline:

- The scope of Critical Discourse Analysis (CDA).

- Main concepts of CDA.

- Techniques and methods of CDA.

- Positive Discourse Analysis (PDA) as a response to CDA.

10.1. The scope of Critical Discourse Analysis

Critical Discourse Analysis (herinafter CDA) is an approach to discourse whose origins are found at the end of the 1970s, in the 'critical linguistics' that emerged (mainly in the UK and Australia) as a reaction against the dominant formal paradigms of the 1960s and 1970s. Indeed, critical linguists (e.g. Fowler et al 1979) focused on the analysis of language as *text* or *discourse* (rather than as decontextualized sets of possible sentences in the Chomskyan fashion), and they based their analytical approach mainly on Halliday's (1978, 1985) systemic/functional grammar[1]. Critical Linguistic studies were based on the premise that grammar is an **ideological** instrument for the categorization and classification of things that happen in the world, a premise which owed much to the theory of linguistic determinism known as the *Sapir/Whorf hypothesis* (Thornborrow, 2002). This hypothesis assumes that the language we use influences the way we think and that no two linguistic systems have the same way of categorizing the world.

From a broader perspective, it can be said that the general lines of CDA are traced back to Aristotle, to the philosophers of the

---

[1] See Chapter 8 for a detailed account of Functionalism.

Enlightenment, to Marx, and more recently to the philosophers of the Frankfurt School (Agger 1992, Rasmussen 1996). Likewise, another line of influence goes back to Althusser (1971), Foucault (1980)[2] and Pêcheux (1982), as well as to the feminist approaches to language and communication.

Teun van Dijk is one of the current key researchers in CDA. He defines the discipline as follows:

> Critical discourse analysis (CDA) is a type of discourse analytical research that primarily studies the way social power abuse, dominance, and inequality are enacted, reproduced, and resisted by text and talk in the social and political context. With such dissident research, critical discourse analysts take explicit position, and thus want to understand, expose, and ultimately resist social inequality. (2001: 352)

Having previously worked on text grammars and psychological theories, van Dijk (2004) explains that one of the reasons why he turned to CDA was because he realized that these grammars and theories had very little to do with the real problems of this world. One of these problems, for instance, is racism; an issue that, from van Dijk's view, has to be studied in relation to discourse due to the fact that it is normally expressed, reproduced or legitimated through text and talk.

The work of Norman Fairclough (1989, 1992a & b, 1995, 2001) presents a comprehensive and programmatic attempt to develop a theory of CDA which links discourse, power and social structure. Fairclough examines the role of social institutions in shaping discourse practices, and argues that language is always shaped by the material and social conditions in which it is produced. From Fairclough's perspective, discourse is a three-dimensional concept which involves 1) *texts* (the objects of linguistic analysis), 2) *discourse practices* (the production, distribution and consumption of texts) and 3) *social practices* (the power relations, ideologies and hegemonic struggles that discourses reproduce, challenge or restructure).

Society and *criticism* are key terms in the critical approaches to the study of language. Ruth Wodak (1989) is another author within this perspective, who defines her approach (which she calls *critical linguistics*) as an interdisciplinary approach to language study with a

---

[2] See Chapter 9.

critical point of view which intends to study language behavior in natural speech situations of social relevance. From an analytical point of view which attempts to expose social inequality and injustice, Wodak places special emphasis on the use of multiple methods and the importance of historical and social aspects.

Wetherell et al. (2001) present CDA as an approach which is based on a view of *semiosis* as an irreducible part of material social processes, semiosis including all forms of meaning-making: visual images, body language and verbal language. Social life is seen as interconnected networks of *social practices*, every practice having a semiotic element (see 9.4.).

From all its premises, it can be deduced that CDA is essentially multidisciplinary. Rather than being a direction or a new school, it aims to offer a different mode of analysis by finding a more or less critical pespective in different areas such as rhetoric, stylistics, sociolinguistics, pragmatics, ethnography, conversation analysis, etc. Consequently, CDA does not have a unitary theoretical framework. It can be said that there are many types of CDA, which can be theoretically and analytically quite diverse. However, all will have a common perspective: they will ask and try to answer questions about the way certain discourse structures are deployed in the reproduction of social dominance, thus featuring such notions as *power, dominance, hegemony, ideology, gender, race,* and *discrimination*, among others. It is an underlying assumption of CDA that in most interactions, speakers bring with them different dispositions with respect to language which are directly related to their social positionings.

The explicit awareness of their role in society is crucial for critical discourse analysts, for they strongly argue that both science and scholarly discourse are an inherent part of the social structure, and are consequently influenced by it as well. Thus, CDA tries to explain discourse structures in terms of the properties of social interaction and social structure, rather than merely to describe them. In particular, CDA pays special attention to the ways discourse structures enact or reproduce relations of **power** and **dominance** in society.

The main tenets of CDA, as summarized by Fairclough & Wodak (1997: 271-80) are the following:

1.   CDA addresses social problems
2.   Power relations are discursive

3. Discourse constitutes society and culture
4. Discourse does ideological work
5. Discourse is historical
6. The link between text and society is mediated
7. Discourse analysis is interpretative and explanatory
8. Discourse is a form of social action

Since CDA believes that discourse is a form of social action, it follows that CDA uses the analysis of discourse as a means to make people aware of several important social and political issues.

CDA intends to bridge the gap between **micro** and **macro levels** of social order. *Power* and *dominance*, for example, are terms that belong to the macrolevel of analysis; *discourse, verbal interaction* or *communication,* belong to the microlevel. Van Dijk (2001b) explains that a racist speech in parliament, for instance, is a discourse at the microlevel of social interaction in the specific situation of a debate, but at the same time and at the macrolevel, it may enact or be a constituent part of legislation or the reproduction of racism.

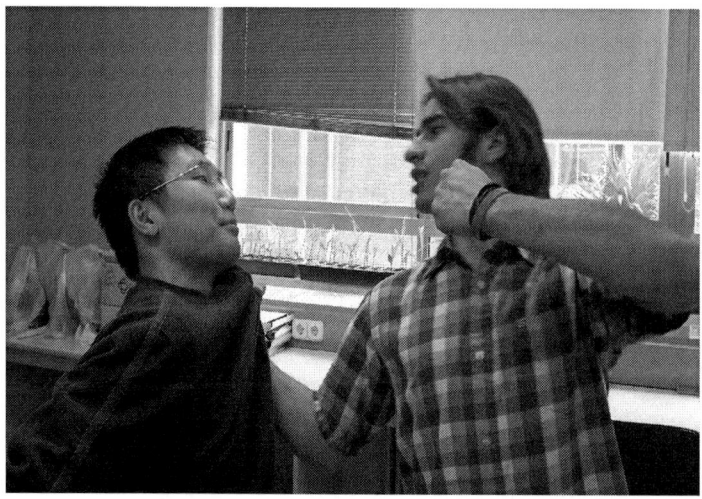

A fight brought on by racist attitudes in High School

Critical discourse analysts argue that most of the studies in critical linguistics and DA neglect **social cognition** (i.e. the social representations in the minds of social actors), an omission which –in their opinion– has been one of the major theoretical shortcomings of discourse research. Consequently, CDA places emphasis on social cognition as the necessary theoretical and empirical 'missing link' between discourse and dominance, by attempting to show the nature of its relationship with discourse and society.

Ideology is also a key term in CDA. It is the belief of critical discourse analysts that language never appears by itself; on the contrary, it always manifests itself as the representative of an ideological system.

Most discourse studies within the CDA approach deal with different aspects of **power**, **domination** and **social inequality**. In particular, we may find research on topics such as *professional power, institutional power, gender inequality, racism, ethnocentrism, the enactment of power through media discourse or through political discourse,* among others.

We shall now proceed to discuss the central topic of **power** in more detail.

10.2. Discourse and power

In a commonsense, non-theoretical description, we may say that **power** is multi-faceted and can take different forms. We generally speak of power as measurable in terms of the amount of political power, military power, physical power, etc. that some person or group has. For instance, we regard the President of a nation as one of the most powerful persons in that nation. Also, in many contexts, men are regarded as having more power than women, and white people more than black people. Power is also associated with rank and status, and thus hierarchies are built around relative positions of political, social or professional power.

In a less commonsense and more academic environment, discourse has been regarded by many scholars as an important site for both constructing and maintaining **power relations**. CDA views power as already belonging to some participants and not to others, and as a condition which is determined by their institutional role and/or their socio-economic status, ethnic identity or gender.

Thus, **power** (and, in particular, *the social power of groups or institutions*) is a central concern in most critical work on discourse. **Social power** –van Dijk (2001) remarks– is defined in terms of **control**. Therefore, the members of a given social group will have power if they are able to control the acts and minds of members of other groups. This ability to control other people's minds and acts presupposes a priviledged access to certain social resources such as force, money, status, fame, knowledge, information, etc., which are not easily available to all human beings.

Different types of power are identified, depending on the various resources employed to exercise such power. The power of the miltary, for example, is based on force; the power of the rich is based on their money, and so on. But, fortunately, as van Dijk states, "...power is seldom absolute. Groups may more or less control other groups, or only control them in specific situations or social domains. Moreover, dominated groups may more or less resist, accept, condone, comply with, or legitimate such power, and even find it 'natural'" (2001b: 355). And precisely because sometimes the enactment of power is acceptable, the power of dominant groups is integrated in laws, rules or habits, in such a way that sometimes power is taken for granted, as can be observed in many racist or sexist discourses which form part of our everyday experience. It is not uncommon to find examples, especially in our modern world, of very effective power enacted by means of persuasion or manipulation, as a strategic way to change the mind of others in the interest of a particular group. This is the main reason for critical discourse analysts's particular interest in focusing on the discursive strategies that legitimate control, thereby legitimating relations of inequality.

Althusser (1971) was one of the first theorists to describe power as a discursive phenomenon, and his work has been highly influential in much of the early work in CDA. He also viewed power as an ideological phenomenon, and claimed that it operates through discourse by constructing particular subject positions for people to occupy, which are sometimes accepted as natural and unchangeable even though they may not be in the best interest of the powerless.

As regards the relationship between power and discourse, then, critical discourse analysts take the following statements as axiomatic:

- Access to specific forms of discourse, such as the discourses of politics, the media or science, is itself a power resource.
- If we are able to influence people's minds by exercising our power, we will indirectly control

their actions.
- Those groups who control most influential discourse also have more chances to control the minds and actions of others.

Hence van Dijk splits up the issue of discursive power into two basic questions for CDA research:

> I. How do (more) powerful groups control public discourse?
> II. How does such discourse control mind and action of (less) powerful groups, and what are the social consequences of such control, such as social inequality? (2001b: 355)

Through this particular approach to research, CDA intends to show results that will distinguish **power abuse** from legitimate and acceptable forms of power. When the members of a given group abuse their power and other groups accept this abuse by acting in the interest of the powerful, critical discourse analysts use the term **hegemony** (Gramsci, 1971). The hegemonic groups constitute the **power elites**, and they have special access to discourse, since they are the groups who have the most to *say*, in contrast to those (powerless) groups who are allowed to say little or nothing. Thus, CDA defines elites in terms of their **symbolic power**, a term borrowed from Bordieu's (1982)[3] metaphor of the symbolic capital. The symbolic power of a given group is then measured by the extent of its members' discursive and communicative scope and resources (van Dijk, 1993).

10.2.1. 'Powerful' discourse structures

So... can discourse be powerful? It certainly can, and in order to analyze the power of discourse, we need to consider not only **how** speakers say what they say, but also **what** it is that they say.

The belief in the existence of more or less powerful ways of speaking, for example, underlies much of the early work in sociolinguistic studies of language and gender. Also, one of the ways in which the elites enact their power is by controlling the

---

[3] See Chapter 9.

context of discourse, i.e. they control the communicative event in all its components: time, place, setting, presence or absence of the participants, etc. Thus, for instance, it is normally the C.E.O.[4] of a company (and not the employees) who calls for a meeting at the time, place and in the circumstances which are convenient for her/him, or it is the professor who makes an appointment with the student, and not viceversa.

CDA is specially concerned with those forms of context control which are legally or morally unacceptable, such as the exclusion of women by men (in any given context), the restrictions put on black people to have access to the press or any powerful institution, or any other kinds of communicative discrimination and marginalization.

These modes of context control and discrimination are also manifested at the level of discourse structures. Hence some opinions are censored or not heard, some points of view are completely ignored: "The discourse itself becomes a 'segregated' structure" (van Dijk, 1993). As a consequence, the less powerful are less quoted, less heard, and less spoken about; their 'voices' are blocked.

At the micro-level of text and talk, we find a more or less consciously controlled and less direct influence of power. Very subtle manifestations of dominance may be found at the syntactic, morphological or phonological level, as could be the case of the use of a given intonation, the use of some rhetorical figures, and, at a broad semantic (pragmatic) level, the turn-taking or the politeness strategies used by speakers, which may overtly or covertly impose the power of the 'speaking' groups over the 'non-speaking' powerless groups.

Indeed, the use of (im)politeness strategies may be very telling about which of the interlocutors is expressing dominance. It is a well-known linguistic fact that those people who are in power feel entitled to be impolite towards their subordinates (Culpeper, 1996); hence the insolent and impolite tone used by members of higher ranks in the military towards the powerless soldiers of a lower rank. This impoliteness (and consequent use of power) may be materialized in a given type of intonation, in the use of ironic discourse, or in the use of certain 'impoliteness markers' (Alba-Juez, 2006, 2007), to name a few possibilities.

Other linguistic strategies which are commonly used to express power directly or indirectly are the use of hedges, hesitations,

---

[4] Chief Executive Officer

interruptions, pauses, laughter, certain specific forms of address, etc. Also, the choice of *topics* and *topic change* is crucial for all discourse. The group who decides the topic to be dealt with and when it should be changed is the group in power, as when men control the topics when in conversation with women, or when teachers decide what the content of their syllabi will be without consulting their students. Controlling the topic generally results in mind control, for topics may influence people's views about what is important information of text or talk. This is one of the reasons why CDA focuses on how discourse structures influence mental representations: since topics influence what people see as most important, these may eventually influence how a given item is defined in terms of a preferred mental model. Thus, for instance, immigration may be restricted if it is presupposed in a parliamentary debate that all refugees are "illegal" (Wodak & van Dijk 2000).

All these strategies may, depending on the circumstances, result in more or less aggressive forms of sexism, racism or other signs of dominance.

10.2.1.1. Example and analysis

Example 1 (taken from Culpeper, 1996), exhibits a case of the use of impoliteness in the context of army recruit training (Private Alves is being humiliated by the Sergeant), where there is a rigid hierarchical power structure and recruits are at the bottom:

1)
        Alves is denied speaking rights. This is clear at the beginning of
        the interview:
        S1: you're going to mess up one of my squad leaders
        PA:

        S1: [indistinct] any way you can how about it=   =don't
        PA: =I=

        S1: bullshit me now Alves you want to jump you want to
        PA:

        S1: jump on somebody=   =JUMP ON ME then…
        PA: =no=   who

        S1:   shut up Alves you're the one who is
        PA: said that sergeant

S1: running your little mouth again you're the one
PA:

S1: intimidating and threatening my squad leaders...
PA:

S1:   bullshit tell that god damn lie to someone
PA: I didn't sergeant

S1: that believes your ass private you've already been
PA:

S1: proven to be a damn habitual liar
PA:

(1996: 360)

The sergeant here feels in power and in total control of Private Alves, a fact that is shown through different mechanisms and strategies: he uses taboo insulting words or expressions, he yells at the recruit (JUMP ON ME...), he interrupts Alves every time he tries to say a word (and therefore he is in control of the turn-taking structure), he gives direct orders by using imperatives (*shut up Alves...*) and he accuses the recruit of being a liar (among other things) without letting him speak in his own defense. This is a clear case of hegemony, where the power elite (the sergeants) have access to discourse (while the powerless recruits do not) and where the powerless group (the recruits) accept the 'abuse' and act in the interest of the powerful by remaining silent or by accepting humiliation.

Thus, and obviously, the group having the symbolic power here is the group of the sergeants. However, it is difficult to judge if their behavior can be labelled as "abusive", for the kind of discourse used by this dominant group is considered to be part of what they consider their job. As Culpeper explains, within the context of an army training camp, it is assumed that recruits should obey orders without hesitation, and the best way to achieve this goal is to "destroy the recruits' individuality and self-esteem, and then rebuild it in the desired mould" (1996: 359). Therefore, the limits for what is to be considered abusive in this environment will be different from those in another context, although this fact does not exclude the possibility of serious abuse or harassment, which many times is caused precisely by the great degree of power that is given to and assumed from the higher positions in the hierarchy.

10.2.2. Other studies on discourse and power

In order to clarify the type of research that a critical view to
discourse analysis can produce on the topic of power, we shall list
and briefly discuss a few of the most representative studies which
may be taken as representative, even though not all the authors
mentioned place themselves within CDA:

- ❖ Edelsky (1981) studied the asymmetrical distribution of
  social power between men and women by examining the
  differential between women and men regarding the amount
  of talk and access to the 'floor' in conversation. This study
  is based on a model of power in interaction which assigns
  more power to those participants who take the most turns.
- ❖ Fishman's (1983) study of white, heterosexual, professional
  couples talking at home reveals that, while the women
  worked harder than the men at maintaining conversations,
  they were however less successful at getting their topics
  introduced into the talk.
- ❖ Harris (1984) examines the function of certain types of
  question formats as a powerful means of controlling
  discourse in British magistrates' courts examinations. She
  concludes that, in this particular context, the propositional
  content of the questions and their syntactic form resulted in
  a highly conducive form of questioning by the examining
  magistrate, who uses this type of questioning in order to
  accuse. Such questioning (which mainly gave rise to short
  yes/no or minimal answers) provided a powerful means of
  controlling the interaction, for they did not allow the
  defendants to introduce their own topics or shape the
  content of what was discussed, and generally when the
  defendants started to produce minimal responses they were
  interrupted by the magistrate.
- ❖ Goodwin (1992) shows that African-American girls engage
  in powerful forms of talk, in an activity known as
  'instigating', in which they bring about public
  confrontations between one of the girls (who is accused of
  having offended another) and another (the offended party).
  According to Goodwin, power is evident in the activity of
  instigating, for it creates a situation where confrontation
  and negotiation are worked out between the participants.
  In addition, she observes that the level of complexity found

in this activity was never found among the boys in her study, and concludes that, in order to study power in female speech, a good starting point would be to see how females use language to orchestrate the important political events in their lives.

❖ An interesting study made by Gal (1992) shows that remaining silent in discursive interaction may also be a powerful strategy. Silence, she explains, can be a resource for the institutionally more powerful participants in certain settings such as interviews, police examinations or religious confession. It can also be used as a form of resistance and protest (as, for instance, the case of seventeenth-century English Quakers, who refused to speak when they were expected to verbally show their ideological commitment). Other authors, such as Kurzon (1992), Gray (1992), Akman (1994), McCarthy & Carter (1994) and Alba-Juez (2001) have also found that silence may be used to gain control of a situation or to express dominance of some sort.

❖ Diamond (1996) argues that the currency of conversation consists of ideas or statements, rather than turns, and is in favor of a view of power as political and consensual in discursive interaction. She studies power and status in the talk between trainers and trainees in a Swiss institute of psychotherapy from the politeness perspective, and concludes that high-rank members use strategies related to 'solidarity' politeness, while low-rank members use strategies associated with 'defence' politeness (Scollon & Scollon, 1981).

❖ Analyzing the participation of men and women in an academic discussion list on the Internet, Herring, Johnson & DiBenedetto (1996) found out that there was a notable gender difference in spite of the supposedly democratic attitude of the World Wide Web. Moreover, the male participants expressed their discontent when there were more women than men contributing to a particular topic.

❖ In an analysis of the reconstruction of sexual consent in a sexual harassment disciplinary tribunal, Ehrlich (1998) argues that the tribunal was conducted on the basis of a typically male view of what is considered to be reasonable resistance to sexual aggression. The tribunal qualified the complainant's expressions of resistance with adjectives such as "deficient" or "inactive", which, in Goodwin's view, is a sign of a lenient treatment of the defendant, based on a masculine view of how resistence to sexual aggression should be, thus displaying power abuse on the part of the members of the tribunal, who were all male.

❖ Dirks (2006) focuses on how the British and German "quality" press dealt with the warfare interests of the US administration in Iraq. She follows a cultural heuristics of research that consists of a social studies approach and the application of pragmalinguistic methods (such as the analysis of frames, conceptual metaphors, speech acts, etc.) from a genre-based perspective. This approach leads her to find empirical evidence for the shaping of policy lines in the papers' front page articles from a comparative intra-European perspective.

10.3. Ideology, social cognition and discourse

Ideology is a key notion in CDA, for it is considered to be the notion that establishes the link between discourse and society. Within CDA, it is Teun van Dijk (1997, 2004) who has developed a theory which intends to specify the internal structures and contents of ideologies.

Van Dijk explains that "ideologies are developed by dominant groups in order to reproduce and legitimate their domination" (1997: 25). Discourse is the medium by which ideologies are communicated in society, thereby reproducing the power and domination of certain groups.

Ideologies resemble natural languages in that they are essentially social: they are shared by the members of a group and they are used to solve the social problem of successful communicative interaction. However, while groups use languages for communication among their own members, ideologies serve not only for internal coordination, but also (and more importantly) to coordinate social interaction with members of other groups.

Members of a group, thus, develop a basic framework that allows them to act as members of such a group: they share a given identity, aims, values, etc., and take it as the general basis which will let them know how to act in normal situations as well as in situations of conflict.

In his study on ideology, van Dijk combines his earlier notions from the cognitive study of discourse (van Dijk & Kintsh, 1983) with later ideas on social cognition, power, racism and the reproduction of power through discourse. In his academic autobiography, he summarizes his view as follows:

> The crucial concept of ideology I proposed is defined in terms of the fundamental cognitive beliefs that are at the basis of the social representations shared by the members of a group. Thus, people may have ideological racist or sexist beliefs (e.g., about inequality) that are at the basis of racist and sexist prejudices shared by the members in their group, and that condition their discourse and other social practices. We thus at the same time are able to link ideologies with discourse, and hence with the ways they are (discursively) reproduced, as well as the ways members of a group represent and reproduce their social position and conditions in their social cognitions and discourse [...] That is, ideologies control social representations of groups, and thus the social practices and discourses of their members. This happens through the ideological control of mental models which in turn, [...] control the meaning and the functions of discourses, interaction and communication. And conversely, ideologies may be 'learned' (and taught) through the generalization of mental models, that is, the personal experiences of social members. (2004: 26-27)

In short, **ideologies** are both *social systems* and *mental representations*. This means that they not only have a social function but also cognitive functions of belief organization. Ideologies are the mental representations that form the basis of **social cognition**, and by social cognition van Dijk means "the shared knowledge and attitudes of a group" (1997: 29). This social cognition in turn influences the specific beliefs of the members of a group, which finally make up the basis of **discourse.**

10.3.1. Ideological analysis: An example

In order to illustrate how practitioners of CDA analyze discourse in terms of ideology, the analysis that van Dijk (1997) makes of the following fragment of a politician's (Mr Rohrabacher's) speech is here reproduced and summarized:

> We need economic growth, business expansion, not more civil rights legislation that is redundant and useless...
> We care about these people living in horrible situations,

whatever their race, and they come in all colors...
[Their horrible situation] Rarely is this a result of bigotry...
They were listening to so-called liberal leaders who were telling
them that they should not try [to get jobs] because they did not have
a chance rather than listening to conservatives who were telling
them to go for it...
This first step is to recognize that racial discrimination plays
only a minor role in the economic tragedy befalling our inner cities.
We need to talk about our economy moving, creating new jobs and
personal economic advancement of our citizens...
Let us defeat this legislation. It is going to hurt those it claims to
help. (1997: 32)

Van Dijk argues that this and other fragments of Mr Rohrabacher's
speech express ideological polarization by making reference to
different groups (liberals and conservatives) and their different
social views of minorities. All discursive structures aim at putting
emphasis on *our good* things, as opposed to *their bad* things. This
principle of positive self-presentation and negative other-
presentation finds its expression at different levels of discourse
description such as:

1   *Topic* selection (e.g., 'We tell them to go for it' vs 'They
    tell them they should not try').
2   *Schematic organization* (the overall argument against civil
    rights legislation: 'we oppose a redundant law, and instead
    propose better job opportunities').
3   *Local meanings*, coherence, implications and presuppositions
    (e.g., 'a welfare system that provides the wrong incentives
    to people who need an inspiration to change, not pressure
    to remain the same' implies that the jobless don't want to
    work, and that their position is caused by welfare and not
    by employers who refuse to hire them); we also find
    disclaimers and denials of racism ('Rarely is this a result of
    bigotry').
4   *Lexicalization* implying our positive and their negative
    properties ('we care about these people' vs. 'obtrusive civil
    rights bill')
5   *Style* (e.g., imitation of popular oral argumentative style:
    'The less fortunate of our fellow citizens. That is who will
    not be helped')
6   *Rhetorical devices*, such as contrasts ('It [the bill] is going
    to hurt those it claims to help'), metaphors ('The job

explosion experienced throughout America during the Reagan years'), hyperboles and euphemisms ('less fortunate of our fellow citizens'). (1997: 33)

This analysis is but one example of CDA, which shows that ideologies may be encoded at all levels and in all the structural properties of discourse and context; a type of analysis which eventually should enable us to fully understand the complex relation between discourse and society.

10.4. Steps to follow when doing CDA

Wetherell et al (2001) propose an analytical framework for doing CDA which is modelled upon Bhaskar's (1986) concept of *explanatory critique*. We reproduce it here as a useful guide for the student or reader who wants to 'embark' upon CDA:

An Analytical framework for CDA

Stage 1: Focus upon a social problem that has a semiotic aspect.
Beginning with a social problem rather than the more conventional 'research question' accords with the critical intent of this approach – the production of knowledge which can lead to emancipatory change.

Stage 2: Identify obstacles to the social problem being tackled.
You can do this through analysis of:
  a) the network of practices it is located within
  b) the relationship of semiosis to other elements within the particular practice(s) concerned
  c) the discourse (the semiosis itself) by means of:
    -   structural analysis: the order of discourse
    -   interactional analysis
    -   interdiscourse analysis
    -   linguistic and semiotic analysis

The objective here is to understand how the problem arises and how it is rooted in the way social life is organized, by focusing on the obstacles to its resolution – on what makes it more or less intractable.

Stage 3: Consider whether the social order (network of practices) 'needs' the problem. The point here is to ask whether those who benefit most from the way social life is now organized have an interest in the problem *not* being resolved.

Stage 4: Identify possible ways past the obstacles. This stage in the framework is a crucial complement to Stage 2 – it looks for hitherto unrealized possibilities for change in the way social life is currently organized.

Stage 5: Reflect critically on the analysis (Stages 1-4). This is not strictly part of Bhaskar's explanatory critique but it is an important addition, requiring the analyst to reflect on where s/he is coming from, and her/his own social positioning.

(2001: 236)

10.5 Major criticisms levelled at CDA

CDA has been the target of a critique made by Schegloff (1997), which triggered a complex debate (Wetherell, 1998; Schegloff, 1998; Billig, 1999a, 1999b and 1999c; Schegloff, 1999a and 1999b) carried out mainly between CDA and CA (Conversation Analysis). Schegloff argues that the type of research carried out by CDA does not include a detailed and systematic analysis of discourse, as is the case with CA. He holds the idea that the work of critical discourse analysts should be grounded in the technical discipline of conversation analysis, and that if this were so, the results of such a technical analysis might turn out to be quite different from what they primarily assumed.

Moreover, Schegloff's main point in this argument is that CDA should not merely *presuppose* contextualization (i.e. it should not presuppose that, for example, being black or being a woman will be evident from the way people write or talk); on the contrary, it should *prove* it by examining what social members actually say and do. If this is not done –Schegloff remarks– contextualization is pointless and has no discursive relevance.

Thus CA is offered by Schegloff as a corrective to the 'grandiosity' of CDA, a grandiosity which is evident, in his opinion, when critical analysts impose their own frames of reference on a world which is already interpreted and constructed by the participants of discourse. This imposition, Schegloff argues, is an act of intellectual hegemony, which seems ironic, considering that it is precisely hegemony that critical discourse analysts want to denounce when doing their job. Thus, reading between the lines, Schegloff suggests that CDA is not as objective a method of analysis as CA is.

Other authors (e.g. Cunningham, 2004) have accused CDA of being 'left-leaning' and thus politically-oriented, which, in their opinion, disqualifies it as scholarship. In an attempt to make opposing positions meet, van Dijk (1999b) notes that the debate between CDA and CA does not imply that these fields are in conflict or that they are imcompatible. On the contrary, he argues that there is valuable CA-oriented research that has a critical perspective and that CDA shares many basic criteria and aims with CA.

Kress (1996) suggests that, in order for CDA to move from mere critical reading and deconstructivism, it should now try to engage in some productive activity. Luke (2002: 98) also writes about "the need to develop a strong positive thesis about discourse and the productive uses of power". Thus, CDA should move towards finding ways to redistribute power, without focusing on the struggle against it. Martin (2007: 84) observes that "these critiques seem to suggest that CDA move in the direction of PS [Peace Sociolinguistics] and related interventions". This circumstance led him to call for the development of *Positive Discourse Analysis*, a novel approach to which we now turn.

10.6. Positive Discourse Analysis

When considering the reach of CDA, Martin and Rose (2003) and Martin (2004, 2007) argue that now we need not so much to concentrate on the negative as on the positive aspects of power. These scholars believe that the analysis should turn to a complementary focus on community, "taking into account how people get together and make room for themselves in the world – in ways that redistribute power without necessarily struggling against it" (Martin, 2004: 183). These observations, in addition to the feeling that a change of direction was necessary in CDA, were the basis for the development of a new perspective on the analysis of discourse: the perspective of *Positive Discourse Analysis* (PDA).

PDA argues for constructive discourse research in order to undo what was an apparent pathological disjunction in 20th-century social

science and humanities: the study and critique of processes which
disempower and oppress. Thus, the aim of PDA is to engage in
"heartening accounts of progress" rather than in "discouraging
analyses of oppression" (Martin, 2004: 184), to focus on
constructive social action, rather than on the deconstruction of
negative social action. Therefore, PDA is concerned with what texts
"'do well' and 'get right' in our eyes" (Macgilchrist, 2007), the
emphasis being put on the discourse we like rather than on the
discourse we wish to criticize.

Examples of the positive analysis of discourse can be found in
the following works:

> Martin (2002 and 2004) considers the role of images and
  evaluative language in promoting reconciliation, focusing
  on indigenous relations in Australia and South Africa.
> Martin & Rose (2003) introduce the reader to this new field
  of research and they analyze some inspirational writing by
  Mandela and Tutu, on the grounds that the study of texts
  concerned with the processes of truth and reconciliation
  takes text analysis to a new and higher dimension.
> Anthonissen (2003) discusses the productive resistance to
  media censorship in apartheid South Africa.
> Martin & Stenglin (2006) present an analysis of the use of
  space in relation to land rights in a gallery of the Museum
  of New Zealand in Wellington.

Doing Positive Discourse Analysis evidently entails taking a
positive stand to the analysis of discourse, a stance that will value
some aspects of social change positively, giving a practical face to
the "interventionist ambitions harboured by critical discourse
analysts" (Martin, 2007: 86). This type of analysis involves the
study of discourses that are not typically associated with CDA, and
even more, it involves considering a new kind of analysis which,
notwithstanding, can draw on the previous findings of CDA.

10.6.1. Example of analysis

As a more detailed example of analysis within PDA, Martin's
(2004) study of **voice** in a discourse dealing with the theme of
reconciliation with Indigenous people in Australia is presented and
summarized herein along the following points:

- **Type of text analyzed**: A government report of the National Inquiry into the "Separation of Aboriginal and Torres Strait Islander Children from Their Families", entitled *Bringing Them Home*. He presents this report as a sign of the emergence of new multimodal genres as agents of social change.

- **Aims of the report**: Martin observes that the way in which the report gives voice to indigenous Australians is remarkable, and that this aim is achived by means of a **multimodal strategy.**

- **Multimodal strategies involved in giving voice to Indigenous Australians:**

  a) A mixture of spoken testimony with bureaucratic writing,
  b) A mixture of language and photographic image[5],
  c) Nominalizations (e.g. *The forcible removal of Indigenous children from their families*),
  d) Inclusion of lists, tables, graphs and maps,
  e) Thematization: Indigenous voices are privileged by means of assuming first position in Parts and Chapters throughout the report. This thematization has the effect of establishing the stance taken by the author(s) of the report, which intends to align readers with the victims of the genocide that is being denounced.

- **Effect of the report**: the above discourse strategies proved to be efficient in achieving the main aim of the report. Its effect was staggering, causing a march for reconciliation of a quarter of a million people across the Harbour Bridge in Sydney, May 2000 (on the third anniversary of the report's release).

---

[5] The text includes a photograph of 6 young pre-school Aboriginal girls in white dresses, who had been kidnapped and were now eligible for adoption by white families. Above the photo is the heading "Homes Are Sought for These Children", and below the photo there are different sub-texts containing different voices (the institution's, the prospective foster parents' and the girls' voices). See Martin (2004), p.186.

Voice is but one of the possible variables or aspects to take into account when doing PDA. Martin (2004) suggests that PDA can also be done by analyzing aspects such as:

- The forms, strategies and mechanisms of **evaluative language**[6], on the grounds that "communities are formed around attitudes to things" and thus "we say what we feel in the expectation that people will empathise, and so align themselves with our feelings" (2004: 188).

- The **power of narrative**: the evaluative structure present in almost every narrative may have the power of aligning values around the social significance of recountable events, and in so doing it can also be used to enact reconciliation, as is the case with the narrative in P. Kelly's popular land rights anthem (1999)[7] entitled "From Little Things Big Things Grow".

10.6.2. Final remarks on PDA

PDA is a novel and very recent approach to the analysis of discourse, and as such, it still has a long way to go in the development of its methodology and tools for analysis. However, this is an approach that has strong foundations, for it is grounded on Systemic Functional Linguistics, as well as on positive values and intentions. It seems appropriate, then, to conclude this section by reflecting upon the quote presented at the beginning of this chapter: Martin's final paragraph in his article entitled *Positive Discourse Analysis: Solidarity and Change*:

> I suppose it would be going too far to propose a 10 year moratorium on deconstructive CDA, in order to get some constructive PDA off the ground. But we do need to move beyond a preoccupation with demonology, beyond a singular focus on semiosis in the service of abusive power – and reconsider power

---

[6] This is so to the point that he has developed a theoretical approach to the study of the language of evaluation: Appraisal Theory. (See Martin and Rose (2003) and Martin and White (2005).

[7] Kelly, P. (1999). *Don't Start Me Talking: Lyrics* 1984-1999. Sydney: Allen & Unwin. Cited in Martin (2004).

communally as well, as it circulates through communities, as they re-align around values, and renovate discourses that enact a better world. Good question, of course, what better is! And how to achieve it? We can start to ask. (2004: 197).

SUMMING UP... (CHAPTER 10)

1. The origins of **CDA** may be traced back to the end of the 1970s, in the 'critical linguistics' that emerged (mainly in the UK and Australia) as a reaction against the dominant formal paradigms of the 1960s and 1970s.

2. CDA can be defined as "a type of discourse analytical research that primarily studies the way social power abuse, dominance, and inequality are enacted, reproduced, and resisted by text and talk in the social and political context" (van Dijk 2001).

3. CDA is essentially **multidisciplinary**. Rather than being a direction or a new school, it aims to offer a different mode of analysis by finding a more or less critical pespective in different areas such as rhetoric, stylistics, sociolinguistics, pragmatics, ethnography, conversation analysis, etc.

4. In particular, CDA pays special attention to the ways discourse structures enact or reproduce relations of **power** and **dominance** in society. Thus, it uses the analysis of discourse as a means to make people aware of several important social and political issues.

5. **Ideology** is also a key term in CDA.   **Ideologies** are both *social systems* and *mental representations*. They are the mental representations that are the basis of **social cognition**. Language/discourse always appears as the representative of an ideological system.

6. CDA views **power** as already belonging to some participants and not to others, and as a condition which is determined by their institutional role and/or their socio-economic status, ethnic identity or gender.

7. The **power elites** have special access to discourse. Thus, CDA defines elites in terms of their **symbolic power** (Bordieu, 1982). The symbolic power of a given group is measured by the extent of its discursive and communicative scope and resources.

8. Power is enacted in discourse at its different macro and micro-levels. It is manifested through both text and context.

9. Somehow in contrast with CDA, **Positive Discourse Analysis (PDA)** argues for constructive discourse research and is concerned with what texts "'do well' and 'get right' in our eyes".
10. The aim of PDA is to **focus on constructive social action**, rather than on the deconstruction of negative social action. This new approach has strong foundations, for it is **grounded on Systemic Functional Linguistics**, as well as on positive values and intentions.
11. The type of analysis done in PDA involves the study of discourses that are not typically associated with CDA, and even more, it involves considering **a new kind of analysis** which, notwithstanding, can draw on the previous findings of CDA.

SELF-EVALUATION QUESTIONS

Choose the answer that best suits the information given in Chapter 10.

1) The origins of CDA are found ...
a) in the U.S.A.
b) in the U.K. and Australia.
c) in France.

2) Critical Linguistic Studies were based on the premise that...
a) grammar is objective.
b) discourse structures can only be studied from a "purely linguistic" perspective.
c) grammar is an ideological instrument.

3) According to Fairclough, discourse involves...
a) texts, discourse practices and social practices.
b) only texts.
c) social practices and context.

4) CDA is essentially...
a) multidisciplinary.
b) monodisciplinary.
c) concerned with the formal aspects of language.

5) Some essential notions of CDA are...
a) surface structure and deep structure.

b) speech acts and speech events.
c) power, dominance, ideology.

6) CDA believes that discourse is...
a) a set of grammatical rules.
b) a form of social action.
c) a type of behavior that has to be criticized.

7) CDA uses the analysis of discourse in order to...
a) make people aware of important social and political issues.
b) facilitate the learning of languages.
c) find linguistic universals.

8) Critical discourse analysts believe that...
a) there is nothing in language beyond the text.
b) language always represents an ideological system.
c) ideology is not an important aspect of language.

9) CDA considers discourse as an important site for...
a) the enactment of power.
b) discovering psychological problems.
c) the study of mental disfunction.

10) *Hegemony* refers to...
a) the eventual success of a social group.
b) the financial capital a social group owns.
c) the abuse of power of a social group.

11) Hegemonic groups...
a) are the ones who control and have special access to discourse.
b) do not have a special interest in accessing discourse.
c) have no contact with the powerless groups.

12) Control and discrimination...
a) cannot be analyzed at the syntactic level in discourse.
b) only manifest themselves at the semantic level.
c) are manifested at the level of discourse structures.

13) Which of these strategies are commonly used to express power?
a) Choice of topic and topic change.
b) Use of hedges, hesitations, interruptions, laughter and pauses.

c) All of the above.

14) Ideologies…
a) do not form part of the structure of a language.
b) are communicated through the medium of discourse.
c) are only found in the discourse of the powerful.

15) Ideologies...
a) have both a social and a cognitive function.
b) do not represent the shared knowledge of a group.
c) are not related to social cognition.

16) Schegloff criticizes CDA for…
a) being too technical.
b) not presupposing contextualization.
c) not including a systematic analysis of discourse.

17) *Positive Discourse Analysis* argues in favor of…
a) constructive discourse research.
b) the negative aspects of power.
c) the study of processes that oppress.

18) When doing PDA, possible variables to take into account are…
a) the evaluative structure of narratives.
b) voice and evaluative language in general.
c) all of the above.

19) PDA is grounded on…
a) Transformational Grammar.
b) Systemic Functional Linguistics.
c) Structural Linguistics.

20) PDA focuses on…
a) the kind of discourse that shows positive values and intentions.
b) discourses that are used to disempower the lower classes.
c) the language of racism and abuse.

PRACTICE

A) *ANALYSIS*: Here are two jokes that you might hear someone tell in some circles in the United States of America. ANALYZE them from the CDA perspective, looking for any specific type of ideology they might be favoring or satirizing. LOOK FOR the discourse structures that are used to express the ideologies in question.

[1]

The Secretary of the Mormon Church in Utah approaches the President of the Church and the following exchange takes place:

Secretary: I have good news and bad news to tell you, Mr. President. I'll start with the good news: **God** is in town.
President: Wonderful. But... what's the bad news?
Secretary: **She** is **black.**

[2]

A favorite uncle is visiting his family when he has a heart attack.
They rush him to the hospital. Later the doctors come out with long   faces.
"It seems his brain is dead but his heart is still beating", they say.
A gasp arises from the family members. "We've never had a liberal in the family before!"

B) *ANALYSIS*: ANALYZE this exchange between a student and a Professor in an American University from the CDA perspective. Do you think the discourse structures used favor any **ideology** in particular? Also, identify and explain the use/abuse of **power**. Do you find any signs of **discourse hegemony**?

Professor M: Yes. The assignment is due May 14th. It's mandatory. (He looks at his watch)

Student: O.K., thank you so much.   Oh, Dr. M, one more thing…
(Professor M looks at his watch again, stands up and walks towards the door)
Student: I have this problem with my scholarship, y' know, and…
Professor M: (looks at his watch again and avoids eye contact with the student). I have a meeting in five minutes…
Student: But it's only one more important thing…
Professor M: (looks at his watch again) SORRY, BUT I'VE GOTTA GO!

C) *ANNOTATING DISCOURSE:* SEARCH for any kind of discourse on the Internet (TV interviews, chat rooms, radio programs, etc.) which you suspect might show a certain ideology and thus might expose the hegemony of a given social group. ANNOTATE A FRAGMENT of such discourse for the purposes of analysis (following the guidelines in Chapter 2).

D) *ANALYSIS:* ANALYZE the fragment using Wetherell's analytical framework, and focusing on any discourse feature (topics, turn-taking, silence, prosodic features, etc.) that you consider relevant in the particular text and context of your data for a critical analyisis.

E) *ANALYSIS*: SEARCH for a piece of discourse that, in your opinion, displays positive values and intentions and, using a PDA perspective, look for the strategies (e.g. voice, evaluative language, etc.) used by the writer/speaker in order to show such positive aspects.

FURTHER READING

Fairclough, 1992

Fairclough, 2001
Martin, 2004
Martin & Rose (2003 [2007]), Chapter 9.
Martín Rojo, L., Pardo, M. L. & R. Whittaker, 1998

Neff, 1997
Thornborrow, 2002
van Dijk, 1997
van Dijk, 1999a
van Dijk, 2001
van Dijk, 2003
van Dijk, 2004
van Dijk, 2008 a & b
van Dijk, 2009
Wetherell, 1998
Wodak & van Dijk, 2000

USEFUL WEBSITES

Critical Discourse Analysis:
http://www.kon.org/archives/forum/15-1/mcgregorcda.html
http://users.utu.fi/bredelli/cda.html

Teach yourself Critical Discourse Studies:
http://www.discourses.org/resources/teachyourself/
Criticisms of CDA:
http://clublet.com/c/c/why?CriticalDiscourseAnalysis

Teun Van Dijk's website: http://www.discourses.org/

Martin's article on PDA:
http://wwww.wagsoft.com/Systemics/MartinPapers/JA-
2004%20Positive%20Dicourse%20Analysis%20Solidarity%20and
%20Change.doc

Macgilchrist's article on PDA:
http://cadaad.org/ejournal/2007/1/macgilchrist

Criticism of PDA:
http://lancastermaze.blogspot.com/2007/02/positive-discourse-
analysis.html

MEDIATED DISCOURSE ANALYSIS

"Everywhere about us in our day-to-day world we see the discourses which shape, manage, entice, and control our actions. Instrumental to the process of shaping those discourses are the objects by which we index our own positions and identities in the world. The traffic light at a busy intersection not only narrowly manages the flow of automobiles through the intersection, it also indexes the municipal regulatory powers and apparatus that have placed the traffic light and which maintain its functioning. Furthermore, as we approach the light and make our choices about stopping or driving right through it, we index ourselves in respect to those regulatory powers and that municipal power apparatus. Mostly, of course, we index ourselves as law-abiding citizens by stopping when instructed to do so."

**Scollon & Scollon, *Discourses in Place.
Language in the Material World***

Chapter Outline:

- Theoretical principles and methods of Mediated Discourse Analysis.

- Central concepts within this approach.

- The analysis of social action from this perspective.

11.1. What is Mediated Discourse Analysis?

Mediated Discourse Analysis (herinafter MDA) is an approach to the study of discourse which focuses more upon human social action than upon texts or discourses. This approach considers technology as mediational means within social actions. Language is not considered the only mediational means; non-verbal communication and physical objects used by an agent in taking an action are mediational means as well. Discourse and human action in social change are its main concerns, and **mediated action** is used as the basic unit of analysis.

As Norris & Jones (2005) point out, the spoken or written texts we produce may have significant social consequences. MDA explores the actions individuals take with texts, as well as the consequences of those actions.

Like other approaches to DA, MDA is theoretically interdisciplinary. It developed out of linguistics and it integrates concepts from mediated action theory, sociocultural psychology, interactional sociolinguistics, critical discourse analysis, anthropological linguistics and intercultural communication.

Mediated discourse analysts work with the underlying assumption that social problems in our contemporary world are inextricably linked to texts. R. Scollon (2001: 1) explains that MDA is a framework for looking at social actions with the following two questions in mind:

1. What is the action going on here?
2. How does discourse figure into these actions?

He also points out that "MDA seeks to develop a theoretical remedy for discourse analysis that operates without reference to social actions on the one hand, and social analysis that operates without reference to discourse on the other" (2001: 1). For example, the action of going out with a friend for a cup of coffee is seen by Scollon as a very complex set of actions which involves many complex discourses "with rampant intertextualities and interdiscursivities" (2001: 1), such as family talk, service encounter talk, international neo-capitalist marketing of coffee, etc.[1]   MDA intends to show all this complexity without presupposing which discourses and actions are the relevant ones in a given particular case.

11.2.   Central concepts in MDA

The following are five central concepts in MDA (Scollon, 2001):

1) **Mediated action**: the unit of analysis in MDA. Analysts focus on the acting of social actors, because the discourses in question are not merely material objects: "they are instantiated in the social world as social action" (Scollon, 2001: 3). According to Scollon, it is unproductive to work with "pure" abstractions. There is no social action without discourse, and there is no discourse without concrete, material actions.

2) **Site of engagement:** the social space where mediated action occurs. The interpretation of a mediated action is located within the social practices which are related in that unique place and moment. Thus the focus is on real-time, irreversible actions rather than on objectivized analyses of discourses.

3) **Mediational means:** the material means (e.g. the body, dress and movements of the material actors) through which mediated action is carried out, which are in dialectical interaction with structures of the habitus. Mediational means are multiple in a single action, and they are

---

[1] See 11.7.

inherently polyvocal, intertextual and interdiscursive. They inevitably carry histories and social structures with them.

4)   **Practice:** MDA takes as a premise that mediated action is only interpretatable within practices. Thus, having lunch at a restaurant, for instance, is interpreted as a different action from having lunch at home, the difference lying both in the practice (for example, who prepares the coffee) and in the mediational means (the decoration of the room, the type of kitchen, etc.).

5)   **Nexus of practice:** The different types of practices (discursive and non-discursive) are interrelated and linked to form nexus of practice. So, for instance, an Italian restaurant nexus of practice would include different things such as *ordering practices* (e.g. we have to be able to distinguish between different types of pizza and pasta), *eating practices* (e.g. alone or with friends), *discursive practices* (e.g. being able to pronounce and understand some Italian terms), *physical spacing practices* (e.g. there is a place for the customers and a place for the restaurant staff), and so on. The concept of the nexus of practice is unbounded, and as such it is always unfinalized. The constellation of practices is what makes for the uniqueness of the site of engagement and the identities thus produced.

11.3. MDA as a theory of social action

Scollon (2001) emphasizes the fact that social problems in our contemporary world are inextricably linked to texts. Much of what we say is accompanied by action and, conversely, most of our actions are accompanied by language.

MDA shares the goals of CDA[2]. However, MDA reformulates the object of study by focusing not on the discourses of social issues but on social action as the grounds of discourse and language.

Thus, the single most important principle in MDA theory is the *principle of social action,* for discourse is not conceived as a system of representation, thought or values, but as **a matter of social actions**. The ecological unit of analysis, i.e. **mediated action** (the person or persons in the moment of taking an action along with the mediational means which are used by them), is a corollary to this

---

[2] See Chapter 10.

principle. All social action is based on tacit, normally unconscious actions which form the different **practices**. An individual's accumulated experience of social actions is what we call the **habitus**[3] (Bourdieu, 1977; 1990) or the **historical-body** (Nishida, 1958).

The starting point for mediated discourse analysts, therefore, is the study of social action, and the analysis of language or discourse only takes place when language is understood to be a significant mediational means for the actions under analysis. Thus, the methodological problem faced by a mediated discourse analyst is not how to accomplish the analysis of a text, but how to accomplish the analysis of a social-mediated action.

11.4. Methods in MDA

MDA includes multiple methods, from ethnographic participant-observation, interviews and questionnaire surveys, to focus groups or the collection of texts and images. The main aim is the identification and analysis of key mediated actions.

Data production activities are organized in three main groups (Scollon, 2005):

1) **Ethnography of communication surveys of key situations and participants:** These surveys differ from the original surveys in the Ethnography of communication in that they are more concerned with problems of social change and thus focus on social issues. The aim of mediated discourse analysts is to enter into the lifeworlds of the group in order to learn which mediated actions in which sites of engagement are crucial in producing social identities and social changes for that group. Therefore the survey intends to obtain information about the participants, the mediational means, the scenes or situations, and the events and actions.

2) **Issue-based surveys of public discourse:** These provide an independent analysis of the significance of topics, mediational means, and mediated actions to cross-check against the ethnography of communication surveys. The

---

[3] See also Chapter 9.

dialectal link between public discourse and personal action is central to MDA.

3) **Public opinion and focus group surveys of issues and situations**: These provide MDA with a means of determining the sociopolitical issues that are central across the public at large. In a later stage they are compared with the analyses of public discourses and those of specific concrete mediated actions taken in specific sites of engagement.

Each type of data can be seen from four different perspectives (S. Scollon, 1998):

1) **Members' generalizations**: These are generally expressed in simple statements such as "We usually do X or Y," and may also be contrasted with generalizations about other groups of people: "Those Xs do P or Q". Members' generalizations are a very important source of data in MDA.

2) **Individual experience:** Members of a social group typically make sweeping generalizations about their group but, if given the chance, they make a disclaimer about these generalizations by stating that they do not do everything their group does because they are different. MDA understands that, even in rather homologous groups, the habitus of individuals may vary widely, and thus it is important to study the range delimited by both individual and group actions.

3) **'Neutral'/'objective' data:** MDA is generally skeptical of objectivized data which eliminates the particularistic characteristics of individual actions. However, introducing a third point of view –that of a distant observer- provides important information for the analysis. For this reason, MDA includes an examination of the position of the analyst and takes recording devices such as cameras, tape recorders and the like as examples of mediational means which can help to complete the information provided by the other two types of group-internal data (members'

generalizations and individual experience).

4) **Playback responses**: A method used in interactional sociolinguistics and other fields by means of which close attention is paid to the linguistic details of social interactions. It can also be used to check transcriptions for accuracy. Playback provides the original participants in a scene with an 'objective' record of their actions, as well as with the analysis developed by an external observer.

11.5.   Mediated social interaction

R. Scollon (1998) argues that the *sender-receiver* model of communication is misleading because it makes us think that the *social interaction* occurring in texts is between the author or producer and the reader or audience. Taking the case of news discourse as an example, this author thus argues that the primary social interactions are among the news producers (e.g.: journalists, photographers, editors) and not between the producers and the audience. News producers prepare a 'spectacle' among themselves which is the primary social interaction. Then MDA sees this spectacle not so much as a communication *to* an audience but as a communication *in front of* an audience.

Likewise, the relationship between producers (authors) and spectators is seen differently. The primary social interaction, from the spectators' point of view, is among the members of the audience, for they may argue against, comment on or assess what they are viewing, but by no means can they be said to be engaged in what they are viewing or hearing.

Thus, from the MDA perspective, **all discourse is mediated and all mediations are discursive**. The difference between this approach and any other approach to discourse lies in the focus of attention, which for MDA is placed on "the actions of social actors in using the texts of communication" (Scollon, 2005).

11.6.   Interdisciplinarity

As noted in 11.1., MDA is an interdisciplinary approach to discourse. Its origins can be found in a Boasian type of linguistics rather than in a Saussurian approach because, like Boas and Sapir, mediated discourse analysts ground their analysis of language in the sociocultural worlds of the people who use language. They are not so much interested in the abstract or structural characteristics of a language, which were the main concern of de Saussure's or Bloomfield's studies.

The integration of many disciplines, however, brings about crucial problems which, according to Scollon (2005), are the following:

a) **Representation and action:** There is a tension between the study of abstract systems of representation and the study of social actors living in real time. MDA uses concepts and theoretical assumptions from neo-Vigotskian sociocultural psychology (such as *mediated action* or *activity theory*) in order to solve this issue. Thus, mediated discourse analysts consider that the habitus of social actors carries with it the life history of the person. Embedded in the mediational means are the histories and the social structures of the world in which they were created.

b) **Linguistic relativity:** There is a tension between the Saussurian assertion about the total arbitrariness of the symbol and the Boasian assertion that symbolic systems embed the histories of mental categorizations of their users. Here MDA turns to the Ethnography of Communication for help, by placing all studies of practice within a broader study of the place of the practice in the whole ecology of the social actor or the social group.

c) **Units of analysis:** Mediated action (i.e. the social actor acting in real time using some mediational means) is taken as the unit of analysis. But using this unit brings about certain problems, such as the question of whether language is a unique mediational means or whether there are other innate cognitive structures underlying other semiotic systems. And there is also the issue around the obvious fact that "all or some mediational means are actually used in very partial representations as social actors take action" (Scollon 2005).

Mediated action: A guided tour of The Globe Theatre in London.

d) **Methodology:** As we saw in 11.4., the nature of MDA calls for methods which are most commonly found in Interactional Sociolinguistics (such as tape-recording, transcription and playback). However, this methodology focuses more on linguistic data than on the mediated action and the social actors, which, according to mediated discourse analysts, may lead to errors of interpretation or analysis. The solution to this problem is then found in ethnographic studies and hence the mediated actions are positioned within a larger sphere of social activity.

e) **The psychology of the social actor:** Mediated discourse analysts believe that much of what we do as social actors has no connection to our capacity to articulate our intentions or goals in acting. Thus the analyst faces the problem of not having a well-grounded analytical basis for attributing a given action to a particular social actor. As Scollon (2005) notes, the question for MDA to resolve at this point is to what extent it is necessary to enter into the psychology of the social actor to produce a mediated discourse analysis.

11.7.   How does MDA analyze discourse?

In order to illustrate how social actions are analyzed in MDA, we shall summarize Scollon's (2001) analysis of the social action of having a cup of coffee with friends. This author does not see this situation as the simple action of drinking a coffee, but as a very complex and nested set of actions (lining up, ordering, paying, looking for a table, etc.). Likewise, the discourse of the conversation among friends is not the only discourse in the action; there are others implied, such as the discourse of service encounters, or that of the international marketing of coffee (he places his actors at a Starbucks® café). He then focuses on the coffee cup, which he considers the primary *mediational means* because, among other things, without the cup there is no such action of 'having a cup of coffee'. Scollon points out that "the cup itself (with its protective sleeve) is an impressive semiotic complex" (2001:2) where at least seven different discourses (Gee 1999) can be found:

1) **The discourse of commercial branding** (a recognizable logo appears twice on the cup and once on the sleeve).
2) **Legal discourse** (the logo is marked as a registered property ® and the sleeve has a copyright © mark).
3) **E-commerce discourse** (the website of the company is indicated).
4) **Consumer correctness discourse** (a text indicates that the company cares for those who grow its coffee and gives a telephone number where consumers can call and make a donation to them).
5) **Environmental correctness discourse** (there is a statement about the sleeve being made of 60% recycled fiber).
6) **Service information discourse** (there is a printed list of possibilities, such as *Decaf, Shots, Milk*, etc., and a handwritten 'L' (for *latte*)).
7) **Manufacturing information discourse** (there is also information about the cup itself, such as the size or product labelling and number).

Scollon remarks that, in this particular case, MDA should try to work out a way to understand the relationships among the actions and the different discourses involved in drinking a cup of coffee.

He then points out (2001: 3):

> Ethnographic observation leads us to believe that, on the whole, except for the odd linguist, the coffee is drunk without much attention being focused on this impressive discursive array on the cup. Correspondingly, the literature has many analyses of such Discourses in public places, from the products of the news industry through the broader popular culture industry, which make scant reference at all to the actual social situations in which these Discourses are engaged in social action. Mediated Discourse Analysis is an attempt to theorize a way in which we can link the Discourse of commercial branding, for example, with the practice of drinking a cup of coffee in conversation without giving undue weight either to the action without reference to the Discourse or to the Discourse without reference to the actions within which it is appropriated.

As can be seen, mediated discourse analysts give great importance to the material place where social actions occur. This is the main concern of *Geosemiotics*, with which we shall deal in the next section.

11.8. Geosemiotics

Mediated discourse analysts have developed a broad and systematic analysis of how language appears in the material world. This broad analytical position has been called *Geosemiotics* and it holds the assumption that a very important aspect of the meaning of all language (whether in a conversation, in a book or on a public traffic sign) is based on the material, concrete, physical placement of that language in the world.

The scholars supporting this position argue that "all instances of language in the world occur in semiotic aggregates –very complex systems of the interaction of multiple semiotic systems" (Scollon & Scollon, 2003: xii). From this perspective, "any human action is a process of selection among many semiotic systems which are always in a kind of dialectical dialogicality with each other" (Scollon & Scollon, 2003: xii). The key to the analysis of any human action is *indexicality*, i.e., the meaning of signs based on their material location.

Hence, all language takes a major part of its meaning from how and where it is placed. All of the signs and symbols index a larger discourse (e.g. the discourse of public transport regulation and the discourse of academia). Geosemiotics entails a broad analysis of discourse, and therefore not only applies to signs, or other symbols posted in different places, but also to signals and messages such as those sent off by our bodies, and whose meaning depends very much on where they are and what they are doing 'in place'.

11.8.1. Indexicality

In order to understand the meaning of any (linguistic) sign we need to ask the following questions (Scollon & Scollon, 2003):

a)   Who has uttered this?
b)   Who is the viewer?
c)   What is the social situation?
d)   Is that part of the material world relevant to such a sign?

These questions can be posed thanks to the property of language called *indexicality*. Indexicality is a universal characteristic of language and it is defined as "the property of the context-dependency of signs, especially language; hence the study of those aspects of meaning which depend on the placement of the sign in the material world" (Scollon & Scollon, 2003: 3).

In Chapter 3[4] we learned how language indexes the world in many ways (e.g. by means of personal pronouns or demonstratives). The indexicality of language allows us to understand, for instance, a sentence like *The examples **below** illustrate the point in question*. In order to understand such a sentence we have to rely upon a semiotics of written language which tells us that 'below' must index or refer to a text which is written within the same document (not in another document or on a piece of paper), or that it does not literally mean 'below' as if it were an object below another object. But the primary interest of MDA is not so much the indexicality in language as the *indexable world*, i.e. the ways in which the sign system of language indexes the other semiotic systems in the world around language.

We signal our meanings by means of **icons** (signs that resemble the objects being signalled), **indexes** (signs which point to or are attached to the object) and **symbols** (signs which are arbitrarily or conventionally associated with the object). For example, the picture

---

[4] See 3.5. (Deixis).

of a woman or a man beside or on a door at a public place is an **icon** that normally indicates that the door leads you into the women's or the men's restrooms. An arrow is an **index** (in public life signs) which indicates direction. The signs of written language are the most common **symbols** in our daily life. However, even when the symbols used in language are used arbitrarily, some of them also have iconic meanings; in fact all of them were originally iconic (but their history has been forgotten). These three types of sign may co-occur, and thus we may have a sign that contains both an icon and an index (e.g. the women's restroom icon together with an arrow indexing the direction to be followed in order to find the restroom), or one that contains all three types (e.g. the picture of a man and a woman, the arrow and the word 'restrooms').

11.8.2. Central elements in Geosemiotics

According to Scollon & Scollon (2003), there are four central elements to be taken into account when doing geosemiotic analysis:

1) **Social actor**: A person who moves and acts in the physical world, and who 'gives off' different signals (such as race, sex, age, etc.).

2) **Interaction order**: The set of social relationships we take up and try to maintain with the other people who are in our presence.

3) **Visual semiotics**: The 'visual frame' of the social action. It deals with aspects such as how the interaction order is represented visually and how placement of visual symbols affects their interpretation.

4) **Place semiotics**: Any human action takes place somewhere in the physical universe. Semiotic spaces (i.e. those spaces which provide pictures, discourses, or actions) are taken into account as well as non-semiotic spaces (i.e. spaces where signs are forbidden).

Thus, from the point of view of Geosemiotics, everything surrounding us may influence our taking particular actions: from our location in a city or on a farm, close to the ocean or to the mountains, to the people with whom we interact or the signs that form part of the whole picture of our social interactions.

As can be seen, MDA takes a holistic approach to the analysis of discourse by considering every element related to and interconnected with the discourse situation and the social action being carried out.

11.9. Example of analysis

We shall use the following picture in order to analyze the social action taking place by exploring the different discourses involved in the action as well as the information regarding its place and time (Geosemiotics).

As pointed out in 11.1., the first questions that mediated discourse analysts raise are:

1) What is the action going on here?
2) How does discourse figure into the action?

Regarding question 1, the action going on is that of a Kindergarten III class at an American school (**site of engagement**). The teacher (one of the **social actors**) is pointing to some written symbols (**mediational means**) on the board and most of the students are listening to and looking at the teacher. The body language (another type of **mediational means**) of one of them (the boy on the left), however, shows that he is temporarily not paying attention to the teacher because he is probably more interested in someone else or something occurring to the right of the picture. We can identify different discourses which form part of the action and which are interrelated:

1- **Oral discourse (exchange between the teacher and the students)**: This is one of the last days of the academic course, and so the teacher is asking the students about their favorite part of the course. They all respond to the question, showing different opinions which the teacher tries to summarize by making a diagram on the board.

2- **Written discourse**: There are different types of written discourse on the different boards and walls of the class:
   a) **Diagramatic discourse:** The oral discourse is intertwined with the written discourse on the board, which the teacher has organized in the form of a diagram and which intends to summarize the main points made by the students. We read that some of their favorite activities were the *garden hat parade,* the *museum field trip,* the *100ᵗʰ day of school, Pilgrim and Native- American day, St. Patrick's day, celebration of learning day* and the *San Isidro Parade.* This list of favorite activities not only signals the preferences of the students but also provides a considerable amount of information about the type of school where the action is taking place. Many aspects could be analyzed in this respect, but for the purpose of illustration, we may say that it is evidently an American school (the language used is English and they celebrate Native-Americans day – therefore showing respect for this group), but there is one point that gives us a clue that the action may not be taking place in America: the fact that one of the favorite activities of the students was the "San Isidro Parade". In effect, this is an American school in Spain, and thus we see that it is a policy of the school to celebrate and show respect not only for American festivities and celebrations, but also for those of the country where the school is located.
   b) **Discourse of rules or regulations**: We see a sign on the

wall (entitled "K-III Rules") that constantly reminds the students of the rules to be followed in class and during interaction with teacher and classmates, which are three (*1. We do not talk when someone else is talking, 2. We are kind to our friends,* and *3. We follow directions*). This sign is in turn related to a bigger sign posted on the entrance wall of the classroom (but does not appear in the picture) which reads: "It's all about respect."

c) **Poetic discourse:** We also see a poster with a nursery rhyme *("With silver bells and cockleshells...")* on the white board behind the teacher, which does not appear to be very related to the action going on at the moment but which nevertheless provides the analyst with some historical information about other actions or activities carried out throughout the school year, which form part of the **habitus** of the actors in the picture and therefore also contribute to the overall meaning of the social action in question.

d) **Language-learning discourse:** On the whiteboard we can partially see a sentence that is part of a language exercise for completion (...because____). This exercise (as well as the poem) does not seem to be of great importance at the moment but provides us with some information about previous actions carried out in the class.

So in the picture analyzed herein both the discursive and non-discursive practices are interconnected, and they constitute the **nexus of practice** of the social action in question. Among the practices observed in the social action taking place we may mention *turn-taking practices* (the students raise their hands to take part in the conversation), *physical spacing practices* (the students are sitting on the floor, the teacher is sitting on a chair in front of the class), *teaching-learning practices* and so on.

It is interesting to observe here that both the teacher and the students are wearing pyjamas, which is not a normal or daily practice in school environments. However, this fact is one more clue for the interpretation of the particular action taking place: the picture was taken on "pizza and pyjama day", and therefore the practice of wearing pyjamas and slippers has to be judged as appropriate and also as explanatory of the relaxed atmosphere that can be observed in the class as a whole.

It is also worth noting that all of the signs analyzed are indexes of a larger discourse. For example, the rules posted on the wall index the larger discourse of school policy, or the language used by the teacher indexes the larger discourse of politically correct institutional language.

As we see, discourse and action are equally important for the interpretation of the situation under analysis. Both the oral and written discourses, as well as the body language of all the participants, are indexes of the action and practices going on. For instance, the teacher's body language shows that she is developing an activity with her students (she's pointing to the board, and her posture indicates that she is 'in command'). Thus it can be observed here, as in all social actions, that the different mediational means (e.g.: body language, texts, way of dressing, oral discourse) found in this action are polyvocal (there is more than one 'voice'), intertextual (different kinds of text are interrelated) and interdiscursive (different discourses intertwine).

SUMMING UP... (CHAPTER 11)

1. MDA is an approach to the study of discourse which focuses on **social action**.
2. Language, as well as non-verbal communication and physical objects used by an agent in carrying out an action, are considered to be **mediational means**.
3. Discourse and human action in social change are its main concern, and **mediated action** is used as the basic unit of analysis.
4. All social action is based on tacit, normally unconscious actions which make up the different **practices**. An individual's accumulated experience of social actions is what we call the **habitus** or the **historical-body**.
5. There are both **discursive** and **non-discursive practices**, which are interconnected and which together constitute the **nexus of practice** of a given social action.
6. MDA includes multiple **methods**, from ethnographic participant-observation, interviews and questionnaire surveys, to focus groups or the collection of texts and images. The main aim is the identification and analysis of key mediated actions.
7. From the point of view of MDA, **all discourse is mediated and all mediations are discursive**.
8. MDA is an **interdisciplinary** approach to discourse.
9. **Geosemiotics** is a broad analytical position taken by MDA, which holds the assumption that a very important aspect of the meaning of all language (whether in a conversation, in a book or on a public traffic sign) is based on the material, concrete, physical placement of that language in the world.
10. The key to the analysis of any human action is **indexicality**, i.e., the meaning of signs based on their material location.
11. We signal our meanings by means of **icons**, **indexes** and **symbols**. These three types of signs may co-occur.
12. Scollon & Scollon (2003) identify four central elements to be taken into account when doing geosemiotic analysis: **social actor, interaction order, visual semiotics and place semiotics**.

SELF-EVALUATION QUESTIONS

Choose the answer that best suits the information given in Chapter 11.

1) MDA mainly focuses on...
a) texts.
b) discourses.
c) discourse and human action in social change.

2) According to MDA...
a) language is the only mediational means.
b) verbal communication and physical objects are also mediational means.
c) only linguistic behavior can be analyzed.

3) MDA is...
a) an interdisciplinary approach to DA.
b) a solely linguistic approach to DA.
c) mainly an intercultural approach to DA.

4) MDA uses...
a) only one method to analyze data.
b) multiple methods to look at data from different perspectives.
c) multiple methods to look at data from a single perspective.

5) MDA analysts base their studies on...
a) the sender-receiver model of communication.
b) a producer-audience model of communication.
c) a social interaction model of communication.

6) MDA analysts are concerned with...
a) the formal aspects of language.
b) exotic cultures and their behavior.
c) social actors and their actions in using the texts of communication.

7) MDA is an approach...
a) which takes ideas and concepts from many other disciplines.

b) based on Bloomfield's studies.

c) with no connection to other disciplines.

8) The unit of analysis used by MDA is...

a) the sentence.

b) mediated action.

c) the text.

9) MDA methodology focuses more on...

a) linguistic data than on the mediated action of social actors.

b) the mediated action of social actors than on linguistic data.

c) psychological considerations than on social ones.

10) MDA analysts give great importance to...

a) the material place where social actions occur.

b) the syntactic analysis of the sentences used by speakers.

c) the psychological mechanisms put in motion when using a language.

11) The systematic analysis of how language appears in the material world is called...

a) Semiotics.

b) Sociolinguistics.

c) Geosemiotics.

12) In geosemiotic analysis...

a) the material and physical placement of language is of utter importance.

b) traffic signs are the main concern.

c) conversation is the focus of attention.

13) Within Geosemiotics, the key to the analysis of human action is...

a) syntax.

b) indexicality.

c) grammar.

14) Geosemiotics...

a) analyzes only signs and symbols posted on different places.

b) focuses on outdoor situations and meanings.

c) entails a very broad analysis of discourse.

15) Indexicality...
a) has to do with the context-dependency of signs.
b) can not be said to be a universal characteristic of language.
c) does not depend on the placement of signs in the material world.

16) MDA is primarily interested in...
a) the indexicality in language.
b) the indexable world.
c) place deixis.

17) What type of sign is this: ?
a) an icon.
b) an index.
c) a symbol.

18) What type of sign is this: ?
a) an icon.
b) an index.
c) a symbol

19) The three types of signs...
a) may not be used together.
b) may co-occur.
c) are not present in the language system.

20) MDA...
a) takes a partial approach to DA.
b) does not pay attention to conditions other than language itself.
c) takes a holistic approach to DA.

PRACTICE

A) *ANALYSIS*: ANALYZE the type(s) of discourse found in the different signs on this road in France. IDENTIFY the *icons, indexes* and *symbol*s, and indicate if there are cases of co-occurrence of two or three types of signs.

B) *ANALYSIS*: IDENTIFY the different discourses found on this inscription in a street of London. ANALYZE the visual and place semiotics of the symbols.

C) *ANALYSIS*: TAKE PICTURES of people in public places and choose one for analysis. IDENTIFY the social actors, the mediational means and the different practices constituting the nexus of practice. Also, INDICATE the different discourses and how they interrelate.

D) *ANALYSIS*: EXAMINE this photograph showing a fragment of a wall in a London Underground station. From the MDA approach to DA,

    a) ANALYZE the type(s) of discourse found in it.

    b) ANALYZE the visual and place semiotics of the symbols.

    c) IDENTIFY and explain the icons, indexes and symbols, and INDICATE if there are cases of co-occurrence of two or three types of signs.

FURTHER READING

Norris & Jones, 2005.
R. Scollon, 1998.
R. Scollon, 2001.
Scollon & Scollon, 2003.
Scollon & Scollon, 2004.

USEFUL WEBSITES

Suzanne Wong Scollon website :
http://www.aptalaska.net/~ron/horn/

Review of R. Scollon and S. Scollon's (2003) *Language in the Material World* :
http://sfl.tjcu.edu.cn/tian/publications/reviews/Discourses%20in%20place%202003.pdf

Application of MDA in a U.S. Air Force study:
http://www.airpower.maxwell.af.mil/airchronicles/apj/apj03/fal03/disler.html
A mediated discourse analysis approach to language attitude research:
http://www.meertens.knaw.nl/ss17/contributions/abstract.php?paperID=744

Rodney Jones' website:
http://144.214.44.26/index.php/people/62-academic-staff/15--jones-rodney-dr

12 FURTHER ISSUES IN DISCOURSE ANALYSIS

"The moment one starts to think of language as discourse, the entire landscape changes, usually, for ever."

McCarthy & Carter, *Language as Discourse*

"Discourse is used for communication: people use utterances to convey information and to lead each other toward an interpretation of meanings and intentions. This role greatly increases the scope of discourse analysis, simply because one has to address how the language of utterances is related to aspects of the communication process (such as knowledge or intentions) that bear an indirect (and controversial) relationship to language per se."

D. Schiffrin, *Approaches to Discourse*

Chapter Outline:

- Units of analysis.

- Discourse types or genres.

- The concepts of *cohesion* and *coherence.*

- Discourse markers and their contribution to cohesion and coherence.

- The concepts of *discourse function* and *discourse strategy.*

12.1. Some important issues of concern for all discourse analysts

As the reader may have noticed, in spite of the noticeable differences existing among the various approaches presented and studied in this book, all of them have, however, common concerns. Considering their importance, we shall try to elucidate some of these in this Chapter. I refer to the following:

- Unit(s) of analysis
- Discourse types
- Cohesion and coherence
- Discourse strategies and functions

12.1.1. Unit(s) of analysis

Discourse analysts have always been on the lookout for a **unit of analysis** that will allow them to describe and explain linguistic phenomena. One of their initial research questions might be simply formulated as: What are my units of analysis going to be? Shall I think in terms of…

- sentences?
- propositions?
- utterances?
- turns?
- speech acts?
- theme/rheme structures?
- social action?
- strategies?
- functions?

As may be inferred from previous chapters, there is not a single or unique unit that can be used for all types of discourse analysis. In general, we may say that scholars have rejected the sentence as a unit, because their studies intend to go precisely 'beyond the sentence', and thus one of the initial (formal) definitions given referred to *a unit of language larger than the clause or sentence* (Lakoff, 1998). But the phenomenon of discourse is more embedded into a functional definition of language ('language in use') than into a formal one, and a functional definition does not say anything about the size of the units. How big, then, can a feature of discourse be? Depending on the level on which they focus, researchers may deal with larger or smaller units. Different approaches work with different units, but the same analyst may handle different units at the same time if s/he considers it appropriate for the purposes of his/her study.

Thus, for instance, we have seen that, whereas for an interactional sociolinguist the main unit of analysis may be the *utterance* or the *(politeness) strategy*, for a mediated discourse analyst this will be *mediated action* (a much broader and larger unit than an *utterance* or a *strategy*).

The term *discourse* is generally applied to dyadic interactions which may be very long, medium-length, or very short: a simple "Hi!" (in a given context and situation) may constitute data for analysis. Lakoff's (1998) definition of **discourse** takes this fact into account. By defining discourse as "A term used to cover all linguistic interactions that follow predictable patterns known implicitly or explicitly to participants and that have a discernible function," she supports the view of discourse as linguistic interaction covering any length (*all linguistic interactions*). And if discourse can cover any length, then the units chosen for analysis will also be greater or smaller depending, among other things, on the type of discourse used as data.

Thus, the type of discourse we choose for analysis will bear a close connection to the type(s) of unit(s) used, and hence the choice of a given discourse type is another of the important concerns of discourse analysts. We now turn to this issue.

12.1.2. Discourse types/ genres

As pointed out in 12.1.1., discourse is intrinsically dyadic, but being dyadic does not imply that it is always reciprocal. For example, in a therapy session, the therapist is entitled to ask her patients about their private life but the patients are not entitled to do the same with the therapist. Thus we could say that non-reciprocality is a characteristic of the type of discourse called *Psychotherapeutic discourse.*

Depending on the analyst's perspective or on the variables taken into account, we may divide the universe of discourse into numerous different types, such as *legal discourse, medical discourse, scientific discourse, computer-mediated discourse* or *family discourse*, to name a few.

Lakoff (1998)[1] provides the following taxonomy in terms of the relationship we see between the forms used and the particular discourse. Discourse may thus be:

- *Formal/informal.*
- *Reciprocal/non-reciprocal.*
- *Spontaneous/non-spontaneous.*
- *Face-to-face telephone conversation.*
- *Public private.*
- *Task-oriented (*discourse oriented towards a particular purpose, e.g. Psychotherapy).
- *Literate* (includes all modes of linguistic communication in writing).
- *Memorable* (intended to last, to go on, to be recorded for the future).
- *Empathic* (we can see what each participant is feeling, e.g.: face-to-face normal conversation, dialogue).
- *Monologic* (one party tends to do most of the talking).
- *Truthful* (designed for the purpose of fact-finding, e.g. psychotherapy, legal court discourse) vs. *fictional discourse* (Searle, 1979b).

---

[1] Personal communication in her *Discourse* class, Georgetown University, Spring 1998.

- *Spoken visual* (gestures, movements, etc.) (Fairclough, 1989).
- *Dyadic/triadic/group* (Various parts can take a role. Writing is generally non-dyadic, but letters are dyadic) (Simmel, 1950).

As noted in Chapter 9, Bakhtin uses the term ***genre*** to refer to the different discourse types, and applies it to the whole range of human linguistic production. He notes that each sphere has its own patterns and that therefore genres are context-based, stable and diverse. However, it should be noted that no discourse belongs to a unique and exclusive type. There are no absolute distinctions among all the different discourse types, and thus we may more properly speak of a continuum of discourse types rather than of separate and distinct categories. For example, a conversation between a professor and a student at the end of a class may be situated at some point between the formal/informal range: there is some level of formality because of the distance and differences in power between the student and her professor, but at the same time the particular situation does not require high levels of formality, thus the analyst will surely find certain features of informal speech in their conversation as well.

Consequently, different categories may be found in the same linguistic event. For example, the speech of a political candidate in a public place may belong to all of the following discourse types: public, formal, non-spontaneous, memorable, spoken and visual (at the same time), group, political, non-reciprocal.

Hodge & Kress (2001: 295) point out that "genres only exist in so far as a social group declares and enforces the rules that constitute them". Thus, a given social group may establish, recognize and name a particular kind of social occasion and the actions of the participants on this occasion are governed by the specific set of practices delineated for it. The texts which are created in the process have a form which codes this set of practices, and this form consolidates as a semiotic category and is therefore recognized as a particular genre.

For the purpose of illustration, in the following sections we shall try to explain, briefly, some of the characteristics of three types of discourse (*political, medical* and *computer-mediated discourse*), as well as the way certain scholars have approached their study.

12.1.2.1. Political discourse

As Wilson (2001) notes, the study of political discourse covers a broad range of subject matter and draws on a wide range of analytic methods. The primary goal of political discourse analysis is to discover and point to the ways in which language is manipulated for specific political purposes. Orwell (1969) analyzes different manners in which language is used to manipulate the thoughts of an audience. For instance, he shows how politicians manipulate the minds of people by using the term "pacification" to refer to the bombing of defenceless villages. Orwell accuses politicians of being responsible for a general decline in the use of the English language, by distorting it and constructing what the British call "political gobbledygook," i.e. complicated language that is difficult to understand. An example of this gobbledygook can be found in President Nixon's Press Secretary's use of the noun-phrase "biosphere overload" to refer to overpopulation, or in the title "The Urban Conservation and Environmental Awareness Work Party" given to an anti-vandalism committee of a British District Council (Neaman & Silver, 1990). Edleman's (1971, 1977, 1988) work also points to the symbolic manipulation of reality for the achievement of political goals. Likewise, Pêcheux (1978, 1982) notes that the meaning of words is transformed in terms of who uses them, so words in a given "discourse formation" (Foucault, 1972) may be interpreted differently within another formation. For example, the interpretation of the phrase "Social Security reform bill" within a liberal environment in the U.S. may differ radically from its interpretation within a conservative environment. This issue is related to Fairclough's general point about not looking at isolated sentences or words, because in most cases it is the context, and not the words themselves, which carry the political message.

Language may be manipulated for political purposes at different levels. Thus, as was shown above, certain words or expressions (lexical level) may be strategically placed and used with certain political aims in mind. Likewise, certain syntactic forms of a given political discourse may be used differently depending on the ideological goals of the text. An example of manipulation at the syntactic level is found in Stubbs' (1996) study on the distribution of ergative[2] forms within two school Geography textbooks. The book in which causation and agency were expressed more

---

[2] Ergatives are verbs which can be transitive or intransitive, and which allow the same nominal group and the same object group in transitive clauses and as subject in intransitive clauses. E.g. Several firms *have closed their factories*, Factories *have been closed*, Factories *have closed* (Stubbs, 1996: 133). Thus ergatives have agentive and nonagentive uses, a fact that allows the speaker/writer to use them differentially for different ideological goals.

frequently was found to be the book whose author adopted an explicit political role.

Interestingly enough, "research on accent clearly indicates that selected phonological variables can carry political loading" (Wilson, 2001: 410). In effect, discourse can also be manipulated at the phonological level in order to achieve certain political objectives. For example, while Margaret Thatcher was Prime Minister of Britain, it was perceived that she modified her speech in very particular ways with the intention of making herself more appealing to voters (Wilson, 2001). Also, in a study by Wilson & Gunn (1983), it was revealed that speakers can be perceived as either more Catholic/Irish/Republican or more Protestant/British/Unionist, by adopting certain alternative phonological forms.

It is clear that all linguistic levels, from lexis to pragmatics, are involved in characterizing political discourse. Most authors within the Social Theory and Critical Discourse Analysis[3] approaches tend to carry out studies of pragmatic aspects within political discourse, such as the use of implicatures, speech acts or metaphors, or the use and abuse of power. Hart (2005) argues in favor of the combination of cognitive linguistics and CDA for the proper analysis of political discourse. Gjierstad (2007) points out the importance of the systematic inclusion of contextual elements in the analysis of (political) discourse, and of the advantages of basing such an analysis on the Scandinavian theory of linguistic polyphony (the ScaPoLine). The theory of linguistic polyphony puts emphasis on the identification of the presence of different points of view in one single utterance. Obeng & Hartford (2008) compile six articles in which a variety of issues connected to discourse as political behavior are discussed, such as the teaching of English as an international language used as a weapon of American hegemony, or the functions and uses of English similes, metaphors, and informal language in the political discourse of Albania before the 1990s.

Other authors also take a critical stance on political discourse but do not belong to either Social Theory or CDA proper. Such is the case of Robin Lakoff (1990, 2000, 2001, 2002), who delves into power and other interesting pragmatic issues. Lakoff (2002), for example, analyzes the vagueness, breeziness and informality of the language used by President Bush to talk about the tragedy of the September 11th, 2001 terrorist attacks on the U.S., as well as his use of 'cowboy-isms' for certain political purposes, among other things.

As was suggested in Chapters 9 and 10, it is now a growing trend in

---

[3] See Chapters 9 and 10.

political discourse to combine social theory and linguistic theory, a trend that can be identified in Fairclough's (e.g. 1992a), van Dijk's (e.g. 1989) or Wodak's (e.g. 1995) work. Thus we are led into the reflection that the discourse used by those who analyze political discourse is also political. In effect, Wilson (2001) points out that some analyses may become as much political as linguistic, and that political discourse is made up of and must allow for both. Moreover, some authors define political discourse in such broad terms that almost any discourse may be considered political.

Much more could be written and said about political discourse, but it would overstep the boundaries of this chapter. Thus, it is now time for us to turn to another genre which has been widely studied by discourse analysts: medical discourse.

12.1.2.2. Medical discourse

There are a considerable number of studies about the discourse of medical encounters. These studies take different approaches or theories (e.g. interactional sociolinguistics, conversation analysis, politeness theory) as a point of departure for their analyses.

A great part of the research on the topic has been directed towards the analysis of power relationships between doctor and patient. Madfes (2002, 2003), for example, finds there are two types of medical discourse practice: a) the traditional (Western) practice, characterized by intrusion and a parallel discourse, in which the doctor always controls the floor of the conversation and often displays power by being uncooperative with respect to the patient's inquiries, and b) the alternative-medicine practice, whose main features are reinforcement and convergence, in which the doctors interact at a more egalitarian level with their patients, trying to maintain face and showing a more open and understanding attitude, not only in their talk but also at the level of body language.

Most studies on medical encounters have been conducted within the context of Western traditional medicine. Helman (1984) describes these encounters as "ritualized" (in an analogy to religious rituals) in the sense that there is a sequence of phases that normally occurs in them. Ten Have (1989), for instance, presents medical encounters as organized into a sequence of six phases: 1) Opening, 2) Complaint, 3) Examination or test, 4) Diagnosis, 5) Treatment of advice, and 6) Closing. Likewise, using Byrne & Long's (1976) model, Heath (1992: 37) proposes the following sequence: I) Relating to the patient, II) Discovering the reason for attendance, III) Conducting a verbal or physical examination or both, IV) Consideration of the patient's condition, V) Detailing treatment or further investigation, and VI) Terminating.

Notwithstanding the ritualized condition of medical encounters, we also find features of conversational discourse in them, because they also have some degree of unpredictability. Indeed, several major analyses (e.g. Frankel, 1979; Heritage, 1989; Maynard, 1991; Ainsworth-Vaughn, 1998a) deal with the question of **genre**, i.e. of whether medical encounters are fundamentally conversational or interview-like. Ferrara (1994) compares conversation with psychotherapy sessions (a type of medical encounter) and he finds differences with respect to the following seven aspects 1) Parity, 2) Reciprocality, 3) Routine recurrence, 4) Bounded time, 5) Restricted topic, 6) Remuneration, and 7) Regulatory responsibility. The first two (*parity* and *reciprocality*) are more a feature of conversation than of medical encounters. The other five features, on the contrary, characterize medical discourse rather than normal conversation. As Ainsworth-Vaughn suggests, medical encounters exist on a continuum between interrogation and friendly conversation, "with a small amount of time devoted to satisfying medical goals" (2001: 458).

The analysis of **frames** (Tannen, 1993; Tannen & Wallat, 1987) has been of most interest to analysts of medical encounters. The interactive behavior of participants constitutes the frame. So by situating a given interaction within a frame, a speaker attempts to constitute the self. Thus if the doctor-patient encounter is framed as part of the medical institution, participants are constituted as doctors, nurses or patients. Story-telling and the use of narrative have been linked with framing in medical discourse. Ainsworth-Vaughn (1998b) suggests that patient's storytelling is used not only to frame but also to mitigate discussion of a serious illness (e.g. cancer), introduce a candidate diagnosis, or validate the patient's experience.

Many studies have shown that questions in medical encounters demonstrate both power-claiming and power-sharing, although most of them argue in favor of a clear predominance of the former over the latter, describing these encounters as highly asymmetrical interviews, with only one person having the right to question (West, 1984; Hein & Wodak, 1987; Weijts, 1993; Alexias 2008).

Another aspect that has been studied within the discourse of medical encounters is **gender**, albeit not sufficiently, as Ainsworth-Vaughn (2001) points out. The few studies that focus on this variable tend to conclude that women are more likely to be cooperative in discourse, while men are more likely to be competitive. Menz and Lalouscheck (2006), for instance, analyze patient-doctor communication in terms of age, gender and cause, and they argue that, since there is evidence of the fact that coronary heart disease is under-diagnosed and under-treated in women, the discourse of physicians should show more support to enhance women's ability to describe the kind and course of symptoms, for it is the patients rather than physicians who "are experts for describing their pain" (2006:150).

All the studies named above concentrate on the area of doctor-patient communication, and therefore their focus is on spoken discourse. The other area on which the medical language literature has tended to concentrate is the area of the language of particular genres of medical discourse, whose focus is mainly written discourse. The written genre that has been given the most attention is the *case history*[4].

Other interesting studies have focused on the lexicon, the syntax and the semantics of medicine. Johnson & Murray (1985) for example, explore the role of euphemisms in medical language, which are used in many cultures, especially when the diagnosis is "bad". Staiano (1986) delves into the grammar of illness and disease and sheds light on the contrast between the construction "I am" (e.g. *I am a diabetic*) and "I have" (e.g. *I have* or *I suffer from diabetes*). The former expression displays an identification of the speaker with the pathology, while the latter (genitive construction) identifies the illness as an external object. Ross (1989) explores the use of metaphors in medical discourse and argues that the fact that disease is viewed as an outrage lays the groundwork for the undoubtedly dominant metaphor of biomedicine, i.e. "Medicine is war" (Lakoff & Johnson, 1980).

12.1.2.3. Computer-mediated discourse

Interpersonal communication via computer networks is a recent phenomenon in the history of humanity, and consequently the analysis of the language used in such type of communication is also recent. This communication type has been called *Computer-mediated discourse* (henceforth CMD), and is defined by Herring as follows:

> *Computer-mediated discourse* is the communication produced when human beings interact with one another by transmitting messages via networked computers. The study of computer-mediated discourse [...] is a specialization within the broader interdisciplinary study of computer-mediated communication (CMC), distinguished by its focus on *language and language use* in computer networked environments, and by its use of methods of discourse analysis to address that focus. (2001: 612)

---

[4] For a detailed description of the characteristics of this genre, see Fleischman (2001).

According to medium, computer-mediated communication is classified in two main modes:

A) **Synchronous**: a mode that requires that both sender and addressee(s) be logged-on simultaneously (e.g. chat, MUDs and MOOs[5]).

B) **Asynchronous**: a mode that does not require that users be logged-on at the same time (e.g. e-mail, usenet newsgroups, listserv discussion lists, etc.).

CMD is considered distinct from writing and speaking due to a number of reasons, among which are:

1. CMD exchanges are normally faster than written exchanges (e.g. letters), but slower than spoken exchanges.
2. CMD allows multiple participants to communicate

---

[5]*MUD* stands for *Multi-User Domain*, which was originally designed as a variation of the *Dungeons and Dragons* game, developed for multi-users on the Internet. *MOO* stands for *MUD, Object-Oriented*. MUDs and MOOs have proliferated and found a comfortable home in education.

simultaneously in a manner that is unknown and impossible to attain through other media.

3. It is a 'private' and public medium at the same time, since it creates the impression of direct and even private exchange of messages, but it also may involve the distribution to an unseen (and frequently unknown) audience.

4. Information is available through the visual channel, and it is typically limited to typed text. Modern systems of communication, however, allow the chats to be accompanied by video-images and sound, in which case it becomes very close to face-to-face communication.

These and other reasons have led participants to think of CMD as a blend of both speaking and writing, albeit still having its own and distinctive features, constraints and potentialities. Precisely this blending of speaking and writing is what causes CMD to be perceived as less correct, complex and coherent than standard written language. In effect, CMD often contains non-standard features which are generally deliberate choices made by the users to economize on typing effort or to mimic spoken language in a creative way (Herring, 2001). Thus, Murray (1990) observes that computer science professionals using CMD delete subject pronouns, determiners and auxiliaries, avoid mixed case (e.g. by not using capital letters), and use abbreviations very frequently. In this respect, some of the main strategies adopted by CMD users are:

- Use of a 'mixed' style (formal/informal – written/spoken).
- Use of acronyms and abbreviations (e.g.: ASAP, FYI, btw, etc.).
- Use of the so-called *electronic utterance* (Sotillo, 2000), i.e. a single clause with complements and adjuncts.
- Use of symbols or emoticons to compensate for the lack of facial expressions, sound, or body language (e.g.: ☺, $$, capital letters to mimic shouting or a higher pitch of the voice: GREAT!!!).
- Use of abridged, concise language.
- Use of *Netiquette* rules[6]: Politeness on the web.

Some authors have described CMD as an *interactionally incoherent*

---

[6] *Netiquette* is network etiquette, i.e. the dos and don'ts of online communication. It covers both common courtesy online and the informal "rules of the road" of cyberspace. An example of these rules can be found at: http://www.albion.com/netiquette/

type of discourse, considering the limitations of computer messaging systems of turn-taking. Herring (2001: 618) explains that the two properties of the computer medium that create obstacles to interaction management are: "1) disrupted turn *adjacency* caused by the fact that messages are posted in the order received by the system, without regard for what they are responding to, and 2) lack of simultaneous *feedback* caused by reduced audiovisual cues."

In spite of the above-mentioned common characteristics of CMD, we cannot say that it is a uniform medium of communication. Language can vary widely in computer-mediated environments depending on different factors, such as situational context or participant demographics (e.g. variables such as *gender, age, social class, geographical location*, etc.). This variation leads us to the conclusion that, despite being mediated by impersonal machines, CMD reflects the social and personal circumstances and realities of its users. As Herring (2001) points out, CMD constitutes social practice in and of itself: participants negotiate, intimidate, joke, flirt (and even have sex or get married) on the Internet.

Scholars studying CMD have focused on different aspects of this type of discourse, such as **power asymmetries** (e.g. the dominance of the United States as the leading source of computer network technology (Yates, 1996)), **gender asymmetries** (e.g. female participants in discussion groups are disproportionately disfavored (Herring, 1996; 1998; 1999)) or **the dominance of the English language** on the Internet (Mattelart, 1996; Yates, 1996).

As regards methodology, Androutsopoulos & Beißwenger (2008) point out that language-focused research on CMD has drawn on methods and key concepts from a variety of research traditions in linguistics, including pragmatics, conversation analysis, sociolinguistics, genre analysis, and the ethnography of communication. These methodologies have been applied fruitfully to study how individuals use linguistic resources to establish contacts, manage interactions, and construct identities within computer networks.

All in all, the discursive negotiation and expression of social relations in cyberspace provide an extremely rich source of data for the study of discourse and social practice. As has already been suggested, different electronic interactions may vary greatly in pragmatic aspects such as *level of formality, use of speech acts, discourse topic* and *topical coherence*. This last aspect, *coherence*, is another of the important issues that – together with cohesion– has been widely studied by discourse analysts. The next section in this chapter touches upon this topic.

12.1.3. Cohesion and coherence

We saw in Chapter 1 that both **cohesion** and **coherence** are part of the seven criteria which are necessary to satisfy the definition of *text* (de Beaugrande & Dressler, 1981). *Cohesion* has to do with the relationships between text and syntax, and *coherence* has to do with the knowledge or cognitive structures that are implied by the language used and that contribute to the overall meaning of a given discourse. Cohesion and coherence are semantic concepts and they are both part of the system of a language.

Seidlhofer & Widdowson (1999) associate *cohesion* to the concept of *text,* and *coherence* to that of *discourse.* These authors make a clear distinction between the concepts of *text* and *discourse* -as opposed to other authors (e.g. Halliday, 1992; Chafe, 1992), who use both terms indistinctly.[7] *Text* is defined by Seidlhofer & Widdowson as "the linguistic product of a discourse process," whereas *discourse* is "the process of conceptual formulation whereby we draw on our linguistic resources to make sense of reality" (1999: 206). Thus, *cohesion* for these authors is a *textual property* and has to do with the textualization of contextual connections. *Coherence*, on the other hand, is the discourse function of realizing those connections, and is a *discoursive property*. A text can therefore have no cohesion but derive a coherent discourse. Conversely, a given text may be cohesive but discourse-incoherent. Examples **a** and **b** illustrate this point in a very simple manner:

a)   I went to Paris last week. And my grandma is a radio hostess.

b)   Great! Oh, no!!

Example **a** is an instance of a cohesive text. We find cohesive devices such as **reference** (*I*) and **conjunction** (*And*), but it is difficult to make a connection between the first clause and the second, and consequently most hearers would catalogue the whole utterance as incoherent (it is hard to find a connection between the fact that the speaker went to Paris and the fact that his grandmother is a radio hostess). Thus, the speaker would most probably be judged as lacking some mental capacities or simply as speaking non-sensically.[8] Contrary to example **a**, example **b** shows no

---

[7] See Chapter 1 for a more detailed account of the use of the terms *text* and *discourse* in DA literature.

[8] However, as the spirit of this book has tried to show, we can never analyze

signs of cohesion (there is no apparent use of reference, substitution or any other cohesive devices), but derives a coherent discourse if we think of the situation in which the two exclamations occurred: A 10-year-old child sees her mother approaching with a bag in her hands and feels happy because she thinks the bag contains the present she has been waiting for, (and so she says *"Great!"*), but immediately after she realizes that the bag holds the books for her to do the homework (and therefore she expresses her disappointment by exclaiming *"Oh, no!!"*).[9]

Let us now examine the concepts of *cohesion* and *coherence* in more detail.

12.1.3.1. Cohesion

All the authors studying the phenomenon of cohesion speak of a set of more or less similar cohesive devices or systems. Halliday & Hasan define *cohesion* as "the set of semantic resources for linking a SENTENCE with what has gone before" (1976:10). Cohesion occurs when one element in the discourse is presupposed by another, i.e., when one element cannot be effectively decoded except by recourse to another element in the same discourse. Some forms of cohesion are realized through the grammar and others through vocabulary. Consequently, Halliday & Hasan (1976) consider two main types of cohesion: 1) *grammatical cohesion,* and 2) *lexical cohesion*, which in turn are divided into five sub-types:

1) **Reference** (grammatical), which has to do with the resources for referring to an element which is recoverable[10] (e.g.: pronouns, comparatives, adverbs *here, then, now*).
2) **Substitution** (grammatical), which refers to a set of place holders that are used to signal an omission (e.g. *do* for verbal groups or *so* for clauses).
3) **Ellipsis** (grammatical), which refers to resources for omitting a clause or part of a clause when it can be assumed (e.g.: *She will go but I won't*, where *go* is omitted in the second clause because it is assumed).

---

utterances out of context, and the same utterance may mean different things depending on the conditions in which it occurs, so we could always find a situation or context where a) could be judged as coherent.

[9] Notice, however, that this example is used in a very simple way to try to illustrate the point these authors want to make, but it could be argued that the cohesion here is given by the intonation or the pragmatic marker used (*Oh, no!!*).

[10] See 3.4.

4) **Conjunction** (both grammatical and lexical), referring to the large inventory of connectors which link clauses in discourse (e.g.: *In addition, however, thus*, etc.).[11]

5) **Lexical cohesion** (lexical), the complement of grammatical cohesion, involving the repetition of lexical items, synonymy, hyponymy and collocation.

Halliday & Hasan note that, in spoken English, some types of grammatical cohesion are also expressed through the **intonation system**. As an example, they explain that in:

> *Did I hurt your feelings? I didn't mean to.*

"the second sentence coheres not only by ellipsis, with *I didn't mean to* presupposing *hurt your feelings*, but also by conjunction, the adversative meaning 'but' being expressed by the tone" (1976: 6).

The relationship between a cohesive item and the item it presupposes in a text is what we call a **cohesive tie**. As Martin (2001) notes, the interpretation of patterns of cohesive ties generally depends on the register, because both the register and the cohesive ties define a text. Halliday & Hasan anticipated this fact in their definition of text:

> The concept of cohesion can therefore be usefully supplemented by that of register, since the two together effectively define a text. A text is a passage of discourse which is coherent in these two regards: it is coherent with respect to the context of situation, and therefore consistent in register; and it is coherent with respect to itself, and therefore cohesive. (1976: 23)

Thus we can conclude that the different discourse types, genres or registers[12] can be identified and distinguished in terms of their cohesive devices. This is one of the reasons why cohesion is an important issue and focus of attention for discourse analysts.

Later studies on cohesion, such as Martin's (1992), reformulated the notion of cohesion as "a set of discourse semantic systems at a more abstract level than lexicogrammar" (Martin, 2001: 37). These semantic systems are the following (summarized from Martin, 2001: 37-38):

- **Identification**, concerned with resources for tracking participants

---

[11] Halliday & Hasan (1976, Chapter 5) consider four main types of conjunctive relations: 1) Additive, 2) Adversative, 3) Causal, and 4) Temporal.

[12] See 12.1.2.

in discourse. It considers the ways in which participants are both introduced into a text and kept track of once introduced.

- **Negotiation**, concerned with resources for the exchange of information and of goods and services in dialogue.
- **Conjunction**, concerned with resources for connecting messages, via addition, comparison, temporality and causality.
- **Ideation**, concerned with the semantics of lexical relations as they are deployed to construe institutional activity.

In Martin's model, the study of texture amounts to the study of patterns of interaction among discourse semantics, lexicogrammar and phonology/graphology in realization. Thus this author aligns the above systems with metafunctions, in the following manner (2001: 39):

- Identification →   textual meaning
- Negotiation →   interpersonal meaning
- Conjunction →   logical meaning
- Ideation →   experiential meaning

To conclude, we shall say that, in very general terms, a given text is cohesive when one or more of these devices or systems (such as ellipsis, conjunction, negotiation, etc.) can be identified, together with their presupposed cohesive ties.

The relationship between cohesion and coherence has always been a central issue in the study of discourse processing (e.g. Taboada, 2004; Yeh, 2004). As Yeh (2004) points out, "cohesion, as surface linguistic features, can not account fully for the coherence of a text" (2004: 243). Coherence mechanisms are deeper and much more "hidden" than those of cohesion, which makes coherence a more abstract and slippery concept as well. Let us now turn to it.

12.1.3.2. Coherence

There are different approaches to the study of **coherence**. Downing (2004) notes that one view sees coherence as a property of what emerges in two collaborating minds during speech production and comprehension (Gernsbacher & Givón, 1995; Linell & Korolija, 1997; Bublitz, 1999). Another view (Schegloff, 1990; Edwards, 1997) sees coherence "as deriving from the notion of discourse as a social event, as action in its own right" (Downing, 2004: 15). The former reflects a cognitive approach to the phenomenon of coherence and the latter, a social one.

De Beaugrande & Dressler note that "there is a continuity of senses among the knowledge activated by the expressions of the text" (1981: 84). This continuity of senses is considered to be the foundation of coherence. Thus, we speak of an 'incoherent' or 'non-sensical' text when we can not find a continuity of sense with it. But the world contains more than the sense of the expressions in the surface text. Elements such as cognitive processes, or the knowledge derived from the participants' experience of the world contribute an important amount of commonsense to the discourse situation or event. There are certain *global patterns* (de Beaugrande & Dressler, 1981) of knowledge and experience (such as *frames* (Minsky, 1975), *schemas* (Bartlett, 1932; Kintsch 1977), *plans* or *scripts* (Schank & Abelson, 1977)), which we all store and activate, and which are crucial when producing or receiving texts. For instance, *frames* are activated when trying to develop a topic, and *schemas* when thinking of how an event sequence will progress. *Plans* have to do with how text users or characters in textual worlds will pursue their goals, and *scripts* with how situations are set up so that certain texts can be presented at the right moment.

Green (1989) sees coherence through the prism of Grice's Cooperative Principle and she states that this principle (and the Relevant Maxim in particular) provides the basis for a natural account of the problem of the coherence of texts. As a consequence of this principle, everything a person says or writes is intended to be necessary, true, and relevant to accomplishing some objective in which both producer and receiver are mutually interested. Thus coherence depends on "the extent to which effort is required to construct a reasonable plan to attribute to the text producer in producing the text" (Green, 1989: 103), which in turn depends on the extent to which each sentence can be interpreted as representing a true, necessary, and relevant contribution to the plan. In this way, Green, like many other authors, shows that coherence is not only a matter of the properties of the text alone, but also of the probability that the receiver(s) will be able to make the necessary inferences to relate the content of the individual sentences or parts of such a text. Therefore, coherence is described as a function of the text-producer's estimate of his audience's beliefs and inferencing capacity, as well as of his acting appropriately on that estimate.

Van Dijk defines coherence in terms of *mental models* (Johnson-Laird, 1983): "…if people are able to construe a possible or plausible model for a sequence or a whole text, then the text is subjectively coherent" (Van Dijk, 2004: 9). This definition, van Dijk remarks, resolves the problem of 'extralinguistic' reference in discourse analysis, because it alludes to the fact that people do not refer so much to the 'real world' but to the "(inter)subjective (re)construction of the world, or a situation in the world in terms of their mental models" (2004: 9). Models let us see that people represent not only what they know about an event, but also what they think and feel in relation to such an event. Thus, it can be concluded that implicit information and inferences in discourse processing are represented in mental models. Interestingly enough, we are also led to infer that what people remember of a text is not precisely its meaning, but the subjective model they have created to represent the particular event in question.

According to van Dijk (2000), there are two main kinds of coherence:

1) *Extensional or referential*: when analyzing the coherence of a text, we examine the relations between its propositions and find a mental model through which it makes sense.

2) *Intensional*: a form of coherence based on meaning, propositions and their functional relations.

Both types of coherence are based not only on conceptual knowledge (e.g. the fact that a cat is an animal), but also on broader world knowledge (e.g. what type of an animal a cat is, where it can be found, what it looks like, etc.).

In spite of the numerous studies on the phenomenon of coherence, the concept is still not fully understood and continues to be a matter of debate. Oftentimes it has been regarded as a fuzzy, vague, and even mystical notion. However, the concept of coherence is a key concept in discourse analysis, and it is precisely the analysis and clarification of this fuzziness what pushes scholars to research the phenomenon in greater depth. In fact, it can be said that coherence is an intrinsically indeterminate notion, due to the fact that it depends on the way which language users ascribe their understanding to what they hear (or read). Coherence can not be found in a text isolated from an interpretation: it is not the texts, but rather the people that cohere. Hence, as Bublitz points out, "coherence is not a state but a process, helped along by a host of interacting factors situated on all levels of communication (from prosodic variation to textual organization, from topic progression to knowledge alignment)" (1999: 2).

Participants of a discursive situation can make it coherent by resorting to different means or strategies. One way of achieving coherence (and also cohesion) is through **discourse/pragmatic markers**. We now turn to them.

12.1.3.3. Discourse markers/pragmatic markers

Discourse markers (herinafter DMs) have been studied by numerous authors and from different discourse perspectives. All these authors, however, have not arrived at a consensus regarding what a DM is. For some, DMs are a kind of *pragmatic marker* (a larger concept) that establishes a conjunctive relation between two sentences (e.g.: Fraser, 1996; 2006). For others (e.g. Schiffrin, 1987; 2001; Romero Trillo, 2006; 2008), the concept of DM is a much broader one, and it includes other pragmatic markers which express not only conjunctive, but other types of relations as well. Earlier works, like Halliday & Hasan's (1976), present a semantic perspective on DMs.[13]

We saw in 12.2.1. that for Halliday & Hasan (1976) *conjunction* is a kind of both lexical and grammatical cohesive device which refers to a range of expressions conveying conjunctive relations. These expressions "express certain meanings which presuppose the presence of other components in the discourse" (1976: 236), and in this sense it can be argued that they also have a deictic nature (as Schiffrin (1987) later claimed). For Halliday & Hasan conjunctive expressions convey four main kinds of meaning:

1) ADDITIVE (e.g.: *and, furthermore, in addition, besides, in the same way*, etc.).
2) ADVERSATIVE (e.g.: *but, yet, though, on the contrary, however*, etc.).
3) CAUSAL (e.g.: *so, then, therefore, consequently, for this purpose*, etc.).
4) TEMPORAL (e.g.: *then, next, after that, finally, to sum up, in short*, etc.).

In spite of the fact that certain expressions are assigned to each of the types of meaning, Halliday & Hasan acknowledge that the meaning of the expressions may vary according to other conditions, different from the semantics of the word or expression in itself. For example, *and* normally has an additive meaning, but it can also convey an adversative relation if it prefaces a proposition whose meaning contrasts with that of a prior proposition, as in:

---

[13] Although they do not speak directly of DMs, their analysis of cohesion includes words and expressions (e.g. *By the way, to sum up, then, thus*, etc.) that have since been called markers by subsequent authors.

She said she wouldn't go. And she finally went!

where *And* can be said to have an adversative meaning equivalent to that of *But*.

Fraser (1990b; 1996; 1998; 2006) places DMs within the broader set of **pragmatic markers** (herinafter PMs). His view differs from Halliday & Hasan's in that it is concerned not so much with the cohesion of text but rather with the meaning of sentences. In Fraser's framework, PMs are expressions that occur as part of a discourse segment but are not part of the propositional content of the message conveyed. There are four types of PMs:

1. BASIC MARKERS (e.g.: performative expressions such as: *I promise, please*, etc.).
2. COMMENTARY MARKERS (e.g.: manner-of-speaking markers such as: *Frankly, bluntly speaking*, etc.).
3. PARALLEL MARKERS (e.g.: conversational management markers such as: w*ell, O.K., now*, etc.).
4. DISCOURSE MARKERS (connectives such as: b*ut, so, then*, etc.).

This taxonomy shows that, in Fraser's view, DMs, are a type of PM and they function as segment *connectives* which belong to any of the following semantic categories:

1. CONTRASTIVE (e.g.: ***but**, although, in contrast to [this/that]*, etc.)
2. ELABORATIVE (e.g.: ***and**, above all, likewise, on top of it all*, etc.)
3. IMPLICATIVE (e.g.: ***so**, after all, for this reason, then, therefore*, etc.)
4. TEMPORAL (e.g.: ***then**, as soon as, finally, first, meanwhile*, etc.)

Thus, Fraser's DMs are roughly equivalent to Halliday & Hasan's conjunctive expressions, but they cannot be said to be on a par with Schiffrin's DMs. Schiffrin's conception of DMs is a rather different one, which reflects her view of discourse as a process of social interaction. She defines discourse markers as sequentially dependent elements that bracket units of talk (1987: 31) and her analysis shows that markers work "at different levels of discourse to connect utterances on either a single plane or across different planes" (2001: 57). She illustrates this fact with the following examples (2001: 57):

(1) a. Yeh, let's get back, because she'll never get home.
(1) b. And they holler Henry!!! 'Cause they really don't know!

Whereas in (1) a *because* connects actions, in (1) b it connects ideas. In (1) a *because* connects a request with the justification for the request, but in (1) b *'Cause* connects two idea units or representations of events.

(2) Jack: [The rabbis preach, ["Don't intermarry"
     Freda: [But I did-   [But I *did* say   those intermarriages
            that we wave in this country are healthy.

Schiffrin explains that (2) has four functions that locate an utterance at the intersection of four planes of talk, because Freda's *but* 1) prefaces an idea unit (that intermarriages are healthy), 2) displays a participation framework (non-aligned with Jack), 3) realizes an action (a rebuttal during an argument) and 4) seeks to establish Freda as a current speaker in an exchange (open a turn at talk).

Schiffrin includes in her repertoire of markers some expressions which are not considered DMs in Fraser's taxonomy, such as *y'know* or *well*. For Fraser, these markers belong to other categories within PMs, but they are not DMs proper.

Schiffrin (1987; 2001) makes three more important points:

- DMs not only display local relationships between adjacent utterances, but also more global relationships across wider spans of discourse.
- DMs are discourse deictic.
- Although DMs have a primary function, their use is multifunctional. This multifunctionality on different planes of discourse helps to create coherence.

Thus we see that DMs are important elements in the creation of cohesive and coherent discourse. For the purposes of illustration, let us analyze the following dyad:

> Fred: Taylor is a woman. However, she is good at
>   interpreting maps.

Tom: Really?

On the one hand, in this example we find **cohesion** devices such as **reference** (*she* refers to *Taylor*) or **conjunction** (*however*) in Fred's utterance, as well as in Tom's (**ellipsis**: Tom's reply could be paraphrased as *Is it real/true that Taylor is good at interpreting maps in spite of the fact that she is a woman?*). On the other hand, it can be observed that the DM *however* also plays an important part in giving **coherence** to the whole discursive situation: the **inference** coming out of this adversative marker is that women in general are not good at interpreting maps. Tom's reply (*Really?*) can also be taken as a marker which signals both men's **mental model**, which depicts women as hopeless map users. Thus, we find a **continuity of senses** in this exchange, given by the participant's capacity to make the necessary inferences related to a given mental model, which in turn leads to the assessment of this particular fragment of discourse as coherent.

The functions of DMs are broad. Their use does not only tell us about their linguistic properties, but also about the cognitive, social and expressive competence of their users. Hence DMs are also seen by researchers as a means to study different discourse **strategies,** which in turn are used to fulfil different and important discourse **functions**. Herein we face another of the concerns of discourse analysts.

12.1.4. Discourse strategies and functions

A final note on **strategies** and **functions** of discourse: The reader will have noticed all throughout this book that much of what discourse analysts do is to search for different strategies which are used to realize different functions of discourse.

Strategy is a key concept in Discourse Analysis, and it may be defined as "an attempt on the part of the speaker to reach (by means of various linguistic procedures) a given communicative aim" (Alba-Juez, 1995: 22). This aim obviously has to do with the function that the strategy is intended to accomplish.

The functions of speech and discourse in general have been studied profusely by many authors from different discourse perspectives. One of the traditional and best-known approaches to the "functions of speech" is Jakobson's (1960), which associates these functions with the six basic components of the communicative event, thus resulting in the following functions:

1. REFERENTIAL (focused on the referential content of the message).
2. EMOTIVE (focused on the speaker's state).
3. CONATIVE (related to the speaker's wishes that the addressee do or think such and such, and used in order to achieve some practical effect).
4. METALINGUISTIC (dealing with the code being used).
5. PHATIC (focused on the channel or on the establishment of bonds of personal union between people).
6. POETIC (concerning the way in which the message is encoded, or the artistic and creative use of language in general).

Halliday's (1976; 1978) more abstract scheme consists of three main functions:

1. EXPERIENTIAL (concerning language as a vehicle to conceptualize and describe our experience).
2. INTERPERSONAL (concerning the relationships among participants and the illocutionary acts used by them).
3. TEXTUAL (concerning messages as organized units of information).

Brown & Yule (1983) point out that the attempts to provide taxonomies of language functions have been vague and confusing, and thus they only describe two very general functions of language:

1. TRANSACTIONAL, which serves in the expression of content.
2. INTERACTIONAL, which serves in expressing social relations and personal attitudes.

The examples of taxonomies of functions shown above suffice to lead us to the conclusion that there is scant agreement on what kinds of functions are involved in human language and on which levels they operate. Most authors find consensus, however, in arguing that it is unlikely that utterances fulfil only one function at a time. The fact is that normally an utterance fulfils several functions simultaneously, and thus it seems reasonable to speak of *tendencies* (e.g. we may say that a given utterance has a *primarily referential function*), rather than of absolute categories that exist to the exclusion of all others. For the purposes of illustration, consider example (a):

(a) *Husband*: Why are you so tense?

     Wife: Tense? Oh, no. I'm not supposed to be tense. I'm
     just your wife. I'm not likely to have feelings of any kind.

The wife's ironic reply in (a) may be said to be primarily **interactional** (in Brown & Yule's terms), but at the same time –and at a lower level of abstraction– it is also fulfilling the function of **verbal attack**, which in turn intends to function as a **reproach**. This example also illustrates the fact that a given strategy (in this case the strategy of *being ironic*) may carry out different functions[14]. Conversely, a given function may be realized by different strategies (e.g. the function of **verbal attack** may be realized not only by the strategy of *being ironic*, but also by *insulting* or simply *ignoring the interlocutor's turn* in conversation).

As with all the topics covered in this course, much more could be said or written about the strategies and functions of discourse. However, for the purposes of the present work, this general view has been deemed sufficient. I encourage the reader to do further research on this or any of the myriad topics found under the umbrella of D.A..

12.2. So… is this all there is to say about DA?

We are finally reaching the end of the book and you might wonder if all the approaches to, and aspects of, DA covered herein are enough. On the one hand, my answer would be that nothing is enough in a discipline like DA, for, as was pointed out in Chapter 1, in a broad sense we could say that there are as many approaches as authors who analyze discourse. Some well-known pragmatic and discursive theories, as for instance, Relevance Theory[15] or the more recent Appraisal Theory[16], have not been covered or explained in this book due to space and planning constraints. On the other hand, it is impossible to cover all the spectrum of knowledge of a discipline (which is in turn multidisciplinary) in only one work.

The reader might have noticed that this book started with two questions (*What is Text Linguistics? What is Discourse Analysis?*) and

---

[14] For a detailed description of the strategies and functions of ironic discourse, see Alba-Juez ([1996] 2001).

[15] See Sperber & Wilson, 1986.

[16] See Martin ([2000] 2003) and Martin & White (2005).

ends with another question (*So… is this all there is to say about D.A.?*), a fact that is symbolic of the essence of this discipline as well as of any other of the fields of human knowledge: we could continue posing questions *ad infinitum* because, as Chafe's quote at the beginning of Chapter 1 suggests, "we are definitely not close to final answers". Thus the intention in this work has been to cover the essentials and to provide the student/reader with the necessary elements for a good initiation into the fascinating enterprise of analyzing discourse. The rest is now in your hands. The possibilities are infinite.

SUMMING UP... (CHAPTER 12)

1. There is not a single or unique unit that can be used for all types of discourse analysis. Different approaches work with different units. Thus, for instance, for an interactional sociolinguist the main unit of analysis may be the *utterance* or the *(politeness) strategy* and for a mediated discourse analyst this will be *mediated action*. But the same analyst may handle different units at the same time if s/he considers it appropriate for the purposes of his/her study.

2. Depending on the analyst's perspective or on the variables taken into account, we may divide the universe of discourse into numerous different types, such as *legal discourse, medical discourse, computer-mediated discourse*, etc. However, no discourse belongs to a unique and exclusive type, and thus we may speak of a continuum of discourse types rather than of separate and distinct categories.

3. When analyzing political discourse, the researchers' primary goal has been to discover the ways in which language is manipulated for specific political purposes.

4. A great part of the research on medical discourse has been directed towards the analysis of power relationships between doctor and patient. Other studies deal with the question of genre, the analysis of frames, the analysis of gender, and with the lexicon, the syntax and the semantics of medical discourse.

5. The study of computer-mediated discourse (CMD) is of recent development, and is considered to be a specialization within the broader interdisciplinary study of computer-mediated communication. This type of discourse has certain particular characteristics, such as the use of a mixed style (spoken/written, formal/informal), use of emoticons, use of abbreviated, concise language, etc. Scholars studying CMD have focused on aspects such as power asymmetries, gender asymmetries, or the dominance of the English language on the Internet.

6. An important concern of discourse analysts has always been to study how a given text or discourse practice achieves cohesion and coherence. Cohesion and coherence are semantic concepts: *Cohesion* has to do with the relationships between text and syntax, and *coherence* has to do with the knowledge or cognitive structures that are implied by the language used and that contribute to the overall meaning of a given discourse.

7. Discourse markers are a relevant topic in DA, and they have been profusely studied for their importance as a means to achieve cohesion and coherence, among other reasons.

8. Much of what discourse analysts do is to search for different strategies which are used to realize different functions of discourse. Both strategy and function are key concepts in DA, because they help the analyst understand the essential motives of linguistic communication.

SELF EVALUATION QUESTIONS

Choose the answer that best suits the information given in Chapter 12.

1)
a) There is a single and unique unit which is used in all kinds of D.A.
b) No analyst uses the same unit of analysis ever.
c) There is not a unique unit that can be used for all types of D.A.

2) Discourse units of analysis...
a) can be larger or smaller than the clause.
b) always have to be larger than the clause.
c) must have a determinate length.

3) Discourse...
a) is intrinsically reciprocal.
b) is intrinsically dyadic.
c) is reciprocal but not dyadic.

4)
a) Every discourse genre belongs to a unique and exclusive type.
b) Genres are context-based and diverse.
c) The different genres are totally distinct and separate categories.

5) Each discourse type has...
a) a given set of practices associated with it.
b) similar discourse practices to the other types.
c) completely separate and distinct practices associated with it.

6) The analysis of political discourse is mainly concerned with...
a) the manipulation of language for specific political purposes.
b) syntactic considerations of language.
c) complicated expressions that mean nothing.

7) By adopting different phonological forms...
a) speakers may be perceived as having different political stances.
b) Margaret Thatcher won the elections.
c) people are thought to be more educated.

8) Language may be manipulated for political purposes at ...
a) the syntactic and the semantic levels.
b) the phonological and the morphological levels.
c) All of the above.

9)
a) The power relationships between doctor and patient is one of the most researched topics within medical discourse analysis.
b) Alternative medicine presents better texts for analysis.
c) All medical discourse is ritualized.

10) Doctor-patient encounters are fundamentally...
a) conversational.
b) interview-like.
c) both a and b.

11) Synchronous computer-mediated communication...
a) does not require that users be logged on at the same time.
b) requires that users be logged on at the same time.
c) are, for instance, e-mail or discussion lists.

12) CMD...
a) does not allow more than two participants at the same time.
b) is both a private and public medium.
d) is always limited to typed text.

13) The so-called "electronic utterance"...
a) is a single clause with complements and adjuncts.
b) is mainly composed of symbols and emoticons.
c) does not follow the rules of politeness.

14) Cohesion...
a) has to do with cognitive structures in general.
b) is associated to the concept of discourse more than to that of text.
c) has to do with the relationships between text and syntax.

15) Reference and ellipsis are...
a) types of coherence.
b) types of conjunction.
c) two cohesive devices.

16) Say whether the element in bold type in the following dyad is an example of:
a) substitution.
b) ellipsis.
c) conjunction.

A: Has Tom arrived?
B: I don't think **so**

17) The cognitive approach views coherence as…
a) deriving from the idea of discourse as a social event.
b) the result of collaborating minds in the speech process.
c) neither of the above.

18) Van dijk defines coherence in terms of…
a) social roles.
b) schemas.
c) mental models.

19) Classify the marker in bold type according to Fraser's taxonomy of pragmatic markers:

A: Do you miss your wife?
B: **To be frank**, I don't.

a)   discourse marker
b)   parallel marker
c)   commentary marker

20) Classify the discourse marker in bold type according to Fraser's taxonomy:
A: She said she didn't want to help me, and **on top of it** she left without saying good-bye.

   a)   elaborative
   b)   implicative
   c)   contrastive

21) Schiffrin points out that discourse markers …
a) only display local relationships.
b) are multifunctional and deictic.

c) only help to create cohesion, not coherence.

22)
a) All authors agree on the same kinds of linguistic function.
b) There is no consensus as to the kinds of linguistic functions.
c) Utterances can only fulfil one function.

PRACTICE

A) *ANALYSIS*: ANALYZE the following e-mail message by answering questions a-e :

From :   John Smith <jsmith@tu.edu>
Sent :   Thursday, April 10, 2005 3:03 PM
To :   "Lauren Dawn" <laurendawn@hotmail.com>
CC :
Subject : Re: Hi there

Lauren:
         I wrote you the day after I returned to say thanks and let you know
I'd arrived safely. It apparently didn't go through. So, again, thanks for
everything.
Let me know when you are coming over this way. And regards to the
family. You've got two very bright and nice sons. You're lucky.

Best regards,
John

a)   What would be (a) possible unit(s) of analysis?   Justify your
     answer.
b)   What type(s) of discourse do we find in this fragment?   What is
     the predominant one?
c)   Can you find any discourse markers? If so, how do they
     contribute to the cohesion and coherence of the discourse in
     question?
d)   What other means are used to achieve cohesion and coherence?
e)   What strategies does the writer of the message use to fulfil what
     functions?

B) *ANALYSIS*: CHOOSE a message, conversation, passage or any kind of text that you might be interested in, and DO THE SAME KIND OF ANALYSIS (answering the same questions) as in Task A.

C) *ANALYSIS*: ANALYZE the following joke in terms of the resources used to achieve **cohesion**. Also, IDENTIFY and EXPLAIN the **cohesive ties** between elements.

Have you been fooling around on me?

1 There was a middle-aged couple that had two stunningly
2 beautiful teen-aged daughters. They decided to try one last time
3 for the son they always wanted. After months of trying, the wife
4 became pregnant and sure enough, nine months later delivered a
5 healthy baby boy. The joyful father rushed to the nursery to see
6 his new son. He took one look and was horrified to see the ugliest
7 child he had ever seen.
8   He went to his wife and said that there was no way that he
9 could be the father of that child. "Look at the two beautiful
10 daughters I fathered." Then he gave her a stern look and asked,
11 "Have you been fooling around on me?" The wife
12 smiled sweetly and said, "Not this time".

FURTHER READING

Alba-Juez, [1996] 2001, Chapters 8 & 9
Alba-Juez, 2006, 2007 & 2009
Bakhtin, 1986
Bublitz, Lenk & Ventola, 1999
Downing, 2004
Halliday, 1976, 1978 & 1985
Halliday & Hasan, 1976
Halliday & Matthiessen, 2004
Herring, 2001, 2009

Jakobson, 1960
Lakoff, 1990a, 1990b
Madfes, 2002, 2003
Tannen, 1993
Wilson, 2001

USEFUL WEBSITES

Discourse types:
Study of psychoanalytic discourse : "A Wittgensteinian Approach to
Discourse Analysis": www.criticism.com/da/lw_da.html

Example of legal discourse:
USA vs. Usama bin Laden Trial Transcripts:
http://cryptome.org/usa-v-ubl-dk3.txt

Medical discourse:
http://www.pantaneto.co.uk/issue2/shachar.htm

http://escholarship.bc.edu/dissertations/AAI3122097/

http://bod.sagepub.com/cgi/content/short/10/4/87

http://interruptions.net/literature/Waitzkin-JHSB89.pdf
http://www.aelfe.org/documents/13_15_Rese%C3%B1a_Fuertes_2.p
df

http://www.allacademic.com/meta/p_mla_apa_research_citation/1/0/9
/0/2/p109024_index.html

Data on different types of discourse can be obtained from electronic
corpora:

The British National Corpus: http://www.natcorp.ox.ac.uk/

The COCA (Corpus of Contemporary American English) corpus:
http://www.americancorpus.org/
The American National Corpus: http://americannationalcorpus.org/

Cohesion and coherence:
http://www.sfs.unituebingen.de/~lothar/TTQM/Scripts/slides2710.pdf

http://www.shakespeare.uk.net/journal/3_2/yeh3_2.htm

Wikipedia entrance for M. A. K. Halliday:
http://en.wikipedia.org/wiki/Michael_Halliday

Brief introduction to Halliday's work:
http://language.la.psu.edu/tifle2002/halliday.html

Bruce Fraser's publications and home page:
www.bu.edu/linguistics/APPLIED/FACULTY/bruce.html

Research on discourse/ pragmatic markers:
http://people.bu.edu/bfraser/

Research on discourse-pragmatic strategies:
http://www.ifeas.unimainz.de/SwaFo/SF_14_05%20Okombo%20Hab
we.pdf

http://www.linguistik-online.de/36_08/odebunmi.html

Sotillo's study on discourse functions in computer-mediated discourse:
http://llt.msu.edu/vol4num1/sotillo/default.html

General resources for Discourse Analysis: This is a website (Teun van Dijk's) where you can find all kinds of information and links to any aspect of discourse analysis: bibliographies, web-sites and discussion lists, societies and organizations for the study of discourse, journals, university programs, research institutes, upcoming conferences and other events, personal web-sites of discourse analysts. Take note!
http://www.discourses.org/

REFERENCES

Agger, B. (1992). *The Discourse of Domination. From the Frankfurt School to Postmodernism.* Evanston, IL: Northwestern University Press.

Ainsworth-Vaughn, N. (1998a). Diagnosis as storytelling. In *Claiming Power in Doctor-Patient Talk.* New York: Oxford University Press, 147-71.

—. (1998b). "Geez where'd you find THAT?": Constructing story and self in oncology encounters. In *Claiming Power in Doctor-Patient Talk.* New York: Oxford University Press, 125-46.

—. (2001). The discourse of medical encounters. In D. Schiffrin, D. Tannen & H. Hamilton (eds.), *Handbook of Discourse Analysis.* Massachusetts & Oxford: Blackwell, 453-69.

Akman, V. (1994). When silence may mean derision. In *Journal of Pragmatics*, 22, 211-18.

Alba-Juez, L. (1995). Irony and the other off record strategies within Politeness Theory. In *Miscelanea: A Journal of English and American Studies*, 16: 13-23.

—. ([1996] 2001). *The Functions and Strategies of Ironic Discourse: An Analysis.* Madrid: Editorial Complutense.

—. (2002). On the influence of the sociological variables P, D and R upon the use of humorous FTAs in two television comedy series. In *Babel A.F.I.A.L.: Aspectos de Filoloxía Inglesa e Alemana, Número Monográfico Extraordinario: Aspectos lingüísticos e literarios do humor.* Vigo: Servicio de Publicacións Universidade de Vigo, 7-23.

—. (2005). *Discourse Analysis for University Students.* Madrid: UNED.

—. (2006). Some pragmatic markers of impoliteness in British English and Peninsular Spanish. In M. Carretero, L. Hidalgo Downing, J. Lavid, E. Martínez Caro, J. Neff, S. Pérez de Ayala & E. Sánchez Pardo (eds.), *A Pleasure of Life in Words: A Festschrift for Angela Downing.* Madrid: Universidad Complutense, 403-19.

—. (2007). Chapter 2: On the impoliteness of some politeness strategies: A study and comparison of the use of some pragmatic markers of impoliteness in British English and American English, Peninsular Spanish and Argentine Spanish. In P. Garcés-Conejos, M. Padilla Cruz, R. Gómez Morón & L. Fernández Amaya (eds.), *Studies in Intercultural, Cognitive and Social Pragmatics.* New Castle upon Tyne, UK: Cambridge Scholars Publishing. 37-56.

—. (2009). 'Little words' in *small talk*: Some considerations on the use of the pragmatic markers *man* in English and *macho/tío* in Peninsular Spanish. In R. P. Leow, H. Cámpos & D. Lardiere (eds.), *Little Words. Their History, Phonology, Syntax, Semantics, Pragmatics and Acquisition.* Washington D.C.: Georgetown University Press.

Alexias, G. (2008). Medical Discourse and Time: Authoritative Reconstruction of Present, Future and Past. In *Social Theory & Health* 6: 167–83.

Althusser, L. (1971). *Lenin and Philosophy and Other Essays.* New York: Monthly Review Press.

Androutsopoulos, J. & Beißwenger, M. (2008). Introduction: Data and Methods in Computer-Mediated Discourse Analysis. In *Language@Internet, 5, Special issue: Data and Methods in Computer-Mediated Discourse Analysis,* article 2.

Anthonissen, C. (2004). Challenging media censoring: writing between the lines in the face of stringent restrictions. In J.R. Martin and R. Wodak (eds.) *Re/Reading the Past: Critical and Functional Perspectives on Time and Value.* Amsterdam: John Benjamins. 91-112.

Aragonés, M., I. Medrano & L. Alba-Juez (2003 [2007]). *Lengua Inglesa I.* Madrid: UNED.

Austin, J.L. (1962). *How to Do Things with Words.* Oxford: Clarendon Press.

Bakhtin, M. (1981). Discourse in the novel. In M. Holquist (ed.), *The Dialogic Imagination.* Austin: University of Texas Press, 259-422.

—. (1986). The problem of genre. In *Speech Genres and Other Late Essays.* Austin: University of Texas Press, 60-102.

Barthes, R. (1967). *Elements of Semiology.* New York: Hill and Wang.

Bar-Hillel, Y. (1954). Indexical Expressions. *Mind*, 63: 359-79.

Bartlett, F. (1932). *Remembering.* Cambridge: Cambridge University Press.

Bauman, R. (2004). *A world of others' words: Cross–cultural perspectives on intertextuality.* Oxford: Blackwell.

Bauman, R. & C. Briggs (1990). Poetics and performance as critical perspectives on language and social life. *Annual Review of Anthropology*, 19: 59-88.

Baynham, M. & S. Slembrouck (1999). Speech representation and institutional discourse. In *Text*, 19/4: 439-57.

Baynham, M. (2006). Performing self, family and community in Moroccan narratives of migration and settlement. In A. de Fina, D. Schiffrin and M. Bamberg (eds.), *Discourse and Identity.* Cambridge: Cambridge University Press. 376-97.

Bell, A. (1999). New stories as narratives. In A. Jaworski and N. Coupland (eds.), *The Discourse Reader*. London & New York: Routledge. 236-51.

Bell, S.E. (2006). Becoming a mother after DES: intensive mothering in spite of it all. In A. de Fina, D. Schiffrin and M. Bamberg (eds.), *Discourse and Identity*. Cambridge: Cambridge University Press. 233-52.

Bernárdez, E. (1999). *¿Qué son las lenguas?* Madrid: Alianza Editorial.

Bhaskar, R. (1986). *Scientific Realism and Human Emancipation.* London: Verso.

Biber, D., S. Conrad & R. Reppen (1998). *Corpus Linguistics. Investigating Language Structure and Use.* Cambridge: Cambridge University Press.

Billig, M. (1999a). Critical Discourse Analysis and Conversation Analysis: an exchange between Michael Billig and Emanuel A. Schegloff. In *Discourse & Society*, 10: 543-82.

—. (1999b). Whose terms? Whose ordinariness? Rhetoric and ideology in Conversation Analysis. In *Discourse & Society*, 10: 543-82.

—. (1999c). Conversation Analysis and the claims of naivety.   In *Discourse & Society,* 10: 572-76.

Bolinger, D. (1952). Linear Modification. *Proceedings of the Modern Language Association* 67: 1117-44.

Bourdieu, P. (1976). The economics of linguistic exchanges. In *Social Science Information*, 16:6 : 645-68.

—. (1977). *Outline of a Theory of Practice.* Cambridge: Cambridge University Press.

—. (1990). *The Logic of Practice.* Stanford: Stanford University Press.

—. (1999 [1991]). Language and Symbolic Power. In A. Jarworski & N. Coupland (eds.), *The Discourse Reader*. London and New York: Routledge, 502-13.

Bravo, D. (1999). ¿Imagen 'positiva' vs. imagen 'negativa'?: pragmática socio-cultural y componentes de face. *Oralia. Análisis del discurso oral*, 2: 155-84.

Brown, G., K.L. Currie & J. Kenworthy (1980). *Questions of Intonation.* London: Croom Helm.

Brown, G. & G. Yule (1983). *Discourse Analysis.* Cambridge: Cambridge University Press.

Brown, P. & S.C. Levinson (1987). *Politeness. Some Universals in Language Usage.* Cambridge: Cambridge University Press.

Bublitz, W. (1999). Views of coherence. In W. Bublitz, U. Lenk & E. Ventola (eds.), *Coherence in Spoken and Written Discourse.* Amsterdam & Philadelphia: John Benjamins, 1-11.

Bublitz, W., U. Lenk & E. Ventola (eds.) (1999). *Coherence in Spoken and Written Discourse*. Amsterdam & Philadelphia: John Benjamins.

Bühler, K. (1934). The deictic field of language and deictic words. Reprinted in R. Jarvella and W. Klein (eds.) (1982), *Speech, Place and Action: Studies of Deixis and Related Topics*. New York: John Wiley, 9-30

Byrne, P.S. & B.E.L. Long (1976). *Doctors talking to patients*. London: HMSO.

Cameron, D. (2001). *Working with Spoken Discourse*. London: Sage.

Candlin, C.N. (1997). General editor's preface. In Gunnarsson, B.-L., Linell, P. and Nordberg, B. (eds.). *The Construction of Professional Discourse*. London: Longman, ix-xiv.

Carabine, J. (2001). Unmarried motherhood 1830-1990: A genealogical analysis. In Wetherell, M, Taylor, S & S.J. Yates (eds.), *Discourse as Data. A Guide for Analysis*. London, Thousand Oaks and New Delhi: Sage and Open University, 267-310.

Carbaugh, D. (2005). *Cultures in conversation*. Mahwah, NJ: Lawrence Erlbaum.

Carlson, G. (2004). Reference. In L. R. Horn & G. Ward (eds.), *The Handbook of Pragmatics*. Oxford: Blackwell, 74-96.

Carston, R. (1995). Quantity maxims and generalized implicature. *Lingua* 96: 213-44.

Chafe, W. (1980). The deployment of consciousness in the production of a narrative. In W. Chafe (ed.), *The Pear Stories: Cognitive, Cultural and Linguistic Aspects of Narrative Production*. Norwood, NJ: Ablex Press, 9-50.

—. (1987). Cognitive constraints on information flow. In R. Tomlin (ed.), *Coherence and Grounding in Discourse*. Amsterdam: John Benjamins, 21-51.

—. (1992). Prosodic and functional units of language. In J. Edwards and M. Lampert (eds.), *Talking Data: Transcription and Coding in Discourse Research*. Hillsdale, NJ: Lawrence Erlbaum Associates.

—. (1994). *Discourse, Consciousness, and Time. The Flow and Displacement of Conscious Experience in Speaking and Writing*. Chicago & London: The University of Chicago Press.

Chomsky, N. (1957). *Syntactic Structures*. The Hague: Mouton.

—. (1965). *Aspects of the Theory of Syntax*. Cambridge: Cambridge University Press.

Covarrubias, P. (2002). *Culture, communication, and cooperation: Interpersonal relations and pronominal address in a Mexican organization*. Lanham, MD: Rowan and Littlefield.

Crystal, D. (1997). *A Dictionary of Linguistics and Phonetics*. Oxford: Blackwell.

Culpeper, J. (1996). Towards an anatomy of impoliteness. *Journal of Pragmatics*, 25: 349-67.

Cunningham, W. (2005) What is CDA? In what ways is it left-leaning? In: http://clublet.com/c/c/why?CriticalDiscourseAnalysis Accessed January 28, 2005.

Danes, F. (1974). Functional Sentence Perspective and the organization of the text. In Danes, F. (ed.), *Papers on Functional Sentence Perspective*. Prague: Academia/The Hague: Mouton, 106-28.

de Beaugrande, R. (1997). *New Foundations for a Science of Text and Discourse: Cognition, Communication, and the Freedom of Access to Knowledge and Society*. Vol. LXI in the series *Advances in Discourse Processes*, R. O. Freedle (ed.). Norwood, NJ: Ablex Publishing.

—. (2002). Plan for Text Linguistics. Basic Questions and Answers. In: http://beaugrande.bizland.com/Course%20plan%20for%20Text%20lin guistics.htm

de Beaugrande, R. & W. Dressler (1981). *Introduction to Text Linguistics*. London & New York: Longman.

de Fina, A. (2006). Group identity, narrative and self-representations. In A. de Fina Schiffrin and M. Bamberg (eds.), *Discourse and Identity*. Cambridge: Cambridge University Press, 351-75.

de Fina, A., D. Schiffrin and M. Bamberg (eds.) (2006). *Discourse and Identity*. Cambridge: Cambridge University Press.

Derrida, J. (1967). *Writing and Difference*. Chicago: University of Chicago Press.

—. (1981). *Dissemination*. Chicago: University of Chicago Press.

Diamond, J. (1996). *Status and Power in Verbal Interaction*. Amsterdam: John Benjamins.

Dirks, U. (2006). Critical discourse analysis of the Iraq conflict in the British and German 'quality' press. *Revista Alicantina de Estudios Ingleses*, 19: 101-123.

Downing, A. (1991). An alternative approach to theme: a systemic-functional perspective. *WORD*, Vol. 42, n° 2, 119-43.

—. (1996). Thematic progression as a functional resource in analysing texts. In M.T. Caneda and J. Pérez (eds.), *Os estudios ingleses no contexto das novas tendencias.* Vigo: Universidad de Vigo, 23-42.

—. (2004). Achieving coherence: Topicality, conceptualizations and action sequences in negotiating conflicting goals. In *Revista Canaria de Estudios Ingleses*, 49: 13-28.

—. (2006). The English pragmatic marker *surely* and its functional counterparts in Spanish. In K. Aijmer & A. M. Simon-Vandenbergen (eds.), *Pragmatic Markers in Contrast*. Amsterdam: Elsevier.

Downing, A. & Locke, P. (1992). *A University Course in English Grammar*. London: Prentice Hall.

Downing, A. & Locke, P. (2006). *English Grammar. A University Course*. Second Edition. London & New York: Routledge.

Du Bois, J. (1993). Meaning without intention: lessons from divination. In J. Hill & Irvine (eds.), *Responsibility and Evidence in Oral Discourse*. Cambridge: Cambridge University Press. 48-71.

Duranti, A. (1993). Intentions, self, and responsibility: an essay in Samoan ethnopragmatics. In: J. Hill & Irvine (eds.), *Responsibility and Evidence in Oral Discourse*. Cambridge: Cambridge University Press, 24-47.

—. (1997). *Linguistic Anthropology*. Cambridge: Cambridge University Press.

Edelsky, C. (1981). Who's got the floor? *Language in Society* 10, 383-421.

Edleman, M. (1971). *Politics as Symbolic Action*. New York: Academic Press.

—. (1977). *Political Language*. New York: Academic Press.

—. (1988). *Constructing the Political Spectacle*. Chicago: University of Chicago Press.

Edwards, J., and Lampert, M. 1993. *Talking Data: Transcription and Coding in Discourse Research*. Hillsdale, NJ: Lawrence Erlbaum Associates.

Ehrlich, S. (1998). The discursive reconstruction of sexual consent. In *Discourse and Society*, 9: 149-71.

Fairclough, N. (1989). *Language and Power*. London: Longman.

—. (1992a). *Discourse and Social Change*. Cambridge: Polity Press.

—. (1992b). Discourse and text: linguistic and intertextual analysis within discourse analysis. In *Discourse and Society*, 3: 192-217.

—. (1995). *Critical Discourse Analysis: The Critical Study of Language*. Harlow, UK: Longman.

—. (2001a). Critical Discourse Analysis as a Method in Social Scientific Research. In R. Wodak & M. Meyer (eds.), *Methods of Critical Discourse Analysis*, London: Sage

—. (2001b). The discourse of new labour: Critical Discourse Analysis. In Wetherell, M, Taylor, S. and S. Yates (eds.), *Discourse as Data*. London, Thousand Oaks, CA & New Delhi: Sage & Open University, 229-66.

Fairclough, N. & R. Wodak (1997). Critical discourse analysis. In T.A. van Dijk (ed.), *Discourse Studies. A Multidisciplinary Introduction*,

Vol. 2. Discourse as Social Interaction. London: Sage, 258-84.

Fasold, R. (1990). *Sociolinguistics of Language.* Oxford: Blackwell.

Ferencik, M. (2007). Exercising politeness: Membership categorisation in a radio phone-in programme. *Pragmatics* 17, 3: 351-70.

Ferrara, K. W. (1994). *Therapeutic Ways with Words.* Oxford Studies in Sociolinguistics. New York: Oxford University Press.

Fillmore, C.J. (1971). Towards a theory of deixis. *The PCCLLU Papers* (Department of Linguistics, University of Hawaii) 3.4: 219-41.

Firbas, J. (1964). On defining the theme in functional sentence analysis. *Travaux Linguistiques de Prague* 1, 267-80.

—. (1986). On the dynamics of written communication in the light of the theory of functional sentence perspective. In Cooper, C. R. and S. Greenbaum (eds.), *Studying Writing.* London: Sage, 40-71 (selected parts).

—. (1992). *Functional Sentence Perspective in Written and Spoken Communication.* Cambridge: Cambridge University Press.

Fish, S. (1980). Is there a text in this class? In *Is There a Text in This Class?* Cambridge: Harvard University Press, 303-21.

Fishman, P. (1983). Interaction: The work women do. In B.Thorne, C. Kramarae & N. Henley (eds.), *Language, Gender, and Society.* Rowley, MA: Newbury House 89-102.

Fitch, K. (1998). *Speaking relationally: Culture, communication, and interpersonal connection.* New York: Guilford.

Fleischman, S. (2001). Language and Medicine. In D. Schiffrin, D. Tannen & H. Hamilton (eds.), *Handbook of Discourse Analysis.* Massachusetts & Oxford: Blackwell, 470-502.

Foucault, M. (1972). *The Archaeology of Knowledge.* London: Tavistock.

—. (1973). *The Birth of the Clinic: An Archaeology of Medical Perception.* London: Tavistock.

—. (1980). *Power/Knowledge: Selected Writings and Other Interviews 1972-1977.* C. Gordon (ed.). New York: Pantheon Books.

—. (1981). *History of Sexuality.* Vol. 1. Harmondsworth: Penguin Books.

—. (1984). Nietsche, genealogy, history. In P. Rabinow (ed.), *The Foucault Reader.* Harmondsworth: Penguin.

Fowler, R, Hodge, G, Kress, G. & T. Trew (1979). *Language and Control.* London: Routledge & Kegan Paul.

Frankel, R. (1979). Talking in interviews: a dispreference for patient-initiated questions in physician-patient encounters. In G. Psathas (ed.), *Everyday Language: Studies in Ethnomethodology.* New York: Irvington, 231-62.

Fraser, B. (1990a). Perspectives on politeness. *Journal of Pragmatics* 14, 219-36.

—. (1990b). An approach to discourse markers. In *Journal of Pragmatics* 14, 383-95.

—. (1996). Pragmatic Markers. *Pragmatics* 6 (2), 167-90.

—. (1998). Contrastive discourse markers in English. In A. Jucker & Y. Ziv (eds.), *Discourse Markers: Description and Theory*. Amsterdam & Philadelphia: John Benjamins, 301-26.

—. (2006). Towards a Theory of Discourse Markers. In K. Fischer (ed.) *Approaches to Discourse Particles*. Bremen: Elsevier. 189-204.

Fraser, B & Nolen, W. (1981). The association of deference with linguistic form. *International Journal of the Sociology of Language* 27, 93-109.

Gal, S. (1992). Language, gender and power: An anthropological view. In K. Hall et al (eds.), *Locating Power*. Berkeley: Berkeley Linguistic Society, 153-61.

Garfinkel, H. (1967). *Studies in Ethnomethodology*. Englewood Cliffs, NJ: Prentice Hall.

—. (1974). The origins of the term 'ethnomethodology'. In R. Turner (ed.), *Ethnomethodology*. Harmondsworth: Penguin, 15-18.

Gee, J. P. (1999, 2nd edition 2005). *An Introduction to Discourse Analysis: Theory and Method*. New York: Routledge.

Gernsbacher, A.M. & T. Givón (1995). Introduction: Coherence as a mental entity. In A.M. Gernsbacher & T. Givón (eds.), *Coherence in Spontaneous Text*. Amsterdam. John Benjamins, viii-viii.

Gjierstad, O. (2007). The Polyphony of Politics: Finding Voices in French Political Discourse. In *Critical Approaches to Discourse Analysis across Disciplines*, vol. 1, (2): 61-78.

Goffman, E. (1959). *The Presentation of Self in Everyday Life*. New York: Anchor Books.

—. (1967). On face work. In E. Goffman (ed.), *Interaction Ritual*. New York: Anchor Books, 5-46.

—. (1971). *Relations in Public*. New York: Basic Books.

—. (1974). *Frame Analysis*. New York: Harper and Row.

—. (1981a). Footing. In *Forms of Talk*. Philadelphia: University of Pennsylvania Press, 124-59.

—. (1981b). Response cries. In *Forms of Talk*. Oxford: Basil Blackwell, 78-122.

Goodwin, M. (1992). Orchestrating Participation in Events: Powerful Talk among African-American Girls. In K. Hall (ed.), *Locating Power: Proceedings of the 1992 Berkeley Women and Language Conference*. Berkeley: Berkeley Women and Language Group, Linguistics

Department, UC-Berkeley, 182-96.

Gramsci, A. (1971). *Selections from the Prison Notebooks*. New York: International Publishers.

Gray, J. (1992). *Men are from Mars, Women are from Venus*. New York: Harper Collins.

Green, G.M. (1989). *Pragmatics and Natural Language Understanding*. Hillsdale, NJ: Lawrence Earlbaum.

Grice, H.P. (1975). Logic and conversation. In P. Cole and J. Morgan (eds., *Syntax and Semantics 3: Speech Acts*. New York: Academic Press, 41-58.

—. (1978). Further notes on logic and conversation. In: P. Cole (ed.), *Syntax and Semantics, 9: Pragmatics*. New York: Academic Press, 113-27.

Grimes, J.E. (1975). *The Thread of Discourse*. The Hague: Mouton.

Gu, Y. (1990). Politeness phenomena in modern Chinese. *Journal of Pragmatics* 14 (2): 237-57.

Gumperz, J. (1981). The linguistic bases of communicative competence. D. Tannen (ed), *Analyzing Discourse: Text and Talk*. Washington, D.C.: Georgetown University Press, 323-34.

—. (1982). *Discourse Strategies*. Cambridge: Cambridge University Press.

Hall, J.K. (1996). Who needs "identity"? In S. Hall and P. du Gay (eds.) *Questions of cultural identity*. London: Sage. 1-17

Halliday, M.A.K. (1967). Notes on transitivity and theme in English: Part 2. *Journal of Linguistics* 3: 199-244.

—. (1976). *System and Function in Language*. London: Oxford University Press.

—. (1978). *Language as Social Semiotic*. London: Edward Arnold.

—. (1985). *An Introduction to Functional Grammar*. London: Edward Arnold.

Halliday, M.A.K. & R. Hasan (1976). *Cohesion in English*. London: Longman.

Halliday M.A.K. & C. Matthiessen (2004). *An Introduction to Functional Grammar* (3rd Edition). London: Arnold.

Hanks, W. (1996). *Language and Communicative Practices*. Oxford: Westview Press.

Harris, Sandra. (1984). Questions as a mode of control in magistrates' courts. *International Journal of the Sociology of Language,* 49: 5-28.

Harris, Z. (1951). *Methods in Structural Linguistics*. Chicago: University of Chicago Press.

—. (1952). Discourse Analysis. *Language* 28: 1-30.

Hart, C. (2005). Analyzing political discourse: Toward a cognitive approach. *Critical Discourse Studies* 2 (2): 189-94.

—. (1992). Diagnosis in the general-practice consultation. In P. Drew and J. Heritage (eds.), *Talk at Work*. Cambridge: Cambridge University Press, 235-67.

Hein, N. & R. Wodak (1987). Medical interviews in internal medicine: some results of an empirical investigation. In *Text*, 7/1: 37-65.

Helman, C. G. (1984). The role of context in primary care. In *Journal of the Royal College of General Practitioners*, 34: 547-50.

Heritage, J. (1984). *Garfinkel and Ethnomethodology*. Oxford: Basil Blackwell.

—. (1989). Current developments in conversation analysis. In D. Roger & P. Bull (eds.), *Conversation*. Philadelphia: Multilingual Matters, 21-47.

Herring, S.C. (1996). Posting in a different voice: Gender and ethics in computer-mediated communication. In C. Ess (ed.), *Computer-Mediated Communication: Linguistic, Social and Cross-Cultural Perspectives*. Amsterdam: John Benjamins, 81-106.

—. (1998). Ideologies of language on the Internet: The case of 'free speech'. Paper presented at the 6th *International Pragmatics Conference*, Reims, France.

—. (1999). The rhetorical dynamics of gender harassment on-line. In L.J. Gurak (ed.), *Information Society* 15(3). Special issue on *The Rhetorics of Gender in Computer-Mediated Communication*, 151-67.

—. (2001). Computer-mediated discourse. In D. Schiffrin, D. Tannen & H. Hamilton (eds.), *Handbook of Discourse Analysis*. Massachusetts & Oxford: Blackwell, 612-34.

—. (2007). A faceted classification scheme for computer-mediated discourse. *Language@Internet, 4*, article 1. http://www.languageatinternet.de/articles/2007/761

—. (In press, 2009). Digital media. In: P. Hogan (ed.), *The Cambridge Encyclopedia of the Language Sciences*. Cambridge: Cambridge University   Press.   Preprint: http://ella.slis.indiana.edu/~herring/digmed.pdf

Herring, S.C., D. Johnson and T. DiBenedetto. (1995). 'This discussion is going too far!' Male resistance to female participation on the Internet. In M. Bucholtz and K. Hall (eds), *Gender Articulated: Language and the Socially Constructed Self*. New York: Routledge, 67-96.

Hirschberg, J. (1991). *A Theory of Scalar Implicature*. New York: Garland.

Hockett, C. & S.A. Altmann (1968). A note on design features. In T. Sebeok (ed.), *Animal Communication*.Bloomington: Indiana University Press, 61-72.

Hodge, R. & G. Kress (2001). Social Semiotics. In M. Wetherell, S. Taylor & S. Yates (eds.), *Discourse Theory and Practice. A Reader.* London, Thousand Oaks and New Delhi: Sage Publications, 294-99.

Holmes, J. (1995). *Women, Men and Politeness.* London: Longman.

Horn, L.R. (2004). Implicature. In L. R. Horn & G. Ward (2004). *The Handbook of Pragmatics.* Oxford: Blackwell Publishing.

Horn, L.R. & G. Ward (2004). *The Handbook of Pragmatics.* Oxford: Blackwell Publishing.

Howarth, D. (2000). *Discourse.* Buckingham: Open University Press.

Hutchby, I. & R. Wooffitt (2008). *Conversation Analysis (2nd Edition).* Cambridge: Polity Press.

Hymes, D. (1962). *The Ethnography of Speaking.* Gladwin & Sturtevant (eds.). Washington, D.C.: Anthropological Society of Washington, 15-83.

—. (1964). *Language in Culture and Society.* New York: Harper & Row Publishers.

—. (1970). On communicative competence. In J. Gumperz and D.Hymes (eds.), *Directions in Sociolinguistics.* Holt Rinehart and Winston.

—. (1972). Toward ethnographies of communication: the analysis of communicative events. In P. Giglioli (ed.), *Language and Social Context.* Harmondsworth: Penguin, 21-43 (excerpts from Hymes, D (1966) Introduction: toward ethnographies of communication). *American Anthropologist*, 66 (6): 12-25.

—. (1974a). Toward ethnographies of communication. *American Anthropologist*, 66, 6. American Anthropological Association, 3-28.

—. (1974b). *Foundations in Sociolinguistics: an Ethnographic Approach.* Philadelphia: University of Pennsylvania Press.

—. (1980). What is Ethnography? In *Language and Education: Ethnolinguistic Essays.* Washington, D.C.: Center for Applied Linguistics.

Iedema, R., Degeling, P., Braithwaite, J & L. White (2004). 'It's an interesting conversation I'm hearing': The doctor as manager. In *Organization Studies*, 25, Nº 1, 15-33.

Jakobson, R. (1960). Linguistics and Poetics. In T. Sebeok (ed.), *Style in Language.* Cambridge: M.I.T. Press.

Jarratt, S. (ed.) (1978). *Betchworth Village Recipes.* Betchworth Village, UK: Parish Partners.

Jaworski, A. & N. Coupland (eds.) (2006), Second Edition. *The Discourse Reader.* London & New York: Routledge.

Jefferson, G. (1979). A technique for inviting laughter and its subsequent acceptance/declination. In G. Psathas (ed.), *Everyday Language:*

Studies in Ethnomethodology. New York: Irvington, 79-96.

Jespersen, O. (1922). *Language: Its Nature, Development and Origin.* London: Allen & Unwin.

—. (1965). *A Modern English Grammar*: Part IV. London: Allen & Unwin.

Johansson, S. & A. Stenström (eds.) (1991). *English Computer Corpora: Selected and Research Guide.* Berlin: Mouton de Gruyter.

Johnson, D. & J.F. Murray (1985). Do doctors mean what they say? In D. Enright (ed.), *Fair of Speech: The Uses of Euphemism.* Oxford: Oxford Univesity Press, 151-58.

Johnson Laird, P.N. (1983). *Mental Models: Towards a Cognitive Science of Language, Interference, and Consciousness.* Cambridge, MA: Harvard University Press.

Johnstone, B. (2002). *Discourse Analysis.* Oxford: Blackwell.

Karttunen, L. & S. Peters. (1975). Conventional implicature in Montague grammar. *Proceedings of the First Annual Meeting of the Berkeley Linguistic Society,* 266-78.

Karttunen, L. & S. Peters. (1979). Conventional implicature. In C.K. Oh & D.A. Dinneen (eds.), *Syntax and Semantics II: Presupposition.* New York: Academic Press, 1-56.

Katriel, T. (2004). *Dialogic moments: From soul talks to talk radio in Israeli culture.* Detroit, MI: Wayne State University Press.

Keith Sawyer, R. (1995). A developmental model of heteroglossic improvisation in children's fantasy play. In *Sociological Studies of Children,* 7, 127-53.

Kiesling, S. (2006). Hegemonic identity-making in narrative. In A. de Fina, D. Schiffrin and M. Bamberg (eds.), *Discourse and Identity.* Cambridge: Cambridge University Press. 261-87.

Kintsh, W. (1977). On comprehending stories. In M. Just & P. Carpenter (eds.), *Cognitive Processes in Comprehension.* Hillsdale, NJ: Erlbaum, 33-62.

Klages, M. (2001). Mikhail Bakhtin. At: http://www.colorado.edu/English/ENGL2012Klages/bakhtin.html

Kress, G. (1996). Representational resources and the production of subjectivity: questions for the theoretical development of Critical Discourse Analysis in a multicultural society. In C. Caldas-Coulthard & M. Coulthard (eds.), *Text and Practices: Readings in Critical Discourse Analysis.* London: Routledge, 15-31.

Kroskrity, P. (2000). Identity. *Journal of Linguistic Anthropology,* 9 (1-2): 111-14.

Kurzon, D. (1992). When silence may mean power. In *Journal of*

Pragmatics 18: 92-95.

Labov, William. 1966. *The Social Stratification of English in New York City.* Washington D.C.: Center for Applied Linguistics.

Labov, W. (1972a). *Sociolinguistic Patterns.* Oxford: Blackwell.

—. (1972b) (ed.). The transformation of experience in narrative syntax. In *Language in the Inner City.* Philadelphia: University of Pennsylvania Press, 354-405.

—. (1981). Speech actions and reactions in personal narrative. In D. Tannen (ed.), *Analyzing Discourse: Text and Talk* (Georgetown University Round Table). Washington, D.C.: Georgetown University Press, 219-47.

—. (1984). Field methods of the project on linguistic change and variation. In J. Baugh & J. Sherzer (eds.). *Language in Use.* Englewood Cliffs, NJ: Prentice Hall, 28-53.

—. (1996). When intuitions fail. *Chicago Linguistic Society: Papers from the Parasession on Theory and Data in Linguistics* 32: 76-106.

—. (1997a). How I got into linguistics, and what I got out of it. Essay at: http://www.ling.upenn.edu/~labov/Papers/How I got.html

—. (1997b). Some further steps in narrative analysis. In *Journal of Narrative and Life History* 7 (1-4): 395-415.

—. (1997c). Narrative analysis: Oral versions of personal experience. In *Journal of Narrative and Life History,* 7 (1-4), 3-38.

—. (2004). Some observations on the Foundation of Linguistics. At: http://www.ling.upenn.edu/~wlabov/Papers/Foundations.html

Labov, E. & J. Waletzky, (1967). Narrative analysis. In J. Helm (ed.), *Essays on the Verbal and Visual Arts.* Seattle: University of Washington Press, 12-44.

Labov, William, P. Cohen, C. Robins and J. Lewis.. 1968. A study of the non-standard English of Negro and Puerto Rican Speakers in New York City. *Cooperative Research Report 3288.* Vols. I and II. Philadelphia: U.S. Regional Survey (Linguistics Laboratory, U. of Philadelphia).

Lacan, J. (1977). *Ecrits. A Selection.* New York: W. W. Norton.

Laclau, E & Mouffe, C. (1985). *Hegemony and Socialist Strategy. Towards a Radical Democratic Policy.* London: Verso.

Lakoff, G. & M. Johnson (1980). *Metaphors We Live By.* Chicago: University of Chicago Press.

Lakoff, R. (1973). The logic of politeness: or, minding your p's and q's. In C. Corum et al. (eds.), *Papers from the ninth regional meeting of the Chicago Linguistic Society.* Chicago: Chicago Linguistic Society, 292-305.

—. (1990). *Talking Power: The Politics of Language. New York:* Basic Books.

—. (1990a). The Talking cure. *Talking Power: The Politics of Language.* New York: Basic Books, 59-83.

—. (1990b). Life and language in court. *Talking Power: The Politics of Language.* New York: Basic Books.

—. (2000). *The Language War.* Berkeley: University of California Press.

—. (2001). The rhetoric of the extraordinary moment: The concession and acceptance speeches of Al Gore and George W. Bush in the 2000 presidential election. *Pragmatics*, 11, N° 3: 309-27.

—. (2002). Finding words for September's Tragedy. At: www.berkeley.edu/news/berkeleyan/2002/03/06lakofhtml.

Lavandera, B. (1988). The social pragmatics of politeness forms. In U. Ammon & N. Dittmar (eds.), *Sociolinguistics. An International Handbook of the Science of Language and Society.* Berlin & New York: Walter de Gruyter, 1196-1205.

Lee Wong, S.M. (1999). *Politeness and Face in Chinese Culture.* Frankfurt: Peter Lang.

Leech, G. (1983). *Principles of Pragmatics.* Singapore: Longman.

—. (2005). Adding Linguistic Annotation. In M. Wynne (ed.), *Developing Linguistic Corpora: A Guide to Good Practice*, Oxford: Oxbow Books: 17-29. Available online at: http://ahds.ac.uk/linguistic-corpora/ [Accessed 2008-05-18].

Levinson, S. (1983). *Pragmatics.* Cambridge: Cambridge University Press.

—. (1987). Putting linguistics on a proper footing: Explorations in Goffman's concepts of participation. In P. Drew & A. Woolton (eds.), *Goffman: An Interdisciplinary Appreciation.* Oxford: Polity Press.

—. (2000). *Presumptive Meanings: The Theory of Generalized Conversational Implicature.* Cambridge, MA: MIT Press.

—. (2004). Deixis. In L. R. Horn & G. Ward (eds.), *The Handbook of Pragmatics.* Oxford: Blackwell.

Linell, P. & N. Korolija (1997). Coherence in multi-party conversation. In T. Givón (ed.), *Conversation: Cognitive, Communicative and Social Perspectives.* Amsterdam & Philadelphia: John Benjamins, 167-206.

Luke, A. (2002). Beyond science and ideology critique: developments in critical discourse analysis. *Annual Review of Applied Linguistics*, 222, 96-110.

Macgilchrist, F. (2007). Positive Discourse Analysis: Contesting dominant discourses by reframing the issues. *Critical Approaches to Discourse Analysis Across Disciplines*, 1 (1): 74-94.

Madfes, I. (2002). La regulación del poder en la entrevista médica. Paper presented in the IX Conference of the Argentine Association of Linguistics. Córdoba, November 2002.

—. (2003). La confrontación de imágenes en una interacción asimétrica: ¿médico y paciente: afiliación o conflicto? In D. Bravo (ed.), *Actas del Primer Coloquio del Programa EDICE.* Stockholm: Stockholms Universitet, 172-85.

Mao, L.R. (1994). Beyond politeness theory: 'face' revisited and renewed. *Journal of Pragmatics* 21 (5): 451-86.

Martin, J.R. (1996). Types of structure: deconstructing notions of constituency in clause and text. In E. H. Hovy and D. R. Scott (ed.), *Computational and Conversational Discourse: Burning Issues. An Interdisciplinary Account.* Heidelberg: Springer (NATO Advanced Science Institute Series F –Computer and System Sciences, Vol. 151: 39-66.

—. ([2000] 2003). Beyond exchange : appraisal systems in English. En S. Hunston & G. Thompson (eds.) *Evaluation in Text. Authorial Stance and the Construction of Discourse.* Oxford : Oxford University Press. 142-75.

—. (2001). Cohesion and Texture. In D. Schiffrin, D. Tannen & H. Hamilton (eds.), *Handbook of Discourse Analysis.* Massachusetts & Oxford: Blackwell, 35-53.

—. (2002). Blessed are the peacemakers: reconciliation and evaluation. In C. Candlin (ed.), *Research and Practice in Professional Discourse.* Hong Kong: City University of Hong Kong Press, 187-227.

—. (2004a). Positive Discourse Analysis: Solidarity and Change. *Revista Canaria de Estudios Ingleses*, 49, 179-200.

—. (2004b). Negotiating difference: ideology and reconciliation. In M. Pütz, J. Neff van Aertselaer & T. van Dijk (eds.), *Communicating Ideologies: Language, Discourse and Social Practice.* Frankfurt: Lang. 85-177.

—. (2007). Comment. *World Englishes* 26 (1): 84-86.

Martin, J.R. & D. Rose (2003, 2nd edition 2007). *Working with Discourse. Meaning Beyond the clause.* London & New York: Continuum.

Martin, J. R. & P.R.R. White (2005). *The Language of Evaluation. Appraisal in English.* New York: Palgrave Macmillan.

Martin, J.R. & M. Stenglin (2006). Materialising reconciliation: negotiating difference in a post-colonial exhibition. In T. Royce and W. Bowcher (eds.), *New Directions in the Analysis of Multimodal Discourse.* Mahwah, NJ: Erlbaum. 215-38.

Martín Rojo, L., Pardo, M. L. & R. Whittaker (1998). El análisis crítico del discurso: Una mirada indisciplinada. En Martín Rojo, L. y R. Whittaker (eds.), *Poder-Decir o el poder de los discursos*. Madrid: Arrecife, 9-33.

Matsumoto, Y. (1988). Reexamination of face. *Journal of Pragmatics* 12: 403-26.

Mattelart, A. (1996). Les enjeux de la globalisation des rèseaux. In *Internet : L'Extase et L'Effroi* (special issue of *Le Monde Diplomatique*), 10-14.

Maybin, J. (2001). Language, struggle and voice: The Bakhtin/Volosinov writings. In Wetherel, M., S. Taylor & S. Yates (eds.), *Discourse Theory and Practice. A Reader*. London, Thousand Oaks and New Delhi: Sage, 64-71.

Maynard, D. W. (1991). Interaction and asymmetry in clinical discourse. In *American Journal of Sociology* 97: 448-95.

McCarthy, M. & R. Carter (1994). *Language as Discourse: Perspectives for Language Teachers*. New York: Longman.

McEnery, T. & A. Wilson (1996). *Corpus Linguistics*. Edinburgh: Edinburgh University Press.

Menz, F. & Lalouscheck, J. (2006). "I can't tell you how much it hurts": Gender-relevant differences in the description of chest pain. In Gotti, M & Salager-Meyer, F. (2006) (eds.). *Advances in Medical Discourse Analysis: Oral and Written Contexts*. Bern: Peter Lang.

Minsky, M. (1975). A framework for representing knowledge. In P. Winston (ed.), *The Psychology of Computer Vision*. New York: McGraw-Hill, 211-77.

Mishler, E. (2006). Narrative and identity: the double arrow of time. In A. de Fina, D. Schiffrin and M. Bamberg (eds.), *Discourse and Identity*. Cambridge: Cambridge University Press. 30-47.

Moita-Lopes, L.P. (2006). On being white, heterosexual and male in a Brazilian school: multiple positionings in oral narratives. In A. de Fina, D. Schiffrin and M. Bamberg (eds.), *Discourse and Identity*. Cambridge: Cambridge University Press. 288-313.

Morris, C.W. (1938). *Foundations of the Theory of Signs*. In O. Neurath, R. Carnap & C. Morris (eds.), *International Encyclopedia of Unified Science*. Chicago: University of Chicago Press, 77-138. (Reprinted in Morris 1971).

—. (1971). *Writings on the General Theory of Signs*. The Hague: Mouton.

Murray, D. E. (1990). CmC. In *English Today* 23: 42-46.

Nafá, L. (2005). *Análisis acústico-discursivo de la entonación en la interpretación simultánea inglés británico-español peninsular. Aplicaciones a la didáctica y la investigación en la interpretación de lenguas*. Tesis Doctoral. Granada: Universidad de Granada.

Neaman, J.S. & Silver, C.G. (1990). *Kind Words*. New York: Facts on File.

Neff-van Aerselaer, J. (1997). *'Aceptarlo con hombría'*. Representations of masculinity in Spanish political discourse. In Johnson, S & Meinhof, U.H. (eds.), *Language and Masculinity*. Oxford: Blackwell, 159-73.

—. (2004). Dialogic turbulence in social change advertising: church versus state in Spain. In M. Pütz, J. Neff-van Aertselaer & T. van Dijk (eds.), *Communicating Ideologies: Multidisciplinary Perspectives on Language, Discourse, and Social Practice*. Amsterdam: Peter Lang, 547-74.

Nishida, K. (1958). *Intelligibility and the Philosophy of Nothingness: Three Philosophical Essays*. R. Shinzinger (trans.). Honolulu: East-West Center Press.

Norris, S. & R. Jones (2005). *Discourse in Action: Introduction to Mediated Discourse Analysis*. London: Routledge.

Nwoye, O. (1992). Linguistic politeness and socio-cultural variations of the notion of face. *Journal of Pragmatics* 18: 309-28.

Obeng, S. G. & B.A.S. Hartford (2008). *Political Discourse Analysis*. Huntinton, NY: Nova Science Publishers.

O'Driscoll, J. (1996). About face: a defence and elaboration of universal dualism. *Journal of Pragmatics* 25 (1): 1-32.

O'Farrell, C. (2005). *Michel Foucault*, London: Sage.

Orwell, G. (1969). Politics and the English language. In W.F. Bolton and D. Crystal (eds.), *The English Language Vol 2: Essays by Linguists and Men of Letters, 1858-1964*. Cambridge: Cambridge University Press: 217-19.

Patrick, P. L. (2004). Some basic things that variationists do or assume. Course materials at:
http://courses.essex.ac.uk/LG/LG554/Principles.VarAnal.html

Pêcheux, M. (1978). Discourse-structure or event. In C. Nelson & L. Grossberg (eds.), *Marxism and the Interpretation of Culture*. London: Macmillan, 251-66.

—. (1982). *Language, Semantics and Ideology*. New York: St. Martin's Press.

Pérez de Ayala, S. (2001). FTA's and Erskine May: Conflicting needs? – Politeness in Question Time. *Journal of Pragmatics*, 33: 143-69.

Prince, E. F. (1992). The ZPG letter: subjects, definiteness, and information status. In S. Thompson and W. Mann (eds), *Discourse Description: Diverse Analyses of a Fundraising Text*. Amsterdam and

Philadelphia: John Benjamins, 295-325.

Quirk, R. et al. (1985). *A Comprehensive Grammar of the English Language*. London: Longman.

Rasmussen, D.M. (ed.) (1996). *The Handbook of Critical Theory*. Oxford: Blackwell.

Reich, S. (1998). Introduction to corpus linguistics: course outline. At: www.uni-koeln.de/phil-fak/englisch/bald/outline.htm

Ribeiro, B.T. (2006). Footing, positioning, voice. Are we talking about the same things? In A. de Fina, D. Schiffrin and M. Bamberg (eds.), *Discourse and Identity*. Cambridge: Cambridge University Press. 48-82.

Romero-Trillo, Jesús (2006). 'Discourse markers'. In *Encyclopedia of Language and Linguistics*. Oxford: Elsevier. 639-42.

—. (2008). Discourse markers/Pragmatic markers. In *SciTopics: Research summaries by experts*, at http://www.scitopics.com/Discourse_Markers_Pragmatic_Markers.html (accessed February 10, 2009).

Ross, J. W. (1989). The militarization of disease: do we really want a war on AIDS? In *Soundings, 72* (1): 39-58.

Sacks, H. (1971). Quoted in Levinson, 1983: 313.

—. (1984). Notes on Methodology. In J.M. Atkinson & J. Heritage (eds.), *Structures of Social Action*. Cambridge: Cambridge University Press, 21-27.

Sacks, H., E. Schegloff & G. Jefferson (1974). A simple systematics for the organization of turn-taking in conversation. *Language* 50, 4: 696-735.

Sapir, E. (1933). Communication. In *Encyclopedia of the Social Sciences*, 4: 78-81.

Saville-Troike, M. (2003). *The Ethnography of Communication: An Introduction (Language in Society)*. London: Blackwell.

Sawyer, R. K. (1995). A developmental model of heteroglossic improvisation in children's fantasy play.In A. Ambert (ed.), *Sociological Studies of Children*, Volume 7: 127-53. Greenwich, CT: JAI Press.

Schank, R. & R. Abelson (1977). *Scripts, Plans, Goals, and Understanding*. Hillsdale, NJ: Erlbaum.

Schegloff, E. (1972). Sequencing in conversational openings. In J. Gumperz & D. Hymes (eds.). *Directions in Sociolinguistics*. New York: Holt, Rinehart & Winston, 346-80.

—. (1991). Reflections on talk and social structure. In D. Boden and D. Zimmerman (eds.), *Talk and Social Structure*. Cambridge: Polity

Press.

—. (1997). Whose text? Whose context? In *Discourse & Society,* 8 (2): 165-87.

—. (1999a). 'Schegloff's texts' as Billig's data: a critical reply. In *Discourse & Society,* 10: 558-72.

—. (1999b). Naivete vs. sophistication or discipline vs. self-indulgence: a rejoinder to Billig. In *Discourse & Society,* 10: 577-82.

—. (2007).*Sequence Organization in Interaction: A Primer in Conversation Analysis, Volume 1,* Cambridge: Cambridge University Press.

Schegloff, E. & H. Sacks (1973). Opening up closings. *Semiotica,* 7 (3/4): 289-327.

Schiffrin, D. (1981). Tense variation in narrative. *Language* 57, 45-62.

—. (1987). *Discourse Markers.* Cambridge: Cambridge University Press.

—. (1994). *Approaches to Discourse.* Oxford: Basil Blackwell.

—. (1996). Narrative as self-portrait. *Language in Society* 25/2, 167-204.

Schiffrin, D., Tannen, D. & Hamilton, H. (eds.) (2001). *Handbook of Discourse Analysis.* Massachusetts & Oxford: Blackwell.

Schiffrin, D. (2006). From linguistic reference to social reality. In A. de Fina, D. Schiffrin and M. Bamberg (eds.), *Discourse and Identity.* Cambridge: Cambridge University Press, 103-31.

Scollon, R. (1998). *Mediated Discourse as Social Interaction: A Study of News Discourse.* London: Longman.

—. (2001). *Mediated Discourse: The Nexus of Practice.* London: Routledge.

—. (2005). Multiple Methods. At: www.aptalaska.net/~ron/FOOD%2005/mda/method.htm

Scollon, R. & S.W. Scollon (1981). *Narrative, Literacy and Face in Interethnic Communication.* Norwood, NJ: Ablex.

Scollon, R. & S. W. Scollon (2003). *Discourses in Place: Language in the Material World.* London & New York: Routledge.

Scollon, R. & S.W. Scollon (2004). *Nexus Analysis: Discourse and the Emerging Internet.* London: Routledge.

Scollon, S. (1998). Methodological Assumptions in Intercultural Communication. In B.L. Hoffer and J. H. Koo (eds.), *Cross-cultural Communication. East and West in the 90s.* Trinity University, San Antonio, TX: Institute for Cross-Cultural Research, 104-09.

Searle, J. (1969). *Speech Acts: An Essay in the Philosophy of Language.* Cambridge: Cambridge University Press.

—. (1975). Indirect Speech Acts. In P. Cole (ed.), *Syntax and Semantics,* Vol. 3: 59-82.

—. (1979a). A Taxonomy of Illocutionary Acts. *Expression and Meaning*. Cambridge: Cambridge University Press.

—. (1979b). On the logical status of fictional discourse. *Expression and Meaning*. Cambridge: Cambridge University Press.

Seidelhofer, B. & H. Widdowson (1999). Coherence in summary: The contexts of appropriate discourse. In W. Bublitz, U. Lenk & E. Ventola (eds.), *Coherence in Spoken and Written Discourse*. Amsterdam & Philadelphia: John Benjamins, 205-20.

Simmel, G. (1950). Sociability, Part 1/III and The expansion of the dyad, Part 2/III & IV (The triad). In K. Wolff (ed.), *The Sociology of Georg Simmel*. New York: Free Press, 40-51.

Slembrouck, S. (2006). What is meant by 'discourse analysis'? Department of English, University of Gent. At: http://bank.rug.ac.be/da/da.htm

Sotillo, S. (2000). Discourse functions and syntactic complexity in synchronous and asynchronous communication. In *Language Learning & Technology*, 4(1): 82-119.

Sperber, D. & D. Wilson (1986). *Relevance. Communication and Cognition*. Oxford: Blackwell.

Staiano, K.V. (1986). *Interpreting Signs of Illness: A Case Study in Medical Semiotics*. Berlin: Mouton de Gruyter.

Stalnaker, R.C. (1974). Pragmatic presuppositions. In M.K. Munitz & P.K. Unger (eds.), *Semantics and Philosophy*. New York: New York University Press. 197-214.

Stubbs, Michael (1996). *Text and corpus analysis*. Oxford: Blackwell.

Svartvik, J. & R. Quirk (eds.) (1980). *A Corpus of English Conversation*. CWK GLEERUP LUND.

Taboada, M. (2004). *Building Coherence and Cohesion: Task-Oriented Dialogue in English and Spanish*. Amsterdam/Philadelphia: John Benjamins.

Tannen, D. (1984). *Conversational Style: Analyzing Talk among Friends*. New Jersey: Ablex Publishing Corporation.

—. (1989). *Talking Voices: Repetition, Dialogue, and Imagery in Conversational Discourse*. Cambridge: Cambridge University Press.

—. (1990). *You Just Don't Understand. Women and Men in Conversation*. New York: Ballantine.

—. (1993). *Framing in Discourse*. New York: Oxford University Press.

—. (2007). *Talking Voices. Repetition, Dialogue, and Imagery in Conversational Discourse* (2nd edition). Cambridge: Cambridge University Press.

Tannen, D. & C. Wallat (1987). Interactive frames and knowledge schemas in interaction: examples from a medical examination interview. In *Social Psychology Quarterly,* 50(2): 205-16.

Taylor, S. (2001). Locating and Conducting Discourse Analytic Research. In: Wetherell, M.; Taylor, S. & S. J. Yates (2001) (eds.). *Discourse as Data: A Guide for Analysis.* London: Sage, 5-48.

ten Have, P. (1989). The consultation as genre. In B. Torode (ed.), *Text and Talk as Social Practice.* Dordrecht: Foris, 115-35.

The Golden Girls: Scripts. (1991). London: Boxtree Limited; Touchstone Pictures and Television.

Thomas, J. (1986). *The Dynamics of Discourse. A Pragmatic Analysis of Confrontational Interaction.* Unpublished Doctoral Dissertation. Lancaster University.

Thornborrow, J. (2002). *Power Talk: Language and Interaction in Institutional Discourse.* London: Longman.

Titscher, S. M., R. Meyer, R. Wodak & E. Vetter (2000). *Methods of Text and Discourse Analysis.* London: Sage.

van Dijk, T. (1977). *Text and Context: Explorations in the Semantics and Pragmatics of Discourse.* London: Longman.

—. (1980). *Macrostructures.* Hillsdale, NJ: Erlbaum.

—. (1985). *Handbook of Discourse Analysis.* 4 Volumes. London: Academic Press.

—. (1989). Structures of discourse and structures of power. In J.A. Anderson (ed.), *Communication Yearbook 12.* Newbury Park, CA: Sage, 163-83.

—. (1993). Principles of critical discourse analysis. In *Discourse and Society*, Vol 4: 249-85.

—. (1999a). Discourse and the denial of racism. In A. Jaworski & N. Coupland (eds.), *The Discourse Reader.* London & New York: Routledge, 541-58.

—. (1999b). Critical Discourse Analysis and Conversation Analysis. Editorial in *Discourse & Society*, 10 (4): 459-60.

—. (2000). Cognitive Discourse Analysis. An Introduction. Version 1.0. at http://www.hum.uva.nl/teun/cogn-dis-anal.htm.

—. (2001). Critical discourse analysis. In D. Schiffrin, D. Tannen & H. Hamilton (eds.), *The Handbook of Discourse Analysis.* Massachusetts & Oxford: Blackwell, 352-71.

—. (2003) *Dominación étnica y racismo discursivo en España y América Latina.* Barcelona: Gedisa.

—. (2004). From Text Grammar to Critical Discourse Analysis. A Brief Academic Autobiography. Version 2.0. At: www.discourses.org [Accessed February 14, 2009].

—. (2008a). *Discourse and Power.* Houndsmills, U.K.: Palgrave.
—. (2008b). *Discourse and Context. A Sociocognitive Approach.* Cambridge: Cambridge University Press.
—. (2009). *Society and Discourse. How Context Controls Text and Talk.* Cambridge: Cambridge University Press.
van Dijk, T. & W. Kintsch (1983). *Strategies of Discourse Comprehension.* New York: Academic Press.
Van Dijk, T, Neff-van Aertselaer, J. & M Pütz (2004). Introduction: Language, Discourse and Ideology. In M. Pütz, J. Neff-van Aertselaer & T. van Dijk (eds.), *Communicating Ideologies: Multidisciplinary Perspectives on Language, Discourse, and Social Practice.* Amsterdam: Peter Lang.
Ward, G. & B.J. Birner (2001). Discourse and Information Structure. In D. Schiffrin, D. Tannen & H. Hamilton (eds.), *The Handbook of Discourse Analysis.* Massachusetts & Oxford: Blackwell Publishers, 119-37.
Watts, R.J. (1992). Linguistic politeness and politic verbal behaviour: reconsidering claims for universality. In Watts. R., Ide, S. and Ehlich K. (eds.), *Politeness in Language: Studies in its History, Theory and Practice.* Berlin: Mouton de Gruyter, 43-69.
—. (2003). *Politeness.* Cambridge: Cambridge University Press.
Weijts, W. (1993). Seeking information. In *Patient Participation in Gynaecological Consultations: Studying Interactional Patterns.* Maastricht: Uniprint Universitaire Drukkerij, 39-64.
Weinreich, U., Labov, W. & M. Herzog (1968). Empirical foundations for a theory of language change. In W. Lehmann & Y. Malkiel (eds.), *Directions for Historical Linguistics.* Austin: University of Texas Press, 97-195.
Werkhofer, K. (1992). Traditional and modern views: the social constitution and the power of politeness. In Watts, R, Ide, S & Ehlich, K. (eds.), *Politeness in Language: Studies in its History, Theory and Practice.* Berlin: Mouton de Gruyter, 155-99.
West, C. (1984). *Routine Complications: Troubles with Talk between Doctors and Patients.* Bloomington: Indiana University Press.
Wetherell, M. (1998). Positioning and interpretative repertoires: conversation analysis and post-structuralism in dialogue. In *Discourse and Society,* 9 (3): 387-412.
Wetherell, M.; Taylor, S. & S. J. Yates (2001a) (eds.). *Discourse Theory and Practice: A Reader.* London: Sage Publications.
Wetherell, M.; S. Taylor & S. J. Yates (2001b) (eds.). *Discourse as Data: A Guide for Analysis.* London: Sage Publications.

Wilson, J. (2001). Political Discourse. In D. Schiffrin, D. Tannen and H. Hamilton (eds.), *Handbook of Discourse Analysis*. Massachusetts & Oxford: Blackwell.

Wilson, T.D. (2002). Alfred Schutz, Phenomenology and research methodology for information behaviour research. Paper delivered at *ISIC4 - Fourth International Conference on Information Seeking in Context*, Universidade Lusiada, Lisbon, Portugal, September 11 to 13, 2002. At: http://informationr.net/tdw/publ/papers/schutz02.html

Winfrey, O. (ed.). *The Oprah Magazine*. October and December 2002 issues.

Wodak, R. (1995). *Disorders of Discourse*. London: Longman.

Wodak, R. & T. van Dijk (eds.) (2000). *Racism at the top*. Klagenfurt: Drava Verlag.

Woofit, R. (2001). Researching Psychic Practitioners: Conversation Analysis. In M. Wetherell et al (eds.), *Discourse as Data: A Guide for Analysis*. London: Sage Publications, 49-92.

Worthan, S. and V. Gadsden (2006). Urban fathers positioning themselves through narrative: an approach to narrative self-construction. In A. de Fina, D. Schiffrin and M. Bamberg (eds.), *Discourse and Identity*. Cambridge: Cambridge University Press. 314-41.

Wynne, M (editor). 2005. Developing Linguistic Corpora: a Guide to Good Practice. Oxford: Oxbow Books. Available online from http://ahds.ac.uk/linguistic- corpora/ [Accessed 2008-05-18].

Yates, S. J. (1996). English in cyberspace. In S. Goodman & D. Graddol (eds.), *Redesigning English: New Texts, New Identities*. London: Routledge, 106-40.

Yeh, C. (2004). The relationship of cohesion and coherence: A contrastive study of English and Chinese. In *Journal of Language and Linguistics*, Vol. 3, 2: 243-260

Yule, G. (1996). *Pragmatics*. Oxford: Oxford University Press.

Zimmerman, D. H. and D.L. Wieder (1970). Ethnomethodology and the problem of order: comment on Denzin. In J. D. Douglas (ed.), *Understanding everyday life: toward the reconstruction of sociological knowledge*. Chicago: Aldine Publishing. 285-98.

CHAPTER 1

1. b
2. a
3. c
4. a
5. c
6. b
7. a
8. b
9. a
10. c
11. a
12. b
13. c
14. b
15. a
16. c
17. a
18. b
19. c
20. a

CHAPTER 2

1. a
2. b
3. a
4. b
5. b
6. b
7. a
8. c
9. a
10. a
11. c
12. a

13. b
14. a
15. c

CHAPTER 3

1.   b
2.   c
3.   c
4.   a
5.   b
6.   a
7.   b
8.   c
9.   c
10. b
11. c
12. b
13. a
14. b
15. a
16. b
17. a
18. b
19. b
20. c
21. b
22. a

CHAPTER 4

1.   b
2.   a
3.   b
4.   c
5.   a
6.   c
7.   a
8.   b
9.   a
10. c

11. b
12. b
13. b
14. b
15. c
16. a
17. a
18. b
19. a
20. c

CHAPTER 5

1. b
2. a
3. c
4. c
5. a
6. b
7. c
8. b
9. a
10. b
11. a
12. c
13. a
14. b
15. a
16. c
17. c

CHAPTER 6

1. c
2. a
3. b
4. a
5. b
6. c
7. b
8. b

9. b
10. c
11. a
12. c
13. b
14. a
15. b

CHAPTER 7

1. b
2. c
3. b
4. c
5. a
6. c
7. a
8. c
9. c
10. a
11. b
12. a
13. c
14. b
15. a
16. a
17. b
18. c

CHAPTER 8

1. b
2. a
3. c
4. b
5. b
6. c
7. b
8. a
9. c
10. c

11. c
12. a
13. b
14. b
15. c

CHAPTER 9

1.   c
2.   b
3.   b
4.   a
5.   c
6.   a
7.   b
8.   c
9.   c
10. a
11. a
12. b
13. a
14. b
15. c
16. c
17. a
18. b
19. a
20. c
21. b

CHAPTER 10

1.   b
2.   c
3.   a
4.   a
5.   c
6.   b
7.   a
8.   b
9.   a

    10. c
    11. a
    12. c
    13. c
    14. b
    15. a
    16. c
    17. a
    18. c
    19. b
    20. a

CHAPTER 11

    1) c
    2) b
    3) a
    4) b
    5) c
    6) c
    7) a
    8) b
    9) b
    10) a
    11) c
    12) a
    13) b
    14) c
    15) a
    16) b
    17) a
    18) b
    19) b
    20) c

CHAPTER 12

1) c
2) a
3) b
4) b
5) a
6) a
7) a
8) c
9) a
10) c
11) b
12) b
13) a
14) c
15) c
16) a
17) b
18) c
19) c
20) a
21) b
22) b

CHAPTER 1

A) Open task
B) Open task
C) Open task

CHAPTER 2

A) Open task

B) a) Open task
b) Open task
c) Open task

CHAPTER 3

A) Open task

B)

a) The first referent in the recipe (**SUPER FISH DISH**) is presented in bold type and capital letters. This is a discourse strategy used to give prominence to it, since it is the main referent of the recipe, i.e. the name of the dish. Most of the other referents in the recipe are introduced in capital letters, as the list of ingredients, constituting the first reference sequence. The use of referents is then continued by using full noun phrases, pronouns and zero pronouns which refer to evoked, familiar or inferable entities, as shown in the following table:

REFERENT	TYPE AND EXPLANATIONS
the fillets of sole	Previously **evoked**, thus **definite** and not very explicit (anaphoric reference), though there is some level of explicitness (specifying they are fillets *of sole*. Thus *fillets* can also be considered a case of **esphoric** reference within the same nominal group).
a few prawns	Though previously **evoked** (**anaphoric** reference), the quantity was not specified, and therefore it is somehow introduced for the first time. Thus the referent is **indefinite** and now more **explicit** as to the quantity needed.
them	Previously **evoked** (**anaphoric** reference), thus now referred to by means of a pronoun, which makes it **inferable** and **familiar** as well.
a fireproof dish	Not previously evoked, thus **indefinite**, but **familiar** for any person who can relate to cooking (**homophoric** reference).
the hard-boiled eggs	Previously **evoked** (**anaphoric** reference), thus **definite.**
mushrooms and (or) tomatoes	Previously **evoked** and **definite** (the definite article *the* has been ellipted in the coordination. Can also be labeled as **familiar** referents (thus **homophoric**).
them	Pronoun. Previously **evoked** referent (**anaphoric**), and therefore, **inferable.**
the fish	Previously **evoked**, **familiar**, **definite** and **inexplicit**. Anaphoric reference.

| cheese sauce | Though previously **evoked,** still **indefinite** (perhaps because the quantity is not specified). Can also be labeled as a **familiar, homophoric** referent. |
| grated cheese | Though previously **evoked (anaphoric** reference), still **indefinite** (perhaps because the quantity is not specified). Can also be labeled as a **familiar (homophoric)** referent. |

NOTE: All referents naming the ingredients can become **exophoric** the moment the recipient is following the instructions of the recipe with the real ingredients on his/her kitchen counter.

Inferable items that have been omitted by using the Ø pronoun:

     i)   the pronoun *it* in:

Cover Ø with cheese sauce and sprinkle Ø liberally with grated cheese.
Bake Ø in oven 375 (Gas n°5) for about 25-30 minutes and until Ø (is) golden brown.
Serve Ø hot.

     ii)   the pronoun *them* in:

Roll up the fillets of sole, enclosing a few prawns in each roll, and season Ø.

b)

1)

    Personal deixis: The use of the possessive adjective *your* in the first exchange between Agnes and her mother is a case of the normal, **non-gestural** use of the adjective (it clearly refers to Agnes' bed). The use of *we* in "All we are is dust in the wind" constitutes a case of the generic, **symbolic** use of the deictic first person plural. The use of *it* in "It seems so pointless…" may be interpreted as an instance of the **non-deictic** use of the pronoun (i.e. as a "void" *it* filling the slot of the subject but having no personal specific reference), or it may be taken as a referent for her mother's previous utterance, in which case it would be an example of **discourse, symbolic deixis**.

Place deixis: The demontratives *this* (**proximal**) and *that* (**distal**) obviously occur in their gestural usage in the second exchange between Agnes and her mother. However, taken as a whole, the expressions *This dust in the wind* and *that dust in the wind* can be taken as examples of **personal, gestural** deixis meaning "I" and "you" (taking Agnes' mother as the deictic center) respectively.

Time deixis: The use of the word *now* constitutes a case of **proximal time deixis**, which also looks as **gestural**, considering the fact that the mother is putting a special emphasis on the word (which is marked in bold type in the comic strip).

Social deixis: The use of *her* in "It's frightening how *her* dust in the wind…" is an example of **social deixis** indicating rank or respect, used in an ironical way and in analogy with expressions like "Her Royal Highness", because no matter how philosophical Agnes may be, she finally has to acknowledge her mother's authority and make her bed. Obviously, it is also an example of **personal, symbolic deixis**, for the whole nominal phrase makes reference to Agnes' mother.

2)

Place deixis: The use of *this* in "This is real life, Agnes! exemplifies a case of **symbolic, proximal place deixis**. *This* (i.e. the world of real life) is here opposed to the fictional, ideal world of novels, which would be the distant, non-proximal world for Agnes' mother. The demonstrative *that* in "Put down that pen…" is an instance of **gestural** (see Agnes' mother's finger pointing at it), **distal place deixis**.

Personal deixis: *Me* in "Listen to me" is a **personal deictic** (first person singular) used in a **symbolic** way. The possessive adjective *your* (in "But your pearls of wisdom…"), the objective pronoun *them* (in "Future readers will find them enthralling!"), and the subjective pronouns *you* in "You go ahead and write" and *we* in "We'll talk later" all exemplify instances of **symbolic, personal deixis**.

Discourse deixis: The demonstrative pronoun *that* in "Oh, my! That is very flattering!" is used as a **discourse deictic** (in its **symbolic** usage) which goes back to Agnes' previous whole utterance, and is obviously an instance of a **distal place deictic** as well. The discourse marker *finally* in "Finally, the word storm…" can be considered as a **symbolic (temporal) discourse deictic**, connecting the previous discourse in Agnes' novel with its final paragraph, and, metaphorically, also connecting the previous situation in the comic strip with its resolution or resulting action (Agnes' mother's rage (metaphorically the "storm" or the "mighty cloud of blather") "evaporated", and therefore Agnes can continue to read in peace.

Time deixis: The comparative adverb *later* should be taken as a **symbolic time deictic** which is relative to the coding time of the speaker (Agnes' mother, in this case).

c)

1)
Line 1: Expressive act (greeting: Larry King greets the caller on the phone).
Line 2: Assertive act but can also be considered an expressive, expressing a psychological state (complimenting: "Gentlemen, the honor is mine"). Expressive act (thanking).
Lines 2 to 5: Directive acts (questions).
Line 6: Directive (question).
Line 7: Assertive (answer).
Line 8: Assertive.
Lines 9-10: Directive (interrupting, somehow "ordering" Maher to stop: "Wait a minute,…". Directive (question: You had some sort of disaster…?).
Lines 11 to 16: Representative, assertive acts.

2)
Line 1: Expressive act (greeting: Larry King greets the second caller on the phone).
Lines 2 and 3: Directive (question). Expressive (thanking).
Line 4: Directive (question).
Lines 5 to 10: Representative, assertive acts.
Line 11: Expressive (apologizing: "Excuse me. It is.").

Lines 11 to 16: Representative, assertive acts.
Lines 17-18: Directive (question).
Lines 19 to 24: Assertive acts (answers).

There seems to be a pattern in the sequence of speech acts for receiving calls from the audience that could be broadly summarized as follows:

TV Host: Expressive act (Greeting).
Caller: Expressives   (Thanking,   complimenting)   and   directives (question(s)).
Guest: Assertives, directives and expressives (all these may form part of the answers to the caller's questions).

d) In fragment 1:

PRESUPPOSITION TRIGGERS	PRESUPPOSITION
little plan B (line 3)	**Existence.** There exists a little plan B which has to do with the administration's Homeland Security Department.
Homeland Security Department (line 3)	**Existence.** There exists a Homeland Security Department.
to stop (line 3)	**Connotation.** The election process is taking place at the moment.
Our 2000 Florida deal (lines 4-5)	**Existence.** There existed a deal in Florida in 2000.
etc...	

In fragment 2:

PRESUPPOSITION TRIGGERS	PRESUPPOSITION
Carbondale, Illinois (line 1)	**Existence.** There is a caller from Carbondale, Illinois .
again (line 2)	**Connotation** Southern voters had voted for the Democrats before.
my (line 8)	**Factive/ Existence:** Maher has a stand-up act on TV, and thus this

	stand up act exists.
dumbest (line11)	**Connotation.** Other parts of the country are less dumb.
The people who are following the compass (line 22)	**Connotation.** Other people are not following the compass.
etc…	

CHAPTER 4

A)

a-c) First of all, it is necessary to situate the microstructure of this call within the macrostructure of a television interview, and in particular, Larry King's interviews. It is customary on the *Larry King Show* to receive calls from viewers some time towards the end of the show. These viewers are expected to ask the guest questions, but they are not normally allowed to participate in the discussion, apparently due to time constraints. At first sight, Larry King's greeting (*Toquerville, Utah, hello*) constitutes a relatively straightforward interactional ritual which opens a period of interpersonal access, but this access is very soon restricted to Mr. King and Mr. Maher; the caller is left aside (and therefore, he turns from the role of *principal* into the role of *bystander*). Even more, very soon in the exchange Mr. King "speaks for the caller" (and thus takes the role of *animator*). This "speaking for another" occurs after Mr. Maher asks the caller "You mean you're talking about on Election Day?" and Larry King immediately answers (without letting the caller intervene) "Yes, in case there's some big occurrence". This remark alters the participation framework of the talk, something that Mr. King can do because he is the host of the show and therefore he is normally the participant with the most power. Thus here King is being the spokesman who produces a message whose content is the responsibility of another, i.e. the *animator* for the caller, who is in the *principal* role (because she was the one who was supposed to be responsible for talking, since Maher asked her the question, not Larry King). At the same time, the fact that Mr. King is speaking for the caller provides some *contextualization cue* as to his and the other interactants' roles and positions within the exchange. Mr. King's changing roles as *principal, animator* and *author* (responsible for, producer, and creator of talk) at different stages of the interview indicate that he has power and he is in charge, to the point that the caller must keep silent even when she's been asked a question. When Bill Maher speaks, he fills the slots of both *author* and *principal* (creator and responsible for talk). In his last intervention he, like King, uses the strategy of "speaking for another" (though in an ironic way) when he mocks the administration (...*this is an administration that has always said, "OK, we're operating under this premise. You can't criticize the administration during a time of war. Oh, and by the way, we're always at war. The war is ongoing"*), in which case he also takes the role of *figure* (the participant that is portrayed by talk).

Another example of Mr. King's use of the power the situational context grants him is when, again, his remark "Wait a minute, you had some sort of disaster you don't want to hold an election if you've got bombs dropping?" alters the participation framework of the talk (he interrupts Bill Maher). These disruptions could be considered hostile by some viewers, for in general TV hosts are expected to respect the turns of both guests and callers; however, King's status as a very well-known television interviewer entitles him to be occasionally impolite. Both callers and viewers normally accept this type of superiority on King's part, so they respond in a positive way and thus *face* is maintained.

B)
1)
Politeness strategy: Off Record (Be ironic)
Maxim being flouted: Quality

2)
Politeness strategy: Off Record (Give hints)
Maxim being flouted: Relevance

3)
Politeness strategy: Off Record (Give association cues)
Maxim being flouted: Relevance

4)
Politeness strategy: Bold on record
Maxim being flouted: None

5)
Politeness strategy: On Record with Negative Politeness
Maxim being flouted: None (it is a *conventionally* indirect request, and therefore, there is no need for the interlocutors to work out the implicature.).

C)
(1) i), ii), iii), iv), v) & vi)

Andrew's reactions and answers to Mr. Martin's (his master) and the family's comments show, among other things, that he interprets everyone's utterances in their literal meaning and from a logical point of view. He lacks a great deal of the pragmatic knowledge which is necessary to judge that, for example, Grace's comment *"I think it sucks"* is a rude one (Scene 2). This is not only a funny scene but also one that makes the reader/watcher aware of all the mechanisms human beings have at their disposal in order to judge social events and adjust their discourse accordingly. The robot lacks these mechanisms and therefore does not know of any social customs that would let him understand that when a servant's master says that "he is fine" in a situation like the one depicted in the scene (Andrew has served the meal and now all the members of the family are eating), he must leave the room and return to the kitchen. Mr. Martin has to make this intention explicit at the end of the exchange and cannot take Andrew's knowledge for granted.

If we look at Andrew's interpretation of Mr. Martin's comment *"We are fine Andrew"*, it can be said that, since Andrew took it literally and could not grasp the meaning beyond the words, it is clear that he could not work out the implicature telling him that Mr. Martin wanted him to go to the kitchen. Mr Martin was flouting both the Quantity and the Manner Maxims, for he was not being as informative as required and he was being obscure, and therefore a normal, human interlocutor would have interpreted *"We are fine"* as a way of asking his interlocutor to leave, considering the context and the relationship between Mr. Martin and Andrew, which is an asymmetrical one.

When analyzing Andrew's discourse in the light of Grice's Cooperative Principle, a question arises as to whether it can be considered to be cooperative, and we come to the conclusion that, even though Andrew always tries to be helpful in many ways, on several occasions he is not cooperative from the pragmatic point of view, as can be seen in Scene 1. When Mr. Martin says *"Good night"*, Andrew is not being cooperative by saying *"It certainly is, sir"*, even though he may sound nice and respectful. He lacks the communicative competence necessary to give the right answer: in this particular case, he does not know that "Good night" is the appropriate and socially accepted answer to "Good night" and that both utterances constitute an *adjacency pair* in which "Good night" is considered the *preferred second* (Sacks, Schegloff & Jefferson, 1974. See chapter 5). The same can be said of Andrew's reply in Scene 2, when Mr. Martin indirectly requests him to go to the kitchen *("We are fine,*

Andrew"), he again interprets the utterance literally, and therefore is not being cooperative by saying *"Indeed you are sir"*. As was mentioned above, Andrew fails to make the necessary implicature which would lead him to the conclusion that his master wants him to leave the room.

With regard to whether or not Andrew is capable of flouting the Maxims of Grice's Cooperative Principle in the same fashion human beings do, it is interesting to note that, if we analyze Andrew's discourse superficially, we would conclude that he never flouts any of the maxims, for he always tells the truth (Quality), he is generally very accurate and does not speak more than required (Quantity), he intends to make relevant contributions, and he generally makes his contribution in a brief and orderly way (Relevance and Manner). But the fact that he cannot flout the Maxims paradoxically shows that he cannot always be cooperative, because, as Grice (1975) himself acknowledged, flouting the Maxims is sometimes a requirement in order to be cooperative. Besides, if we analyze the general principle as put by Grice: *"Make your contribution such as is required, at the stage at which it occurs, by the accepted purpose or direction of the talk exchange in which you are engaged"* (1975: 45), we will clearly see that in most cases Andrew lacks precisely the necessary criteria to determine whether his contribution is "such as is required", "by the accepted purpose or direction of the talk exchange in which he is engaged". Therefore, he also flouts the Maxims but in a different way from that of a normal human being.

Since Andrew cannot work out implicatures, he does not have the capacity to understand *off record FTAs* (B & L, 1987) like *"We are fine, Andrew"* (Scene 2). To use an everyday expression, we could say that Andrew cannot "read between the lines". The human brain makes a great number of complex and intricate connections and inferences that Andrew's computer brain cannot make at his stage of development.

But, can we say that Andrew is "polite"? If we think of politeness in terms of the social-norm view (Fraser, 1990), we will probably be able to say that Andrew is polite. He generally follows the social norms of accepted behavior: he always wants to help *("One is glad to be of service")*, he uses *"Thank you"* and *"Please"* when expected to, and always tries to please the family he works for. In fact, he is a robot and he's been programmed to that effect. But if we think of politeness from the face-saving perspective, that is, from the view that being polite entails being able to use a set of on record and off record strategies (B & L, 1987), we will clearly see that Andrew's politeness is restricted to *bald on record* and *on record with positive and negative politeness strategies*. Andrew finds it very difficult to go off record and to understand people when they do so. His use of language is restricted to truth conditional logic (remember he is a robot and his mind is a computer) and consequently he has no ability to flout the Maxims intentionally, nor can he understand or interpret the messages intended by other people when they flout the Maxims. But Andrew can handle some politeness strategies; for instance, he goes *on record with negative politeness* when he addresses Mr. Martin, which makes him sound respectful and non-imposing. But even when going on record, Andrew lacks, at least partially, the necessary information every normal speaker of English has. A clear example of this fact is found in Scene 1, where his response to "Good night" (*"It certainly is, sir"*) shows us that he does not know the socially accepted rule that tells us that the correct response to "Good night" is "Good night". He then flouts the maxim of quantity (saying more than necessary) unintentionally by falling into what he himself calls *"an infinite verbal loop"* by answering *"Good night"* again and again, following his master's instruction to the letter.

(2) Open task.

CHAPTER 5

A)   This verbal interchange has the typical **overall organization** of a telephone call, distributed in the following manner:

1. **Opening section**: T1, T2 & T3
2. **Main body**: *Topic slot 1*: T5, T6, T7 & T8 (There is only one topic slot in this conversation)
3. **Closing section**: T9, T10 & T11

The *opening* of this telephone conversation contains the typical *summons-answer* **adjacency pair** (constituted by the telephone ringing (T1 and T2), followed by a *greeting-greeting* pair (T2 and T3)). As we can see, the utterance "Hello" in T2 constitutes the second (preferred) part of the first adjacency pair, but at the same time it is the first part of the second one. T3 has the (preferred) second part of the greeting in T2, but at the same time it starts another adjacency pair where a *request* is the first part and the *granting* of the request is the second (preferred) part: The Police Officer asks about Mr. Rowlings, and he agrees to talk to the Police Officer by acknowledging his identity in T4. Immediately after, still on the same turn, Mr. Rowlings starts the next adjacency pair (*question/answer*) which is completed in T5 by the Police Officer, who subsequently starts the next adjacency pair in the same turn. In spite of the fact that the Officer uses the verb "to invite" ("*…and we are **inviting** you to collaborate with our Corps*") the first part of this pair is not an invitation but a request (the Officer here is a bit "tricky" in order for his request not to sound too imposing). Mr Rowlings understands that the Officer is asking for money, and he delays the granting the request by asking a question (*Well,… how much would that be?*) which introduces a *question-answer* **insertion sequence** (in T6 & T7) , making the answer to the request in T5 appear separately (not adjacent to it) in T8. The question in T6 may be taken to be a *pre-acceptance* (**pre-sequence**) of the request, in the sense that the granting of the request is conditioned to the answer of the question (i.e. to the amount of money requested), and therefore, it also constitutes a conversational strategy to show the Officer that he is not willing to give him a large amount of money right away. The request having been granted to some degree, in T9 and T10 we find an example of a *thanking/acceptance of thanks* adjacency pair which could be considered as the *pre-closing* (**pre-sequence**) of the telephone conversation. The *closing* is made through a *greeting/greeting* pair in T10 & T11.

B)

a) & b) The fragment from *Hannity & Colmes* contains 14 turns and 13 TRPs. Some of these transition places can be identified by all the linguistic qualities or devices provided in the guidelines for analysis, but others can not. For instance, it can be said that the transition from T1 to T2 displays all of the devices: *syntactic* (there is sentence completion), *intonational* (although the transcript has no prosodic annotation here, the turn ends with a yes/no question with a rising intonation), *semantic* (the question contains a complete proposition) and pragmatic (there is more than one speech act in the turn, the final one being a question that gives the floor to the interviewee, and therefore it can be said that there is pragmatic unity in the whole turn). However, we do not find these characteristics in the transitions from T2 to T3, T3 to T4 and T12 to T13 because in all three cases we find one of the interlocutors interrupting the other and consequently the sentences, intonation, propositions and speech acts involved are broken.

c) T1 and T2 constitute a *question/answer* adjacency pair whose second part contains an insertion sequence with an interruption followed by a *request/granting of the request* adjacency pair (*Let me finish/Go ahead. Go ahead.*). The answer to the question in T1 continues in T6, and T7 can be said to be a backchannelling turn (*I understand your point*) which serves the purpose of letting the speaker know that his interlocutor is hearing and that he understands his answer, which continues in T8. T9 and T10, as well as T11 and T12, are again *question/answer* adjacency pairs, but the second part of the second pair (T12) is not complete because Hannity interrupts (T13) and starts another adjacency pair which could be labelled as *assertion/agreement*, T14 being the *agreement* or second part.

d) There are no examples of self-repair in this text, although T12 could be mistaken as a case of *other-initiated repair* of what Hannity says in T11. However, the repair is not about Hannity's mistake in talking but about Hannity's thoughts and beliefs, which are completely opposite to Kennedy's.

All along this interview, it is noticeable that Hannity is the one who always controls the floor by allocating the turn to his interviewee or by interrupting his turn without major consideration. They are discussing political matters and it is obvious that the interlocutors have opposite ideas and belong to different political parties, thus Hannity takes advantage of his power as the TV show host, and controls the floor all the time as one of the strategies to prove Kennedy wrong.

B) Open task

CHAPTER 6
A)

	Television interview
SETTING	The house of Edmund Lewis in the Isle of Mull (Scotland), in a televised interview during the early 2000s.
PARTICIPANTS	**W**: T.V. show interviewer and hostess. **E**: Poet and novelist Edwin Lewis. The audience (it is present and influences the whole communicative practice even if they do not participate).
ENDS	Entertainment **W** intends to provide her audience with information about E. Lewis. **E** intends to collaborate with the TV hostess and (probably) also intends to show his best face to the audience.
ACT SEQUENCE	**W**: Greeting/welcome/introduction of guest **E**: clarification/request **W**: description of setting/question **E**: answer **W**: question **E**: answer **W**: question (requests clarification) **E**: answer (provides clarification) **W**: question **E**: answer **W**: anticipation of information **E**: giving additional information **W**: question **E**: answer/question **W**: answer **E**: giving additional information **W**: question **E**: answer

	W: Question **E**: Answer
KEY	Serious but not solemn. Relaxed, entertaining and somewhat light-hearted.
INSTRUMENTALITIES	Oral, face-to-face standard British English.
NORMS	Interaction based on need of entertaining the audience by providing information about guest. Interviewer should ask questions and interviewee should answer them following the accepted rules of politeness. One of the accepted general norms could be, for example, that the interviewer should not intrude on the writer's private life.
GENRE	Journalistic, television interview discourse. Relatively wide range of topics.

b) In this dialogue we find, as well as in the dialogue analysed in 6.7., that the ACTS, ENDS, KEY and GENRE are all related to one another. The range is wider here, because the aim of the interview (ENDS) allows for a greater variety of topics to be covered, albeit always within the range of the interviewee's career and personal opinions.

c) The sequence of acts is long but restricted almost exclusively to questions and answers (asking for, and giving information), which is to be expected, considering the nature of the Speech Event (a television interview). Interviews always consist of questions and answers because normally the main aim of this type of interview is to make the interviewee known to the audience so they can learn more about his professional and personal life. This sequence of questions and answers is also related to the NORMS of this type of conversational exchange, which have to do with entertaining and providing the audience with information about the guest (interviewee). It is also normally expected that both interviewer and interviewee observe certain rules of politeness, a fact that is in turn related to the KEY of the practice, which has to be serious but at the same time should serve the purpose of entertaining, and therefore it does not have to be solemn, but relaxed, amusing and somewhat light-hearted. Obviously, the INSTRUMENTALITIES go hand in hand with the KEY and the other elements of communication: television interviews are normally verbal, oral types of exchange; in this case the variety is standard British English and the GENRE of the practice can be located within journalistic discourse, and in particular, within the type of discourse used in television face-to-face interviews.

B)

	Chat-room encounter
SETTING	Cyberspace/a chat room, in July 2002.
PARTICIPANTS	**Kimberly-Tood** (moderator who screens the questions of the fans and passes them along to Melissa). **Melissa Joan Hart** (actress/ celebrity speaker who answers all the questions). **Salem the cat, lindauer, MDi, A. Lopez, Mster Magoo** and **Mmy** (Melissa's fans).
ENDS	For the fans, the end is to learn more about the life, opinions, likes and dislikes of Melissa. The overall purpose of the chat is to put a celebrity in touch with the public, to facilitate communication between a famous character and her group of fans, and to use her as a role-model (in this case in particular, regarding bike safety).
ACT SEQUENCE	**K-T**: Presents new speaker (Salem the Cat) with question. **M**: answers question (lines 3-5) **K-T**: presents new speaker (lindauer) with question **M**: answers question

	K-T: presents new speaker (MDi) with question **M**: answers question **K-T**: presents another question from Salem the Cat **M**: answers question **K-T**: presents new speaker (A. Lopez) with question **M**: answers question (lines 19-22) **K-T**: presents new speaker (Mster Magoo) with question **M**: answers question **K-T**: presents new speaker (Mmy) with question **M**: answers question (lines 28-29). There is a strict sequence of question/answer adjacency pairs related to the particular nature of this chat room encounter (a group of fans who have the opportunity to chat with their favorite actress, and thus want to ask as many questions as possible, which she is willing to answer promptly). The whole chat is not reproduced here, but the same structure is observed all over, with the exception of the introductory and concluding greetings.
K EY	Relaxed, light-hearted, friendly.
I NSTRUMENTALITIES	Written, synchronous, computer-mediated American English.
N ORMS	The turns to ask questions to the actress are allotted by the presenter, Kimberly-Todd. The fans are allowed to ask

	questions in an orderly way and Melissa is expected to answer them. The language used should fit the norms for chat-room colloquial English and follow the rules of netiquette (politeness on the web). Written formal conventions are not expected to be followed (thus the use of abbreviations (e.g. *fav.* for favorite), symbols (e.g. @), acronyms (e.g.NIN), avoidance of capital letters (e.g. "i" for *I*), "sensational" spellings (e.g. "U" for *you*, "thru" for *through*), etc.
G ENRE	Informal, computer-mediated discourse (chat-room discourse). Relatively wide range of topics, although the main topic of the whole interview is "bike safety".

CHAPTER 7

A)

Joke **a** (*Don't Leave'Em Hanging*) is a narrative which starts with an **orientation**, i.e. a clause or clauses whose function is the identification of the time, place, persons, their activity or the situation. In this case the orientation gives us information about the main characters of the story (Ralph and Edna) and their status as patients in a mental hospital (place). There is no **abstract** in this narration. However, it could be argued that, in a way, the title of the joke constitutes its abstract, but we have to consider that in this case the title is not part of the narration per se. When people tell jokes, they do not normally give a title to them. So perhaps a distinction should be made between the spoken and the written versions of the same joke. The orientation is followed by the **complicating action** (i.e.

the clauses describing the different events of the story), and the events of the action are followed by Edna's final reply (*He didn't hang himself. I put him there to dry...*) which constitutes the **most reportable event**, i.e. the **result or resolution** of the narrative.

This joke does not contain all six elements or parts identified in narratives (see 7.2.), but it has the essential characteristic of this type of discourse: its temporal sequence. The joke recapitulates experience in the same order as the supposedly original events. However, we know the events did not occur in real life precisely because of the fact that it is a joke, so in this respect the narrative in jokes differs from the narratives of personal experience that Labov describes in many of his papers. Therefore we may say that *credibility* is not an important factor for jokes to be successful. What counts here is that the most reportable event (in this case *He didn't hang himself. I put him there to dry...*) contains a reasonable amount of humor and/or wit for the joke to be worth telling and for the speaker to be given the floor for as long as it is necessary to tell the joke.

Joke **b** (*Take Off My Clothes*) is much shorter than joke **a**. It only contains three clauses. The first two constitute the **complicating action**, but at the same time they contain some elements of **orientation** (Who? → *my wife and I*; Where? → *home*; When? → *the other night*). The last clause can be said to be the most reportable event (and in this case, for being a joke, the funniest), i.e. the **resolution** (*Then she told me never to wear her clothes again*) because it is the witty clause which constitutes the key to the understanding of the previous events, and it is precisely the clause that makes the narration a joke.

Thus, jokes **a** and **b** are very similar in that they both have three of the elements found in narratives (*orientation, complicating action* and *resolution*, and both have the prototypical **temporal structure** of narratives. There is very little **descriptive structure** in these two jokes. As was explained in 7.2.1., descriptions play a background function in narratives. Since neither of the jokes contains explicit evaluation clauses, it can be said that there is no **evaluation structure** in them. Perhaps this could be taken as one of the differences between jokes and narratives of personal experience: there is generally no intention of evaluation in jokes, for their main target is not to judge, but to entertain. However, jokes can also contain morals of some sort (and consequently some form of evaluation), depending on the context and situation in which they are told. But in order to draw firm conclusions on the topic, we would have to follow all the steps of Variational Analysis, including quantitative analysis, a task which goes beyond the aims of this book.

B)

As can be seen, the joke in **B** (*White House Visitors*) has a different structure from the two jokes in **A** above. We can not classify this one as *narrative* because it lacks the fundamental feature of narratives: its sequential structure. The structure of this joke is mainly **descriptive** (the description of a tourist in the White House) and there is no sequence of events. This joke consists only of an Adjacency Pair of the type Question/Answer, in which the question mainly describes the subject named in the answer (tourist) in such a way that makes it inferable to the hearer that the rest of the people who live in the White House are **not** honest, ethical, intellectual, law-abiding or truthful (which constitutes the essence of the joke).

Therefore, from the variationist point of view, we cannot say that all jokes have the same structure or even belong to the same discourse type.

C)

The first three clauses of this narrative constitute its **orientation**, considering that they explain the state of events when the narrator was dating Ethan (Who? → *the narrator and Ethan*; When? → *when she was younger*; What were the characters like? → *the narrator was stupid and clumsy (according to Ethan); Ethan was very critical of her; her family hated him*). **The complicating action** starts with the clause *One weekend, when he was away, I met Will at a party and we completely hit it off*. The **most reportable event**, i.e., the **result or resolution**, is the fact that she broke up with Ethan and started dating Will, a fact that resulted in the present state of their being happily married (**coda**). Thus, this is a more complete narrative than those in A, in the sense that it has more elements: Orientation-Complicating action-Resolution-Coda.

Apart from the essential and prevailing **temporal structure** (clearly seen in the temporal clauses of the *complicating action* and *resolution*), in this narrative we also find elements of a **descriptive structure** (when the narrator describes herself, Ethan and Will), as well as of an **evaluative structure**: it is clear that the narrator evaluates the situation in favor of Will, rather than Ethan. Her **point of view** can clearly be noticed in that she puts the blame on Ethan and the praise on Will.

This is a prototypical narrative of personal experience, and therefore the element of **credibility** is important: it is assumed that what the narrator is telling her audience/interlocutor(s) is true, and because of this (as well as because all love stories seem to have a certain appeal to people) it is worth being told.

CHAPTER 8

A)

a) **Marked theme**: *Out* (circumstantial adjunct)
b) **Unmarked theme**: *Susan*
c) **Unmarked theme**: *Are you* (Finite + subject is the normal first constituent in polar interrogatives)
d) **Marked theme**: *Never* (circumstantial adjunct)
e) **Marked theme**: *Right* (subject complement)

B)

a) **Multiple themes**: *Hey* (**non-experiential**, interpersonal, pragmatic marker of attention); *dude* (**non-experiential**, interpersonal, vocative); *give* (**experiential**, verb)
b) *I*: **Experiential** theme (subject); *However*: **Non-experiential** theme: (textual; discourse marker)
c) *She*: **Experiential** theme (subject).
d) *That kid*: **Detached theme** (left-dislocation).
e) The Rolling Stones: **Detached theme** (Absolute theme).

C)

1 *President, 'I* have 'admiration for the 'accomplishment of 'scientific
Multiple theme **Rheme**

Given   **New**

2 research in developing 'medicines which have 'proved of 'great 'benefit.
Rheme
New

3 *Yet 'also, I* have a 'healthy 'scepticism 'both of our 'pharmaceutical
Multiple Themes **Rheme**

Given   **New**

industry and ´our… of our ´exaggerated ´confidence in ´some of its

Rheme

New

4 ´products, ´many of which ´cause a ´great deal more ´harm than the

Rheme

New

5 ´illegal ´recreational drugs which ´attract the ´bulk of ´public ´attention.

Rheme

New

6   *And for ´that reason, it* would be ´wrong to place ´more

      Multiple Theme   **Rheme**

          New   **Given**

´unnecessary burdens and ´regulations upon food ´supplements and the

Rheme

New

8 ´health- ´food shops that ´sell them. Many ´believe these ´products to

                Theme   **Rheme**

                Given   **New**

9 be ´beneficial, and *at ´least* they ´don´t cause ´harm. I   ´regard

         Theme   **Rheme**   **Theme** **Rheme**

           Given   **New**   **Given** **New**

10 ´homeopathic ´medicines in the ´same   ´way. Today we have ´more

      Rheme   **Theme**   **Rheme**

      New   **Given**   **New**

11 ′patients who ′are better ′informed than ′ever ′before and ′*that*′s a

Rheme	Theme
New	Given

12 ′good   thing. I ′want people to have ′access to ′objective information

Rheme	Theme	Rheme
New	Given	New

13 about ′medicines   and ′about ′treatment. *But ′that*'s quite ′different

Rheme	Multiple themes	Rheme
New	Given	New

14 from ′opening the ′door to the ′direct ′advertising of ′medicines.

Rheme
New

15 *The ′result*, I ′fear, will ′not be better public ′information, but

Theme	Rheme
Given	New

16 ′greater public ′confusion, ′stimulated by the ′marketing techniques

Rheme
New

17 of a ′used-′car salesman.

Rheme/ New

The thematic and information structures have been only **broadly** marked herein, in the knowledge that in fact the structure is much more complex than what the general Theme-Rheme and Given-New labels can show. These labels have been assigned here to the main clauses, without considering those in the dependent clauses. Another important thing to remark before the analysis is the fact that, as was noted in 8.3., the analysis of information units as consisting of only one tonic prominence is idealistic and simplistic. As can be observed in the text included in this exercise, tone groups have more than one prominence in most cases. Having said this, we can proceed to provide some general guidelines as to the interpretation of this particular text.

As regards the thematic structure of this lecture, we find instances of multiple themes, such as *President, I* (Non-experiential theme (vocative) + experiential theme), *Yet also, I* (Non-experiential themes (conjunctive + conjunctive) + experiential theme), or *But that* (Non-experiential (conjunctive) + experiential theme). There are cases of *thematization*, as is the case of the adjunct *For that reason* (line 6) which is fronted in order to set the scene circumstancially for the upcoming information. This fact makes the speaker treat this information as New by giving tonic prominence to it. Also, the adjunct *Today* is fronted (line 10) in order to set up a framework of time. In line 14 we observe that the subordinate clause has been thematized (*The result...*): here the unmarked version would be *I fear that the result...*

It is observed in this text that there is great variation in the length of tone units, a fact that depends on factors such as speed of utterance, familiarity with the content of the message, the syntactic structures and lexical items chosen or other situational and/or personal factors such as self-confidence. Thus, within the information marked as New, we find in fact (and in most cases) more than one tonic prominence. We may interpret this as several intonation units or as an information unit with several intonation nuclei. Pitch prominence and pitch movement (intonation) are given in general to those words that are considered to carry the heaviest information load, or those implying a given contrast, such as *that* (referring to the fact of having information about medicines) in line 13; an element that is contrasted with *direct advertising,* which is also given special prominence.

Most of the themes of the main clauses in this text coincide with the Given. However, in the final and concluding clause, the speaker plays with both the thematic and information structures in order to present a criticizing and ironic comment: as noted above, the subject of the subordinate clause is fronted, emphasizing the phrase *The result,* in order to show the displeasure of the speaker with the results of the previously criticized policy of the direct advertising of medicines. As we can see, the next and final focus is placed on the words *greater, confusion* and *used car salesman* (within the subordinate clause), which directly and sarcastically refer to the thematized phrase *The result* in the main clause. Consequently, the organization of the thematic and information structures of this text helps us realize the communicative intentions of the speaker, i.e. to criticize a given policy in favor of another.

Many more aspects of the given text could be analyzed here with respect to the thematic and information structures, which I invite the student to reflect upon. (See TASK C in Chapter 8 for the completely annotated corpus. Here it has been simplified in order to make the general thematic structure clear).

D) Open task

E) Open task

CHAPTER 9

A) Open task

B) The main points that could be made regarding the comparison between CA and Post-structural Theory are the following:

a) **The context: which aspects are considered relevant or not?**
A post-structuralist or critical analyst would focus on the history of the social practices around his/her topic of research, as well as in all the political and sociological aspects related to the discourse in question. A conversation analyist, on the contrary would require very little background information about the broader social context, for it is not considered necessary for a successful analysis. Schegloff (1991) claims that the only context we need to understand discourse is what is evident and relevant to the participants as revealed by their talk, so by no means a conversation analyst would resort to, for example, so much historical information as a post-structural analyst would.

b) **The relationship of discourse with the real world, the objective truth and the results of its generalization**
Foucaldian analysis claims that discourse constitutes reality because it studies the material and the cultural together, a claim which is part of the **constructionist theory of meaning.** For post-structuralists and post-modernists there are no absolute truths. Truth is always relative to the discourse or language game of the moment. The set of knowledge/power relations which produces the truths of one historical period will inevitably change and be replaced by other truths in another period. Thus, post-structuralists (and all critical perspectives in general) are against universal

truths or absolute ethical positions.

A conversation analyst, on the contrary, would be more in favor of a belief in social scientific investigation as a truth –seeking process, on the grounds that good scientific practice should be objective and should discover real patterns, not invented patterns which can not be replicated or found again by another researcher.

More precisely, conversation analysts (and ethnomethodologists) would claim to take an even-handed and non-judgemental perspective. They are not interested in evaluating the truth or falsity of what people say, but in the organization of their talk.

c) **The position of analysts with respect to the topic: Are they politically engaged?**

All discourse analysis perspectives that are critical necessary take a politically-engaged stance. A critical or politically engaged stance of some kind is probably the most common position among discourse analysts, especially Foucauldians, critical sociolinguists, ethnographers of communication and Bakhtinian-influenced scholars.

However, conversation analysts reject the view that critique should be built into the analytic process. Schegloff (1997) argues that a critical stance in discourse research is not just bad scholarship but also bad politics. From Schegloff perspective, post-structuralism and critical analysts in general, conduct a type of research that is biased and at the same time prevents them from seeing clearly what their object of analysis is. Conversation analysts view DA as a technical discipline, and thus consider science as a different kind of activity from politics. Academics, in their view, are researchers, not politicians.

C) Open task

D)

Basically, we may speak of two main voices in this narrative: the voice of women and the voice of men. The reasons for saying that a computer should be a masculine or a feminine noun are used to express both male and female ideas (and criticisms) about the opposite sex. The voice of the narrator is also important, because, even when it seems to be the compromising voice at the beginning, at the end s/he acknowledges that the women's arguments won. The reader/hearer/analyst might argue, then, that the narrator has to be a woman (and that, therefore, this is a piece of discourse where the ideologies of women are defended), but this argument could be counter-argued, because it could very well come from a man who wants to show his empathy with women. There is also the voice of the institution: the school, which shapes the discourse used by the teacher, to which the narrator has to adjust. A more rigurous research should be made of the origins of the narration, in which other voices should be examined and other questions should be asked, such as: Who is the real, original narrator? Who sent this joke as an e-mail message? What intentions might the sender have had in sending the message to a particular friend? What might have motivated the sender to send the message in the first place? What does this joke/narration mean in the whole context of asynchronic computer-mediated communication?

Thus, in order to give a proper post-structuralist bakhtinian treatment to the analysis, we should do further research about the total historical discourse practice in question, which I invite the students/readers to engage in, if they want to pursue the topic.

CHAPTER 10

A)

[1]

In order to analyze and interpret this joke, we need to have a minimal knowledge about the Mormon Church, as well as some historical knowledge of its beliefs/traditions. As many critical discourse analysts have remarked, in order to do CDA we need to have a historical perspective of certain social practices. In this case, the average American who hears this joke will have the social cognition about the fact that in a not very distant past, the Mormon Church did not admit black people as possible members, and that it authorized male poligamy. Thus, the members of this group may be regarded as representatives of a racist and chauvinistic ideology, which lends itself to satire. In order to make this fact evident and, at the same time present an opposition to that ideology, the joke teller uses satire, which is manifested at the discourse structural level in several ways.

The examination of thematic and organization structure (combined with a critical approach) proves useful for the analysis of this joke. If we look at the two pieces of news delivered by the Secretary of the Church, we will see that he uses *God* as the theme of both utterances, but that he plays with the thematic and organization structures in a fashion that reveals his ideology and at the same time makes the joke funny. The structures of both utterances are the following:

God	is in town
Theme	**Rheme**
Hearer-Given/ Discourse New	**New**

She	is black
Theme	**Rheme**
1) Hearer and discourse-Given	**New**
2) Hearer and discourse-New	

In the first piece of news the *theme* deals with both *given* and *new* information: God is 'hearer-given' (the hearer has the concept of God in his/her mind) but 'discourse new' (it is introduced here for the first time). The *rheme*, as expected, contains *new* information (that God is **in town**). In the second piece of news –the one that makes the joke funny and at the same time critical of the ideology represented by the Mormon Church– there is an evident play on the expected and the unexpected. The *theme* refers to God as well, so here we may say that the *theme* is both *hearer and discourse-given*, but instead of the expected "he", we hear a "she", which makes the *theme* become new information in some respects, even when God was named before. So we could divide the information structure analysis into two parts, which correspond to the two different kinds of information being delivered: on the one hand (1) *She* refers to God, which is *hearer given* and *discourse given* (because the Secretary talked about God before), but on the other hand (2) the fact that God is a "she" is shocking, and therefore constitutes both *hearer and discourse-new* information.

The information in the *rheme* is also new (as might be expected) and also contributes to the implied criticism and joke (it is bad news for a Mormon to say that God is a woman and, moreover, that she is black). Thus both the *theme* and the *rheme* of the second utterance contain new information which in turn expresses an ideology that is nowadays considered not 'politically correct', and thus it is to be criticized and laughed at in the context of the joke.

[2]

This joke also reflects the ideology of the person who tells it, and in this respect it differs from joke [1] because the reflected ideology is not criticized but supported, for this kind of joke is more likely to be told by a Republican, that is, the party which in the USA opposes the liberals, who are the group that is ridiculed and criticized here.

The analysis of **implicature,** together with a critical perspective, can be used to explain how the ideology is expressed: Although not said explicitly, the last utterance of the joke ("We've never had a liberal in the family before!") carries the implicature that liberals are people whose brain is dead in spite of the fact that their hearts are still beating. The speaker is here violating both the Quantity (by not saying explicitly that liberals have no brains) and the Manner (by being ambiguous) Maxims of the Cooperative Principle, and in doing so the listener is led to think that s/he is doing it for some reason, which triggers the above-mentioned implicature.

Thus, the violation of the Maxims proves that this joke expresses a biased view of a political party, thereby implying that the opposing party is better and, on the contrary, has brains. The manipulation of some discourse strategies allows the person telling the joke to present a negative image of the Democrats (liberals) and a positive image of the Republicans, which will eventually – from a CDA perspective – bring about the manipulation of the hearers' minds.

B) Open task

C) The exchange between the professor and her student here reproduces the **power relations** between these two social roles within the academic world. As we saw in Chapter 10, CDA views semiosis as an irreducible part of material social processes which includes all forms of meaning-making. In this case, the **semiosis** of the professor's body language when she looks at her watch, or when she heads towards the door in the middle of the conversation with the student, is indicative of the **social inequality** between professor and student, and of the professor's use and abuse of the power she has over the student. The same can be said about the professor's raising of her voice at the end of the exchange (in capital letters). If, for instance, Professor M's interlocutor had been the Dean of that particular school, both her verbal and body languages would have been different. The **hegemonic discourse** would have been completely in the hands of the Dean, who has more **symbolic power** than the professor because s/he is part of a higher **power elite** in that particular social frame.

Consequently, the discourse used in the exchange favors the ideology that, within the university sphere, professors are more powerful than students and can say and do what they want when interacting with them, which makes the relationship between these two interlocutors asymmetrical, with more **symbolic power** and

hegemony on the part of the professor. It is more accepted for professors to behave impolitely towards students than viceversa, whether students like it or not. And even when we know that they do not like it, they tacitly accept that hegemony, because the professors have access to social resources such as knowledge, force, status and – most important– the students' final grades, which allow them to control the students' minds and acts up to a certain extent. So if the professor does not want to cooperate in helping the student with her scholarship problem, the student has little or no power to complain or demand more attention from the professor. She just has to accept Professor M's impoliteness silently and be careful not to say anything else that could increase the professor's annoyance, because that could turn out to have very negative effects on her final grades or on her academic life in general.

In short, the professor shows her power and hegemonic control in this exchange by: a) constantly looking at her watch (thus showing her impatience explicitly); b) raising her voice to the student; and c) not answering the student's question, thus being uncooperative. All of these are elements of the discursive situation which are indicative of a given attitude and stance on the part of the teacher which in turn reveal her social/academic status (any observer would know who the professor was and who the student was without previous knowledge about their identity), her symbolic power and, consequently, the hegemonic control of her discourse.

D) Open task

E) Open task

CHAPTER 11

A) All the signs in the picture show the **discourse of public transport regulation**, which in turn also includes the **discourse of the municipal authority** of this particular place in France. The meaning of these signs depends upon different forms of indexicality which locate language and discourse in the physical world. We find the three different types of signs:

- Icons→ the plane which signals the way to the airport, the drawing of a port, which accompanies the words "Le port Monaco"

- Indexes→ all the arrows in the different signs
- Symbols→ all the words and numbers

The three types of sign co-occur on the big blue sign which indicates the direction to *Nice, Cote d'Azur* and *Le Port Monaco*. The white sign combines symbols and indexes. The round speed limit signs are accompanied by a triangular sign with an index on top. It is important to remember here that, as noted in 11.8.1., signs are rarely 'pure', and consequently most of them have characteristics of the other two types (e.g. the symbols used for written language are frequently iconic as well).

Reading and understanding these signs is a practice which forms part of the nexus of practice of drivers not only in France but in the rest of the world.

B)   We find the following types of discourse on the inscription:

- Historical information discourse (designer, time and circumstances in which it was built).
- Architectural discourse (there is also information about how it was constructed and about its structure).
- Discourse related to general information about The Monument given to visitors (opening and closing hours, admission fees).
- Discourse of street directions (directions are given as to how to get to *St. Magnus the Martyr*).

Visual semiotics: the inscription is placed on The Monument, and therefore the reader understands that the information given refers to it. The fact that this inscription is in this particular place of London (The City) also adds extra information to the whole image, which would be understood differently if it were in a different location. The inscription has a sober type of letter –no colors and no icons–, which gives it a 'formal' and serious appearance, in accordance to the seriousness of the monument and the respect expected to be felt for it and for its history.

Place semiotics: The inscription is placed at the base of The Monument, and the rest of the monument speaks for itself, without the need for any other symbols or signs. The architectural style of The Monument is in fact a sign which provides a lot of meaning, together with the place where it is located (The City of London, where the Great Fire occurred in 1666. The

Monument was built to commemorate this fire). Also, the inscription is placed at a height which is accessible to the human eye, this fact being a sign that there is an intention and expectation of interaction with all visitors and passersby.

C) Open task

D) As we have seen, within MDA language is not considered the only mediational means. Non-verbal communication and physical objects are taken as mediational means as well. In this particular picture, we see two signs which operate as **mediational means** within a specific **site of engagement**: an underground station where thousands of people come and go every day (**mediated action**) and, in their rush, they need to be informed and oriented as to the stations the tube takes them to, as well as the directions they have to follow in order to get to their final places of destination, once in the station. The two signs on this wall of the Baker Street station in London are **indexical** of the site of engagement, the part of the material world where the action is taking place. Even when these signs are not part of the possible conversations the people in the station might be holding, they are part of the total discursive situation and they help the analyst by giving the necessary background information in order to understand it.

The first sign (to the left) is an **icon** which is indexical of the most important attraction for tourists on Baker Street: the Sherlock Holmes Museum, at 221b Baker Street, where, according to the stories written by Sir Arthur Conan Doyle, the famous fictional characters of Detective Sherlock Holmes and Dr. John Watson lived in Victorian times. On the second sign (to the right) we find a combination of **icon** and **symbols**, for the typical icon used in London for the underground stations has the name (in written language symbols) corresponding to this particular station on the horizontal bar that cuts the circle of the icon in two semicircles.

As regards the type(s) of discourse, it can be said that in this picture we mainly find the graphic discourse of directions in public places (which in this case informs the people as to where they are and what they will find once they get out of the station), but we should also remark that there is a kind of cultural/intellectual graphic discourse, manifested on the icon in the shape of Sherlock Holmes' head, which cannot be understood or interpreted by people from foreign cultures who are not acquainted with the literary works of Sir Arthur Conan Doyle.

CHAPTER 12

A)

a) Depending on the approach taken, we could work with different units of analysis. We could say that the e-mail message is a large unit in itself, which, as we saw in Chapter 12, has certain characteristics (mixed style (formal/informal; spoken/written, etc.). E-mail messages usually have two main kinds of information: 1) the information provided at the heading (addresser, date and time of the message, addressee, subject, etc.) and 2) the message itself. The relationship between these two parts contributes to the coherence of the whole message in that the former provides the addressee with information that will help her make sense of the information in the latter.

However, if the researcher wants to analyze further, it will be useful to choose a smaller unit. S/he could choose, for instance, the *speech act* and thus s/he will reach the conclusion that the main speech acts in this message are:

Excusing oneself (Lauren had told John in her previous message that she was surprised to not have received any news from him after he left, so that is why he excuses himself by saying that he had written a message but it didn't go through).
Thanking
Offering (By saying "Let me know when you are coming over this way" he implies that he intends to return Lauren's hospitality when she visits him).
Sending regards
Complimenting
Greeting

The message also has coherence insofar as we connect it with a previous one sent by Lauren, which can be inferred from the fact that in the *subject* section of the message we see that John's is a reply to Lauren's message entitled "Hi there". Thus the whole message can be considered a speech act, i.e. that of *replying*.

Another possible approach to analyze this message could take the *politeness strategy* as a unit of analysis, and thus we could say that John's first statement apparently looks like a direct, on record statement, but in fact it shows the use of an indirect, off record strategy in order to apologize for the fact that he didn't write before (e.g. the adverb *apparently* may be considered to be a *hedge* to elude certain responsibility for the previous absence of response). The rest of the message can be said to contain instances of the use of *on record with positive politeness* strategies, i.e., strategies aiming at the positive face of the addressee (e.g. complimenting: "You've got two very bright and nice sons", "You're lucky").

We could take other perspectives, and so, for example, we could analyze this discourse as a *social practice* within the Mediated Discourse Analysis approach and consider *mediated action* as the unit of analysis. But I leave this and other possibilities in the hands of the creative student or reader of this book.

b) We may say that the discourse under analysis is primarily *Computer-mediated discourse* (See 12.1.2.3.), but of course it has features of other types of discourse, such as written, epistolary discourse, or oral, informal, everyday conversation.

c) We find three discourse markers in this message:

1) So: Causative conjunction
2) Again: Elaborative, additive conjunction
3) And: Elaborative, additive conjunction

The three conjunctions contribute to the cohesion of the message by linking clauses and ideas. Additionally, they also contribute to the coherence of the whole situation by relating (in the case of *so* and *again*) the ideas in this message to those expressed by Lauren in her previous (inferred) message, and thus help to make sense of the whole situation.

d) With respect to cohesion, we find examples of reference (e.g. use of pronouns (*I, you, it*), substitution (*everything*, referring to Lauren's hospitality), ellipsis (e.g. *And* (give my) *regards to the family*), etc.

With respect to coherence, we may say that both addresser and addressee share certain mental frames and knowledge of the world (e.g. about situations when it is deemed appropriate to express gratitude or to ask for excuses) which makes the whole message a coherent piece.

Much more could be said about coherence and cohesion, but for the purposes of this exercise, the above remarks should suffice. We leave other considerations open to the reader's judgement.

e) We provide here only a few examples:

STRATEGIES	DISCOURSE FUNCTIONS
Be indirect, excuse yourself	Opening the message
Express gratitude	Topic closure
Offer future hospitality	Topic change

C) **Open task**

D) In this joke we find examples of both grammatical and lexical cohesion. The table below shows some of the expressions in the joke with the types of cohesion and their cohesive ties:

EXPRESSIONS	TYPE OF COHESION	COHESION TIES WITH...
They (lines 2 and 3)	Reference/identification And also: Lexical cohesion (repetition of *they* in lines 2 and 3)	a middle-aged couple (line 1)
After months of trying (to have a baby) (line 3)	Ellipsis	...to try one last time for the son they always wanted (lines 2, 3)
The wife (lines 3 and 11)	Reference/identification And also: Lexical cohesion (repetition of *the wife* in lines 3 and 11)	a middle-aged couple (line 1) (Here the type of reference is *bridging* (see Chapter 3), i.e. a kind of inferred anaphoric reference –we infer that in a couple there is a wife)

The joyful father (line 5)	Reference/identification	a middle-aged couple (line 1) and …delivered a healthy baby boy (lines 4-5) (Here the type of reference is again *bridging*, because we infer that in a couple there is a husband, who eventually became a father after the wife delivered a baby)
He (lines 6, 8, 10)	Reference/ identification And also: Lexical cohesion (repetition of *he*)	The joyful father (line 5)
A healthy baby boy (line 5)	Reference /identification And also: Lexical cohesion (between *baby boy* and *son*)	The son they always wanted (line 3)
The ugliest child he had ever seen (lines 6-7)	Reference/ identification And also: Lexical cohesion (among the synonymous *son, baby, boy, child*)	a healthy baby boy (lines 4-5), which in turn refers back to *the son they always wanted* (line 3)
That child (line 9)	Reference/identification And also: Lexical cohesion (among the synonymous *son, baby, boy, child*)	The ugliest child he had ever seen (lines 6-7), which in turn refers back to *a healthy baby boy* (lines 4-5), which in turn refers back to *the son they always wanted* (line 3)

The two beautiful daughters (lines 9-10)	Reference/identification And also: Lexical cohesion (repetition of *beautiful daughters*)	Two stunningly beautiful teen-aged daughters (lines 1-2)
Then (line 10)	Conjunction	The preceding clauses (the husband's comment to his wife about his disbelief that such an ugly boy could be his)
"(I have) Not (been fooling around on you) this time" (line 12)	Ellipsis	Have you been fooling around on me? (line 11)

CONCEPTUAL INDEX